OXYGEN RADICALS AND TISSUE INJURY

Proceedings of a Brook Lodge Symposium
Augusta, Michigan, U.S.A.
April 27 to 29, 1987

Barry Halliwell
Editor

Dorothy J. Marshall
Managing Editor

Martha M. Tacker
Manuscript Editor

Program Committee

J.Kenneth Gibson, *Chairman*
J.Mark Braughler
Peter Chelune
Edward D. Hall
Gary Mahnke
Peter A. Ward

Library of Congress Cataloging in Publication Data

Oxygen radicals and tissue injury.

    1. Free radicals (Chemistry)—Physiological effect—
Congresses.   2. Superoxide—Physiological effect—
Congresses.   3. Active oxygen in the body—Congresses.
4. Pathology, Molecular—Congresses.   I. Halliwell,
Barry.
RB170.097   1988   616.07   88-21390
ISBN 0-913822-15-9

**Published for The Upjohn Company by the Federation of American Societies for
Experimental Biology, 9650 Rockville Pike, Bethesda, Maryland 20814, U.S.A., 1988**

Upjohn

CONTENTS

Papers were presented by the authors shown in boldface type.

PREFACE

Basic research during the past decade has heightened our awareness of the role of oxygen radicals in various pathophysiological processes. The biomedical literature reflects the explosion of interest in oxygen radical biology as it applies to the understanding and treatment of human diseases. This is not only true concerning acute tissue injury caused by trauma or ischemia, but oxygen radical injury is being linked to many chronic diseases as well. The critical molecular components of free radical biology and the biological interrelationships of these components in mediating tissue injury are being unraveled so that their significance can be better understood and exploited by biomedical scientists and clinicians. Consequently, it is now possible to envision the development of unique pharmacological agents with free radical scavenging or antioxidant properties for use in the treatment of human disease and injury.

To more effectively pursue this exciting avenue of disease intervention, The Upjohn Company sponsored a Brook Lodge conference in April 1987 to assemble current experimental and theoretical information on the formation of oxygen radicals, their subsequent reactions, and their relation to tissue injury in various organ systems. The conference clearly demonstrated the multidisciplinary nature of successful free radical research and the value of basic scientific research in supporting the development of new therapeutic interventions.

Because space limitations prohibited open attendance of the conference, we thought other scientists and clinicians with broad interests in biomedical research and its clinical applications might benefit from receiving a copy of the proceedings. We, therefore, arranged with the Federation of American Societies for Experimental Biology (FASEB) to distribute this monograph to its members.

We are grateful to Dr. Peter Ward for his contributions to the early planning of the conference and the selection of speakers. We acknowledge the assistance of Dr. Gerald Zins and Dr. Roy Hudson, directors of Upjohn Cardiovascular Diseases Research and Central Nervous System Diseases Research, respectively. Their enthusiastic support made this conference possible.

J.M.Braughler
J.K.Gibson
E.D.Hall

1988

THE BIOLOGY OF OXYGEN RADICALS: General Concepts

Irwin Fridovich

After two decades of oxygen radical research, it is clear that superoxide can be formed in biological systems and can form other reactive species by a variety of reactions. The primary biological defense against the damage these highly reactive radicals can cause is the enzyme team comprising the superoxide dismutase, catalase, and peroxidase enzymes. The persistent idea that superoxide acts through formation of the hydroxyl radical is reconsidered, and ways superoxide can act directly or through formation of more highly reactive species are described. Paraquat toxicity requires conditions suitable for superoxide formation, and the bacteriostatic and bactericidal actions of paraquat can now be explained in terms of superoxide action. Superoxide is being implicated as a major factor in more and more medical conditions, and ways to protect from or ameliorate its damaging effects would be highly desirable. A complex of deferoxamine and manganese that mimics superoxide dismutase action appears promising. The two decades of oxygen radical research not only have clarified our concept of oxygen radical chemistry and biochemistry, but have laid a solid foundation for practical application of this knowledge.

TWO DECADES of oxygen radical research have led to some clear-cut conclusions. 1) Superoxide ($O_2^{\cdot-}$) is produced in vivo by enzymatic, spontaneous, and photochemical oxidation reactions. 2) The dismutation of $O_2^{\cdot-}$ to H_2O_2 and O_2, which can occur spontaneously or be catalyzed by certain metal salts and complexes, is facilitated in vivo by specific defensive enzymes called superoxide dismutases (SODs). A few oxygen-tolerant organisms do not contain SODs. Notable among these are the *Lactobacillaceae*, which accumulate as much as 30 mM Mn^{II} within their cells and which use low molecular weight complexes of Mn^{II} as functional replacements for SODs. 3) Amino acid sequence homologies indicate two families of SODs. One of these is composed of the Cu,ZnSODs and the other of MnSODs and FeSODs. All of these SODs catalyze the same reaction and do so with comparable efficiency. Their distribution among extant organisms and organelles reflects a complex evolutionary history, not yet fully delineated. 4) Increased steady state levels of $O_2^{\cdot-}$, whether due to elevated rate of production or to decreased enzymatic scavenging, result in cessation of growth, mutagenesis, and cell death. 5) $O_2^{\cdot-}$ can exert deleterious effects directly or by engendering more potent oxidants, such as by protonation, by reaction with vanadate or manganous salts, or by a metal salt-catalyzed interaction with H_2O_2. In the latter case, binding of the catalytic metal cations to target macromolecules or to biomembranes greatly increases the selectivity of the damage. 6) $O_2^{\cdot-}$ is an active participant in a number of physiological and pathological processes, and exogenous SOD is often protective. Availability of abundant supplies of recombinant SOD, of the glycoprotein extracellular SOD, and ultimately of a stable, membrane-permeant, nontoxic, low molecular weight mimic of SOD may provide the basis for major advances in medical practice.

The two decades of effort invested in basic research into the biology of oxygen radicals seem certain to yield practical benefits, in addition to the conceptual clarifications which have already been achieved.

SUPEROXIDE AND SUPEROXIDE DISMUTASES

$O_2^{\cdot-}$ is a frequently encountered intermediate of dioxygen reduction in both biotic and abiotic systems. It can be produced by radiolysis, photosensitized oxidations and autoxidations, and by some enzyme-catalyzed oxidations. It is capable of initiating and propagating free-radical chain reactions and of damaging cell components, both by direct and by indirect actions. Defenses are required.

The primary defense, found in virtually all facultatively or obligatorily aerobic cells, is provided by metalloenzymes called superoxide dismutases. They specifically and efficiently catalyze conversion of $O_2^{\cdot-}$ into H_2O_2 plus O_2. Three distinct types of SODs, falling into two evolutionary families, have been described. The first of these enzymes to be discovered contains Cu^{II} and Zn^{II} at the active sites. These Cu,ZnSODs are ordinarily found in the cytosol of eukaryotic cells, but also occur in a small subset of bacteria (1-5) and in the extracellular fluid of mammals (6). Cu,ZnSODs from any source exhibit considerable sequence homology, but are unrelated, in an evolutionary sense, to the SODs containing Mn^{III} or Fe^{III} at their active sites.

All known SODs catalyze the same reaction with approximately equal efficiency. The MnSODs and FeSODs are usually found in prokaryotes, which may contain one or both of these enzymes. MnSODs and FeSODs, from any source, exhibit extensive sequence homology (7). The presence of a MnSOD in mitochondria is in accord with the proposed symbiotic origin of mitochondria. In *Escherichia coli*, FeSOD and MnSOD are products of distinct genes and exhibit

From Department of Biochemistry, Duke University, Durham, North Carolina, USA.

Address correspondence to Dr. Irwin Fridovich, Department of Biochemistry, Duke University Medical Center, Durham, North Carolina 27710, USA.

catalytic activity only when the correct metal is at the active site. In contrast, *Bacterioides fragilis* and *Propionibacterium shermanii* produce a single active SOD which may contain Mn[III] or Fe[III], depending on growth conditions. In *E. coli* the FeSOD appears to be constitutive and is present whether the cells have been grown aerobically or anaerobically, whereas the MnSOD is under repression control and is not ordinarily present in anaerobically grown cells. Imposition of an oxidative stress, through elevation of PO_2 or by addition of compounds such as viologens or quinones, which can mediate O_2^{-} production within the cells, enhances biosynthesis of MnSOD. *E. coli* can be induced to produce MnSOD under anaerobic conditions by the presence of chelating agents, and this has tentatively been explained in terms of an iron-containing repressor protein (8). FeSOD, although usually restricted to prokaryotes, has been found in a few families of plants.

There are a few oxygen-tolerant organisms which do not contain SOD. Among these are certain lactobacilli (9), acholeplasmas (10), and neisserias (11). The lack of SOD in *Lactobacillus plantarum* has been explained (12). This organism grows best in a Mn[II]-rich medium, and it concentrates Mn[II] to intracellular levels of about 30 mM. When these cells are starved of Mn[II], they become oxygen-intolerant and exceedingly sensitive to quinones, such as plumbagin, which can mediate increased intracellular production of O_2^{-}. Complexes of Mn[II] with metabolic intermediates, such as lactate or malate, catalyze the dismutation of O_2^{-}, although not nearly as efficiently as do the SODs. It appears that, in *L. plantarum*, Mn[II] serves as a functional replacement for SOD.

DISPOSING OF PEROXIDES

H_2O_2 is produced by the dismutation of O_2^{-} and by a number of oxidases. It is a strong oxidant in its own right and, furthermore, can be reduced by Fe[II], Cu[I], and other reductants to yield the devastatingly reactive hydroxyl radical, $\cdot OH$. Accumulation of H_2O_2 is prevented by catalases and peroxidases. Catalases dismute H_2O_2 into H_2O plus O_2, and peroxidases catalyze the reduction of H_2O_2 to water. Among the electron donors used by different peroxidases are alcohols, phenols, amines, thiols, NADPH, leuco-dyes, and halides. Most catalases and peroxidases are heme proteins, but there are exceptions. Thus, lactobacilli and related bacteria that cannot synthesize heme produce a catalase containing manganese at its active site. Glutathione peroxidase, which can reduce alkyl hydroperoxides as well as H_2O_2, contains selenocysteine at its active site.

SODs, catalases, and peroxidases must be viewed as members of a defensive team, whose combined purpose is to minimize exposure of the cell to the reactive intermediates of dioxygen reduction. They are also mutually protective. Thus, O_2^{-} can inhibit catalases and peroxidases (13-17), and H_2O_2 can inactivate Cu,ZnSOD and FeSOD. SODs would therefore protect catalases and peroxidases against O_2^{-}, while being protected by them against H_2O_2. To the extent that this defensive team falls short of perfection, back-up systems are required. Such back-up is provided by antioxidants such as a-tocopherol, which terminate free-radical chain reactions, and by a host of repair systems, which strive to undo the damage that has been done.

O_2^{-} OR $\cdot OH$: DAMAGING SPECIES?

Because O_2^{-} is not indiscriminately reactive and because O_2^{-} plus H_2O_2 can, in the presence of catalytic Fe[III] or Cu[II], give rise to $\cdot OH$ or to species of comparable reactivity, the idea that O_2^{-} exerts deleterious effects only by way of $\cdot OH$ has taken hold (18). There are numerous indications that O_2^{-} can cause mischief quite independently of mediation by $\cdot OH$. Some of these have already been reviewed (19), but the prevailing view appears not to have been significantly shaken. It is therefore important to renew consideration of instances in which O_2^{-} itself exerts deleterious effects.

O_2^{-} protonates to $HO_2^{\cdot}$, with a pKa of 4.8. $HO_2^{\cdot}$ is a stronger oxidant than O_2^{-} and will directly attack polyunsaturated fatty acids (20). Protons are concentrated in specific cellular microenvironments, and substantial local conversions of O_2^{-} to $HO_2^{\cdot}$ must therefore be anticipated. The interiors of lysosomes and of phagosomes are acidified relative to the rest of the cell. Electrostatic forces will concentrate cations, including protons, adjacent to anionic interfaces, such as the surfaces of biological membranes. O_2^{-} entering such microenvironments will protonate to $HO_2^{\cdot}$ and thereby gain oxidizing potential.

There are a number of small molecules which rapidly react with O_2^{-}, even without the assistance of prior protonation. These include catechols, catecholamines, bile pigments, a-tocopherol, ascorbate, and other enediols, including the enediol forms of simple sugars such as the trioses (19,21).

Reduction of the iron in ferritin allows its escape into free solution. Green and Mazur (22) noted that the xanthine oxidase reaction caused a dioxygen-stimulated release of iron from ferritin, which was not inhibited by catalase. The subsequent availability of SOD allowed demonstration that the O_2^{-} made by the xanthine oxidase reaction was responsible for this mobilization of iron (23,24). Iron released from ferritin, by the action of O_2^{-}, was then found to

UPJOHN SYMPOSIUM / OXYGEN RADICALS April 1987

facilitate lipid peroxidation (25). Hence, inappropriate mobilization of iron from ferritin is another mechanism by which $O_2^{\cdot-}$ can cause damage to living systems.

Just as association of $O_2^{\cdot-}$ with H^+ increases its oxidizing potential, its association with other cationic centers can do likewise. An example of this mechanism that exacerbates the reactivity of $O_2^{\cdot-}$ is provided by vanadate (vanadium, V). Thus, vanadate catalyzes oxidation of NADPH by $O_2^{\cdot-}$ and it does so by formation of a V^{IV} peroxyl adduct, which can cause univalent oxidation of NADPH. The resultant pyridinyl radical rapidly reduces dioxygen to $O_2^{\cdot-}$, providing the basis for an ongoing chain reaction (26,27), as follows:

$$V^V + O_2^{\cdot-} \rightleftharpoons V^{IV}\text{-OO}^\cdot \qquad [1]$$
$$V^{IV}\text{-OO}^\cdot + NADPH \rightleftharpoons V^{IV}\text{-OOH} + NADP^\cdot \qquad [2]$$
$$NADP^\cdot + O_2 \rightleftharpoons NADP^+ + O_2^{\cdot-} \qquad [3]$$
$$V^{IV}\text{-OOH} + H^+ \rightleftharpoons V^V + H_2O_2 \qquad [4]$$

This process has been shown to account for the vanadate stimulation of NADPH oxidation by biological membranes (28). A number of sugars and sugar phosphates can reduce V^V to V^{IV}, and V^{IV} can reduce dioxygen to yield $O_2^{\cdot-}$. It follows that V^V plus sugars will, under aerobic conditions, generate $O_2^{\cdot-}$, which in the presence of V^V will then initiate the oxidation of NADPH (29).

Mn^{II} forms an adduct with $O_2^{\cdot-}$, much as vanadate does (30).

$$Mn^{II} + O_2^{\cdot-} \rightleftharpoons Mn^{I}\text{-OO}^\cdot \qquad [5]$$

$Mn^{I}\text{-OO}^\cdot$ can either act as an oxidant directly or, in the presence of chelating agents capable of stabilizing Mn^{III}, can yield Mn^{III} which, in turn, acts as an oxidant. This is illustrated by reactions 6 through 9.

$$Mn^{I}\text{-OO}^\cdot + NADPH \rightleftharpoons Mn^{I}\text{-OOH} + NADP^\cdot \qquad [6]$$
$$Mn^{I}\text{-OOH} + H^+ \rightleftharpoons Mn^{II} + H_2O_2 \qquad [7]$$
$$Ligand\text{-}Mn^{I}\text{-OO}^\cdot + 2H+ \rightleftharpoons Ligand\text{-}Mn^{III} + H_2O_2 \qquad [8]$$
$$Ligand\text{-}Mn^{III} + NADPH \rightleftharpoons Ligand\text{-}Mn^{II} + NADP^\cdot + H^+ \qquad [9]$$

If the ligand shown in reactions [8] and [9] markedly stabilizes Mn^{III}, it may limit the ability of Mn^{III} to oxidize electron donors (reaction 9). Thus manganese^{III}-pyrophosphate is unable to oxidize NADPH. The oxidation of Mn^{II} by $O_2^{\cdot-}$ and the subsequent oxidation of biological reductants by $Mn^{I}\text{-OO}^\cdot$ or by Mn^{III} as a function of the ligands available have been explored (31).

These effects of protons, vanadate, and manganous salts are merely illustrative. It seems likely that the complex interior of cells provides other opportunities for increasing the oxidizing potential of $O_2^{\cdot-}$ through association with cationic centers.

$O_2^{\cdot-}$ must be recognized as able to cause damage by means that do not involve production of the hydroxyl radical.

$O_2^{\cdot-}$: BACTERIOSTATIC AND BACTERICIDAL

Paraquat is actively taken up by a variety of cell types and can, within the cell, be reduced univalently at the expense of NADPH and under the catalytic influence of diaphorase enzymes. Since the paraquat monocation radical rapidly reduces O_2 to $O_2^{\cdot-}$, the stage is set for increased intracellular production of $O_2^{\cdot-}$. If $O_2^{\cdot-}$ damages cells, then one might anticipate that paraquat toxicity should be dependent upon both dioxygen and a source of electrons and should be diminished by elevation of intracellular levels of SOD. These expectations have all been affirmed, yet there was some apparent disagreement about whether paraquat could exert lethal effects or was merely bacteriostatic.

In a low-salt medium, $1.0\,\mu M$ paraquat inhibits the growth of E. coli without imposing lethality, whereas 1.0 mM paraquat exerts a bactericidal effect The bacteriostatic effect of low levels of paraquat is overcome by supplementing the medium with yeast extract, but the bactericidal action of high concentrations of paraquat is not influenced by nutritional supplementation (32).

$O_2^{\cdot-}$ can thus exert two quite different effects on E. coli. At low fluxes, it inactivates an enzyme or enzymes required for the biosynthesis of small molecules that are essential for growth and that are present in yeast extract. One of these superoxide-sensitive enzymes is dihydroxyacid dehydratase, which serves in the biosynthesis of branched-chain amino acids (33,34). High fluxes of $O_2^{\cdot-}$ must, in contrast, damage essential cellular components such as DNA or membranes, leading to cell death. The mutagenic effect of paraquat is oxygen-dependent and is opposed by elevated intracellular levels of SOD (35), and SOD-deficient E. coli exhibits an increased rate of spontaneous mutagenesis (36). Hence $O_2^{\cdot-}$, by some mechanism, damages DNA. Membranes are subject to attack by both $O_2^{\cdot-}$ and by $\cdot OH$, as shown through the use of spin probes (37,38).

A NEW MIMIC OF SOD ACTIVITY

$O_2^{\cdot-}$ has been implicated as a major factor in the toxicity of hyperoxia, the oxygen-dependent toxicities of viologens and quinones, inflammation, radiation damage, tumor promotion, and reperfusion injury. In many of these instances, SOD has been shown to exert a protective or ameliorative effect. A low molecular weight mimic of SOD activity, which might be able to cross cell membranes, should be very useful.

Numerous complexes of Cu^{II} have been studied.

The problem with complexes of Cu^{II} is that many proteins, particularly those bearing active thiol groups, tightly bind Cu^{II} and are inactivated by it. The SOD-like activity of the copper^{II}-salicylate complex is thus eliminated by bovine serum albumin. We have prepared a complex from deferoxamine (desferrioxamine B methanesulfonate) and Mn^{IV} which, in contrast, retains full activity in the presence of serum albumin or of the mixed soluble proteins present in a dialyzed extract of *L. plantarum*. We find that this complex protects a unicellular green alga against the toxicity of paraquat (39). Further probing of the utility of this complex in both plants and animals is underway.

ACKNOWLEDGMENT

It is impossible, because of limitations of space, to provide proper documentation of all of the statements made in this brief review. The reader who requires more complete documentation can find it in the following reviews (19,40-45).

REFERENCES

1. Puget K, Michelson AM. Isolation of a new copper-containing superoxide dismutase, bacteriocuprein. Biochem Biophys Res Commun 1974:58:830-838.

2. Steffens GJ, Bannister JV, Bannister WH, et al. The primary structure of Cu-Zn superoxide dismutase from *Photobacterium leiognathi*: evidence for a separate evolution of Cu-Zn superoxide dismutase in bacteria. Hoppe Seylers Z Physiol Chem 1983:364:675-690.

3. Dunlap PV, Steinman HM. Strain variation in bacteriocuprein superoxide dismutase from symbiotic *Photobacterium leiognathi*. J Bacteriol 1986:165:393-398.

4. Steinman HM. Copper-zinc superoxide dismutase from *Caulobacter crescentis* CB15: a novel bacteriocuprein form of the enzyme. J Biol Chem 1982:257:10283-10293.

5. Steinman HM. Bacteriocuprein superoxide dismutases in pseudomonads. J Bacteriol 1985:162:1255-1260.

6. Marklund SL. Human copper-containing superoxide dismutase of high molecular weight. Proc Nat Acad Sci USA 1982:79:7634-7638.

7. Steinman HM. Superoxide dismutases: protein chemistry and structure-function relationships. In: LW Oberley, ed. Superoxide dismutase. Boca Raton, Florida: CRC Press, 1982:11-68.

8. Moody CS, Hassan HM. Anaerobic biosynthesis of the manganese-containing superoxide dismutase in *Escherichia coli*. J Biol Chem 1984:259:12821-12825.

9. Archibald FS, Fridovich I. Manganese, superoxide dismutase and oxygen tolerance in some lactic acid bacteria. J Bacteriol 1981:146:928-936.

10. Lynch RE, Cole BC. *Mycoplasma pneumoniae*: a pathogen which manufacturers superoxide but lacks superoxide dismutase. Dev Biochem 1980:11B:49-56.

11. Archibald FS, Duong MN. Superoxide dismutase and oxygen toxicity defenses in the genus *Neisseria*. Infect Immun 1986:51:631-641.

12. Archibald FS, Fridovich I. Manganese and defenses against oxygen toxicity in *Lactobacillus plantarum*. J Bacteriol 1981:145:442-451.

13. Odajima T, Yamazaki I. Myeloperoxidase of the leukocyte of normal blood. III. The reaction of ferric myeloperoxidase with superoxide anion. Biochim Biophys Acta 1972:284:355-359.

14. Rister M, Baehner RL. The alteration of superoxide dismutase, catalase, glutathione peroxidase, and NAD(P)H cytochrome *c* reductase in guinea pig polymorphonuclear leukocytes and alveolar macrophages during hyperoxia. J Clin Invest 1976:58:1174-1184.

15. Kono Y, Fridovich I. Superoxide radical inhibits catalase. J Biol Chem 1982:257:5751-5754.

16. Kono Y, Fridovich I. Inhibition and reactivation of Mn-catalase: implications for valence changes at the active site manganese. J Biol Chem 1983:258:13646-13648.

17. Blum J, Fridovich I. Inactivation of glutathione peroxidase by superoxide radical. Arch Biochem Biophys 1985:240:500-508.

18. Aust SD, White BC. Iron chelation prevents tissue injury following ischemia. Adv Free Rad Biol Med 1985:1:1-17.

19. Fridovich I. Biological effects of the superoxide radical. Arch Biochem Biophys 1986:247:1-11.

20. Bielski BHJ, Arudi RL, Sutherland MW. A study of the reactivity of perhydroxyl radical/superoxide ion with unsaturated fatty acids. J Biol Chem 1983:258:4759-4761.

21. Mashino T, Fridovich I. Superoxide radical initiates the autoxidation of dihydroxy acetone. Arch Biochem Biophys 1987:254:547-554.

22. Green S, Mazur A. Relation of uric acid metabolism to release of iron from hepatic ferritin. J Biol Chem 1957:227:653-668.

23. Williams DM, Lee GR, Cartwright GE. Role of superoxide anion radical in reduction of ferritin iron by xanthine oxidase. J Clin Invest 1974:53:665-667.

24. Biemond P, van Eijk HG, Swaak AJ, Koster JF. Iron mobilization from ferritin by superoxide derived from stimulated polymorphonuclear leukocytes: possible mechanism in inflammation diseases. J Clin Invest 1984:73:1576-1579.

25. Thomas CE, Aust SD. Rat liver microsomal NADPH-dependent release of iron from ferritin and lipid peroxidation. J Free Rad Biol Med 1985:1:293-300.

26. Darr D, Fridovich I. Vanadate and molybdate stimulate the oxidation of NADH by superoxide radical. Arch Biochem Biophys 1984:532:562-565.

27. Liochev S, Fridovich I. Further studies of the mechanism of the enhancement of NADH oxidation by vanadate. J Free Rad Biol Med 1985:1:287-292.

28. Liochev S, Fridovich I. The vanadate-stimulated oxidation of NAD(P)H by biomembranes is a superoxide-initiated free-radical chain-reaction. Arch Biochem Biophys 1986:250:139-145.

29. Liochev S, Fridovich I. The oxidation of NADH by vanadate plus sugars. Biochim Biophys Acta 1987:924:319-322.

30. Bielski BHJ, Chan PC. Products of reaction of superoxide and hydroxyl radicals with Mn^{2+} cation. J Amer Chem Soc 1978:100:1920-1921.

31. Archibald FS, Fridovich I. The scavenging of superoxide radical by manganous complexes: in vitro. Arch Biochem Biophys 1982:214:452-463.

32. Kitzler J, Fridovich I. The effects of paraquat on *Escherichia coli*: distinction between bacteriostasis and lethality. Free Rad Biol Med 1987:2:245-248.

33. Brown OR, Seither RL. Oxygen and redox-active drugs: shared toxicity sites. Fund Appl Toxicol 1983:3:209-214.

34. Kuo CF, Mashino T, Fridovich I. α,β-Dihydroxy-isovalerate dehydratase: a superoxide-sensitive enzyme. J Biol Chem 1987:262:4724-4727.

35. Moody CS, Hassan HM. Mutagenicity of oxygen free-radicals. Proc Nat Acad Sci USA 1982:79:2855-2859.

36. Farr SB, D'Ari R, Touati D. Oxygen-dependent mutagenesis in *Escherichia coli* lacking superoxide dismutase. Proc Nat Acad Sci USA 1986:83:8268-8272.

37. Rosen GM, Barber MJ, Rauckman EJ. Disruption of erythrocyte membranal organization by superoxide. J Biol Chem 1983:258:2225-2228.

38. Freeman BA, Rosen GM, Barber MJ. Superoxide perturbation of the organization of vascular endothelium-cell membrane. J Biol Chem 1986:261:6590-6593.

39. Rabinowitch HD, Privalle CT, Fridovich I. Effects of paraquat on the green alga *Dunaliella salina*: protection by a mimic of superoxide dismutase, Desferal-Mn(IV). Free Rad Biol Med 1987:3:125-131.

40. Fridovich I. Superoxide dismutases. Adv Enzymol 1986:58:61-97.

41. Taylor AE, Matalon S, Ward P, eds. Physiology of oxygen radicals. Baltimore:Williams & Wilkins, 1986.

42. Weiss SJ. Oxygen, ischemia and inflammation. Acta Physiol Scand Suppl 1986:548:9-37.

43. Sies H, ed. Oxidative stress. New York:Academic Press, 1985.

44. Granger DN, Hollwarth ME, Parks DA. Ischemia-reperfusion injury: role of oxygen-derived free radicals. Acta Physiol Scand Suppl 1986:548: 47-63.

45. McCord JM. Superoxide radical: a likely link between reperfusion injury and inflammation. Adv Free Rad Biol Med 1986:2:325-345.

QUESTIONS AND COMMENTS

Dr. Donald Borg: If $O_2^{\cdot-}$ or its conjugate acid, $HO_2^{\cdot}$, which will not manifest strong nucleophilic behavior in the aprotic membrane interior, passes through or into some membranes, what relevance, if any, does superoxide's nucleophilicity in aprotic media have to $O_2^{\cdot-}$ toxicity in membranes or at hydrophobic protein (enzyme) surfaces in vivo?

Dr. Irwin Fridovich: I do not think it likely that $O_2^{\cdot-}$ will enter the low dielectric environments found within lipid bilayers or within globular proteins. Hence, it appears to me that the very great nucleophilicity of $O_2^{\cdot-}$ in aprotic solvents, although of considerable interest to organic chemists, need not concern biochemists or physiologists.

Dr. Barry Halliwell: Marklund has recently suggested that extracellular SOD exists bound to endothelial cell surfaces and that the low activity of extracellular SOD in extracellular fluids is merely due to detached enzyme. What is your opinion of this proposal?

Dr. Irwin Fridovich: Since Marklund has shown that extracellular SOD has considerable affinity for heparin and, indeed, has used heparin-affinity chromatography as a purification procedure for extracellular SOD, I consider this proposal to be entirely sensible.

Dr. Gerald Cohen: The solvent channel that leads $O_2^{\cdot-}$ to the active site of Cu,ZnSOD is quite narrow. Is ferrocyanide small enough to fit, so that it could indeed be oxidized by SOD?

Dr. Irwin Fridovich: Cu,ZnSOD catalyzes the oxidation of ferrocyanide by $O_2^{\cdot-}$. Inactivation of the Cu,ZnSOD by prior treatment with H_2O_2 or by heating eliminates this activity. We must therefore conclude that ferrocyanide does gain access to the active-site channel, albeit not as easily as does $O_2^{\cdot-}$, since the rate of the ferrocyanide oxidation reaction is much slower than the rate of the usual superoxide dismutation reaction. We facilitate it by using 50 μg/mL of the enzyme and 50 mM ferrocyanide.

Dr. Gerald Cohen: This ferrocyanide oxidation experiment with SOD has "opened Pandora's box." Can we now seriously consider the potential for SOD to mediate cellular damage under certain unusual circumstances, such as in trisomy 21?

Dr. Irwin Fridovich: Yes, this possibility, which was first considered by Sinet and Michelson over a decade ago, must now be reexamined. It seems entirely possible that the Cu,ZnSOD could use $O_2^{\cdot-}$ as an oxidant towards a variety of substrates. This will have to be explored both in vitro and in vivo.

I. CHEMISTRY

Barry Halliwell, *Session Chairman*

LIPID PEROXIDATION: Some Problems and Concepts

John M. C. Gutteridge

Lipid peroxidation, a simple sequence of events first described some 40 years ago, has become an unnecessarily complicated topic in the biomedical literature because of the imprecise use of terms and the inadequate control and standardization of reaction and measurement conditions. This paper addresses several questions concerning the basic mechanisms of lipid peroxidation. Two of the most contentious issues are initiation of lipid peroxidation and the exact role of iron complexes in this event. The study of lipid peroxidation urgently needs new and much improved methods of detection and measurement before definitive answers can be given. Some of the pitfalls in the use of current methods, particularly the thiobarbituric acid reaction and conjugated diene measurement, are discussed briefly.

ELEGANT STUDIES measuring the autoxidation of a natural oil were performed using oxygen uptake measurements in the early 19th century (reviewed in reference 1). However, it was not until the 1940s, as a result of work by Farmer and his collaborators at the British Rubber Producers Association research laboratories, that our present concepts of lipid autoxidation were formed. There was an explosion of biological interest in lipid autoxidation, or lipid peroxidation as it is now more widely known, during the 1960s. More recent studies have consolidated and evaluated many of the suggestions made. **Table 1** (2-36) lists some of the important events associated with the development of our understanding of lipid peroxidation.

Today several questions concerning lipid peroxidation remain unanswered. This short review addresses these questions.

NONENZYMIC LIPID PEROXIDATION

A free radical ($R^{\cdot}$) that has sufficient energy to abstract a hydrogen atom from a methylene carbon of an unsaturated fatty acid (LH) can initiate a chain reaction in bulk lipid. The resulting carbon-centered radical ($L^{\cdot}$) reacts rapidly with molecular oxygen ($k = 10^9$-10^{10} M^{-1}s^{-1}) (37) to form a peroxy radical ($LO_2^{\cdot}$), which itself can abstract a hydrogen atom from an unsaturated fatty acid, leaving a carbon-centered radical and a lipid hydroperoxide (LOOH).

$$LH + R^{\cdot} \rightarrow L^{\cdot} + RH \qquad \text{Initiation} \qquad [1]$$

From National Institute for Biological Standards and Control, United Kingdom.

Address correspondence to Dr. J.M.C. Gutteridge, Division of Chemistry, National Institute for Biological Standards and Control, Blanche Lane, South Mimms, Potters Bar, Hertfordshire, EN6 3QG, United Kingdom.

$$L^{\cdot} + O_2 \rightarrow LO_2^{\cdot}$$
$$LH + LO_2^{\cdot} \rightarrow LOOH + L^{\cdot} \qquad \text{Propagation} \qquad [2]$$

$$L^{\cdot} + L^{\cdot} \rightarrow LL$$
$$LO_2^{\cdot} + LO_2^{\cdot} \rightarrow LOOL + O_2 \qquad \text{Termination} \qquad [3]$$
$$LO_2^{\cdot} + L^{\cdot} \rightarrow LOOL$$

The free-radical chain reaction propagates until two free radicals destroy each other to terminate the chain (reaction 3). Hydroperoxides and cyclized endoperoxides, formed as a consequence of the chain reaction, are important when considering the mode of action of iron complexes in lipid peroxidation, which I will discuss later.

In nonenzymic lipid peroxidation, the peroxy radicals last long enough to be able to move to new fatty acid molecules since they can readily be intercepted and scavenged by a variety of different antioxidants. Peroxidic products of the chain reaction (LOOH) are a complex mixture of isomers.

ENZYMIC PEROXIDATION

Enzymic peroxidation should only refer to the generation of lipid peroxidation products at the active center of an enzyme. The hydroperoxides and endoperoxides produced are stereospecific and have important biological functions. The enzymes cyclooxygenase and lipoxygenase catalyze enzymic peroxidation according to these criteria. Free radicals are probably important intermediates in the reaction, but are localized to the active centers of the proteins. During the formation of endoperoxides by cyclooxygenase, a powerful oxidant (O_x) is generated, which is amenable to scavenging by antioxidants (38).

ENZYMIC REDOX CYCLING OF IRON IN NONENZYMIC PEROXIDATION

Iron has long been known to be important in lipid peroxidation reactions for reasons that will be discussed in the next section. Redox cycling of iron greatly promotes lipid peroxidation, and enzymes such as cytochrome P450 reductase in the presence of NADPH can reduce iron complexes (19), as can the superoxide ($O_2^{\cdot-}$) generated by mixtures of xanthine oxidase and its substrates (20). In this way the enzyme is performing a function no different from that of ascorbic acid, so stress on the enzymic nature

Table 1. Some Important Contributors to Our Understanding of Lipid Peroxidation*

1940s-50s	Chemical sequence of unsaturated fatty acid autoxidation: Farmer, Bolland, Sutton, Bateman, Gee, TenHave, Koch, Ingold (2-6).
1950s-60s	Biological implications of lipid peroxidation: Tappel, Bernheim, McCay, Harman, Mead, Mengel, Barber (7-13).
1960s	Chemical toxicity as related to lipid peroxidation: Recknagel, Slater, Comporti, Dianzani, Di Luzio, Orrenius (14-18).
1960s	Enzyme-promoted lipid peroxidation: Hochstein and Ernster, McCord and Fridovich (19,20).
1960s	Biological importance of metal complexes in lipid peroxidation: Uri, Wills, Hochstein, Aust, O'Brien (21-25a).
1960s	Enzymic peroxidation by cyclooxygenase and lipoxygenase: Hamberg and Samuelsson, Nugteren and Hazelhof (26-28).
1960s	Water-soluble biologically active products of lipid peroxidation: Baker and Wilson, Schauenstein and Esterbauer (29,30).
1970s	Formation of biologically active peroxides by autoxidation of fatty acids: Pryor, Porter (31,32).
1970s-80s	Biomedical importance of reactive iron and copper complexes in lipid peroxidation: Dormandy, Gutteridge and Halliwell (33-36).

* This table is not intended to be a comprehensive list of contributors to the field of lipid peroxidation or a list of specialists who have contributed to our knowledge of the chemistry of free radicals and metal ions.

of this reaction is inappropriate. The free-radical chain reaction is exactly as described in equation 2, and no stereospecific products are formed.

The important question that now arises is, what is the initiator R· of the reaction shown in equation 1?

THE IMPORTANCE OF IRON IN LIPID PEROXIDATION

The role of iron in lipid peroxidation is at present one of the most contentious issues. Most of the senior workers in the field appear to agree about the mechanisms involved, but there is considerable confusion about the descriptive terminology used. The review by Holman in 1954 (1) states that "The first chain must be initiated by some nonperoxidic free radical or by stray radiation. Parallel oxidation chains are initiated by radicals formed by decomposition of hydroperoxide." Lipid peroxidation has always lived with this dichotomy of meaning of *initiation*, although most writers fail to indicate to which initiation reaction they are referring, i.e., the first one or subsequent ones. In my view, *initiation* should only be used for the former (first chain initiation), whereas peroxide decomposition that

starts another chain reaction would be better described as *stimulation* of lipid peroxidation.

Initiation of Peroxidation by Ferrous Ions

Iron ions are themselves free radicals (39), and ferrous ions can take part in electron transfer reactions with molecular oxygen (equation 4).

$$Fe^{2+} + O_2 \rightleftharpoons Fe^{3+} - O_2^{·-} \rightleftharpoons Fe^{3+} + O_2^{·-} \qquad [4]$$

Generation of $O_2^{·-}$ by any source in the presence of iron ions can lead to the formation of hydroxyl radicals ($·OH$) by Fenton chemistry (equations 4-6).

$$2O_2^{·-} + 2H^+ \rightarrow H_2O_2 + O_2 \qquad [5]$$

$$Fe^{2+} + H_2O_2 \rightarrow OH^- + Fe^{3+} + ·OH \qquad [6]$$

High-energy radiation studies have shown that the ·OH produced in free solution can initiate lipid peroxidation by hydrogen abstraction (equation 7) (40) as can $HO_2·$ in purified fatty acid (41).

$$LH + ·OH \rightarrow L· + H_2O \qquad [7]$$

There is, therefore, no reason why superoxide-dependent Fenton chemistry should not also initiate lipid peroxidation in this way. Whether reaction 4 is an initiating reaction for lipid peroxidation was debated as early as 1956 by Uri (21). In spite of these considerations, careful studies using superoxide-dependent Fenton chemistry ($O_2^{·-}$ providing the H_2O_2 and also reducing Fe^{3+} to Fe^{2+}) have unequivocally failed to show any significant involvement of the ·OH in microsomal or liposomal peroxidation systems, as tested by scavengers (42). Yet, ·OH is certainly formed in these systems, since it can be detected by spin trapping (43) and by deoxyribose degradation (42). How can this incongruency be explained?

Stimulation of Peroxidation by Iron Complexes

The most important point to consider when attempting to study initiation reactions is the purity of the lipid preparation. The purchase of high-purity (99.9%) fatty acids is no safeguard against the presence of substantial amounts of lipid peroxides, since purity refers to the presence of other fatty acids. All commercial and biological samples of unsaturated fatty acids certainly contain from trace to large amounts of peroxidized material (44). The addition of an iron complex to such preparations will stimulate peroxidation by a peroxide-decomposition reaction, which generates alkoxy ($LO·$) and peroxy ($LO_2·$) radicals (equation 8).

$$2LOOH \xrightarrow[\text{complexes}]{\text{iron}} LO^{\cdot} + LO_2^{\cdot} + H_2O \qquad [8]$$

The rate constant for this reaction has been given as 1.5×10^3 $M^{-1}s^{-1}$ (45), which is higher than the rate constant for reaction of ferrous ions with H_2O_2 in the Fenton reaction (76 $M^{-1}s^{-1}$) (46). Consequently, iron complexes preferentially stimulate peroxidation by lipid decomposition reactions because there is usually plenty of lipid hydroperoxide present.

Attempts are often made to purify lipids by using methods developed for lipid chemistry. These include chemical reduction of the peroxides present (47), solvent partition of the peroxide and lipid (48), and column chromatography (49). However, although these offer some improvement, they are inadequate to completely remove peroxides, which is necessary to study the first initiation. Complete removal is very difficult (50) and, in one laboratory, 48 low-temperature, anaerobic recrystallizations were needed to obtain lipid suitable for mechanistic studies (B.H.J. Bielski, personal communication).

The answer to the question I posed earlier is, then, that to the best of my knowledge, no experiments have yet satisfactorily tested the role of ferrous ions in the first-chain initiation of lipid peroxidation by $\cdot OH$ formation since there have always been peroxides present that can be decomposed by added metal ions.

THE IMPORTANCE OF COMPLEXING IRON

Iron-Oxygen Complexes

The intermediate formed in equation 4 is the perferryl ion, a resonance hybrid of $Fe^{3+}-O_2^{\cdot -}$ and $Fe^{2+}-O_2$. Perferryl has been widely implicated as an initiating species (51-54) since the concept was first introduced by Hochstein (19,24). However, perferryl's ability to abstract a hydrogen atom from a methylene carbon has never been established, and its participation on energetic grounds is doubtful (55,56). Iron in the ferryl ion (FeO^{2+}) is considerably more reactive than in the perferryl ion, and the ferryl ion has been considered an alternative to the $\cdot OH$ in Fenton chemistry (57). Now that these iron complexes can be made in the laboratory, sound experimentation with totally peroxide-free lipid is urgently required to verify initiation reactions. All the iron complexes described would, however, be expected to stimulate lipid peroxidation by decomposing peroxides (58).

The rate of peroxidation appears to be maximal when the ratio of ferrous ion to ferric ion is one to one (59). Studies by Aust and colleagues have demonstrated that there is also an essential requirement for ferric ions in order for ferrous ions to stimulate lipid peroxidation maximally. They proposed a ferrous-dioxygen-ferric complex as an

Table 2. The Effect of $\cdot OH$ Scavengers on Phospholipid Peroxidation Stimulated by Different Ratios of EDTA to Ferrous Ion*

	TBA Reactivity[+]			
	EDTA:Fe^{2+} (1:1)		EDTA:Fe^{2+} (0.5:1)	
Addition	A532	Inhibition (%)	A532	Inhibition (%)
Control (lipid + EDTA + Fe^{2+})	0.365	--	0.426	--
Formate (11.1 mM)	0.195	47	0.541	0
Ethanol (11.1 mM)	0.164	55	0.455	0
Butan-1-ol (11.1 mM)	0.171	53	0.422	1
Urea (1.11 mM)	0.372	0	0.471	0
Thiourea (1.11 mM)	0.219	40	0.455	0
Glucose (11.1 mM)	0.229	37	0.516	0
Mannitol (11.1 mM)	0.178	51	0.463	0
Tris (11.1 mM)	0.253	31	0.438	0
Propyl gallate (0.22 mM)	0.083	77	0.127	70
SOD (0.006 mg/mL)	0.188	49	0.303	29
Catalase (0.036 mg/mL)	0.188	49	0.406	5
Albumin (0.03 mg/mL)	0.348	5	0.401	6

* These data were extracted from reference 65.
† TBA = thiobarbituric acid. Reactivity was measured by absorbance at 532 nm.

initiating species (60). However, the vital experiments using peroxide-free lipid have not yet been performed to substantiate initiation, so it could well be that this complex is exceptionally effective at decomposing lipid peroxides.

Iron Chelates

Ferric ions rapidly precipitate out of neutral aerobic solution to form insoluble ferric hydroxides, and it was recognized some time ago that complexing iron with ligands such as ADP or EDTA (19,25) overcame this problem. Complexing with EDTA thus helps to keep iron in a reactive form in solution and may favorably alter the redox potential of the iron (61,62). Depending on its molar ratio to iron, EDTA can either stimulate or inhibit lipid peroxidation (63). EDTA promotes the autoxidation of ferrous ions and formation of $\cdot OH$ (64), but EDTA can inhibit lipid peroxide decomposition (65). Based on these observations, it was reasoned that by carefully adjusting the ratio of EDTA to iron, it might be possible to inhibit the iron-dependent decomposition of contaminating lipid peroxides and yet enhance the autoxidation of ferrous ions to form $\cdot OH$ radicals by Fenton chemistry (65). **Table 2** shows that at a molar

EDTA-to-ferrous ion ratio of 1:1 the peroxidation of phospholipid liposomes became inhibited by ·OH scavengers, suggesting that it was substantially dependent on ·OH. Variations from this ratio returned peroxidation to a route independent of ·OH (65). This indirect approach, with a nonbiological system, supports the view that if lipid hydroperoxides were absent from unsaturated fatty acids, then the role of ·OH produced by Fenton chemistry in the initiation of lipid peroxidation (as I have defined it) would become obvious, and scavengers of ·OH would then inhibit initiation.

Iron Proteins

The heme moiety, both free and protein bound, can enhance the rate of lipid peroxidation (66-68), a property ascribed to its ability to decompose lipid peroxides. Recent reports have suggested that heme proteins form a reactive species able to initiate lipid peroxidation by hydrogen abstraction (69-71). Even if these experiments are repeated with fatty acids free of lipid peroxides, care must be taken that a Fenton reaction does not occur using iron ions *released* from heme proteins by H_2O_2 (72).

The iron-storage protein ferritin holds up to 4,500 moles of iron ion per mole of protein and stimulates lipid peroxidation (73). Ascorbate enhances the rate of ferritin-stimulated lipid peroxidation, and the iron released from ferritin has been measured (74). Iron is stored in the ferritin molecule in the ferric state but is released in the ferrous form. Mazur and colleagues (75) demonstrated the release of iron from ferritin by xanthine oxidase. It was later proposed that this could occur through the iron-reducing properties of $O_2^{·-}$ (76). The ability of $O_2^{·-}$ to release iron from ferritin was demonstrated by Biemond et al (77) and later confirmed (78). The ability of ferritin to stimulate lipid peroxidation appears, therefore, to be relatively uncontroversial. Hemosiderin, an iron-lipid-protein complex, is thought to be a degradation product of ferritin. Recently, O'Connell and colleagues (79) suggested that the in vivo conversion of ferritin to hemosiderin may represent a protective mechanism against iron toxicity, since the iron in hemosiderin is considerably less reactive than in ferritin. Evidence to support this is the inability of hemosiderin to release iron to bleomycin over a wide pH range (80) and the poor ability of hemosiderin iron to stimulate lipid peroxidation (81).

The iron-transport protein transferrin binds 2 moles of ferric ion per mole of protein with high affinity. Under normal conditions, human plasma transferrin is less than 30% loaded with iron, retaining a considerable iron-binding capacity. The ability to bind iron gives the protein a potent antioxidant activity towards iron-stimulated lipid peroxidation (82). Iron can be released from transferrin at low pH values in vivo (83), and the abnormal release of iron from transferrin occurs in synovial fluids from some arthritic patients (84).

The protein lactoferrin has iron-binding properties similar to transferrin, although its ability to hold iron at low pH values is much greater. It is normally only partly iron loaded and also acts as an antioxidant. There has been considerable debate about the role of these two proteins as promoters of the Fenton reaction. However, a recent assessment of the reaction conditions used in previous studies concludes that neither protein is a promoter at pH 7.4 unless an iron chelator is present and the proteins have been incorrectly loaded with iron (85).

Loosely Bound Iron

It is well recognized that cells contain an iron pool associated with low molecular mass compounds from which iron is withdrawn for the synthesis of iron-containing proteins (86). Providing that the integrity of the cell remains intact, enzymes such as the superoxide dismutases, catalase, and glutathione peroxidase (selenium enzyme) effectively remove $O_2^{·-}$ and H_2O_2 from the cell, preferably before they can come into contact with the low molecular mass iron pool and catalyze ·OH formation. Extracellular fluids do not contain significant amounts of these enzymes, but are subjected to fluxes of $O_2^{·-}$ and H_2O_2, e.g., from activated phagocytic cells. Extracellular fluids have apparently evolved different antioxidant protective mechanisms whereby metal complexes are prevented from interacting with reduced oxygen intermediates. Transferrin and lactoferrin bind ferric ions with high affinity; haptoglobins and hemopexin bind hemoglobin and hemin; and albumin binds copper ions (82,87,88). In addition, the copper-containing protein ceruloplasmin catalyzes the oxidation of ferrous ions to the ferric state with the complete reduction of oxygen to water (ferroxidase activity) (76). The appearance of complexable, loosely bound iron or copper ions in extracellular fluids may reflect a potential for oxidant stress. Recently, assays based on chelation have been developed to measure such forms of iron and copper in biological systems (35,80,89). **Table 3** summarizes findings in some extracellular fluids (35,90-95).

ORGANIZATION OF LIPIDS IN THE SUBSTRATE

The physical state of lipids can profoundly affect the rate of peroxidation. Indeed, the importance of structure and steric organization was recognized in the 1960s (reviewed in reference 96).

UPJOHN SYMPOSIUM / OXYGEN RADICALS April 1987

Micelles and Liposomes

Fatty acids in aqueous dispersion orientate into micelles, with limited structure and a diameter usually less than 200 Å. Their hydrocarbon chains face inward, attempting to avoid water, leaving the polar groups on the surface. Phospholipids can also form micelles, but their favored structure in aqueous dispersion is the lipid bilayer or liposome. Liposomes of different sizes can be prepared. They provide a model fluid membrane serving as a permeability barrier in which molecules of large molecular mass can be entrapped. Fundamental differences in the behavior of micelles and liposomes towards oxidant stress have been observed and described in two detailed papers by Aust and colleagues (97,98). These authors highlighted the complexity of interrelationships between substrate, complexed iron, and iron-reducing systems. If catalase is added to peroxidizing lipid, diene conjugation measurements must be used with care. Catalase can nonspecifically decompose hydroperoxides to give a loss of diene conjugation, a result that could be interpreted as inhibition of peroxidation by the removal of H_2O_2 (48). Mannitol, another widely used inhibitor of ·OH participation, has metal-binding properties (99) that could inhibit lipid peroxidation in a nonscavenging way (100).

The effect of structural organization of the substrate on peroxidation can also be illustrated with different metal ions. A cobaltous (Co^{2+}) salt readily stimulates peroxidation of micelles (22), but has no effect on bovine brain phospholipid liposomes (J.M.C. Gutteridge, unpublished data). Aluminum salts greatly potentiate ferrous-stimulated peroxidation of red blood cells and liposomes, but have little or no effect on micelles (101). Comparable membrane effects have been observed with the metal ions calcium (102), zinc (103), lead, and cadmium (G.J. Quinlan, B. Halliwell, C. Moorhouse, and J.M.C. Gutteridge, unpublished data).

Microsomes

Despite their attractive name, microsomes are not organelles but are artefactual debris. They are formed when the cell plasma membrane and endoplasmic reticulum are disrupted and form vesicles upon homogenization of the tissue. As they form, these vesicles encapsulate various amounts of soluble proteins, including superoxide dismutase (SOD) and catalase. Microsomes seem to have acquired a special importance to workers in the lipid peroxidation field, and animals from almost every species have been killed to provide rather insignificant information on the peroxidation of its microsomes. In contrast to data on micelles and

Table 3. Loosely Bound Iron Detected in Some Body Fluids*

Body Fluid	Iron (μM)	Reference
SERUM		
Normal (25)	0	35
Rheumatoid arthritis (21)	0	35
Osteoarthritis (10)	0	35
Hemochromatosis (7)	4.3 ± 6.7	90
SYNOVIAL FLUID		
Rheumatoid arthritis (21)	3.1 ± 1.9	35,91
Osteoarthritis (22)	0.37 ± 1.1	35,91
CEREBROSPINAL FLUID		
Normal	1.84 ± 1.3	35,92
Neuronal ceroid lipofuscinoses (All types) (15)	5.37 ± 2.0	35,92
Multiple sclerosis (6)	1.75 ± 0.8	35,92
Epilepsy (5)	2.48 ± 1.9	35,92
Meningism due to treatment with iron dextran (1)	36.0	93
Cerebral and ocular toxicity due to treatment with deferoxamine (1)	0	94
SWEAT FLUID		
Arm fluid (12)	0.72 ± 2.5	95
Trunk fluid (10)	4.62 ± 2.9	95
PLEURAL EXUDATE		
Rat (inflammatory) (2)	0.85	35
EYE VITREOUS HUMOR		
Rabbit (3 pooled samples)†	4.80	NP**
COLOSTRUM		
Bovine (3)†	0	NP
Bovine (1)†	16.3	NP

* Number of samples assayed are given in parentheses. All assays were performed on stored samples. The bleomycin-iron assays were carried out using unbuffered reagents.
† Conditions of collection not known.
** NP = Unpublished data from the author's laboratory. I am grateful to Drs. D. Armstrong and E. Griffiths for gifts of samples used in these studies.

liposomes, information obtained from microsomes is, for some reason, considered to be more biologically relevant--a concept that may be grossly misplaced. It is perhaps time for more studies to be carried out on purified preparations of biological membranes, e.g., the plasma membrane. Apart from providing a lipid substrate and an enzyme that can reduce Fe^{3+} complexes, the advantages of microsomes are limited by the many complications microsomes introduce (104). Microsomes have considerable biological variability because they are not pure membranes, and during formation they will include different amounts of cytosolic enzymes. Microsomes are, perhaps, more useful when used to study lipid peroxidation accompanied by cytochrome P450 hydroxylations (105).

MOLECULAR SPECIES   DETECTION SYSTEMS

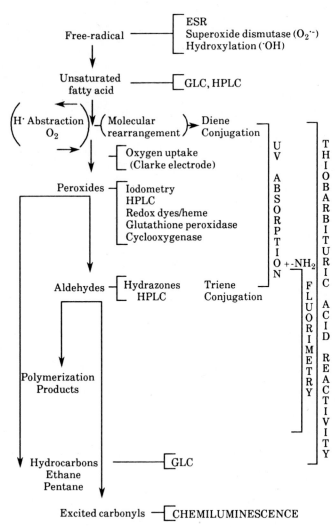

Figure 1. Detection and measurement of lipid peroxidation.

Red Blood Cells

Erythrocytes are the most readily available of all human cells, yet they are probably the most atypical cells for studying free radical reactions. The normal red blood cell contains high concentrations of ferrous ions, oxygen, and polyunsaturated fatty acids, yet it is resistant to oxidative damage. The normal human red blood cell deals with hydrogen peroxide by using two enzymes, glutathione peroxidase and catalase. Glutathione peroxidase removes physiological (micromolar) concentrations of hydrogen peroxide (106), whereas catalase can protect hemoglobin and lipids from oxidation even when the cell is insulted with 10 M (100 volume) hydrogen peroxide.

The standard test for red blood cell peroxidation is to incubate washed red blood cells (in a buffer containing azide to inhibit catalase) with 10 mM H_2O_2 (107) and measure the resulting thiobarbituric acid (TBA) reactive products (108). This technique

has no parallels for in vivo oxidant stress and will not detect cellular deficiencies of protective enzymes or of reducing molecules like NADPH and reduced glutathione (GSH). It can, however, detect subtle changes in membrane vitamin E (108,109) and in the fatty acid composition of the membrane (110).

The red blood cell is, however, susceptible to oxidant stress in vivo in several conditions (reviewed in reference 111). Diseases such as glucose-6-phosphate dehydrogenase deficiency, thalassemia, and the hemoglobinopathy sickle cell anemia leave the red blood cell vulnerable to oxidant stress. Interestingly, the occurrence of these diseases follows the global distribution of malaria. The malarial parasite is highly sensitive to oxidant stress, and the host cell may have a protective advantage by increasing its oxidative susceptibility (111). Another example of oxidant stress occurs in the fetal red blood cell, which is adapted for life in utero at a low oxygen concentration. Upon birth into a higher oxygen concentration, the red blood cells are subjected to oxidant stress, leading to "physiological" hemolysis and "physiological" hyperbilirubinemia of the newborn.

MEASUREMENT OF LIPID PEROXIDATION

Several possible approaches to the detection and measurement of lipid peroxidation are shown in **Figure 1**. These methods have been recently reviewed (39,112), and special comment will be made only about diene conjugation measurement and the TBA reaction.

Diene Conjugation

An ultraviolet absorbance corresponding to the conjugated double bond was first observed in autoxidizing fish oil in 1943 (2) and has been widely used since then as a marker of peroxidation in bulk lipids. The measurement of diene conjugation in biological material is complex, and two recent developments deserve special comment. In 1984 Dormandy and colleagues (113) reported that the main material absorbing at the wavelength of diene conjugates in human plasma was a non-oxygen-containing linoleic acid isomer. They suggested that the carbon-centered linoleic acid radical, when formed in vivo, reacts preferentially with protein and not with dioxygen. Doubts have been raised about the validity of this fatty acid isomer as a specific marker of peroxidation (114). Nevertheless, studies from Dormandy's laboratory (115) show that, whatever its origin (radical or enzymic), the linoleic acid product can be a marker of certain abnormal disease processes.

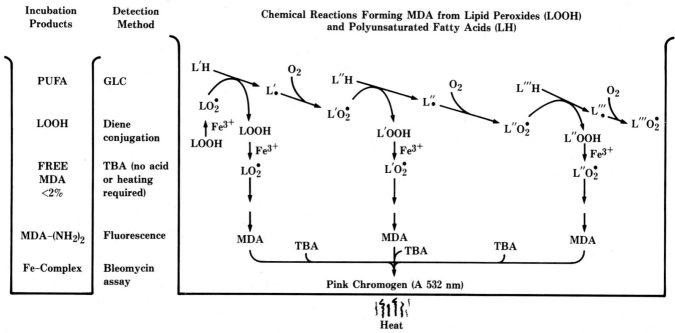

Incubation Products	Detection Method	Chemical Reactions Forming MDA from Lipid Peroxides (LOOH) and Polyunsaturated Fatty Acids (LH)
PUFA	GLC	
LOOH	Diene conjugation	
FREE MDA <2%	TBA (no acid or heating required)	
MDA-(NH$_2$)$_2$	Fluorescence	
Fe-Complex	Bleomycin assay	

Figure 2. Malondialdehyde (MDA) can be formed by lipid peroxidation during the incubation and to a much greater extent during the acid-heat enhanced chemical reactions of lipid peroxides (LOOH) and polyunsaturated fatty acids (LH) in the thiobarbituric acid (TBA) reaction.

By applying second derivative spectra to diene conjugates, Corongiu and colleagues (116,117) have achieved greater sensitivity and separation of peroxidic isomers in relatively simple systems, but the method has yet to be evaluated in more complex biological material.

Thiobarbituric Acid Reactivity

The TBA reaction was first applied to biological material by Kohn and Liversedge in 1944 (118) and has been widely used as a measure of lipid peroxidation in food products, fatty acids, and membranes. As long ago as 1958 it was shown that most (98%) of the TBA-reactive material present in peroxidized fish oil was released from precursors of malondialdehyde (MDA) during the acid-heating stage of the test (119,120). In other words, less than 2% of the MDA reacting with TBA was present in the incubation mixture in a free form, a view entirely supported by my work and confirmed by other experimentation (121). However, Esterbauer and colleagues, using high performance liquid chromatographic (HPLC) techniques, found substantial amounts of free MDA after processing material from peroxidized microsomes (122, 123), although this MDA does not appear to contribute greatly to the formation of fluorescent aminoiminopropene Schiff bases (124). If microsomes are unique in producing large amounts of free MDA, then they might be considered atypical models for tissue peroxidation. It may be that microsomes produce lipid peroxides that are very sensitive to

decomposition, yielding MDA on thin layer chromatographic (TLC) plates and HPLC columns.

The widely held assumption that the amount of MDA measured in the TBA test reflects the amount of free MDA present in the incubation mixture has led to wild claims about the toxicity of MDA in vivo. A simple method is needed to measure free MDA, without the lipid peroxides in the test material decomposing on silica gel (125) or other column materials that contain catalytic iron complexes (126). **Figure 2** attempts to illustrate differences between the incubation reaction of lipid peroxidation and the changes that occur during the chemical heating stage of the TBA test. As the figure shows, the heating reaction amplifies the peroxidation already begun. Some of the pitfalls of the TBA assay have recently been discussed in detail (127).

LIPID PEROXIDATION: CAUSE OR CONSEQUENCE OF TISSUE DAMAGE?

After tissue damage of any kind, it is highly likely that dead or dying cells will undergo lipid peroxidation more readily than normal cells. This has led to the frequent observation that products of lipid peroxidation accompany a multiplicity of disease processes. The question then arises whether lipid peroxidation is a cause or a consequence of tissue damage (128).

The initiation of lipid peroxidation is, by definition, a consequence of some kind of radical attack on the lipid. This may perhaps lead to an exacerbation or amplification of radical damage. At present, the evidence available does not strongly support lipid peroxidation as a major pathway to tissue damage in most degenerative diseases; greatly improved methods are required before a definitive answer to the question can be given.

Lipid peroxidation, chemically defined some 40 years ago as a simple sequence of events, has become an unnecessarily complicated subject by the imprecise use of terms and the inadequate standardization and control of reaction and measurement conditions.

ACKNOWLEDGMENT

I am grateful to Dr. Barry Halliwell for his helpful discussions.

REFERENCES

1. Holman RT. Autoxidation of fats and related substances. In: Holman RT, Lundberg WO, Malkin T, eds. Progress in the chemistry of fats and other lipids; vol 2. London: Pergamon Press, 1954:51-98.

2. Farmer EH, Sutton DA. The course of autoxidation reactions in polyisoprenes and allied compounds. Part V. Observations on fish-oil acids. J Chem Soc 1943:122-125.

3. Bolland JL, Koch HP. The course of autoxidation reactions in polyisoprenes and allied compounds. Part IX. The primary thermal oxidation product of ethyl linoleate. J Chem Soc 1945:445-447.

4. Bateman L, Bolland JL, Gee G. Determination of absolute rate constants for olefinic oxidations by measurement of photochemical pre- and after effects. II. At "low" oxygen pressures. Trans Faraday Soc 1951:47:1274-1285.

5. Bolland JL, TenHave P. Kinetic studies in the chemistry of rubber and related materials. IV. The inhibitory effect of hydroquinone on the thermal oxidation of ethyl linoleate. Trans Faraday Soc 1947:43:201-210.

6. Ingold KU. The influence of alkali on the oxidation of Tetralin. Can J Chem 1956:34:600-608.

7. Tappel AL. Studies of the mechanism of vitamin E action. II. Inhibition of unsaturated fatty acid oxidation catalyzed by hematin compounds. Arch Biochem Biophys 1954:50:473-485.

8. Bernheim F, Wilbur KM, Kenaston CB. The effect of oxidized fatty acids on the activity of certain oxidative enzymes. Arch Biochem Biophys 1952:38:177-184.

9. May E, Poyer JL, McCay PB. Lipid alterations occurring in microsomes during the enzymic oxidation of TPNH. Biochem Biophys Res Commun 1965:19:166-170.

10. Harman D. Aging: a theory based on free radical and radiation chemistry. J Gerontol 1956:11:298-300.

11. Mead JF. The irradiation-induced autoxidation of linoleic acid. Science 1952:115:470-472.

12. Mengel CE, Kann HE. Effects of in vivo hyperoxia on erythrocytes. 3. In vivo peroxidation of erythrocyte lipid. J Clin Invest 1966:45:1150-1158.

13. Barber AA. Inhibition of lipid peroxide formation by vertebrate blood serum. Arch Biochem Biophys 1961:92:38-43.

14. Recknagel RO. Carbon tetrachloride hepatoxicity. Pharmacol Rev 1967:19:145-208.

15. Slater TF. Free radical mechanisms in tissue injury. London: Pion, 1972:283p.

16. Comporti M, Saccocci C, Dianzani MU. Effect of CCl_4 in vitro and in vivo on lipid peroxidation of rat liver homogenates and subcellular fractions. Enzymologia 1965:29:185-205.

17. Di Luzio NR, Costales F. Inhibition of the ethanol and carbon tetrachloride induced fatty liver by antioxidants. Exp Mol Path 1965:4:141-154.

18. Orrenius S, Dallner G, Ernster L. Inhibition of the TPNH-linked lipid peroxidation of liver microsomes by drugs undergoing oxidative demethylation. Biochem Biophys Res Commun 1964:14:329-334.

19. Hochstein P, Ernster L. ADP-activated lipid peroxidation coupled to the TPNH oxidase system of microsomes. Biochem Biophys Res Commun 1963:12:388-394.

20. McCord JM, Fridovich I. Superoxide dismutase on enzymic function for erythrocuprein (hemocuprein). J Biol Chem 1969:244:6049-6055.

21. Uri N. Metal ion catalysis and polarity of environment in the aerobic oxidation of unsaturated fatty acids. Nature 1956:177:1177-1178.

22. Wills ED. Mechanisms of lipid peroxide formation in tissues: role of metals and haematin proteins in the catalysis of the oxidation of unsaturated fatty acids. Biochim Biophys Acta 1965:98:238-251.

23. Wills ED. Lipid peroxide formation in microsomes: the role of non-haem iron. Biochem J 1969:113:325-332.

24. Hochstein P, Nordenbrand K, Ernster L. Evidence for the involvement of iron in the ADP-activated peroxidation of lipids in microsomes and mitochondria. Biochem Biophys Res Comm 1964:14:323-328.

25. Pederson TC, Buege JA, Aust SD. Microsomal electron transport: The role of reduced nicotinamide adenine dinucleotide phosphate-cytochrome c reductase in liver microsomal lipid peroxidation. J Biol Chem 1973:248:7134-7141.

25a. O'Brien PJ. Intracellular mechanisms for the decompositions of lipid peroxide I. Decomposition of a lipid peroxide by metal ions, heme compounds and nucleophiles. Can J Biochem 1969:47:485-492.

26. Hamberg M, Svensson J, Samuelsson B. Thromboxanes: a new group of biologically active compounds derived from prostaglandin endoperoxides. Proc Natl Acad Sci USA 1975:72:2994-2998.

27. Hamberg M, Samuelsson B. Detection and isolation of an endoperoxide intermediate in prostaglandin biosynthesis. Proc Natl Acad Sci USA 1973:70:899-903.

28. Nugteren DH, Hazelhof E. Isolation and properties of intermediates in prostaglandin biosynthesis. Biochim Biophys Acta 1973:326:448-461.

29. Baker N, Wilson L. Water-soluble inhibitor(s) of tumor respiration formed from ultraviolet-induced oxidation of linoleic and linolenic acids. J Lipid Res 1966:7:349-356.

30. Schauenstein E, Esterbauer H, Zollner H. Aldehydes in biological systems: their natural occurrence and biological activities. Pion: London, 1977:1-205.

31. Pryor WA, Stanley JP, Blair E. Autoxidation of polyunsaturated fatty acids. II. A suggested mechanism for the formation of TBA-reactive materials from prostaglandin-like endoperoxides. Lipids 1976:11:370-379.

32. Porter NA, Wolf RA, Yarbro EM, Weenen H. The

autoxidation of arachidonic acid: formation of the proposed SRS-A intermediate. Biochem Biophys Res Commun 1979:89:1058-1064.

33. Stocks J, Gutteridge JMC, Sharp RJ, Dormandy TL. The inhibition of lipid autoxidation by human serum and its relation to serum proteins and alpha-tocopherol. Clin Sci Mol Med 1974:47:223-233.

34. Dormandy TL. Free-radical oxidation and antioxidants. Lancet 1978:i:647-650.

35. Gutteridge JMC, Rowley DA, Halliwell B. Superoxide-dependent formation of hydroxyl radicals in the presence of iron salts: detection of "free" iron in biological systems by using bleomycin-dependent degradation of DNA. Biochem J 1981:199:263-265.

36. Halliwell B, Gutteridge JMC. The importance of free radicals and catalytic metal ions in human disease. Mol Aspects Med 1985:8:89-193.

37. Pryor WA. The role of free radical reactions in biological systems. In: Pryor WA, ed. Free radicals in biology; vol 1. New York: Academic Press, 1976.

38. Egan RW, Paxton J, Kuehl FA. Mechanism for irreversible self-deactivation of prostaglandin synthetase. J Biol Chem 1976:251:7329-7335.

39. Halliwell B, Gutteridge JMC. Free radicals in biology and medicine. Oxford: Oxford University Press, 1985.

40. Raleigh JA, Kremers W, Gaboury B. Dose-rate and oxygen effects in models of lipid membranes: linoleic acid. Int J Radiat Biol 1977:31:203-213.

41. Bielski BHJ, Arudi RL, Sutherland MW. A study of the reactivity of HO_2/O_2^- with unsaturated fatty acids. J Biol Chem 1983:258:4759-4761.

42. Gutteridge JMC. The role of superoxide and hydroxyl radicals in phospholipid peroxidation catalysed by iron salts. FEBS Lett 1982:150:454-458.

43. Noguchi T, Nakano M. Effect of ferrous ions on microsomal phospholipid peroxidation and related light emission. Biochim Biophys Acta 1974:368:446-455.

44. Gutteridge JMC, Kerry PJ. Detection by fluorescence of peroxides and carbonyls in samples of arachidonic acid. Brit J Pharmac 1982:76:459-461.

45. Garnier-Suillerot A, Tosi L, Paniago E. Kinetic and mechanism of vesicle lipoperoxide decomposition by Fe(II). Biochim Biophys Acta 1984:794:307-312.

46. Hardwick TJ. The rate constant of the reaction between ferrous ions and hydrogen peroxide in acid solutions. Can J Chem 1957:35:428-436.

47. Pace-Asciak C, Nashat M. Catabolism of an isolated purified intermediate of prostaglandin biosynthesis by regions of the adult rat kidney. Biochim Biophys Acta 1975:388:243-252.

48. Gutteridge JMC, Beard AP, Quinlan G. Superoxide-dependent lipid peroxidation: problems with the use of catalase as a specific probe for Fenton-derived hydroxyl radicals. Biochem Biophys Res Commun 1983:117:901-907.

49. Gardner HW. Isolation of a pure isomer of linoleic acid hydroperoxide. Lipids 1975:10:248-252.

50. Arudi RL, Sutherland MW, Bielski BHJ. Purification of oleic acid and linoleic acid. J Lipid Res 1983:24:485-488.

51. Pederson TC, Aust SD. The mechanism of liver microsomal lipid peroxidation. Biochim Biophys Acta 1975:385:232-241.

52. Svingen BA, O'Neal FO, Aust SD. The role of superoxide and singlet oxygen in lipid peroxidation. Photochem Photobiol 1978:28:803-809.

53. Tien M, Svingen BA, Aust SD. Initiation of lipid peroxidation by perferryl complexes. In: Rodgers MAJ, Powell EL, eds. Oxygen and oxy-radicals in chemistry and biology. New York: Academic Press, 1981:147-152.

54. Sugioka K, Nakano H, Nakano M, Tero-Kubota S, Ikegami Y. Generation of hydroxyl radicals during the enzymatic reductions of the Fe^{3+}-ADP-phosphate-adriamycin and Fe^{3+}-ADP-EDTA systems: less involvement of hydroxyl radical and a great importance of proposed perferryl ion complexes in lipid peroxidation. Biochim Biophys Acta 1983:753:411-421.

55. Halliwell B, Pasternack RF, De Rycker J. Interaction of the superoxide radical with peroxidase and with other iron complexes. In: King TE, Mason HS, Morrison M, eds. Oxidases and related redox systems. Oxford: Pergamon Press, 1982:733-744.

56. Yokota K, Yamazaki I. The activity of the horseradish peroxidase compound III. Biochem Biophys Res Commun 1965:18:48-53.

57. Koppenol WH. The reaction of ferrous EDTA with hydrogen peroxide: evidence against hydroxyl radical formation. J Free Rad Biol Med 1985:1:281-285.

58. Gutteridge JMC, Halliwell B, Rowley DA. Catalytic iron complexes in biological material: a potential for oxygen radical damage. Life Chem Rep 1984:suppl 2:15-26.

59. Ernster L, Nordenbrand K. Microsomal lipid peroxidation: mechanism and some biomedical implications. In: Yaqi K, ed. Lipid peroxides in biology and medicine. New York: Academic Press, 1982:55-79.

60. Bucher JR, Ming T, Aust SD. The requirement for ferric in the initiation of lipid peroxidation by chelated ferrous iron. Biochem Biophys Res Commun 1983:111:777-784.

61. Grootveld M, Halliwell B. An aromatic hydroxylation assay for hydroxyl radicals utilizing high performance liquid chromatography (HPLC): use to investigate the effect of EDTA on the Fenton reaction. Free Rad Res Commun 1986:1:243-250.

62. Aust SD, Morehouse LA, Thomas CE. Role of metals in oxygen radical reactions. J Free Rad Biol Med 1985:1:3-25.

63. Gutteridge JMC, Richmond R, Halliwell B. Inhibition of the iron-catalysed formation of hydroxyl radicals from superoxide and of lipid peroxidation by desferrioxamine. Biochem J 1979:184:469-472.

64. Cohen G, Sinet PM. Fenton's reagent—once more revisited. In: Bannister JV, Hill HAO, eds. Chemical and biochemical aspects of superoxide and superoxide dismutase. Amsterdam: Elsevier, 1980:27-37.

65. Gutteridge JMC. Ferrous ion-EDTA-stimulated phospholipid peroxidation: a reaction changing from alkoxyl-radical- to hydroxyl-radical-dependent initiation. Biochem J 1984:224:697-701.

66. Tappel AL. The mechanism of the oxidation of unsaturated fatty acids catalyzed by hematin compounds. Arch Biochem Biophys 1953:44:378-395.

67. Tappel AL. Unsaturated lipid oxidation catalyzed by hematin compounds. J Biol Chem 1955:217:721-733.

68. Kaschnitz RM, Hatefi Y. Lipid oxidation in biological membranes: electron transfer proteins as initiators of lipid autoxidation. Arch Biochem Biophys 1975:171:292-304.

69. Sadrzadeh SM, Graf E, Panter SS, Hallaway PE, Eaton JW. Hemoglobin, a biologic Fenton reagent. J Biol Chem 1984:259:14354-14356.

70. Kanner J, Harel S. Initiation of membrane lipid peroxidation by activated metmyoglobin and methemoglobin. Arch Biochem Biophys 1985:237:314-321.

71. Grisham MB. Myoglobin-catalyzed hydrogen peroxide dependent arachidonic acid peroxidation. J Free Rad Biol Med 1985:1:227-232.

72. Gutteridge JMC. Iron promoters of the Fenton reaction and lipid peroxidation can be released from haemoglobin by peroxides. FEBS Lett 1986:201:291-295.

73. Wills ED. Mechanisms of lipid peroxide formation in animal tissues. Biochem J 1966:99:667-676.

74. Gutteridge JMC, Halliwell B, Harrison P, Treffry A, Blake DR. Effect of ferritin containing fractions with different iron loading on lipid peroxidation. Biochem J 1983:209:557-560.

75. Mazur A, Green S, Saha A, Carleton A. Mechanism of release of ferritin iron in vivo by xanthine oxidase. J Clin Invest 1958:37:1809-1817.

76. Gutteridge JMC, Stocks J. Ceruloplasmin: physiological and pathological perspectives. CRC Crit Rev in Clin Lab Sci 1981:14:257-329.

77. Biemond P, van Eijk HG, Swaak AJG, Koster JF. Iron mobilization from ferritin by superoxide derived from stimulated polymorphonuclear leukocytes: possible mechanism in inflammation diseases. J Clin Invest 1984:73:1576-1579.

78. Thomas CE, Morehouse LA, Aust SD. Ferritin and superoxide-dependent lipid peroxidation. J Biol Chem 1985:260:3275-3280.

79. O'Connell MJ, Halliwell B, Moorhouse CP, Aruoma OI, Baum H, Peters TJ. Formation of hydroxyl radicals in the presence of ferritin and haemosiderin. Biochem J 1986:234:727-731.

80. Gutteridge JMC, Hou Y. Iron complexes and their reactivity in the bleomycin assay for radical-promoting loosely-bound iron. Free Rad Res Commun 1986:2:143-151.

81. O'Connell MJ, Ward RJ, Baum H, Peters TJ. The role of iron in ferritin and haemosiderin-mediated lipid peroxidation in liposomes. Biochem J 1985:229:135-139.

82. Gutteridge JMC, Paterson SK, Segal AW, Halliwell B. Inhibition of lipid peroxidation by the iron-binding protein lactoferrin. Biochem J 1981:199:259-261.

83. Halliwell B, Gutteridge JMC, Blake DR. Metal ions and oxygen radical reactions in human inflammatory joint disease. Philos Trans R Soc: Lond(Biol) 1985:311:659-671.

84. Gutteridge JMC. Bleomycin-detectable iron in knee-joint synovial fluid from arthritic patients and its relationship to the extracellular antioxidant activities of caeruloplasmin, transferrin and lactoferrin. Biochem J 1987:245:415-421.

85. Aruoma OI, Halliwell B. Superoxide-dependent and ascorbate-dependent formation of hydroxyl radicals from hydrogen peroxide in the presence of iron. Are lactoferrin and transferrin promoters of hydroxyl-radical generation? Biochem J 1987:241:273-278.

86. Jacobs A. Low molecular weight intracellular iron transport compounds. Blood 1977:50:433-439.

87. Gutteridge JMC. Antioxidant properties of the proteins caeruloplasmin albumin and transferrin: a study of their activity in serum and synovial fluid from patients with rheumatoid arthritis. Biochim Biophys Acta 1986:869:119-127.

88. Gutteridge JMC. The antioxidant activity of haptoglobin towards haemoglobin-stimulated lipid peroxidation. Biochim Biophys Acta 1987:917:219-223.

89. Gutteridge JMC. Copper-phenanthroline-induced site-specific oxygen-radical damage to DNA: detection of loosely bound trace copper in biological fluids. Biochem J 1984:218:983-985.

90. Gutteridge JMC, Rowley DA, Griffiths E, Halliwell B. Low-molecular weight iron complexes and oxygen radical reactions in idiopathic haemochromatosis. Clin Sci 1985:68:463-467.

91. Rowley DA, Gutteridge JMC, Blake D, Farr M, Halliwell B. Lipid peroxidation in rheumatoid arthritis: thiobarbituric acid-reactive material and catalytic iron salts in synovial fluids from rheumatoid patients. Clin Sci 1984:66:691-695.

92. Gutteridge JMC, Rowley D, Halliwell B, Westermarck T. Increased non-protein-bound iron and decreased protection against superoxide radical damage in cerebrospinal fluid from patients with neuronal ceroid lipofuscinoses. Lancet 1982:ii:459-460.

93. Shuttleworth D, Spence C, Slade R. Meningism due to intravenous iron dextran. Lancet 1983:ii:435.

94. Blake DR, Winyard P, Lunec J, et al. Cerebral and ocular toxicity induced by desferrioxamine. Quart J Med 1985:219:345-355.

95. Gutteridge JMC, Rowley DA, Halliwell B, Cooper DF, Heeley DM. Copper and iron complexes catalytic for oxygen radical reactions in sweat from human athletes. Clin Chim Acta 1985:145:267-273.

96. Wolman M. Biological peroxidation of lipids and membranes. Isr J Med Sci 1975:11:1-236.

97. Tien M, Svingen BA, Aust SD. An investigation into the role of hydroxyl radical in xanthine oxidase-dependent lipid peroxidation. Arch Biochem Biophys 1982:216:142-151.

98. Tien M, Morehouse LA, Bucher JR, Aust SD. The multiple effects of ethylenediaminetetraacetate in several model lipid peroxidation systems. Arch Biochem Biophys 1982:218:450-458.

99. Bourne EJ, Nery R, Weigel H. Metal chelates of polyhydroxy compounds. Chem Ind 1959:998-999.

100. Gutteridge JMC. Ferrous salt-promoted damage to deoxyribose and benzoate: the increased effectiveness of hydroxyl radical scavengers in the presence of EDTA. Biochem J 1987:243:709-714.

101. Gutteridge JMC, Quinlan GJ, Clark I, Halliwell B. Aluminium salts accelerate peroxidation of membrane lipids stimulated by iron salts. Biochim Biophys Acta 1985:835:441-447.

102. Gutteridge JMC. The effect of calcium on phospholipid peroxidation. Biochem Biophys Res Commun 1977:74:529-537.

103. Girotti AW, Thomas JP, Jordan JE. Inhibitory effect of zinc(II) on free radical lipid peroxidation in erythrocyte membranes. J Free Rad Biol Med 1985:1:395-401.

104. Koster JF, Biemond P, Mantfoort A, Stam H. The involvement of free radicals in pathological conditions. Life Chem Rep 1986:3:323-351.

105. Ekstrom G, Ingelman-Sundberg M. Mechanisms of lipid peroxidation dependent upon cytochrome P-450 LM_2. Eur J Biochem 1986:158:195-201.

106. Cohen G, Hochstein P. Glutathione peroxidase: the primary agent for the elimination of hydrogen peroxide in erythrocytes. Biochemistry 1963:2:1420-1428.

107. Stocks J, Dormandy TL. The autoxidation of human red cell lipids induced by hydrogen peroxide. Brit J Haematol 1971:20:95-111.

108. Bunyan J, Green J, Edwin EE, Diplock AT. Studies on vitamin E. 5. Lipid peroxidation in dialuric acid-induced haemolysis of vitamin E-deficient erythrocytes. Biochem J 1960:77:47-51.

109. Abrams BA, Gutteridge JMC, Stocks J, Friedman M, Dormandy TL. Vitamin E in neonatal hyperbilirubinemia. Arch Dis Childhood 1973:48:721-724.

110. Gutteridge JMC. The measurement of fatty-acid patterns by GLC and their application to red blood cell studies. Med Lab Sci 1978:35:31-38.

111. Clark IA, Cowden WB. Antimalarials. In: Sies H, ed. Oxidant stress. New York: Academic Press, 1985:131-149.

112. Girotti AW. Mechanisms of lipid peroxidation. J Free Rad Biol Med 1985:1:87-95.

113. Cawood P, Wickens DG, Iversen SA, Braganza JM, Dormandy TL. The nature of diene conjugation in human serum, bile and duodenal juice. FEBS Lett 1983:162:239-243.

114. Thompson S, Smith MT. Measurement of the diene conjugated form of linoleic acid in plasma by high performance liquid chromatography: a questionable non-invasive assay of free radical activity? Chem Biol Interact 1985:55:357-366.

115. Braganza JM, Wickens DG, Cawood P, Dormandy TL. Lipid peroxidation (free-radical-oxidation) products in bile from patients with pancreatic disease. Lancet 1983:ii:375-378.

116. Corongiu FP, Milia A. An improved and simple method for determining diene conjugation in autoxidized polyunsaturated fatty acids. Chem Biol Interact 1983:44:289-297.

117. Corongiu FP, Poli G, Dianzani MU, Cheeseman KH, Slater TF. Lipid peroxidation and molecular damage to polyunsaturated fatty acids in rat liver: recognition of two classes of hydroperoxides formed under conditions in vivo. Chem Biol Interact 1986:59:147-155.

118. Kohn HI, Liversedge M. On a new aerobic metabolite whose production by brain is inhibited by apomorphine, emetine, ergotamine, epinephrine and menadione. J Pharmacol Exp Ther 1944:82:292-300.

119. Dahle LK, Hill EG, Holman RT. The thiobarbituric acid reaction and the autoxidation of polyunsaturated fatty acid methyl esters. Arch Biochem Biophys 1962:98:253-261.

120. Sinnhuber RO, Yu TC, Chang YT. Characterization of the red pigment formed in the 2-thiobarbituric acid determination of oxidative rancidity. Food Res 1958:23:626-633.

121. Frankel EN. Chemistry of free radical and singlet oxidation of lipids. Prog Lipid Res 1984:23:197-222.

122. Esterbauer H, Slater TF. The quantitative estimation by high performance liquid chromatography of free malonaldehyde produced by peroxidizing microsomes. IRCS Med Sci Libr Compend 1981:9:749-750.

123. Esterbauer H, Cheeseman KH, Dianzani MU, Poli G, Slater TF. Separation and characterization of the aldehydic products of lipid peroxidation stimulated by ADP-Fe^{2+} in rat liver microsomes. Biochem J 1982:208:129-140.

124. Esterbauer H, Koller E, Slee RG, Koster JF. Possible involvement of the lipid-peroxidation product 4-hydroxy-nonenal in the formation of fluorescent chromolipids. Biochem J 1986:239:405-409.

125. Christophersen BO. Formation of monohydroxy-polyenic fatty acids from lipid peroxides by a glutathione peroxidase. Biochim Biophys Acta 1968:164:35-46.

126. Porter WL, Levasseur LA, Henick AS. Effects of surface concentration, metals and acid synergists on autoxidation of linoleic acid monolayers on silica. Lipids 1972:7:699-709.

127. Gutteridge JMC, Quinlan G. Malondialdehyde formation from lipid peroxides in the thiobarbituric acid test: the role of lipid radicals, iron salts and metal chelators. J Appl Biochem 1983:5:293-299.

128. Halliwell B, Gutteridge JMC. Lipid peroxidation, oxygen radicals, cell damage and antioxidant therapy. Lancet 1984:i:1396-1397.

QUESTIONS AND COMMENTS

Dr. Frank Bell: There is considerable interest these days in the possible role of peroxidized lipids in damaging the arterial wall and contributing to the atherogenic process. In this regard, do you have any comments on the role of low density lipoproteins (LDL) in carrying peroxidized lipids into the vessel wall, and can you comment on the propensity of LDL-lipid to undergo peroxidation during circulation in the plasma?

Dr. John Gutteridge: I have no in vivo data on the transport of oxidized lipid by lipoproteins. However, when removed from their plasma environment, lipoproteins readily peroxidize. Indeed, even in their plasma environment, storage of samples leads to a copper-mediated peroxidation of lipoprotein. It appears that proteolysis of ceruloplasmin releases copper to cause this peroxidation. The copper-lipid(oxidized)-protein complex in human plasma is known as "ferroxidase II."

Dr. Irwin Fridovich: Xanthine oxidase plus xanthine in phosphate buffer with EDTA will cause oxidation of arachidonic acid dispersed with octyl sulfate. This lipid oxidation is inhibited by SOD, catalase, deferoxamine, mannitol, or ethanol. Would you try to explain all of this in view of your presentation?

Dr. John Gutteridge: Providing you can inhibit or slow down the decomposition of lipid hydroperoxides with EDTA, yet allow the Fenton reaction to continue, the role of ·OH in the initiation of peroxidation will become obvious. Alternatively, the lipid must be completely free of peroxide contamination. However, some caution must be exercised when using catalase as a specific probe for H_2O_2 and measuring its response by diene conjugation. Catalase can nonspecifically decompose hydroperoxides and thereby decrease the observed level of conjugated dienes, and this might be interpreted as removal of H_2O_2. Similarly, mannitol might bind iron, and ethanol can alter the micelle structure.

IRON AND IRON-DERIVED RADICALS

Donald C. Borg and Karen M. Schaich

The need for iron catalysis of Fenton-like reactions that initiate cytotoxic free radical reactions is now recognized, but the mechanism of iron involvement is not clear. This paper addresses three issues: whether the various valence states of iron play a role in membrane lipid oxidation, whether Fenton reactions can occur within lipid phases to initiate lipid oxidation or are largely confined to the external membrane surface, and whether iron bound to deferoxamine can support Fenton reactions. The conclusions, based in part on the authors' research, challenge some of the usual lines of thought and emphasize the importance of considering the microenvironment in developing possible mechanisms for cytotoxic reactions.

IT IS WELL ESTABLISHED that iron plays an important role in initiating and catalyzing a variety of free radical reactions that contribute to oxygen-dependent tissue injury. Mechanisms of iron involvement in the underlying processes are not fully elucidated, but there is a growing consensus that oxidative tissue damage is supported by submicromolar to micromolar levels of nonheme cellular iron, often mobilized from ferritin stores (1,2). Although an obligatory requirement for iron catalysis was disputed until recently (1,3), cyclical Fenton-like reactions with H_2O_2 to produce extremely reactive and potentially toxic hydroxyl radicals ($\cdot OH$) are now recognized to be the driving force initiating cascades of cytotoxic free radical reactions.

Equation 1 represents the Fenton reaction. We

$$Fe^{2+} + H_2O_2 \rightarrow Fe^{3+} + \cdot OH + OH^- \qquad [1]$$

use the term "Fenton-like" to refer to similar reactions of complexed or chelated iron. Fenton "cycling" occurs when the ferric product is reduced back to ferrous form by superoxide ($O_2^{\cdot -}$) or other one-electron reductants (equation 2).

$$Fe^{3+} + O_2^{\cdot -} \text{ (or } AH^\cdot \text{ or } DH_2) \rightarrow$$
$$Fe^{2+} + O_2 \text{(or } A + H^+ \text{ or } DH^\cdot + H^+) \qquad [2]$$

We consider here three questions regarding the participation of iron in oxygen radical reactions leading to tissue injury; two of the questions deal with iron and lipid oxidation.

From Brookhaven National Laboratory, Upton, Long Island, New York, USA.

Address correspondence to Dr. Donald C. Borg, Medical Research Center, Brookhaven National Laboratory, Upton, Long Island, New York 11973, USA.

IRON VALENCE AND LIPID OXIDATION

Membrane lipid peroxidation, an important part of oxidative tissue injury, can be an effect as well as a cause of reactions culminating in cytotoxicity (1,4,5). Initiation or amplification of lipid peroxidation by iron compounds has long been known, and the reactions responsible for modulation of lipid oxidation by iron are an active focus of current research. It is clear that $\cdot OH$ can initiate lipid peroxidation in homogeneous reaction systems (6) and that conditions consistent with Fenton-like generation of $\cdot OH$ are often associated with lipid peroxidation in vivo (5), but the precise nature of iron's role, if any, in initiating lipid oxidation remains elusive (see the paper by Gutteridge in this volume).

Lipid peroxidation is a well-known free-radical chain reaction that has no intrinsic metal requirement. A representative initiating reaction is shown in equation 3, where L represents lipid.

$$LH + \cdot OH \text{ (or } LO^\cdot) \rightarrow L^\cdot + H_2O \text{ (or } LOH) \qquad [3]$$

The chain propagation cycle is shown in equations 4 and 5.

$$L^\cdot + O_2 \text{—(very fast)} \rightarrow LOO^\cdot \qquad [4]$$
$$LH + LOO^\cdot \text{—(very slow)} \rightarrow L^\cdot + LOOH \qquad [5]$$

Nonetheless, iron compounds can increase the rate of lipid oxidation dramatically by converting lipid hydroperoxides (LOOH), the metastable products of the propagation cycle, to reactive alkoxyl (LO$^\cdot$) or peroxyl (LOO$^\cdot$) radicals, which can initiate new reaction chains, a process called chain branching (1,7). For example, the alkoxy or peroxy radicals produced in equation 6 and 7 can (re)initiate lipid peroxidation by reactions 3 and 5.

$$LOOH + Fe^{2+} \text{—(fast)} \rightarrow LO^\cdot + OH^- + Fe^{3+} \qquad [6]$$
$$LOOH + Fe^{3+} \text{—(slow)} \rightarrow LOO^\cdot + H^+ + Fe^{2+} \qquad [7]$$

In studying chain reactions in systems in which there are many potentially competing reactions for chain initiation, branching, and termination, one must take into account not only the relative but also the absolute concentrations of metals and other reactants because the balance between competing reactions depends strongly upon absolute concentrations. This is particularly critical when high concentrations of metals are used in experimental models of reaction systems that have access only to trace concentrations (i.e., a few micromolar or less) in their native states. At high concentrations, metals shift from being repeatedly cycled catalysts to serving as stoichiometric reactants, and they may also exhibit dominant chain termination behavior, which is not seen at all at low concentrations (8,9).

An important chain-terminating reaction of ferrous complexes is shown in equation 8.

$$Fe^{2+} + LOO\cdot + H^+ -(fast)\rightarrow Fe^{3+} + LOOH \qquad [8]$$

Other "antioxidant" actions of high levels of ferrous compounds may include the following:

$$Fe^{2+} + \cdot OH + H^+ -(very\ fast)\rightarrow Fe^{3+} + H_2O \qquad [9]$$
$$Fe^{2+} + LO\cdot + H^+ -(very\ fast)\rightarrow Fe^{3+} + LOH \qquad [10]$$

Equation 9 decreases primary initiation reactions, and equation 10 inhibits chain branching.

Increasing concentrations of H_2O_2 can also convert these same strong oxidants to less reactive species by way of the following reactions:

$$H_2O_2 + \cdot OH -(fast)\rightarrow HO_2\cdot + H_2O \qquad [11]$$
$$H_2O_2 + LO\cdot \rightarrow HO_2\cdot + LOH \qquad [12]$$

When radicals ($L\cdot$) can be oxidized by the ferric complexes present (equation 13), high concentrations of the ferric species can act as chain terminators because the reaction competing for ferric ion (equation 14) is very slow.

$$Fe^{3+} + L\cdot \rightarrow Fe^{2+} + L^+ \qquad [13]$$
$$Fe^{3+} + H_2O_2 -(very\ slow)\rightarrow HO_2\cdot + Fe^{2+} + H^+ \qquad [14]$$

These considerations were largely overlooked in some recent investigations seeking to determine whether *initiation* of lipid peroxidation is caused by ·OH from Fenton reactions (e.g., see the paper by Aust in this volume). Using brain synaptosomes in one case (10) and liposomes prepared from reconstituted microsomal lipids in another (11), these studies suggested that the ratio of Fe^{3+} to Fe^{2+} is a critical determinant of iron pro-oxidant activity and that this action appears to be unrelated to ·OH generation or to the decomposition of preformed lipid hydroperoxides. However, the consequences of changing the Fe^{3+} to Fe^{2+} ratio were mistakenly attributed to effects on reaction initiation when, at concentrations of 200 micromolar (roughly 100 times physiological concentrations), chain branching and termination behavior dominates.

A second reaction characteristic that was insufficiently accounted for in these studies (10,11) may have contributed further to underestimating the overwhelming dominance of chain propagating reactions relative to primary initiation reactions in determining the overall behavior of the lipid oxidation systems. Once lipid oxidation has commenced, the accumulating lipid hydroperoxides (LOOH) favorably compete with H_2O_2 for both ferrous and ferric iron because the reaction rates of iron in both valence states are much greater for LOOH (12) (see the chain branching reactions in equations 6 and 7). Only when interactions of iron with the products of lipid oxidation are inhibited by separating the reactants (e.g., by chelation with the lipophobic chelator EDTA) does the underlying primary initiation by ·OH become apparent (12).

Yet another factor must be taken into account when assessing the role of ·OH reactions with macromolecular or particulate targets: the extraordinarily high reactivity of ·OH. Because of this, ·OH does not survive for more than a few collisions after its formation, and its reactions are intrinsically "site specific." That is, the potential substrates for ·OH oxidation are within, at most, a few tens of angstroms from the site of ·OH production (1,13). This implies that Fenton-generated ·OH must react at the sites where iron is bound. Thus, for ·OH to attack vesicles, iron must be present on the membrane surface or within the lipid environment. Fenton reactions forming ·OH from iron and H_2O_2 in the suspending medium are ineffective or may even be protective if the concentrations of H_2O_2 or of reactive reducing equivalents are rate limiting. This was clearly recognized in another study (14) of metal effects on lipid oxidation wherein it was concluded that $O_2^{\cdot-}$ and H_2O_2 from xanthine oxidase plus iron bound to different complexing agents caused crosslinking of membrane proteins in erythrocyte ghosts through the intermediacy of site-specific ·OH production at the membrane surface.

The authors cited previously (10,11) concluded that ·OH initiation of lipid peroxidation had not occurred because the interventions designed to alter Fenton-like generation of ·OH and the actual measurements of ·OH fluxes in the suspending media correlated poorly, or not at all, with the amount of lipid oxidation. However, these conclusions cannot be accepted with confidence because there was insufficient appreciation that the characteristics of the primary initiation reactions were no longer reflected by the overall responses of their rapidly oxidizing, multibranched chain reacting systems to one or more of three experimental factors: 1) changing ratios of Fe^{3+} to Fe^{2+}, 2) responses to ·OH scavengers, and 3) amounts of ·OH formed in the fluid phase. Each of these three factors, to the extent they were effective at all, operated primarily not upon initiation reactions but upon propagation, where they altered the reactions of Fe^{2+} and Fe^{3+} with chain-initiating LOOH or with chain-carrying LOO· radicals.

Regardless of possible misinterpretations in terms of initiation reactions, the apparent requirements for Fe^{3+} are intriguing. At least to some extent they are illusory, because in both sets of experiments most protocols involved replacement of Fe^{2+} by Fe^{3+} with total concentrations of iron at the extremely unphysiological concentration of 200 micromolar. Hence, the well-known inhibition of iron-dependent oxidative chain reactions by excessive concentrations of either ferrous or ferric species (caused by their competition for chain-carrying peroxy radicals or carbon-centered radicals as discussed previously) could provide relief (from Fe^{2+} inhibition) rather than actual stimulation by Fe^{3+} as the latter displaced the former from 200 micromolar levels.

To explain the apparent requirements for mixtures of valence states to optimize iron stimulation of lipid oxidation or to reconcile reaction kinetics apparently inconsistent with straightforward ·OH chemistry, higher valence oxides of iron, such as ferryl (FeO^{2+} or $Fe(OH)_2^{2+}$) or ferrous peroxide ($Fe(H_2O_2)^{2+}$), have been invoked as the proximate reactants initiating chain reactions or causing lipid oxidation (8-11,15). Nevertheless, not until the past year (15) has spectroscopic identification been claimed for a putative nonheme ferryl reaction intermediate under physiological reaction conditions, and it was pointed out long ago (8) that "kinetic analysis alone cannot produce direct proof for the existence and reactions of ferryl ion." Even the chromophoric reaction intermediate recently detected by stopped flow spectrophotometry (15) in an alleged ferryl-producing reduction of H_2O_2 by ferrous chelates may be attributable to ·OH instead. According to our analysis, a radical may have been formed on the organic ligand carrying the ferric product of the same Fenton reaction that gave rise to the ·OH. This would represent site-specific back reaction of the ·OH formed in the solvent cage of that reaction.

INITIATION OF LIPID OXIDATION: IN OR ON MEMBRANES?

Up to this point we have commented, sceptically in some cases, on reports from other groups. Without undertaking to explain all the findings reported, we have expressed lack of conviction that a good case exists to reject Fenton-type ·OH formation as the "primordial" initiator of lipid oxidation in the model systems studied, but we have not yet given any positive experimental evidence in support of that notion. With that aim in mind, we reasoned that it was important to determine experimentally whether

Fenton-like formation of ·OH can occur in a lipid phase.

Although there are many reports of lipid oxidation initiated under conditions where Fenton-like reactions are thought to occur, it has been correctly noted that "the evidence that ·OH is formed under conditions that exist biologically is indirect" (15). Furthermore, the shallow penetration of a lipid bilayer that would be expected of ·OH, before that highly electrophilic and indiscriminately reactive radical disappeared, provides good reason to question whether ·OH generated externally could penetrate to the hydrophobic membrane interior where the lipid chains are confined. There is evidence, however, that iron on the membrane surface can lead to the production of *some* effective initiator of lipid peroxidation: iron–ascorbate reactions (prolific sources of ·OH) lead to liposome oxidation when the membrane surface charge is neutral or negative and iron ions are not repelled from contact or binding, but not when the charge is positive (16). It has also been concluded (14) that most or all of the ability of zinc ions to protect erythrocyte ghosts from undergoing lipid peroxidation in media containing soluble Fenton systems resides in the displacement of iron from membrane binding sites by zinc.

It is not feasible to confine strongly oxidizing Fenton systems within vesicles because confinement will be breached and the systems will be partially released into the medium secondary to lipid oxidation. Although bulk lipids are weak surrogates for structurally organized membrane bilayers with hydrophobic centers of oriented lipids, exterior polar headgroups and, in cells, a further exterior thicket of glycoprotein filaments, they may provide experimental access to environments with hydrophobicity comparable to membrane interiors. Our earlier work (3), however, showed differences in the proticities of bulk lipids. In reacting with stilbene dibromide in aprotic media, $O_2^{·-}$ acts as a strong nucleophile, causing dehydro-dehalogenation with the formation of a blue chromophore; but in protic environments, $O_2^{·-}$ is a weak electron transfer agent, and no color reaction occurs. By that criterion, bulk oleic acid is a weakly protic medium, but its methyl ester and the methyl ester of linoleic acid are aprotic (3). Although we assumed that the proticity of membrane interiors might resemble that of esters, we did not know, so we studied Fenton reactions in both bulk fatty acids and in lipid esters.

To have a Fenton reaction, H_2O_2 and Fe^{2+} (or Fe^{3+} and a reducing agent) must be present. The questions to be answered, then, are whether all the reactants can penetrate a membrane or a lipid phase and, if so, whether the reaction "goes" in a lipid, hydrophobic environment.

We have shown that H_2O_2 diffuses through

membranes (17), and our present research indicates that up to 10% of H_2O_2 in the aqueous phase partitions into bulk lipid (18). Iron salts and low molecular weight complexes partition from water into oleic acid at concentrations in the micromolar range (**Table 1**). Although systematic studies of iron distribution as a function of iron concentration have yet to be done, it is likely the data in Table 1 represent saturation values rather than partition coefficients.

When millimolar amounts of iron were present in the aqueous phase, the valence of the metal did not affect the solubility in lipid except for ADP chelates of iron, where the ferric form was more lipophilic. As expected, EDTA and DTPA (diethylenetriamine-pentaacetate) are only sparingly soluble in lipid. (In fact, EDTA washes can be used to remove metals from oils.) Optical absorption spectra indicate that the iron complexes with ADP and deferoxamine transfer as chelates to oleic acid.

To study Fenton reactions in lipid phases, we dissolved the spin traps DMPO (5,5-dimethyl-1-pyrroline-*N*-oxide) or PBN (phenyl-*tert*-butyl nitrone) in neat fatty acids or esters, and separately partitioned H_2O_2, iron compounds, and hydroxylamine (as a lipid-soluble reducing agent, when necessary) into the same lipids. All solutions and lipids were sparged and then maintained under argon. To start the reactions, aliquots from each of the lipid phases were mixed, and radical production was monitored by electron paramagnetic resonance (EPR). As we have reported (1,3), when Fenton reactions, either with Fe^{2+} or with Fe^{3+} and a reducing agent, were run in protic oleic acid, the well-known four-line 1:2:2:1 signal of a ·OH adduct was produced with DMPO. When oleic acid was incubated with iron before DMPO was added, the peroxy radical was trapped (1,3), and when the Fenton reaction or iron incubation was allowed to proceed for some time, complex spectra were obtained with alkyl, alkoxy, peroxy, and, in some cases, hydroxyl radical adducts. Thus the reaction system behaves as would be expected according to the classical chemistry of lipid oxidation.

It is possible to follow the changes in ·OH adduct concentrations with time by fixing the magnetic field on one of the center lines of the EPR signal, and this was done to follow the Fenton-like reactions of ferric chloride, "free" and chelated by ADP, EDTA, and DTPA. **Figure 1** shows that, of the three chelates, ADP supported Fenton kinetics in oleic acid at rates approaching that of the ferric salt, whereas EDTA and DTPA chelates reacted much more slowly and provided lower total adduct concentrations. There are three possible explanations for this: 1) the absolute concentrations of chelates partitioned into the oleic acid are not the same (Table 1); 2) EDTA and DTPA are known to react rapidly with ·OH and may have competed with DMPO for the hydroxyl radicals while they were being formed close to the chelates; or 3) the redox characteristics of the three chelates may be different in oleic acid than in water. Probably all of these factors contribute to the observed behavior.

Table 1. Partitioning of Iron from Water into Oleic Acid and Methyl Linoleate*

	Iron (μM) in Lipid Phase and Ferric/Ferrous Ratios					
	Oleic Acid			Methyl Linoleate		
Iron Complex	Ferric	Ferrous	Ratio	Ferric	Ferrous	Ratio
Ammonium sulfate	5.90	6.00	0.98	0.28	0.30	0.93
Chloride	3.50	3.50	1.00	--	--	--
Citrate	0.09	3.40	0.03	--	--	--
Sulfate	3.50	3.50	1.00	--	--	--
ADP†	>18	6.30	>3	0.64	0.19	3.37
EDTA**	0.40	0.54	0.74	0.02	~0	--
DTPA††	0.11	~0	--	~0	~0	--
Deferoxamine	>18	--	--	0.56	--	--

* 1 mM solutions of iron with 10% excess of complexing agent were vortexed with an equal volume of lipid, the phases were separated by centrifugation, and the oil phase was analyzed by atomic absorption (using a furnace with deuterium arc background correction). Concentrations were calculated for the oil phase after corrections for the diluent used (tetrahydrofuran) and for solvent blanks (lipid vortexed with water).

† Adenosine diphosphate (with ammonium sulfate)

** Ethylenediaminetetraacetate

†† Diethylenetriaminepentaacetate

When the reactions were run in aprotic lauric, oleic, or linoleic methyl esters instead of the more protic acids, DMPO gave signals consisting almost entirely of lipid alkyl and sometimes peroxy radical adducts, with weak, if any, contributions from ·OH (**Figure 2**). Especially with linoleate, the signals changed with time, indicating changes of radical species and varying proportions of different radicals (1). These experiments suggest either that the ·OH adduct is not stable in aprotic media (we are not aware of data which indicate this to be so) or that ·OH reactions with aprotic lipids are much faster than those with protic lipids. This raises a more general question we are now investigating: What are the preferred targets for reaction with ·OH in membranes, where most fatty acids are present as esters?

Have these results answered the question of whether Fenton reactions occur within lipid phases and initiate lipid oxidation? Clearly, the chemistry occurs; all the "makings" for compartmentalized Fenton reactions are present in the model systems, and ·OH is produced. Oxidized species of lipid also

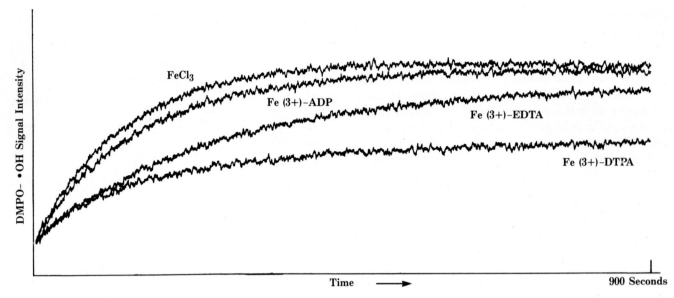

Figure 1. EPR time curves for production of the ·OH spin adduct of DMPO during Fenton reactions in oleic acid. 0.1 mM solutions of $FeCl_3$ or its chelates with ADP (1:17 Fe:ADP molar ratio), EDTA (1:1.1), and DTPA (1:1.1) were partitioned into oleic acid (see text). Final concentrations of reaction components: DMPO, 44 mM; H_2O_2, ~220 mM. EPR parameters: power, 5 mW; modulation amplitude, 0.5 G (at 100 kHz).

can be spin trapped (Figure 2), indicating that lipid oxidation occurs, and changing envelopes of spin-trapped lipid species over time (1) strongly suggest that the characteristic chain reactions of lipid peroxidation have been established with the traces of oxygen that remain. Quantification of this lipid oxidation is in progress.

Hence, intramembranous formation of ·OH appears feasible in vivo provided that appropriately complexed nonheme iron is available and endogenous reducing sources can replace the hydroxylamine used in our models. However, whether chain propagation through lipid bilayers or free radical damage to embedded macromolecules will predominate in biological membranes depends upon the character of the nearby lipid and upon the microenvironment of the binding site for the redox-active metal.

BOUND IRON AND THE FENTON REACTION

It is currently thought that ferric iron bound to deferoxamine (desferrioxamine B methanesulfonate) to form ferrioxamine cannot participate in the reaction cycles that generate ·OH from H_2O_2. However, an apparently paradoxical enhancement of lung damage and mortality in an animal experiment designed to show deferoxamine protection against oxidizing injury by paraquat (19) led us to re-evaluate the redox chemistry of deferoxamine in the presence and absence of traces of iron.

Although deferoxamine itself showed no reduction wave by cyclic voltammetry on a glassy carbon electrode, its ferric chelate, ferrioxamine, was reduced reversibly at $E^{\circ\prime} = -0.42$ volts (K.M. Schaich,

C.A. Linkous, and D.C. Borg, unpublished data). It is important to note that this is within the range of cellular reducing power, and, indeed, we found that under anoxic conditions ferrioxamine can be reduced stoichiometrically by paraquat radical and also by hypoxanthine/xanthine oxidase to a colorless product (20; K.M. Schaich, C.A. Linkous, and D.C. Borg, unpublished data). Solutions of this reduced species reoxidized instantly upon exposure to air, regenerating orange-red ferrioxamine (absorption maximum at 430 nm).

The low $E^{\circ\prime}$ suggests that the iron center in reduced ferrioxamine might directly reduce H_2O_2, affording a Fenton-like production of ·OH. This was confirmed in two ways: 1) by monitoring the disappearance of H_2O_2 with an oxidase-type electrode, and 2) by observing the characteristic EPR spectrum of the ·OH spin adduct of DMPO, as depicted by the uppermost tracing (A) of **Figure 3** (20; K.M. Schaich, C.A. Linkous, and D.C. Borg, unpublished data).

Other recordings in Figure 3 confirm the dynamic nature of reaction systems that present competitive pathways to highly reactive oxygen radical intermediates and how precariously their toxic potential may be balanced between excesses of either oxidizing or reducing capacity (21). The second spectrum (B) shows an example of oxidizing capacity in excess: when an aliquot of anoxic, reduced ferrioxamine is added to an aerobic solution of H_2O_2 and DMPO, O_2 and H_2O_2 compete for its oxidation, and the production of ·OH is markedly decreased. (With appropriate adjustments of reactant concentrations, one can arrange for ·OH to be undetectable.) Since ·OH has a high cytotoxic potential when generated in vivo, this presents the apparent paradox of high oxygen tension serving as an antioxidant in a reaction involving toxic oxygen radicals. The paradox is resolved upon recognition that in this reaction system O_2 supports a detoxifying pathway.

The third trace (C) in Figure 3 was taken from a reaction in which ethanol, as well as H_2O_2 and DMPO, was present in the solution added to reduced ferrioxamine. It shows the superimposed spectra of two spin adducts of DMPO: that from ·OH and that from the *a*-hydroxyethyl radical produced by reaction

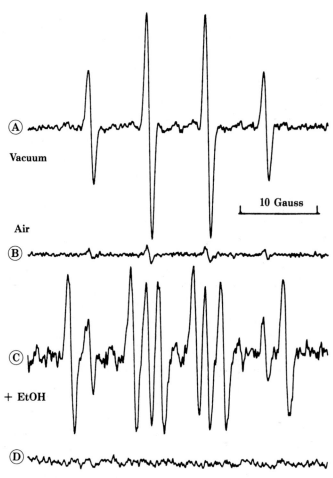

Figure 3. DMPO spin trapping of ·OH produced in the reduction of H_2O_2 by ferrioxamine (FOA) previously reduced by paraquat radical cation (PQ^{+}·). (0.1 mM FOA was reduced by >0.1 mM PQ^{+}·, but no PQ^{+}· remained at the time of final mixing prior to recording of EPR spectra.) Final concentrations of reaction components: FOA, 0.037 mM; H_2O_2, 80 mM; DMPO, 65 mM; and ethanol, when present, 3 mM. X-band EPR parameters: power, 5 mW; modulation amplitude, 1.6 G (at 100 kHz).

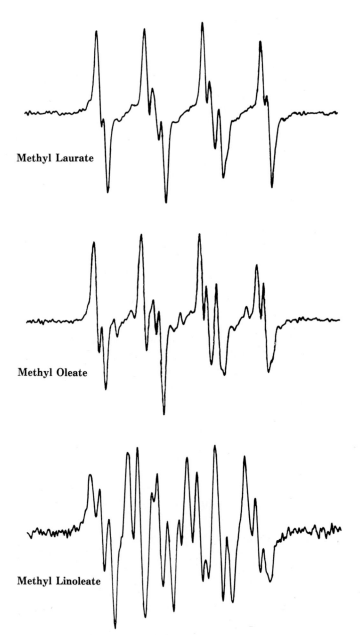

Figure 2. EPR spectra of DMPO spin adducts formed during Fenton reactions in methyl esters of lipids. Argon-purged $FeCl_3$ (1 mM), H_2O_2 (30%), and $NH_2OH·HCl$ (10%) were each partitioned into equal volumes of lipid ester, the phases were separated by centrifugation, and aliquots of the lipid phases were mixed with DMPO (350 mM) dissolved in lipid ester.

of ·OH with ethanol. This helps confirm the presence of authentic ·OH and also denotes the presence of a competitive reaction path for ·OH. Even more instructive, however, is the *absence* of any signal when the reaction was run with a larger aliquot of reduced ferrioxamine (not shown). There is no signal because excess reduced ferrioxamine scavenges oxidizing ·OH and also reduces the spin adducts, which are nitroxide (aminoxyl) radicals, to hydroxylamines or even more reduced diamagnetic products. This illustrates reducing excess in the delicate balance cited in the previous paragraph (21).

Taking into account these results, plus some additional features of the experimental systems, we conclude that a pro-oxidant enhancement of oxidative cytotoxicity may occur when relatively high concentrations of deferoxamine-chelated iron have access in vivo to mobile, strong reducing substances or to reducing enzymes under low oxygen tension (so that $\cdot$OH production from H_2O_2 by reduced ferrioxamine can compete with its autoxidation) (20). Both hypoxia and elevated levels of the reducing enzyme xanthine oxidase exist after postischemic reperfusion, while localized hypoxia in the presence of very strongly reducing small molecules occurs during poisoning by paraquat and related compounds and in the presence of readily autoxidizable metabolites from various nitro compounds and other xenobiotics. Under these conditions, therefore, a biphasic antioxidant/pro-oxidant behavior of deferoxamine as a function of dose is a real possibility (21) despite prevailing assumptions to the contrary. Such an outcome should be carefully considered when planning treatment with deferoxamine (20; K.M. Schaich, C.A. Linkous, and D.C. Borg, unpublished data). Even in biochemical reactions, neither the failure of deferoxamine to suppress an oxidative outcome nor the actual enhancement by deferoxamine of such a response can be considered sufficient evidence to rule out an iron-dependent process without other supporting information (20).

CONCLUSIONS

We have discussed some reactions of iron and iron-derived oxygen radicals that may be important in the production or treatment of tissue injury. Our conclusions challenge, to some extent, the usual lines of thought in this field of research. Insofar as they are borne out by subsequent developments, the lessons they teach are two: Think fast, and think small! In other words, think of the many fast reactions that can rapidly alter the production and fate of highly reactive intermediates, and when considering the impact of competitive reactions on such species, think how they affect the microenvironment (on the molecular scale) "seen" by each reactive molecule.

ACKNOWLEDGMENT

Brookhaven National Laboratory is operated for the U.S. Department of Energy under Contract No. DE-AC-02-76CH00016.

REFERENCES

1. Borg DC, Schaich KM. Cytotoxicity from coupled redox cycling of autoxidizing xenobiotics and metals: a selective critical review and commentary on work-in-progress. Isr J Chem 1984:24:38-53.

2. Aust SD, Morehouse LA, Thomas CE. Role of metals in oxygen radical reactions. J Free Rad Biol Med 1985:1:3-25.

3. Borg DC, Schaich KM, Forman A. Autoxidative cytotoxicity: Is there metal-independent formation of hydroxyl radicals? Are there "crypto-hydroxyl" radicals? In: Bors W, Saran M, Tait D, eds. Oxygen radicals in chemistry and biology, Berlin: Walter de Gruyter, 1984:123-9 (and discussion, p.105).

4. Halliwell B, Gutteridge JMC. Free radicals in biology and medicine. Oxford:Clarendon Press, 1985.

5. Halliwell B, Gutteridge JMC. Oxygen free radicals and iron in relation to biology and medicine: some problems and concepts. Arch Biochem Biophys 1986:246:501-14.

6. Hasegawa K, Patterson LK. Pulse radiolysis studies in model lipid systems: formation and behavior of peroxy radicals in fatty acids. Photochem Photobiol 1978:28:817-23.

7. Borg DC, Schaich KM, Elmore JJ Jr, Bell JA. Cytotoxic reactions of free radical species of oxygen. Photochem Photobiol 1978:28:887-907.

8. Barb WG, Baxendale JH, George P, Hargrave KR. Reactions of ferrous and ferric ions with hydrogen peroxide. Part I. The ferrous ion reaction. Trans Faraday Soc 1951:47:462-500.

9. Barb WG, Baxendale JH, George P, Hargrave KR. Reactions of ferrous and ferric ions with hydrogen peroxide. Part II. The ferric ion reaction. Trans Faraday Soc 1951:47:591-616.

10. Braughler JM, Duncan LA, Chase RL. The involvement of iron in lipid peroxidation. Importance of ferric to ferrous ratios in initiation. J Biol Chem 1986:261:10282-10289.

11. Minotti G, Aust SD. The requirement for iron(III) in the initiation of lipid peroxidation by iron(II) and hydrogen peroxide. J Biol Chem 1987:262:1098-1104.

12. Gutteridge JMC. Lipid peroxidation initiated by superoxide-dependent hydroxyl radicals using complexed iron and hydrogen peroxide. FEBS Lett 1984:172:245-249.

13. Goldstein S, Czapski G. The role and mechanism of metal ions and their complexes in enhancing damage in biological systems or in protecting these systems from the toxicity of $O_2^{\cdot-}$. J Free Rad Biol Med 1986:2:3-11.

14. Girotti AW, Thomas JP, Jordan JE. Xanthine oxidase-catalyzed crosslinking of cell membrane proteins. Arch Biochem Biophys 1986:251:639-653.

15. Rush JD, Koppenol WH. The reaction between ferrous polyaminocarboxylate complexes and hydrogen peroxide: an investigation of the reaction intermediates by stopped flow spectrophotometry. J Inorg Biochem 1987:29:199-215.

16. Kunimoto M, Inoue K, Nojima S. Effect of ferrous ion and ascorbate-induced lipid peroxidation on liposomal membranes. Biochem Biophys Acta 1981:646:169-178.

17. Frimer A, Forman A, Borg DC. H_2O_2 diffusion through liposomes. Isr J Chem 1983:23:442-445.

18. Schaich KM, Borg DC. Fenton reactions in lipid phases. Lipids 1988:23:(in press).

19. Osheroff MR, Schaich KM, Drew RT, Borg DC. Failure of desferrioxamine to modify the toxicity of paraquat in rats. J Free Rad Biol Med 1985:1:71-82.

20. Borg DC, Schaich KM. Pro-oxidant action of desferrioxamine: Fenton-like production of hydroxyl radicals by reduced ferrioxamine. J Free Rad Biol Med 1986:2:237-243.

21. Borg DC, Schaich KM. Pro-oxidant action of antioxidants. In: Miquel J, ed. Handbook of biomedicine of free radicals and antioxidants. Boca Raton: CRC Press, 1988:(in press).

SOURCES OF IRON FOR LIPID PEROXIDATION IN BIOLOGICAL SYSTEMS

Steven D. Aust

Iron is the transition metal most likely involved in lipid peroxidation in biological systems. Evidence is presented that iron can catalyze lipid peroxidation directly and that both the ferric and ferrous states of iron are required. Studies suggest that the most likely source of iron for biological lipid peroxidation is the iron storage protein ferritin. Iron can be released from ferritin by superoxide and organic radicals and by redox cycling chemicals. This paper also discusses the roles of oxidizing and reducing agents, various kinds of chelators, and the pH in determining the ratio of ferric to ferrous iron and thus the likelihood of lipid peroxidation within the cell.

SINCE THE REACTION of molecular oxygen with nonactivated organic molecules is spin forbidden, initiation of lipid peroxidation requires either the generation of very reactive species of oxygen or the presence of complexes of oxygen with a transition metal. We propose that iron is the transition metal most likely involved in the initiation of lipid peroxidation because it generally leads to a partial reduction of oxygen. This situation would require careful control of iron absorption, transport, and storage by iron-containing proteins, e.g., transferrin and ferritin. These proteins provide iron cations for lipid peroxidation only when the iron is released under conditions appropriate for the iron to initiate peroxidation of lipids. The same is probably true for other iron-containing biomolecules, such as hemoglobin.

We propose that the iron-storage protein ferritin initiates lipid peroxidation because its ferric stores are reductively released by both superoxide (O_2^{-}) and organic radicals. However, simple release of iron from ferritin is, by itself, insufficient to cause lipid peroxidation. Our data suggest that initiation requires the formation of a ferrous iron–oxygen species–ferric iron complex. Consequently, our suggested mechanism requires not only the release of iron from ferritin but the simultaneous presence of both Fe^{2+} and Fe^{3+} for initiation of lipid peroxidation. Reductants may be required to keep part of the iron in the ferrous state, while oxidants would be needed to maintain some iron in the ferric state. The O_2^{-} can act as both a reductant and, indirectly, as an oxidant since it produces H_2O_2 by dismutation.

The redox activity of iron is also influenced by pH and chelation. Chelators such as EDTA, which allow

rapid oxidation of ferrous iron, restrict availability of the ferrous ion and thereby inhibit lipid peroxidation. Some chelators, such as the ferrous-selective bathophenanthroline, prevent iron oxidation, whereas some ferric iron chelates are readily reduced by cellular reductants and maintain iron in the ferrous state. In either case, lipid peroxidation would be inhibited due to the lack of ferric ions.

Excessive release of iron from sources such as ferritin, the formation of inappropriate low molecular weight chelates, or loss of cellular reducing capacity could result in the oxidation of cellular components such as polyunsaturated fatty acids. It is apparent that the availability of iron and its ultimate biological effects depend on its redox chemistry, the "redox tone" of the cell, and access to cellular and tissue structures.

ROLE OF IRON IN LIPID PEROXIDATION

The experimental requirement for iron in both enzymatic and nonenzymatic lipid peroxidation was demonstrated in the original papers that described the phenomenon [1,2]. Other transition metals, either alone or coupled with other metals, can substitute for iron under appropriate conditions. The mechanism by which iron initiates lipid peroxidation remains controversial. A popular theory is that it participates in a superoxide-driven Haber-Weiss reaction. However, lipid peroxidation can be initiated by various systems that do not involve O_2^{-}. An example is liver microsomal NADPH-dependent lipid peroxidation, which requires iron but is apparently not affected by endogenous superoxide dismutase or catalase. There is probably a direct reduction of iron by NADPH-cytochrome P450 reductase [3].

With phospholipid liposomes, it is possible to initiate lipid peroxidation upon the addition of only ferrous iron, but it only occurs after a substantial lag period [4]. We have observed that the lag period can be abolished by the addition of ferric iron [4] or by oxidation of a portion of the ferrous iron [5]. These and other observations have led us to propose that both ferrous and ferric iron are required for lipid peroxidation.

If this hypothesis is correct, it is necessary to consider the factors that affect the redox activity of iron. These include the concentration of iron oxidants and reductants, the pH, and the nature of the iron chelator(s). These factors are included in the scheme shown in **Figure 1**. Starting with ferrous iron alone, lipid peroxidation only occurs after oxidation of a

From Department of Biochemistry, Michigan State University, East Lansing, Michigan, USA.

Address correspondence to Dr. Steven D. Aust, Biotechnology Center, Utah State University, Logan, Utah 84322-4430, USA.

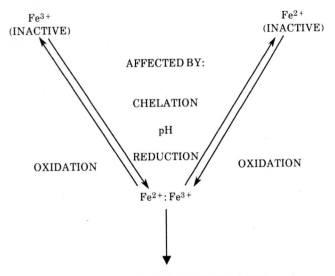

Figure 1. Scheme for the proposed role of iron in lipid peroxidation including the effects of pH, chelation, oxidation, and reduction.

fraction of the ferrous iron to the ferric form. Oxidation can be by autoxidation or by oxidants such as $O_2^{\cdot-}$, hydrogen peroxide (H_2O_2), or lipid hydroperoxides. Starting with ferric iron, it is necessary to include a reductant. It would appear that almost any reductant, including $O_2^{\cdot-}$ (6) or thiols (7), will suffice, providing that the rate of reduction does not exceed the rate of iron oxidation so as to maintain an effective concentration of the ferrous–ferric complex. Excessive oxidation or reduction would preclude significant formation of the ferrous–ferric complex, thereby resulting in little lipid peroxidation.

In the absence of chelating agent, the rate of ferrous autoxidation is greater at higher pH (8). Anions with low affinity for ferrous iron have little affect on the rate of iron autoxidation (9), but chelators with oxygen donor atoms enhance autoxidation (10,11). Also important is the effect of chelators on reduction catalyzed directly by an enzyme. A chelate may or may not be a substrate for a particular enzyme.

PHYSIOLOGICAL SOURCES OF IRON

Iron biochemistry is very complex and not completely understood (12). Iron must be absorbed in the ferrous state and transported in the ferric state by transferrin. After receptor-mediated endocytosis of transferrin, the iron is somehow transferred in an acidic, endocytic vesicle to the iron-storage protein ferritin or is perhaps transferred directly to iron-requiring biosynthetic pathways. Most investigators postulate the need for a low molecular weight chelator to transfer iron to appropriate biosynthetic enzymes, such as ferrochelatase, in cells. This low molecular weight "iron pool" may, in fact, be the most important

pool of redox active iron available to catalyze the destructive oxidation of biomolecules. It is interesting to note that iron-requiring systems seem to require the addition of iron in the ferrous form (13), perhaps because of the ready hydrolysis of ferric iron, especially at neutral pH.

Ultimately, the majority of intracellular iron is deposited in ferritin (14). Ferritin can contain as much as 4500 ions of iron per complex, although it is usually not saturated (15). A small amount of ferritin exists in plasma, but the amount can increase dramatically in various pathological conditions (16).

Another major pool of iron, in terms of amount, is present in various heme proteins, mostly hemoglobin and myoglobin. Because of its juxtaposition with oxygen and membranes that are quite susceptible to lipid peroxidation, it can only be assumed that evolution has provided heme proteins that are not a good source of iron for the catalysis of lipid peroxidation. However, Gutteridge (17) has shown that iron can be released from hemoglobin, presumably catalyzed by H_2O_2, to induce lipid peroxidation.

It seems unlikely that "free" iron exists in biological systems, most likely because of its reactivity. But iron must be transferred from either transferrin or ferritin to iron-containing cellular components such as heme or iron-containing enzymes. Interestingly, these systems are usually saturated by very small amounts of iron (18). Several low molecular weight chelates of iron have been proposed (19-22), and there is biological evidence of their existence (23,24). Since iron is released from ferritin by reduction (15), it would appear that this putative chelator binds and maintains the ferrous state so as to prevent iron-catalyzed oxidation of cellular components. It is also reasonable to propose that a cellular reductant assists in maintaining the low molecular weight chelate in the ferrous form, to ensure that it remains inactive as regards lipid peroxidation. Conversely, excessive oxidation of iron, e.g., by H_2O_2, may generate the ferric iron required for lipid peroxidation. It therefore seems important to identify and characterize the low molecular weight chelate of iron in tissues.

RELEASE OF IRON FROM TRANSFERRIN

Transferrin, the major iron transport protein, contains only two iron binding sites and binds iron in association with bicarbonate, forming a ternary complex that does not dissociate easily (14). Protonating, reducing, and chelating agents can promote iron release from transferrin (25-28). It would appear that iron-saturated transferrin can support hydroxyl radical ($\cdot OH$) formation and lipid

Table 1. Factors Affecting the Release of Iron from Transferrin by Xanthine Oxidase*

| Addition | Iron Release (nmol Fe^{3+}/min) | | | |
	pH 7.0	pH 6.0	pH 5.0	pH 4.5
None	0	0.02	0.02	0.03
ADP	0.01	0.03	0.06	0.13
Xanthine/Xanthine oxidase	0.02	0.04	0.07	0.07
Xanthine/Xanthine oxidase + ADP	0.06	0.18	0.28	0.35

* All incubations contained transferrin (30 μM) in 0.3 M NaCl at 25°C at the pH indicated. Xanthine (0.33 mM), xanthine oxidase (0.05 U/mL), and ADP (80 μM) were added as indicated. Rates of iron release promoted by xanthine oxidase were normalized to a constant rate of O_2^{-} generation. (Data reprinted from reference 33 with permission of Pergamon Journals, Inc.)

Table 2. Effect of Superoxide Dismutase (SOD) on Aerobic, Paraquat-Dependent Release of Iron from Ferritin*

| Ferritin (nmol Fe^{3+}) | Iron Release (nmol Fe^{2+}/min) | |
	−SOD	+SOD
Native ferritin, 1.50 mg (1410)	1.76	0.54
Iron-induced ferritin, 1.50 mg (4800)	1.44	0.72

* Reaction mixtures (1 mL final volume) contained NADPH-cytochrome P450 reductase (0.10 U), paraquat (1 mM), catalase (500 U), bathophenanthroline sulfonate (1 mM), the amount and type of rat liver ferritin indicated, and, where indicated, superoxide dismutase (500 U) in 50 mM NaCl, pH 7.0. Reactions were initiated with NADPH (0.5 mM) and monitored at 530 nm. (Data reprinted from reference 37 with permission of the American Society of Biological Chemists.)

peroxidation, whereas partially iron-saturated transferrin inhibits ·OH formation (29-32).

We studied iron release from transferrin and lipid peroxidation in a system where xanthine oxidase generated O_2^{-} and H_2O_2 (33). Iron was only slowly released from transferrin when incubated with xanthine oxidase (**Table 1**). Iron release was increased when ADP was included and when the pH was lowered. However, these conditions were not conducive to significant rates of lipid peroxidation (not shown). The pH optimum is near 7 for NADPH-cytochrome P450 reductase-dependent lipid peroxidation (34), whereas it is near 6 for a xanthine oxidase- and transferrin-dependent lipid peroxidation (33). As the pH was lowered below 6, the rate of iron release from transferrin increased, but the rate of lipid peroxidation decreased.

RELEASE OF IRON FROM FERRITIN

Upon first analysis, ferritin would appear to be better than transferrin as a source of iron to catalyze the oxidation of lipids or other substances. Ferritin can contain up to 4500 ferric ions per ferritin complex, stored as ferric hydroxide micelles complexed with phosphate (14). Iron is mobilized from ferritin by reduction, but the physiological reductant remains unknown. Chelating agents are required along with reductant, but, again, the physiological low molecular weight chelator is unknown.

When ferritin was incubated with xanthine and xanthine oxidase, slow but significant rates of iron release were observed (35). Superoxide dismutase completely blocked iron release, whereas catalase slightly stimulated release. In these experiments, 2,2'-dipyridyl was included to chelate the iron and provide a chromophore for assay of iron release.

When paraquat and NADPH-cytochrome P450 reductase were used as the superoxide-generating system (36,37), we found that superoxide dismutase would not completely inhibit the release of iron from ferritin (**Table 2**). In addition, more extensive release of iron was observed in the paraquat-dependent superoxide-generating system than with xanthine oxidase. When this system was incubated anaerobically, rapid and complete release of iron from ferritin was observed (**Table 3**). This led to the realization that the paraquat radical itself was a very effective reductant of iron in ferritin.

A further investigation of iron release from ferritin led to the discovery that other bipyridyls (37), the anthracycline antibiotics (38), and various other chemicals capable of being reduced by one electron are able to catalyze iron release (39) (**Table 4**).

XANTHINE OXIDASE- AND FERRITIN-DEPENDENT LIPID PEROXIDATION

The similarities in the conditions under which iron is released from ferritin and under which lipid

Table 3. Anaerobic Iron Release from Ferritin by Paraquat at Various Ferritin Concentrations*

Ferritin Fe^{3+} Added (nmol)	Total Fe^{3+} Reduced (nmol)
0	0.21
25	26.1
50	50.4
75	74.9
100	96.1

* Reaction mixtures (1 mL final volume) contained NADPH-cytochrome P450 reductase (0.1 U), paraquat (0.25 mM), bathophenanthroline sulfonate (1 mM), glucose (5 mM), glucose oxidase (10 U), catalase (500 U), and various amounts of rat liver ferritin, as indicated, in 50 mM NaCl, pH 7.0. Reactions were initiated by the addition of NADPH (0.5 mM) and continuously monitored at 530 nm until no further formation of the bathophenanthroline sulfonate-Fe^{2+} complex was observed. Results are the averages of two separate experiments. (Data reprinted from reference 37 with permission of the American Society of Biological Chemists.)

Table 4. Anaerobic Release of Iron From Ferritin and Oxidation of NADPH by Various Redox Active Compounds*

Addition	Iron Released (nmol/min)	NADPH Oxidized (nmol/min)	NADPH Oxidized/ Iron Released
None	0.23	0.80	3.47
Paraquat	22.22	30.54	1.37
Benzyl viologen	18.97	30.54	1.61
Diquat	27.82	30.54	1.10
Triphenyltetrazolium	8.13	25.72	3.16
Nitrofurantoin	3.88	14.47	3.72
Adriamycin	7.27	14.47	1.99
Daunomycin	11.40	24.11	2.25
Diaziquone	0.25	11.25	45.00

* Reaction mixtures for iron release studies (1 mL final volume) contained NADPH-cytochrome P450 reductase (0.1 U), horse spleen ferritin (500 μM Fe), bathophenanthroline sulfonate (1 mM) or *ortho*-phenanthroline (1 mM), glucose (5 mM), glucose oxidase (10 U), catalase (500 U), and the added compound (0.25 mM each) in 50 mM NaCl, pH 7.0. Reactions were initated by the addition of NADPH (0.5 mM) and monitored spectrophotometrically at 510 nm (when *ortho*-phenanthroline was used) or 530 nm (when bathophenanthroline was used). For NADPH oxidation studies, the chelator was omitted, the amount of NADPH was 0.2 mM, and the decrease in absorbance at 340 nm was monitored. (Data reprinted from reference 39 with permission of the *Annals of Emergency Medicine*.)

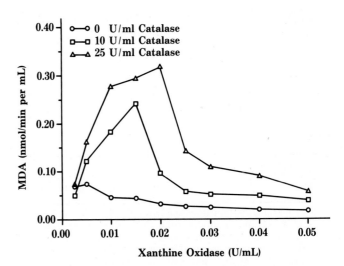

Figure 2. Xanthine oxidase- and ferritin-dependent peroxidation of phospholipids. Reaction mixtures (5 mL final volume) contained phospholipid liposomes (lipid phosphate 1 μmol/mL), rat liver ferritin (200 μmol Fe^{3+}), ADP (1 mmol), xanthine (0.33 mmol), and various concentrations of xanthine oxidase in 50 mM NaCl, pH 7.0. Three experiments were conducted with either 0, 10, or 25 units of catalase per mL. Peroxidation was initiated by the addition of xanthine oxidase, and aliquots from the reaction mixtures were assayed for malondialdehyde (MDA) by the thiobarbituric acid method.

peroxidation begins are striking. Both require reducing and chelating agents. Gutteridge et al (40) described ascorbate- and ferritin-dependent lipid peroxidation, and Wills (41) reported a nonenzymatic lipid peroxidation system using ferritin as the source of iron. Xanthine oxidase is often used as a source of $O_2^{\cdot-}$ and H_2O_2 for the oxidation of many biomolecules including lipid. Both Mazur et al (42,43) and Topham et al (44) proposed that xanthine dehydrogenase, the NAD^+-requiring dehydrogenase form of xanthine oxidase, could catalyze the release of iron from ferritin by direct reduction.

Since lipid peroxidation is often attributed to a superoxide-driven Haber-Weiss reaction, we used xanthine oxidase to study ferritin-dependent lipid peroxidation (35). Lipid peroxidation could be demonstrated, but activity was extremely low when iron release was substantial (35). Since xanthine oxidase produces both $O_2^{\cdot-}$ and H_2O_2, and since we only observe lipid peroxidation when both ferrous and ferric iron are present, we reasoned that the H_2O_2 might oxidize the iron before it could initiate lipid peroxidation. This hypothesis gained support from the observation that catalase stimulated lipid peroxidation (**Figure 2**). The amount of catalase required to stimulate lipid peroxidation maximally increased as the amount of xanthine oxidase was increased.

The ability of catalase to stimulate xanthine

oxidase- and ferritin-dependent lipid peroxidation would suggest that the $\cdot$OH, produced as the ferrous ion was being oxidized by H_2O_2, did not contribute significantly to lipid peroxidation in our system. Further evidence that this might be the case was that chemicals which should have selectively intercepted the $\cdot$OH, such as mannitol, had no effect on peroxidation (37). In an extensive study of ferrous iron and hydrogen peroxide-dependent lipid peroxidation (5), we found further evidence that in our lipid peroxidation system, maximum rates of lipid peroxidation occur at an equal molar ratio of ferrous and ferric iron and that the ferric form is generated by the oxidation of ferrous iron by H_2O_2. In our experiments, there was no correlation between conditions that gave optimum rates of lipid peroxidation and that bleached *p*-nitrosodimethylaniline, presumably catalyzed by the $\cdot$OH (45).

EFFECT OF DIQUAT ON LIVER FERRITIN AND CHELATABLE IRON

The redox-cycling hepatotoxin diquat was used to test the hypothesis that ferritin might be a physiological source of iron. Diquat undergoes redox cycling through reduction by NADPH-cytochrome P450 reductase (37); hepatotoxicity is decreased by treatment of animals with the iron chelator deferoxamine (desferrioxamine B methanesulfonate) (46). In our experiments (D.W. Reif, I.L.P Beales, C.E. Thomas, and S.D. Aust, unpublished data), rats

Table 5. Effect of Diquat on Concentrations of Ferritin and Iron in the Rat Liver

	Concentration in Liver	
Compound and Experiment No.	Control	Diquat
Ferritin (µg/g wet wt)		
Experiment 1	60.8 ± 3.9	72.1 ± 6.8*
Experiment 2	58.6 ± 3.1	71.6 ± 2.5*
Ferritin Iron (nmol/g wet wt)		
Experiment 1	142 ± 11	112 ± 14
Experiment 2	132 ± 11	106 ± 5*
Chelatable Iron (nmol/g wet wt)		
Experiment 1	14 ± 6	46 ± 9†
Experiment 2	29 ± 5	67 ± 9†

* Different from control by Student's t test, $P < 0.05$.
† Different from control by adjusted t test, $P < 0.05$.

were treated with 20 mg of diquat per kg body weight and killed 36 hours later. Their livers were carefully excised, perfused, and analyzed for chelatable iron associated with low molecular weight compounds, total ferritin content (47), and the amount of iron in ferritin. Interestingly, the observed increase in the amount of chelatable iron in the liver of diquat-treated rats (**Table 5**) nearly corresponded to the decrease in iron in ferritin. The amount of ferritin per gram of liver (wet weight) increased, but liver weights decreased so the total amount of ferritin per liver did not change after exposure to diquat. These results suggest that iron may be removed from ferritin in vivo by redox cycling chemicals.

CONCLUSION

Iron meets the transition metal requirement for lipid peroxidation and can be derived quite readily by ferritin exposed to $O_2^{\cdot-}$ or organic radicals. Evidence is presented which suggests that iron can directly catalyze lipid peroxidation. Also, exposure of animals to a redox cycling chemical increased the concentration of chelatable iron in the liver and decreased the amount of iron in ferritin by a corresponding amount. Future research should be directed towards the low molecular weight forms of chelated iron and their properties, and the possibility that oxidative stress might occur by induction of excessive levels of this form of iron or an inability to keep this iron reduced.

ACKNOWLEDGMENT

The contributions of many associates, postdoctoral students, and graduate students are gratefully acknowledged. Although specific authorship is difficult to assign, their collective contributions are gratefully acknowledged. Research support has been provided by the National Institutes of Health (GM-33443 and HL-33543). I also thank Teresa Vollmer and her assistants for preparing this manuscript and those leading to it.

REFERENCES

1. Hochstein P, Nordenbrand K, Ernster L. Evidence for the involvement of iron in the ADP-activated peroxidation of lipids in microsomes and membranes. Biochem Biophys Res Comm 1964:14:323-328.

2. Wills ED. Mechanisms of lipid peroxide formation in tissues: role of metals and haematin proteins in the catalysis of the oxidation of unsaturated fatty acids. Biochim Biophys Acta 1965:98:238-251.

3. Morehouse LA, Thomas CE, Aust SD. Superoxide generation by NADPH-cytochrome P-450 reductase: the effect of iron chelators and the role of superoxide in microsomal lipid peroxidation. Arch Biochem Biophys 1984:232:366-377.

4. Bucher JR, Tien M, Aust SD. The requirement for ferric in the initiation of lipid peroxidation by chelated ferrous iron. Biochem Biophys Res Commun 1983:111:777-784.

5. Minotti G, Aust SD. The requirement for iron(III) in the initiation of lipid peroxidation by iron(II) and hydrogen peroxide. J Biol Chem 1987:262:1098-1104.

6. Tien M, Svingen BA, Aust SD. Superoxide dependent lipid peroxidation. Fed Proc 1981:40:179-182.

7. Tien M, Bucher JR, Aust SD. Thiol-dependent lipid peroxidation. Biochem Biophys Res Commun 1982:107:279-285.

8. Goto K, Tamura H, Nagayama M. The mechanism of oxygenation of ferrous ion in neutral solution. Inorg Chem 1970:9:963-964.

9. Lambeth DO, Ericson GR, Yorek MA, Ray PD. Implications for in vitro studies of the autoxidation of ferrous ion and iron-catalyzed autoxidation of dithiothreitol. Biochim Biophys Acta 1982:719:501-508.

10. Cher M, Davidson N. The kinetics of the oxygenation of ferrous iron in phosphoric acid solution. J Am Chem Soc 1954:77:793-798.

11. Harris DC, Aisen P. Facilitation of Fe(II) autoxidation by Fe(III) complexing agents. Biochim Biophys Acta 1973:329:156-158.

12. Harrison PM. Ferritin: an iron-storage molecule. Semin Hematol 1977:14:55-70.

13. Jones MS, Jones OTG. The structural organization of haem synthesis in rat liver mitochondria. Biochem J 1969:113:507-514.

14. Aisen P, Listowsky I. Iron transport and storage proteins. In: Snell EE, Boyer PD, Meister A, Richardson CC, eds. Annual review of biochemistry. Palo Alto:Annual Reviews, Inc., 1980:49:357-393.

15. Theil EC. Ferritin: structure, function, and regulation. In: Theil EC, Eichhorn GL, Marzili LG, eds. Iron binding proteins without cofactors or sulfur clusters; vol 5. New York:Elsevier, 1983:1-38.

16. Aisen P, Liskowsky I. Iron transport and storage proteins. Ann Rev Biochem 1980:49:357-393.

17. Gutteridge JMC. Iron promoters of the Fenton reaction and lipid peroxidation can be released from haemoglobin by peroxides. FEBS Lett 1986:201:291-295.

18. Camadro J-M, Ibraham NG, Levere RD. Kinetic studies of human liver ferrochelatase: role of endogenous metals. J Biol Chem 1984:259:5678-5682.

19. Jacobs A. Low molecular weight intracellular iron transport compounds. Blood 1977:50:433-439.

20. Bartlett GR. Phosphate compounds in rat erythrocytes and reticulocytes. Biochem Biophys Res Comm 1976:70:1055-1062.

21. Pollack S, Campana T. Low molecular weight non-heme iron and a highly labeled heme pool in the reticulocyte. Blood 1980:56:564-566.

22. Morley CGD, Bezkorovainy A. Identification of the iron chelate in hepatocyte cytosol. IRCS Med Sci Biochem 1983:11:1106-1107.

23. Jones RL, Grady RW, Sonette MP, Cerami A. Host-associated iron transfer-factor in normal humans and patients with transfusion siderosis. J Lab Clin Med 1986:107:431-438.

24. Jones RL, Peterson CM, Grady RW, Cerami A. Low molecular weight iron-binding factor from mammalian tissue that potentiates bacterial growth. J Exp Med 1980:151:418-428.

25. Carver FJ, Frieden E. Factors affecting the adenosine triphosphate induced release of iron from transferrin. Biochem 1978:17:167-172.

26. Kojima N, Bates GW. The reduction and release of iron from Fe^{3+} transferrin CO_3^{2-}. J Biol Chem 1979:254:8847-8854.

27. Morgan EH. Studies on the mechanism of iron release from transferrin. Biochim Biophys Acta 1979:580:312-326.

28. Pollack S, Vanderhoff G, Lasky F. Iron removal from transferrin: an experimental study. Biochem Biophys Acta 1977:497:481-487.

29. Baldwin DA, Jenny ER, Aisen P. The effect of human serum transferrin and milk lactoferrin on hydroxyl radical formation from superoxide and hydrogen peroxide. J Biol Chem 1984:259:13391-13394.

30. Winterbourn CC. Lactoferrin-catalysed hydroxyl radical production. Additional requirement for a chelating agent. Biochem J 1983:210:15-19.

31. Motohashi N, Mori I. Superoxide-dependent formation of hydroxyl radical catalyzed by transferrin. FEBS Lett 1983:157:197-199.

32. Gutteridge JMC, Rowley DA, Halliwell B. Superoxide-dependent formation of hydroxyl radicals and lipid peroxidation in the presence of iron salts: detection of catalytic iron and antioxidant activity in extracellular fluids. Biochem J 1982:206:605-609.

33. Saito M, Morehouse LA, Aust SD. Transferrin-dependent lipid peroxidation. J Free Rad Biol Med 1986:2:99-105.

34. Pederson TC, Buege JA, Aust SD. Microsomal electron transport: the role of reduced nicotinamide adenine dinucleotide phosphate-cytochrome c reductase in liver microsomal lipid peroxidation. J Biol Chem 1973:248:7134-7141.

35. Thomas CE, Morehouse LA, Aust SD. Ferritin and superoxide-dependent lipid peroxidation. J Biol Chem 1985:260:3275-3280.

36. Saito M, Thomas CE, Aust SD. Paraquat and ferritin-dependent lipid peroxidation. J Free Rad Biol Med 1985:1:179-185.

37. Thomas CE, Aust SD. Reductive release of iron from ferritin by cation free radicals of paraquat and other bipyridyls. J Biol Chem 1986:261:13064-13070.

38. Thomas CE, Aust SD. Release of iron from ferritin by cardiotoxic anthracycline antibiotics. Arch Biochem Biophys 1986:248:648-689.

39. Thomas CE, Aust SD. Free radicals and environmental toxins. Ann Emerg Med 1986:15:1075-1083.

40. Gutteridge JM, Halliwell B, Treffry A, Harrison PM, Blake D. Effect of ferritin-containing fractions with different iron loading on lipid peroxidation. Biochem J 1983:209:557-560.

41. Wills ED. Mechanisms of lipid peroxide formation in animal tissues. Biochem J 1966:99:667-676.

42. Mazur A, Carleton A. Hepatic xanthine oxidase and ferritin iron in the developing rat. Blood 1965:26:317-322.

43. Mazur A, Green S, Saha A, Carleton A. Mechanism of release of ferritin iron in vivo by xanthine oxidase. J Clin Invest 1958:37:1809-1817.

44. Topham RW, Walker MC, Calisch MP. Liver xanthine dehydrogenase and iron mobilization. Biochem Biophys Res Commun 1982:109:1240-1246.

45. Bors W, Michel C, Saran M. On the nature of biochemically generated hydroxyl radicals: studies using the bleaching of p-nitrosodimethylaniline as a direct assay method. Eur J Biochem 1979:95:621-627.

46. Smith CV, Hughes H, Lauterburg BH, Mitchell JR. Oxidant stress and hepatic necrosis in rats treated with diquat. J Pharmacol Exp Ther 1985:235:172-177.

47. Thomas CE, Aust SD. Rat liver microsomal NADPH-dependent release of iron from ferritin and lipid peroxidation. J Free Rad Biol Med 1985:1:293-300.

QUESTIONS AND COMMENTS

Dr. Donald Borg: Your recent and preceding work on lipid peroxidation shows a marked stimulation of the overall process in vesicles, but not in homogeneous solution/dispersion, by iron in mixed ferric-ferrous valence state. Candidate chemical reactions to explain the rapid stimulatory effect of the ferric component remain elusive. Can you suggest any reaction or explanation other than your prior suggestions of an iron complex or ferryl or ferro peroxide complex?

Dr. Steven Aust: Unfortunately, I cannot. I have a feeling that we are working on what we called lipid hydroperoxide-dependent lipid peroxidation, but cannot prove it. When we add lipid or organic hydroperoxides, we only need to add ferrous iron to get lipid peroxidation, and our lipid hydroperoxides are stable to ferric iron under our conditions, neutral pH.

Dr. Donald Borg: What, in your view, is the plausibility of the following speculation: that the known, but slow, reaction of ferric iron on hydroperoxides turns from being a virtue (that is, producing a relatively unreactive reaction product) into a vice to initiate new foci of peroxidation elsewhere in the vesicle?

Dr. Steven Aust: As I stated, we only need ferrous iron when we start with some hydroperoxide, and in our system, ferric iron when added alone has no effects that we can detect. In every lipid peroxidation system we have studied, both ferrous and ferric iron seems to be required except when we use a pure Fenton's system and detergent-dispersed lipid.

Dr. Donald Borg: Consider the reaction Fe^{3+}–complex + LOOH → Fe^{2+}–complex + LOO· + H^+, where LOOH is a lipid hydroperoxide and LOO· is a lipid peroxy radical. Because LOO· is a long-lived radical, existing tens of seconds on the average, it has an excellent likelihood of undergoing the following reaction, LOO· + LH → LOOH + L·, to initiate new *foci* of chain oxidation at distant sites on the vesicle, thus causing the wildfire of peroxidation to rapidly engulf the whole vesicle, as it were.

Dr. Steven Aust: Again, we see no lipid peroxidation or decomposition of lipid hydroperoxides when only ferric iron is added. In this regard, liver microsomal lipid peroxidation may give us some clues because lipid hydroperoxides in microsomes react very readily with cytochrome P450 in the ferric form, and one only needs lipid hydroperoxides to get good rates of lipid peroxidation. However, lipid peroxidation occurred in microsomes only with the addition of ferrous iron.

Dr. Irwin Fridovich: The rate of $O_2^{\cdot-}$ production by xanthine oxidase is very sensitive to Po_2. Hence, O_2 depletion during the xanthine oxidase reaction is an important variable. In addition, H_2O_2 inactivates xanthine oxidase. Could your effects of catalase be explained in these terms, i.e., slowing O_2 depletion and protecting xanthine oxidase?

Dr. Steven Aust: We always use a highly aerated system and have never seen oxygen depletion. We have observed this problem in spectrophotometric assays conducted in 1-mL cuvettes, but never in a 25-mL beaker with 5 milliliters of media on a shaker. Also, we always determine the rate of $O_2^{\cdot-}$ production by xanthine oxidase in the conditions of our systems.

Dr. John Gutteridge: We agree entirely with your experimental data that ·OH radicals are not required for microsomal or liposomal lipid peroxidation. However, in none of your systems are you really studying first-chain initiation. It is also very easy to release iron from hemoglobin by peroxides. I have reviewed the data in my paper [Gutteridge JMC. Lipid peroxidation: some problems and concepts. This volume.].

INTRACELLULAR PRODUCTION OF OXYGEN-DERIVED FREE RADICALS

Aron B. Fisher

At normal oxygenation, the reactive oxygen species produced intracellularly by a variety of enzymatic and nonenzymatic reactions are scavenged by antioxidant mechanisms. During hyperoxia, however, the increased production of oxygen metabolites appears to overwhelm these defenses, resulting in tissue damage. This increased production likely comes from nonenzymatic reactions because most oxygen-dependent enzymatic reactions are saturated with oxygen at normal Po_2. Studies with isolated organelles suggest that, under normal conditions, reactive oxygen species are produced by the reaction of oxygen with the reduced flavin or ubisemiquinone produced during electron transfer in the respiratory chain. Additional oxidants are produced by the microsomal fraction and other organelles. Studies at high oxygen pressures show increased production rates for partially reduced oxygen products in various subcellular fractions. Extrapolation of findings in organelles to intact organs must be made with caution. Although no direct evidence exists for increased radical production during hyperoxia in vivo, this paper reviews indirect evidence for production in the intact lung during pulmonary hyperoxia. Similar studies of the herbicide paraquat suggest that intracellular production of oxygen radicals may also explain the toxicity of certain exogenous compounds.

IT IS NOW GENERALLY ACCEPTED that the toxicity of oxygen at increased partial pressure is due to the generation of oxygen-derived free radicals (1). Thus, while eukaryotic life is impossible without adequate oxygen, exposure to elevated concentrations of oxygen results in progressive and lethal damage to the lungs and other organs. The rationale for this paper is the following hypothesis: cell and tissue damage results when, during hyperoxia, the increased intracellular production of oxygen-derived free radicals exceeds the capacity of the antioxidant defenses to remove oxidants and of the repair processes to restore oxidized components, resulting in disorganization of intracellular enzymes and membranes (**Figure 1**). The inflammatory response that generally follows tissue damage due to elevated oxygen tension may amplify the primary insult This mechanism for oxidant damage also serves as a model for a variety of drugs, chemicals, and environmental agents which exert their toxicity through oxygen radical mechanisms.

OXYGEN-DERIVED RADICALS

The bulk of oxygen reduction in most cells occurs by the mitochondrial cytochrome oxidase pathway. In this reaction, four electrons are transferred from reduced cytochrome c through the heme and copper ion prosthetic groups of cytochrome oxidase to molecular oxygen without the release of partially reduced intermediates. However, several other oxidations result in univalent reduction of oxygen to produce superoxide ($O_2^{\cdot-}$) or divalent reduction to generate hydrogen peroxide (H_2O_2). Superoxide can generate hydroperoxy radical ($HO_2^{\cdot}$) by protonation (pKa 4.8), H_2O_2 by dismutation, and hydroxyl radical ($\cdot OH$) and perhaps singlet oxygen by interaction with H_2O_2 in the presence of iron (2,3). H_2O_2, while not a free radical, represents a partially reduced oxygen metabolite; singlet O_2 is a spin-altered form of oxygen. These oxygen-derived metabolites are considered together because of their common increased reactivity for biomolecules compared with the reactivity of ground-state oxygen.

BIOLOGICAL GENERATION OF SUPEROXIDE

Enzymatic Reactions

Superoxide can be generated by both enzymatic and nonenzymatic reactions. The distribution and activity of the enzymatic pathways varies with different cell types depending on their specialized function. This paper surveys reactions that are relevant to mammalian systems.

A prototype reaction is the one catalyzed by NADPH oxidase in the plasma membrane of polymorphonuclear leukocytes and macrophages (4,5):

$$NADPH + 2O_2 \rightarrow NADP^+ + 2O_2^{\cdot-} + H^{\cdot} \qquad [1]$$

This reaction releases $O_2^{\cdot-}$ into the extracellular space or within a phagocytic vacuole. However, this enzyme is present only in phagocytes and, therefore, does not contribute to the intracellular oxidant load in most cells.

Urate oxidase is a peroxisomal enzyme which generates H_2O_2 during the conversion of urate to allantoin:

$$urate + H_2O + O_2 \rightarrow allantoin + H_2O_2 + CO_2 \qquad [2]$$

D-Amino acid oxidase, also a peroxisomal enzyme, generates H_2O_2 and a keto acid:

$$\text{D-}RCHNH_2COOH + H_2O + O_2 \rightarrow$$
$$RCOCOOH + H_2O_2 + NH_3 \qquad [3]$$

From Institute for Environmental Medicine, University of Pennsylvania, Philadelphia, Pennsylvania, USA.

Address correspondence to Dr. Aron B. Fisher, Institute for Environmental Medicine, University of Pennsylvania School of Medicine, 14 John Morgan Building, 36th Street and Hamilton Walk, Philadelphia, Pennsylvania 19104-6068, USA.

Other peroxisomal enzymes, such as glycolate oxidase and L-hydroxyacid oxidase, also generate H_2O_2.

Xanthine oxidase and aldehyde oxidase are flavoproteins containing FAD, iron–sulfur centers, and molybdenum that can undergo redox cycling. Molecular oxygen can serve as an efficient oxidizing substrate for these enzymes leading to the production of both $O_2^{\cdot-}$ and H_2O_2. These enzymes show little substrate specificity. In a typical reaction, xanthine oxidase generates $O_2^{\cdot-}$ and H_2O_2 during the conversion of hypoxanthine to xanthine and then to uric acid:

$$\text{hypoxanthine} + H_2O + O_2 \rightarrow \text{xanthine} + H_2O_2 \,(\text{or } O_2^{\cdot-}) \quad [4]$$

$$\text{xanthine} + H_2O + O_2 \rightarrow \text{uric acid} + H_2O_2 \,(\text{or } O_2^{\cdot-}) \quad [5]$$

The relative proportions of H_2O_2 and $O_2^{\cdot-}$ produced vary with pH and P_{O_2} (6). Xanthine oxidase has a relatively widespread cellular distribution and has recently come under increasing investigation because of the important observation that it can be converted from a dehydrogenase (non-superoxide producing) to the oxidase form during tissue hypoxia (7). Aldehyde oxidase is present in liver cytosol and has a similar reaction mechanism:

$$RCHO + H_2O + O_2 \rightarrow RCOOH + H_2O_2 \,(\text{or } O_2^{\cdot-}) \quad [6]$$

Monoamine oxidase is a flavin-containing enzyme in the outer mitochondrial membrane. A typical reaction is shown in equation 7.

$$\begin{aligned}\text{5-hydroxytryptamine} + H_2O + O_2 \rightarrow \\ \text{5-hydroxyindoleacetic acid} + H_2O_2 + NH_3\end{aligned} \quad [7]$$

Although the production of oxygen-derived radicals by these enzymes is of biological interest, their role in the genesis of oxygen-induced damage at elevated oxygen tensions is probably minor, as discussed below.

Nonenzymatic Reactions

Superoxide is also generated by nonenzymatic reactions involving the autoxidation of cellular components by molecular oxygen. The role of Fe^{2+} in the production of free radicals has been described at this Symposium (see the paper by Borg and Schaich in this volume). Quinone and catechol are biologically relevant chemical groups highly susceptible to autoxidation; radical production from autoxidation of thiols, hydropterins, flavins, and hemoglobin has also been demonstrated (8-13). Some of these biologically important compounds, such as the catechol epinephrine, are found in extracellular fluids as well

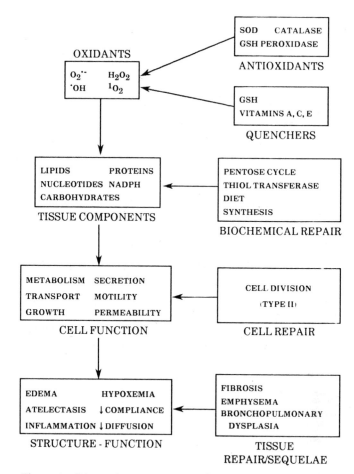

Figure 1. Schematic representation of the sequence of changes in pulmonary oxygen toxicity. The boxes on the left indicate levels of response to oxidants with oxidation of cell components followed by alteration of cell function and organ structure. The boxes on the right indicate defense mechanisms corresponding to each level of oxidant stress. ($^1O_2$ is singlet oxygen.)

as intracellularly and thus could contribute to $O_2^{\cdot-}$ production at both sites.

A major source of $O_2^{\cdot-}$ production in the intact cell appears to be related to the autoxidation of chemically reactive components produced during reductive processes associated with the mitochondrial and microsomal electron transport systems (14,15). The transport of electrons from substrate through the mitochondrial respiratory chain involves the sequential reduction of flavoproteins, ubiquinone, and mitochondrial cytochromes. Although two electrons are transferred from the substrate to the respiratory chain, the reduction of ubiquinone (and possibly flavin) occurs by a single electron transfer (16). The ubisemiquinone generated is, in large part, reoxidized by the cytochrome b complex, but may also react with molecular oxygen to generate $O_2^{\cdot-}$ (17) (**Figure 2**).

The role of electron transport in the production of partially reduced oxygen products has been demonstrated by increased H_2O_2 production after the addition of various metabolizable substrates to isolated mitochondria (18). Inhibitors (such as

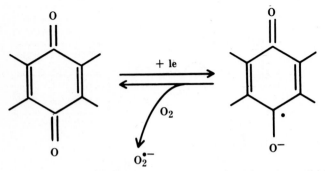

Figure 2. Mechanism of $O_2^{\cdot-}$ production by the autoxidation of the reduced quinone form of mitochondrial ubiquinone. Ubiquinone is reduced in a one-electron transfer to form the ubisemiquinone radical, which is reoxidized with molecular oxygen.

Table 1. H_2O_2 Production in Rat Liver Organelles*

| | | H_2O_2 Production | |
Fraction	Substrate	Organelle (nmol/min per mg of protein)	Intact Liver[†] (nmol/min per g of liver)
Mitochondria	succinate	0.50	12
Microsomes	NADPH	1.70	42
Peroxisomes	uric acid	5.0	30**
Cytosol	endogenous	0.1	4
			(Total) 88

* Data from reference 21.
[†] Extrapolation based on organelle content of liver.
** Estimated rate based on the assumption that 30% of intraorganelle H_2O_2 escapes catalase to diffuse to the cytoplasm.

antimycin A or cyanide) that block the transfer of electrons along the respiratory chain to the terminal oxidase increase the concentration of reduced intermediates and result in increased rates of $O_2^{\cdot-}$ production (18). Measurement of H_2O_2 production by ubiquinone-depleted and -repleted mitochondria has provided evidence that this reaction is the major source of mitochondrial $O_2^{\cdot-}$ (18). Superoxide may also be generated by autoxidation of reduced flavoprotein dehydrogenases in the mitochondrial respiratory chain, although this mechanism appears to be quantitatively less important than the ubiquinone reaction (14). The $O_2^{\cdot-}$ generated in the mitochondria is converted, in large part, to H_2O_2 by the action of mitochondrial superoxide dismutase (SOD) (19).

The electron transport system of endoplasmic reticulum (cytochrome P450 linked) can also generate $O_2^{\cdot-}$ (20). This pathway is distributed selectively, but is present in a wide spectrum of mammalian cell types. Normal electron transport in this pathway involves transfer of an electron from reduced flavin to the cytochrome P450–substrate complex. A second electron is then transferred through this complex to molecular oxygen. Production of $O_2^{\cdot-}$ may occur through autoxidation of the partially reduced flavin cofactor or because of "leakage" of electrons from the enzyme–substrate complex to molecular oxygen.

Subcellular Sites of Superoxide Production

The above considerations indicate that partially reduced oxygen metabolites can be produced at a variety of subcellular sites. These include the mitochondria (ubiquinone and flavoprotein), endoplasmic reticulum (cytochrome P450), peroxisomes (urate oxidase, D-amino acid oxidase), plasma membrane and phagosomes (NADPH oxidase), nuclear membrane, and cytoplasm (xanthine oxidase, aldehyde oxidase, soluble components). The relative rates of $O_2^{\cdot-}$ production by these organelles may vary with the concentration of the enzymes in

various cell types and the availability of substrates and cofactors. Boveris et al (21) have measured rates of H_2O_2 production from various substrates by isolated rat liver organelles. Extrapolation of these results to the intact liver (recognizing the major pitfalls in this exercise) suggested that the microsomal compartment made the greatest contribution to the intracellular oxidant load, followed by peroxisomes, mitochondria, and cytosol (**Table 1**). The total H_2O_2 production rate of 88 nmol/min per gram of liver would account for approximately 5% of liver uptake of molecular oxygen.

H_2O_2 can cross biological membranes and, because of limited reactivity, both H_2O_2 and $O_2^{\cdot-}$ may diffuse some distance from their sites of production. Consequently, radical generation by subcellular compartments may have consequences for the whole cell. Contribution to the cellular oxidant pool is modified by the enzymatic processes for dismutation of $O_2^{\cdot-}$ by SOD in mitochondria and cytosol and removal of H_2O_2 by catalase in peroxisomes and by glutathione peroxidase in cytosol. It has been estimated that the steady state concentrations in the normal aerobic liver cell are 10^{-12} to 10^{-11} M $O_2^{\cdot-}$ and 10^{-9} to 10^{-7} M H_2O_2 (14). Hydroperoxyradical, which is more reactive than $O_2^{\cdot-}$, would have a concentration of 10^{-15} to 10^{-14} M, as dictated by its pKa. The much more reactive $\cdot$OH and singlet O_2 are consumed nearer their sites of production, and their intracellular half-lives have been estimated at 10^{-9} seconds and 10^{-6} seconds, respectively (22).

Effect of PO₂ on Production of Oxygen-Derived Radicals

The above discussion has focused on those metabolic reactions that produce $O_2^{\cdot-}$ under conditions of normal oxygenation. The basis for the

Table 2. Effect of Hyperoxia on H_2O_2 Production By Porcine Lung Organelles and Extrapolation to Whole Lung*

	H_2O_2 Production	
	Control	1 atm O_2
Mitochondria		
nmol/min per mg of protein	0.045	0.6
nmol/min per g of lung	0.22	2.9
Microsomes		
nmol/min per mg of protein	2.2	4.8
nmol/min per g of lung	9.0	19.7

* Data from reference 24.

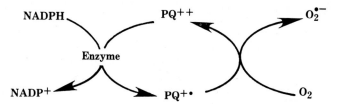

Figure 3. Mechanism of paraquat (PQ) toxicity by "redox cycling." PQ is reduced by an NADPH-dependent microsomal enzyme. The paraquat radical can autoxidize with regeneration of PQ and the production of $O_2^{\cdot-}$.

"free-radical" theory of oxygen toxicity is the increased production of oxygen radicals during hyperoxia. Consequently, an important factor for understanding oxygen toxicity is to consider those reactions in which $O_2^{\cdot-}$ (or H_2O_2) production increases as a function of PO_2. The enzymatic reactions in which molecular oxygen is a substrate probably show little increase in free radical production with hyperoxia since, with the possible exception of peroxisomes, the affinity for oxygen is sufficiently great that the enzyme is saturated with oxygen at normal PO_2. Because of this and their limited distribution, the enzymatic reactions probably have only a minor role in the pathogenesis of oxygen toxicity.

On the other hand, autoxidation involves molecular oxygen directly in reactions in which the rate of autoxidation (and $O_2^{\cdot-}$ production) should be directly proportional to oxygen concentration. Thus, intracellular hyperoxia would be expected to increase significantly the rate of intracellular generation of oxygen-derived radicals. An important feature of this mechanism is the continued reduction of autoxidized species by reducing equivalents provided, for example, by mitochondrial or microsomal respiratory chain carriers. This, in essence, produces 'redox-cycling' with continuous production of oxygen radicals.

Studies with isolated mitochondia, submitochondrial particles, microsomes, and nuclei have demonstrated an increased rate of production of partially reduced oxygen products during hyperoxia (18,23-26). Maximal rates of H_2O_2 release increased approximately ninefold in isolated porcine lung mitochondria and twofold in porcine lung microsomes when PO_2 was increased from 140 to 700 mm Hg (**Table 2**). Based on organelle content of lung tissue, the maximal microsomal H_2O_2 production in the intact organ was estimated to be sixfold greater than that of the mitochondria at a PO_2 of 700 mm Hg. Obviously, these extrapolations to intact tissue have a great degree of uncertainty.

OXYGEN-DERIVED FREE RADICALS FROM DRUGS AND CHEMICALS

The redox cycling described above involves metabolic reduction of endogenous compounds followed by autoxidation with generation of $O_2^{\cdot-}$. A wide variety of exogenous drugs and chemicals are also capable of enzymatic reduction and $O_2^{\cdot-}$ generation on autoxidation. One example is the herbicide paraquat, a bipyridal compound that is accumulated by some cells (lung epithelium, in particular) and is enzymatically reduced by an NADPH-dependent enzyme of the endoplasmic reticulum (27). Autoxidation of the reduced compound generates $O_2^{\cdot-}$ and is the apparent basis for the cellular toxicity of paraquat (**Figure 3**) (28). Other agents which show similar redox cycling as the basis for cellular toxicity include adriamycin, bleomycin, streptonigrin, dialuric acid, nitrofurantoin, and related compounds (29,30).

EVIDENCE FOR IN VIVO GENERATION OF OXYGEN RADICALS DURING PULMONARY HYPEROXIA

The above studies utilizing isolated enzymes or subcellular organelles have indicated the potential sources of oxygen-derived free radicals within intact cells and have suggested possible mechanisms for increased radical production during hyperoxia. Confirmation of these pathways within an intact organ is difficult because radicals generated intracellularly are scavenged by antioxidant defense mechanisms or react with intracellular biomolecules. However, indirect evidence for the generation of free radicals has been obtained through evaluation of the metabolic effects of hyperoxia.

We have utilized an isolated perfused rat lung preparation in a hyperbaric chamber equilibrated with a PO_2 of 5 atm (PO_2 approximately 3700 mm Hg) (31). This represents the approximate intracellular PO_2 since the lung alveolar cells are in equilibrium with the gas in the alveolar space. The lungs were perfused with Krebs-Ringer bicarbonate solution containing 5 mM glucose and a 3% solution of bovine serum albumin that was free of fatty acids. Because

Table 3. Effect of Hyperbaric O_2 on Metabolism in the Isolated Perfused Rat Lung

	GSSG Release (nmol/min per g of lung)	NADPH Production* (nmol/min per g of lung)
Control (0.2 atm O_2)	0.9 ± 0.2	240 ± 40
Hyperbaric $O_2^\dagger$	1.5 ± 0.2**	433 ± 20**
Reference	(32)	(31)

* Reducing equivalents generated via the pentose cycle of glucose metabolism.
$\dagger$ Hyperbaric pressure was 4.1 atm for GSSG experiments and 5 atm for NADPH experiments.
** $P < 0.05$ vs. control

Table 4. Effect of Paraquat on Metabolism in the Isolated Perfused Rat Lung*

	GSSG Release (nmol/min per g of lung†)	NADPH Production (nmol/min per g of lung)
Control	0.094 ± 0.039	113 ± 7
Paraquat**	$0.55 \pm 1.3^{\dagger\dagger}$	$320 \pm 35^{\dagger\dagger}$

* Data from references 33 and 34.
$\dagger$ Rat lung assumed to weigh 1.5 g.
** Paraquat was 1 mM for GSSG release and 1.5 mM for NADPH production.
$\dagger\dagger$ $P < 0.05$ vs. control

the lung was isolated and perfused with an artificial medium, extracellular reactions were unlikely to contribute significantly to the production of oxygen radicals. Using radioactive glucose, we were able to measure rates of carbon flux via mitochondrial pathways and via the pentose cycle. These studies (31) showed no significant change in mitochondrial activity at 5 atm O_2 (vs. 0.2 atm O_2), but an 80% increase in CO_2 (and NADPH) production via the pentose pathway (**Table 3**). In parallel experiments performed by Nishiki et al (32), the efflux of oxidized glutathione (GSSG) into the perfusate was found to increase by 67% at 4.1 atm O_2 (Table 3).

We have interpreted these findings with the perfused lung to indicate increased intracellular generation of partially reduced oxygen products. A major pathway for scavenging the increased radical load is catalyzed by glutathione peroxidase, which reduces H_2O_2 (or lipid peroxide) by means of reduced glutathione (GSH). The cell membrane is somewhat more permeable to GSSG than to GSH and, consequently, the oxidized product appears in the perfusate (32). At the same time, the intracellular reduction of GSSG via glutathione reductase requires NADPH; this substrate is generated in the lung predominantly via the pentose shunt pathway of glucose metabolism (31). The increased GSSG efflux and increased pentose cycle activity during hyperoxia are compatible with an increased oxidant load. It should be noted that increased pentose cycle activity would tend to diminish GSSG efflux so that these measurements in part reflect competing processes.

Similar studies were carried out using the isolated perfused lung to study the generation of oxygen radicals during perfusion with paraquat (33,34). In the presence of paraquat, CO_2 (and NADPH) production via the pentose cycle increased approximately threefold and the rate of GSSG efflux increased approximately sixfold (**Table 4**). The dependence of GSSG efflux on glutathione peroxidase activity was demonstrated by the absence of increased GSSG efflux during paraquat infusion of lungs from rats with selenium (glutathione peroxidase) deficiency (34).

SUMMARY

The primary mechanism of oxygen toxicity appears to be the intracellular generation of oxygen metabolites ($O_2^{\cdot-}$ and H_2O_2), which then generate more reactive species and result in tissue damage. Major sources of intracellular radicals during hyperoxia are the autoxidation of ubiquinone and flavoproteins that are enzymatically reduced as a result of metabolic activity in the mitochondria and endoplasmic reticulum. Studies in the isolated perfused rat lung have demonstrated a rapid alteration of lung metabolism upon hyperbaric oxygenation, with increased activity of glutathione peroxidase and the pentose shunt pathway. An increase in the intracellular rate of oxygen radical generation due to redox cycling may also account for the toxicity of a variety of drugs and chemicals, as illustrated by the herbicide paraquat.

ACKNOWLEDGMENT

I thank Dr. Henry Forman for helpful discussion.

REFERENCES

1. Freeman BA, Crapo JD. Biology of disease: free radicals and tissue injury. Lab Invest 1982:47:412-426.

2. McCord JM, Day ED Jr. Superoxide-dependent production of hydroxyl radical catalyzed by iron-EDTA complex. FEBS Lett 1978:86:139-142.

3. Winterbourn CC. Comparison of superoxide with other reducing agents in the biological production of hydroxyl radicals. Biochem J 1979:182:625-628.

4. Forman HJ, Nelson J, Fisher AB. Rat alveolar macrophages require NADPH for superoxide production in the respiratory burst. Effect of NADPH depletion by paraquat. J Biol Chem 1980:255:9879-9883.

5. Gabig TG, Kipnes RS, Babior BM. Solubilization of the O_2^{-}-forming activity responsible for the respiratory burst in human neutrophils. J Biol Chem 1978:253:6663-6665.

6. Kellogg EW III, Fridovich I. Superoxide, hydrogen peroxide and singlet oxygen in lipid peroxidation by xanthine oxidase system. J Biol Chem 1975:250:8812-8817.

7. Granger DN, Rutili G, McCord JM. Superoxide radicals in feline intestinal ischemia. Gastroenterology 1981:81:22-29.

8. Fisher DB, Kaufman S. Tetrahydropterin oxidation without hydroxylation catalyzed by rat liver phenylalanine hydroxylase. J Biol Chem 1973:248:4300-4304.

9. Massey V, Strickland S, Mayhew SG, et al. The production of superoxide anion radicals in the reaction of reduced flavins and flavoproteins with molecular oxygen. Biochem Biophys Res Commun 1969:36:891-897.

10. Misra HP, Fridovich I. The univalent reduction of oxygen by reduced flavins and quinones. J Biol Chem 1972:247:188-192.

11. Misra HP, Fridovich I. The role of superoxide anion in the autoxidation of epinephrine and a simple assay for superoxide dismutase. J Biol Chem 1972:247:3170-3175.

12. Misra HP, Fridovich I. The generation of superoxide radical during the autoxidation of hemoglobin. J Biol Chem 1972:247:6960-6962.

13. Misra HP. Generation of superoxide free radical during the autoxidation of thiols. J Biol Chem 1974:249:2151-2155.

14. Chance B, Sies H, Boveris A. Hydroperoxide metabolism in mammalian organs. Physiol Rev 1979:59:527-605.

15. Forman HJ, Boveris A. Superoxide radical and hydrogen peroxide in mitochondria. In: Pryor WA, ed. Free radicals in biology; vol. 5. New York: Academic Press, 1982:65-90.

16. Nagaoka S, Yu L, King TE. Characterization of ubisemiquinone radical in the cytochrome b-c_1 segment of the mitochondrial respiratory chain. Arch Biochem Biophys 1981:208:334-343.

17. Cadenas E, Boveris A, Ragan CI, Stoppani HO. Production of superoxide radicals and hydrogen peroxide by NADH-ubiquinone reductase and ubiquinol-cytochrome c reductase from beef-heart mitochondria. Arch Biochem Biophys 1977:180:248-257.

18. Boveris A, Chance B. The mitochondrial generation of hydrogen peroxide: general properties and effect of hyperbaric oxygen. Biochem J 1973:134:707-716.

19. Loschen G, Azzi A, Richter C, Flohe L. Superoxide radicals as precursors of mitochondrial hydrogen peroxide. FEBS Lett 1974:42:68-72.

20. Sligar SG, Lipscomb JD, Debrunner PG, Gunsalus IC. Superoxide anion production by the autoxidation of cytochrome P-450$_{cam}$. Biochem Biophys Res Commun 1974:61:290-296.

21. Boveris A, Oshino N, Chance B. The cellular production of hydrogen peroxide. Biochem J 1972:128:617-630.

22. Pryor WA. Oxy-radicals and related species: their formation, lifetimes, and reactions. Ann Rev Physiol 1986:48:657-667.

23. Freeman BA, Crapo JD. Hyperoxia increases oxygen radical production in rat lungs and lung mitochondria. J Biol Chem 1981:256:10986-10992.

24. Turrens JF, Freeman BA, Crapo JD. Hyperoxia increases H_2O_2 release by lung mitochondria and microsomes. Arch Biochem Biophys 1982:217:411-421.

25. Turrens JF, Freeman BA, Levitt JG, Crapo JD. The effect of hyperoxia on superoxide production by lung submitochondrial particles. Arch Biochem Biophys 1982:217:401-410.

26. Yusa T, Crapo JD, Freeman BA. Hyperoxia enhances lung and liver nuclear superoxide generation. Biochem Biophys Acta 1984:798:167-174.

27. Forman HJ, Aldrich TK, Posner MA, Fisher AB. Differential paraquat uptake and redox kinetics of rat granular pneumocytes and alveolar macrophages. J Pharmacol Exp Ther 1982:221:428-433.

28. Bus JS, Aust SD, Gibson JE. Superoxide and singlet oxygen-catalyzed lipid peroxidation as a possible mechanism for paraquat (methyl viologen) toxicity. Biochem Biophys Res Commun 1974:58:749-755.

29. Cohen G, Heikkila RE. The generation of hydrogen peroxide, superoxide radical and hydroxyl radical by 6-hydroxydopamine, dialuric acid and related cytotoxic agents. J Biol Chem 1974:249:2447-2452.

30. Goodman J, Hochstein P. Generation of free radicals and lipid peroxidation by redox cycling of adriamycin and daunomycin. Biochem Biophys Res Commun 1977:77:797-803.

31. Bassett DJ, Fisher AB. Glucose metabolism in rat lung during exposure to hyperbaric O_2. J Appl Physiol 1979:46:943-949.

32. Nishiki K, Jamieson D, Oshino N, Chance B. Oxygen toxicity in the perfused rat liver and lung under hyperbaric conditions. Biochem J 1976:160:343-355.

33. Bassett DJ, Fisher AB. Alteration of glucose metabolism during perfusion of rat lung with paraquat. Am J Physiol 1978:234:E653-E659.

34. Glass M, Sutherland MW, Forman HJ, Fisher AB. Selenium deficiency potentiates paraquat-induced lipid peroxidation in isolated perfused rat lung. J Appl Physiol 1985:59:619-622.

QUESTIONS AND COMMENTS

Dr. Gerald Cohen: In the hyperbaric lung experiments, the export of GSSG is approximately 0.5 μmol/g per minute, whereas the pentose shunt is increased by 200 μmol/g per minute. Does this mean that the exported GSSG constitutes only 0.25% of that formed?

Dr. Aron B. Fisher: That is difficult to quantitate because we do not know the fraction of NADPH utilized for the glutathione reductase reaction versus other reactions utilizing NADPH such as the NADH/NADPH transhydrogenase. It is safe to say that the fraction of GSSG that is exported is small.

II. OXYGEN RADICALS FROM PHAGOCYTIC CELLS

Joe M. McCord, *Session Chairman*

THE RESPIRATORY BURST OXIDASE OF THE HUMAN NEUTROPHIL

Bernard M. Babior, John T. Curnutte, and Naoki Okamura

When neutrophils are exposed to appropriate stimuli, they begin to manufacture large quantities of superoxide, the precursor of a group of powerful oxidants that are used by these cells as microbicidal agents. The enzyme responsible for superoxide production is the *respiratory burst oxidase*, a membrane-bound flavoprotein, dormant in unstimulated cells, that catalyzes the reduction of oxygen to superoxide at the expense of NADPH. Purification of the oxidase suggests that it is a heterotrimer containing subunits of M_r 66 000, 48 000, and 32 000. A dimeric (M_r 54 000 and 22 000) heme protein, designated cytochrome b_{558}, is also related to the respiratory burst, as indicated by the finding that the gene that is defective in the most common variety of chronic granulomatous disease encodes the larger of the two subunits of the cytochrome; the nature of the relationship has not yet been unequivocally established. Activation of the respiratory burst oxidase has been studied in a cell-free system and shown to require both membrane-associated and cytosolic factors. Protein phosphorylation is also involved in some way in activation of the oxidase.

NEUTROPHILS AND OTHER PHAGOCYTES are uniquely endowed with the capacity to manufacture large quantities of powerful oxidizing agents when they encounter opsonized bacteria, the complement fragment C5a, or other appropriate stimuli (1,2). Because the onset of oxidant production is associated with an abrupt increase in phagocyte oxygen consumption, the metabolic event that gives rise to these oxidants has come to be known as the *respiratory burst*. The oxidants compose a highly complex mixture that includes H_2O_2, oxidized halogens (OCl^-, chloramines (3-5)) and oxidizing radicals (e.g., hydroxyl radical, $\cdot OH$ (6,7)). Their function is to aid the phagocyte in the destruction of invading microorganisms. Although these oxidants are manufactured by the phagocyte strictly for internal use, some of them leak into the surrounding tissues, where they inflict various types of damage as an undesirable but unavoidable side effect of their antimicrobial activity.

The ultimate source of all these microbicidal oxidants is the superoxide radical ($O_2^{\cdot-}$), which phagocytes produce in remarkable quantities, but only after stimulation; resting cells make little or no $O_2^{\cdot-}$. The production of $O_2^{\cdot-}$ is accomplished by the one-electron reduction of oxygen at the expense of NADPH:

$$2\,O_2 + NADPH \rightarrow 2\,O_2^{\cdot-} + NADP^+ + H^+ \qquad [1]$$

From Research Institute of Scripps Clinic, La Jolla, California, USA.

Address correspondence to Dr. Bernard M. Babior, Department of Basic and Clinical Research, Research Institute of Scripps Clinic, 10666 North Torrey Pines Road, La Jolla, California 92037, USA.

From $O_2^{\cdot-}$, the microbicidal oxidants are produced in the following sequence of reactions:

$$2\,O_2^{\cdot-} + 2\,H^+ \rightarrow H_2O_2 + O_2 \qquad [2]$$

$$H_2O_2 + Cl^- \rightarrow OCl^- + OH^- \qquad [3]$$
(catalyzed by myeloperoxidase)

$$OCl^- + RNH_2 \rightarrow RNHCl^- + OH^- \qquad [4]$$

$$O_2^{\cdot-} + ROOH \rightarrow RO^\cdot + OH^- + O_2 \qquad [5]$$
(catalyzed by Fe or Cu)

$$XH + RO^\cdot \rightarrow X^\cdot + ROH \qquad [6]$$

Because many biological substances are capable of participating in the last three of these reactions, a large number of oxidants of broadly varying reactivities can be formed via this sequence.

The *respiratory burst oxidase* is the enzyme that catalyzes the reduction of oxygen to $O_2^{\cdot-}$ (equation 1). It is dormant in resting phagocytes, but comes to life when the cells are activated. A great deal of effort has been devoted to studying the properties and mechanism of activation of this unique oxidase. In the following paragraphs, the current state of knowledge about this enzyme will be briefly surveyed.

PROPERTIES OF THE OXIDASE

The respiratory burst oxidase was first described by Rossi and Zatti (8) as an activity in a particulate fraction from guinea pig neutrophils that catalyzed the reaction of NADPH with oxygen. A similar activity was subsequently found in a particulate fraction from human neutrophils (9,10). The latter activity was unequivocally shown to correspond to the human respiratory burst oxidase based on the following observations: a) one of the products of the reaction was $O_2^{\cdot-}$ (10); b) the activity was present in particles from activated but not resting neutrophils (10); and, most conclusively, c) the activity was missing from particles prepared from activated neutrophils isolated from patients with chronic granulomatous disease, an inherited disorder (more accurately, a group of inherited disorders) in which phagocytes are unable to express a respiratory burst (9,11).

Experiments with the superoxide-forming particles defined the location of the respiratory burst oxidase and established certain of its kinetic

Table 1. Properties of the Respiratory Burst Oxidase

REACTION: $2 O_2 + NADPH \rightarrow 2 O_2^{\cdot-} + NADP^+ + H^+$

LOCATION: Plasma membrane

REQUIREMENTS: FAD
                Phospholipid
                Heme (possibly)

KINETIC PARAMETERS:

	K_m (μM)
NADPH	40
NADH	1000
O_2	10
FAD	0.06
pH optimum	7.0-7.5

parameters. By separating the particulate preparation into its component subcellular fractions, it was possible to show that the oxidase resides in the plasma membrane (12). Further experiments suggested that it is situated in the inner leaflet of the membrane with its pyridine nucleotide binding site extending into the cytoplasm (13). Studies of its catalytic activity showed that the oxidase could use either NADPH or NADH as substrate, but that it preferred the former (the K_m values for NADPH and NADH are about 40 μM and about 1000 μM, respectively (2)). The K_m for oxygen was found to be about 10 μM (14,15), equivalent to the oxygen concentration in buffer under an atmosphere of 1% oxygen; the oxidase is thus able to generate microbicidal oxidants even at the relatively low oxygen tensions prevailing at infected sites. Finally, the enzyme was shown to be active over a broad pH range, with an optimum between pH 7.0 and 7.5 (10).

The superoxide-forming activity was solubilized with the aid of non-ionic detergents in the presence of a highly polar organic solvent (ethylene glycol was used initially) (16,17). With the solubilized oxidase, a requirement for phospholipid became apparent. A very limited study of specificity found that this requirement could be fulfilled by phosphatidylethanolamine, but not by phosphatidylcholine or phosphatidylserine (17). A not unexpected requirement for a flavin cofactor was also demonstrated. The physiological cofactor was shown to be FAD, for which the oxidase has very high affinity, as indicated by its K_m of 0.06 μM (18,19). The oxidase-bound flavin was detectable by electron spin resonance (ESR) spectrometry of the reduced enzyme (20); titration of this ESR signal indicated that the redox potential of the flavin was 280 mV. FAD could be replaced by 8-chloroFAD or 1-deazaFAD, and poorly by FMN, but 5-deazaFAD, which can only transfer electrons in pairs, was found to be a powerful inhibitor of the enzyme (21). The properties of the respiratory burst oxidase are summarized in **Table 1**.

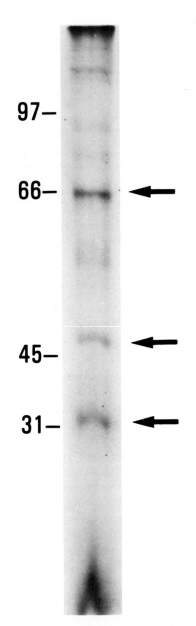

Figure 1. Sodium dodecyl sulfate-polyacrylamide gel electrophoresis of the purified respiratory burst oxidase.

Purification of the superoxide-forming activity, difficult because of the very poor stability of the solubilized enzyme, was finally achieved by "dye-affinity" chromatography (22). The specific activity of the purified oxidase was about 8 μmol $O_2^{\cdot-}$/min per mg of protein. The purified material gave a single major band on nondenaturing gel electrophoresis, but showed three prominent bands (plus minor contaminants) on sodium dodecyl sulfate-polyacrylamide gel electrophoresis (SDS-PAGE) (**Figure 1**). These three bands, at M_r approximately 66 000, 48 000, and 32 000, were also seen when the major band from the nondenaturing gel was re-electrophoresed on SDS-PAGE. Affinity-labeling experiments suggested that the M_r 66 000 band contained the NADPH binding site. Measurements of redox cofactors in the purified material showed three moles of FAD per mole of enzyme, but only negligible amounts of FMN, heme, and ubiquinone. Metals were not assayed. These results suggest that the purified oxidase is an FAD-containing heterotrimer of M_r 150 000 that reduces oxygen to $O_2^{\cdot-}$ with a turnover number of 1000-2000 min^{-1}.

CYTOCHROME b$_{558}$

The absence of heme from the purified oxidase was somewhat of a surprise because in human neutrophils and other phagocytes the relationship of a heme protein to the respiratory burst has been securely established. This heme protein, designated "cytochrome b$_{558}$," was discovered by Hattori in 1961 (23), but its significance was only recognized when Segal and his associates (24) found it to be missing in certain patients with chronic granulomatous disease, thereby demonstrating its connection with the respiratory burst. Subsequent studies have focused on its spectral and redox properties and, more recently, on its structure.

Cytochrome b$_{558}$ is by far the most abundant heme protein in human neutrophils. (Myeloperoxidase is actually the most abundant tetrapyrrole-bearing protein in the neutrophil, but it cannot be considered a heme protein because its prosthetic group is a chlorin, not a porphyrin (25)). Most of the cytochrome b$_{558}$ is located in the specific granules, one of the two populations of granules in the neutrophil, but about 20% is found in the plasma membrane (26). The cytochrome is easily recognized by its characteristic spectrum, which in its reduced (Fe^{2+}) form shows peaks at 528 and 558 nm, along with a Soret peak at 426 nm (27,28) that shifts to 418 nm when the protein is oxidized (**Figure 2**) (28). It has an unusually low redox potential of -245 mV (27), and, like other low-potential heme proteins, forms complexes with carbon monoxide (27,29,30) and alkyl isonitriles (31). It has recently been purified and shown to be a heterodimer composed of peptides of M_r 22 000 and 54 000 (32,33); the larger peptide is glycosylated (34). Of great interest is the recent finding (35) that the M_r 54 000 peptide is encoded by the gene that is defective in the most common variety of chronic granulomatous disease (the X-linked cytochrome b$_{558}$-negative variety). The cloning of that gene was a milestone in molecular genetics because it represented the first instance in which a gene responsible for an inherited disease was cloned in the absence of information about its product (36).

There is at present some controversy about the function of cytochrome b$_{558}$. Many, but not all, workers believe that it is the terminal electron carrier in a short electron transport chain resembling the

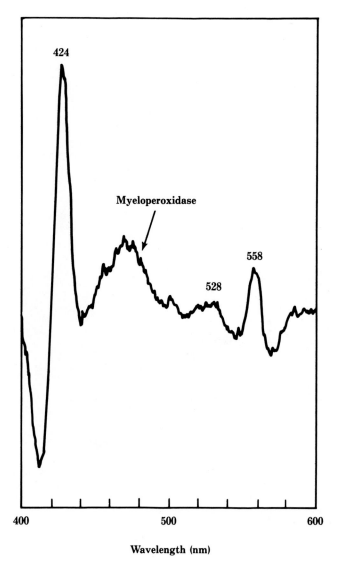

Figure 2. Difference spectrum (dithionite-reduced minus oxidized) of cytochrome b$_{558}$.

cytochrome P450–P450 reductase system. The principal evidence supporting this notion is that the cytochrome in intact neutrophils is reduced when the cells are activated under N_2; that cytochrome in homogenates from resting and activated neutrophils is reduced by NADPH; and that the reduced cytochrome is rapidly ($t_{1/2} = 5$ msec) oxidized by O_2 (28,37,38). There are, however, a number of findings that conflict with this idea (2), including the absence of heme from purified oxidase as discussed above, and, perhaps the most telling of all, the demonstration that neutrophils entirely devoid of detectable cytochrome b$_{558}$ are able to manufacture $O_2^{\cdot-}$ at near normal rates (39). Further work is clearly needed to resolve the role of cytochrome b$_{558}$.

ACTIVATION OF THE OXIDASE

Perhaps most interesting of all is the question of how the oxidase is converted from a dormant to an

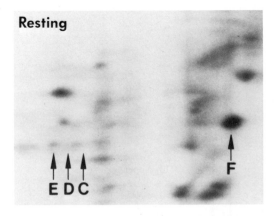

Resting

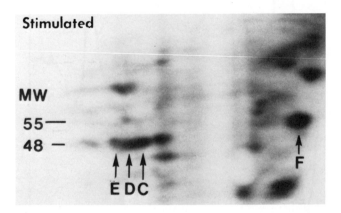

Stimulated

MW

55 —
48 —

Figure 3. Phosphorylation of the M_r 48 000 phosphoprotein group during neutrophil activation. Stimulated cells were treated for 2 minutes with phorbol myristate acetate. C, D and E indicate the three proteins of the M_r 48 000 group. F is a marker protein whose level of phosphorylation is not affected by stimulation.

active state. Until quite recently, this was a very difficult question to address because the enzyme could only be activated in intact cells, which are poorly suited for detailed biochemical analysis. Three years ago, however, several groups of investigators, working independently, showed that the respiratory burst oxidase could be activated by the addition of certain anionic detergents to a cell-free homogenate of neutrophils or macrophages (40-43). This system is now being profitably exploited to elucidate the molecular basis for the activation of the oxidase.

Characterization of the cell-free activating system is still at an early stage. An analysis of requirements showed that the oxidase could be activated not only by arachidonic acid, the detergent originally used for this purpose, but also by sodium dodecyl sulfate (SDS) and by sodium dodecyl sulfonate (44). Apart from the detergent, the only low molecular weight component needed for oxidase activation was Mg^{2+}. Activation occurred in the absence of added nucleotides such as ATP (45, but see 46), and Ca^{2+} inhibited the process. The proteins required for activation were found in both the plasma membrane and the cytosol; the latter

requirement was rather unexpected, because prior to the development of the cell-free activating system, all the elements assumed to be necessary for the operation of the respiratory burst oxidase (receptors, G proteins, protein kinase C, and the oxidase itself) were known to be found in the plasma membrane. Within the past few months the entire system, including its membrane-associated proteins, has been brought into a fully soluble form (47), and it should soon be possible to begin purifying and characterizing all the components of the system.

The cytosolic factor has already been partially characterized (45,46). On gel filtration, it was found to migrate in two locations, showing apparent molecular weights of 40 000 and 240 000. This result suggests that it may exist in a polymerized and depolymerized form. The molecular weights and the lack of calcium requirement distinguish the cytosolic factor from protein kinase C, as does the fact that oxidase activation in the cell-free system requires no ATP. Perhaps most important is the finding that the cytosolic factor is lacking in neutrophils from patients with the autosomally transmitted, cytochrome b_{558}-positive variety of chronic granulomatous disease (48). This finding not only identifies the molecular lesion in that form of chronic granulomatous disease, but also establishes that the cytosolic factor is required for the normal oxidase activation process and is not just an artifact of a peculiar experimental system.

Possible clues to the mechanism of activation of the oxidase have also been obtained from studies of neutrophil protein phosphorylation. Neutrophils can incorporate ^{32}P into various proteins in patterns that differ between resting and stimulated cells. In the context of the respiratory burst, a group of three M_r 48 000 proteins with isoelectric points in the vicinity of neutrality (**Figure 3**) is of particular interest. The state of phosphorylation of these proteins reflects the state of activation of the neutrophil, in that the proteins take up ^{32}P when the neutrophils are exposed to activating agents, lose the label when the cells return to the resting state, and take it up again on reactivation (49). Recently this phosphorylation has been shown to be abnormal in at least two varieties of chronic granulomatous disease. In activated cells from patients with the X-linked cytochrome b_{558}-negative form of the disease, the most acidic of the three M_r 48 000 proteins cannot be detected on the autoradiogram, whereas in cells from patients with the autosomal cytochrome b_{558}-positive variety, none of the three proteins is detected (49,50). These findings clearly connect the M_r 48 000 protein group to the respiratory burst oxidase. The nature of their relationship to this enzyme and its activating system, however, remains to be determined.

REFERENCES

1. Babior BM. Oxygen-dependent microbial killing by phagocytes. N Engl J Med 1978:298:659-68, 721-725.

2. Curnutte JT, Babior BM. Chronic granulomatous disease. In: Harris H, Hirschhorn K, eds. Advances in human genetics; vol 16. New York: Plenum, 1987:229-297.

3. Klebanoff SJ. Myeloperoxidase-halide-hydrogen peroxide antibacterial system. J Bacteriol 1968:95:2131-2138.

4. Thomas EL. Myeloperoxidase, hydrogen peroxide, chloride antimicrobial system: nitrogen-chlorine derivatives of bacterial components in bactericidal action against Escherichia coli. Infect Immunity 1979:23:522-531.

5. Weiss SJ, Klein R, Slivka A, Wei M. Chlorination of taurine by human neutrophils: evidence for hypochlorous acid generation. J Clin Invest 1982:70:598-607.

6. Rosen H, Klebanoff SJ. Hydroxyl radical generation by polymorphonuclear leukocytes measured by electron spin resonance spectroscopy. J Clin Invest 1979:64:1725-1729.

7. Britigan BE, Rosen GM, Chai Y, Cohen MS. Do human neutrophils make hydroxyl radical? Determination of free radicals generated by human neutrophils activated with a soluble or particulate stimulus using electron paramagnetic resonance spectrometry. J Biol Chem 1986:261:4426-4431.

8. Rossi F, Zatti M. Biochemical aspects of phagocytosis in polymorphonuclear leucocytes: NADH and NADPH oxidation by the granules of resting and phagocytizing cells. Experientia 1964:20:21-23.

9. Hohn DC, Lehrer RI. NADPH oxidase deficiency in X-linked chronic granulomatous disease. J Clin Invest 1975:55:707-713.

10. Babior BM, Curnutte JT, McMurrich BJ. The particulate superoxide-forming system from human neutrophils: properties of the system and further evidence supporting its participation in the respiratory burst. J Clin Invest 1976:58:989-996.

11. Curnutte JT, Kipnes RS, Babior BM. Defect in pyridine nucleotide dependent superoxide production by a particulate fraction from the granulocytes of patients with chronic granulomatous disease. N Engl J Med 1975:293:628-632.

12. Dewald B, Baggiolini M, Curnutte JT, Babior BM. Subcellular localization of the superoxide-forming enzyme in human neutrophils. J Clin Invest 1979:63:21-29.

13. Babior GL, Rosin RE, McMurrich BJ, Peters WA, Babior BM. Arrangement of the respiratory burst oxidase in the plasma membrane of the neutrophil. J Clin Invest 1981:67:1724-1728.

14. Gabig TG, Bearman SI, Babior BM. Effects of oxygen tension and pH on the respiratory burst of human neutrophils. Blood 1979:53:1133-1139.

15. Kakinuma K, Kaneda M. Apparent Km of leukocyte O_2^- and H_2O_2 forming enzyme for oxygen. In: Rossi F, Patriarca P, eds. Biochemistry and function of phagocytes. London: Plenum, 1982:351-360.

16. Gabig TG, Kipnes RS, Babior BM. Solubilization of the O_2^--forming activity responsible for the respiratory burst in human neutrophils. J Biol Chem 1978:253:6663-6665.

17. Gabig TG, Babior BM. The O_2^--forming oxidase responsible for the respiratory burst in human neutrophils: properties of the solubilized enzyme. J Biol Chem 1979:254:9070-9074.

18. Babior BM, Peters WA. The O_2^--producing enzyme of human neutrophils: further properties. J Biol Chem 1981:256:2321-2323.

19. Wakeyama H, Takeshige K, Minakami S. NADPH-dependent reduction of 2,6-dichlorophenol-indophenol by the phagocytic vesicles of pig polymorphonuclear leucocytes. Biochem J 1983:210:577-581.

20. Kakinuma K, Kaneda M, Chiba T, Ohnishi T. Electron spin resonance studies on a flavoprotein in neutrophil plasma membranes: redox potentials of the flavin and its participation in NADPH oxidase. J Biol Chem 1986:261:9426-9432.

21. Light DR, Walsh C, O'Callahan AM, Goetzl EJ, Tauber AI. Characteristics of the cofactor requirements for the superoxide-generating NADPH oxidase of human polymorphonuclear leukocytes. Biochemistry 1981:20:1468-1476.

22. Glass GA, DeLisle DM, DeTogni P, et al. The respiratory burst oxidase of human neutrophils. J Biol Chem 1986:261:13247-13251.

23. Hattori H. Studies on the labile, stabile nadi oxidase and peroxidase staining reactions in the isolated particles of horse granulocytes. Nagoya J Med Sci 1961:23:362-378.

24. Segal AW, Jones OTG, Webster D, Allison AC. Absence of a newly described cytochrome b from neutrophils of patients with chronic granulomatous disease. Lancet 1978:ii:446-449.

25. Babcock GT, Ingle RT, Oertling WA, et al. Raman characterization of human leukocyte myeloperoxidase EC-1.11.1.7 and bovine spleen green haemoprotein: insight into chromophore structure and evidence that the chromophores of myeloperoxidase are equivalent. Biochim Biophys Acta 1985:828:58-66.

26. Borregaard K, Heiple JM, Simon ER, Clark RA. Subcellular localization of the b-cytochrome component of the human neutrophil microbicidal oxidase: translocation during activation. J Cell Biol 1983:97:52-61.

27. Cross AR, Jones OTG, Harper AM, Segal AW. Oxidation-reduction properties of the cytochrome b found in the plasma membrane fraction of human neutrophils: a possible oxidase in the respiratory burst. Biochem J 1981:194:599-606.

28. Gabig TG, Schervish EW, Santinga JT. Functional relationship of the cytochrome b to the superoxide-generating oxidase of human neutrophils. J Biol Chem 1982:257:4114-4119.

29. Lutter R, van Schaik MLJ, van Zwieten R, Wever R, Roos D, Hamers MN. Purification and partial characterization of the b-type cytochrome from human polymorphonuclear leukocytes. J Biol Chem 1985:260:2237-2244.

30. Morel F, Vignais PV. Examination of the oxidase function of the b-type cytochrome in human polymorphonuclear leukocytes. Biochim Biophys Acta 1984:764:213-225.

31. Cross AR, Parkinson JF, Jones OTG. The superoxide-generating oxidase of leucocytes: NADPH-dependent reduction of flavin and cytochrome b in solubilized preparations. Biochem J 1984:223:337-344.

32. Segal AW. Absence of both cytochrome b-245 subunits from neutrophils in X-linked chronic granulomatous disease. Nature 1987:326:88-91.

33. Parkos CA, Allen RA, Cochrane CG, Jesaitis AJ. Purified cytochrome b from human granulocyte plasma membrane is comprised of two polypeptides with relative molecular weights of 91,000 and 22,000. J Clin Invest 1987:80:732-742.

34. Harper AM, Chaplin MF, Segal AW. Cytochrome b-245 from human neutrophils is a glycoprotein. Biochem J 1985:227:783-788.

35. Dinauer MC, Orkin SH, Brown R, Jesaitis AJ, Parkos CA. The glycoprotein encoded by the X-linked chronic granulomatous disease locus is a component of the neutrophil cytochrome b complex. Nature 1987:327:717-720.

36. Royer-Pokora B, Kunkel LM, Monaco AP, et al. Cloning the gene for an inherited human disorder–chronic granulomatous disease–on the basis of its chromosomal location. Nature 1986:322:32-38.

37. Cross AR, Higson FK, Jones OTG, Harper AM, Segal AW. The enzymic reduction and kinetics of oxidation of cytochrome b-245 of neutrophils. Biochem J 1982:204:479-485.

38. Cross AR, Jones OTG, Garcia R, Segal AW. The association of FAD with the cytochrome b-245 of human neutrophils. Biochem J 1982:208:759-763.

39. Ezekowitz RAB, Orkin SH, Newburger PE. Recombinant interferon-gamma augments phagocyte superoxide production and X-CGD gene expression in X-linked "variant" chronic granulomatous disease. J Clin Invest 1987:80:1009-1016.

40. Bromberg Y, Pick E. Unsaturated fatty acids stimulate NADPH-dependent superoxide production by cell-free system derived from macrophages. Cell Immunol 1984:88:213-221.

41. Curnutte JT. Activation of human neutrophil nicotinamide adenine dinucleotide phosphate, reduced (triphosphopyridine nucleotide, reduced) oxidase by arachidonic acid in a cell-free system. J Clin Invest 1985:75:1740-1743.

42. McPhail LC, Shirley PS, Clayton CC, Snyderman R. Activation of the respiratory burst enzyme from human neutrophils in a cell-free system: evidence for a soluble cofactor. J Clin Invest 1985:75:1735-1739.

43. Heyneman RA, Vercauteren RE. Activation of a NADPH oxidase from horse polymorphonuclear leukocytes in a cell-free system. J Leukocyte Biol 1984:36:751-759.

44. Bromberg Y, Pick E. Activation of NADPH-dependent superoxide production in a cell-free system by sodium dodecyl sulfate. J Biol Chem 1985:260:13539-13545.

45. Curnutte JT, Kuver R, Scott PJ. Activation of neutrophil NADPH oxidase in a cell-free serum: partial purification of components and characterization of the activation process. J Biol Chem 1987:262:5563-5569.

46. Clark RA, Leidal KG, Pearson DW, Nauseef WM. NADPH oxidase of human neutrophils. Subcellular localization and characterization of an arachidonate-activatable superoxide-generating system. J Biol Chem 1987:262:4065-4074.

47. Curnutte JT, Kuver R, Babior BM. Activation of the respiratory burst oxidase in a fully soluble system from human neutrophils. J Biol Chem 1987:262:6450-6452.

48. Curnutte JT, Berkow RL, Roberts RL, Shurin SB, Scott PJ. Chronic granulomatous disease due to a defect in the cytosolic factor required for the nicotinamide adenine dinucleotide phosphate oxidase activation. J Clin Invest 1988:81:606-610.

49. Hayakawa T, Suzuki K, Suzuki S, Andrews PC, Babior BM. A possible role for protein phosphorylation in the activation of the respiratory burst in human neutrophils: evidence from studies with cells from patients with chronic granulomatous disease. J Biol Chem 1986:261:9109-9115.

50. Segal AW, Heyworth PG, Cockcroft S, Barrowman MM. Stimulated neutrophils from patients with autosomal recessive chronic granulomatous disease fail to phosphorylate a Mr-44,000 protein. Nature 1985:316:547-549.

CELLULAR AND BIOCHEMICAL EVENTS IN OXIDANT INJURY

Charles G. Cochrane, Ingrid U. Schraufstatter, Paul Hyslop, and Janis Jackson

Studies of the cellular and biochemical events involved in oxidant damage of cells during the inflammatory process are reviewed. Addition of H_2O_2 or activated human neutrophils to several types of target cells quickly decreased ATP levels. This decrease was related to diminished activity of mitochondria and inactivation of the glycolytic enzyme glyceraldehyde-3-phosphate dehydrogenase by H_2O_2 directly and through a decrease in NAD levels subsequent to increased activity of poly(ADP-ribose) polymerase. This increased polymerase activity was associated with DNA damage that could be measured within 20 seconds of exposing target cells to oxidants such as H_2O_2 and stimulated leukocytes. Of the oxidants generated in the inflammatory process, H_2O_2 appears to be the one most likely to penetrate target cells. Studies with isolated DNA show that H_2O_2 generates hydroxyl radical ($\cdot OH$) by a Fenton reaction in the vicinity of the DNA and that the amount of $\cdot OH$ formed correlates with the percentage of DNA strand breaks. Additional studies supporting the concept that unsaturated fatty acids may also induce DNA damage are briefly discussed.

UNDERSTANDING THE MECHANISMS by which oxidants damage cells and tissues during the inflammatory process has been hampered by a lack of information about the primary targets of oxidants in the cells and tissues, the precise oxidant species responsible for the damage to these targets, and the biochemical mechanisms of injury that are set into motion by damage of the primary targets. In previous studies we have defined several cellular targets of oxidants. These studies have been conducted utilizing stimulated leukocytes, oxidants such as hydrogen peroxide (H_2O_2) or hypochlorous acid (HOCl), and superoxide ($O_2^{\cdot -}$) produced by xanthine oxidase. As targets of the oxidants, we have used the $P388D_1$ murine macrophage cell line, the GM1380 human fibroblast cell line, human peripheral lymphocytes, monocytes and neutrophils, endothelial cell lines, and rabbit alveolar macrophages.

Our initial studies defined several primary targets of the oxidants: cellular membranes, DNA, glyceraldehyde-3-phosphate dehydrogenase (GAPDH; an enzyme of the glycolytic pathway), Ca^{2+} reservoirs, and mitochondria (**Figure 1**). An initial observation was that, within five minutes of adding H_2O_2 or activated human neutrophils to target cells, ATP levels began to fall in a dose-dependent fashion (**Figure 2**) (1). A diminished synthesis rather than an increased catabolism of ATP was responsible (2), and so the glycolytic and mitochondrial pathways of ATP formation came under scrutiny. Assessment of

From Department of Immunology, Research Institute of Scripps Clinic, La Jolla, California, USA.

Address correspondence to Dr. C. G. Cochrane, Department of Immunology, Research Institute of Scripps Clinic, 10666 North Torrey Pines Road, La Jolla, California 92037, USA.

components of the glycolytic pathway revealed fivefold to tenfold increases in glyceraldehyde-3-phosphate and dihydroxyacetone phosphate concentrations after exposure to H_2O_2 (100 to $500\,\mu M$). Lactate formation decreased threefold to fivefold at these concentrations of H_2O_2. Each enzyme of the glycolytic pathway, except for GAPDH, maintained near normal V_{max} and K_m values for its substrate (2). Two reasons for the exception were apparent: H_2O_2 directly inhibits GAPDH (2,3), and it depletes the amount of the essential cofactor, NAD (**Figure 3**) (4). In vitro, H_2O_2 directly inactivates GAPDH, possibly by forming a disulfide linkage between cysteine 149 and the spatially related cysteine 153. The diminished levels of NAD and the partial inactivation of GAPDH led to a precipitous fall in the glycolytic synthesis of ATP (2).

Mechanisms responsible for the decrease in NAD levels in the target cells were then studied. Poly(ADP-ribose) polymerase is a major enzyme using NAD as substrate (equation 1):

$$NAD \xrightarrow{\text{poly(ADP-ribose) polymerase}} \text{Nicotinamide} + \text{poly(ADP-ribose)} \text{ (or (ADP-ribose)–proteins)} \quad [1]$$

We therefore examined the activity of this enzyme by measuring levels of nicotinamide, which freely diffuses from the cell, and ADP-ribosylation of proteins within the cell after exposure to H_2O_2. Both nicotinamide release and ADP-ribosylation of proteins (many of which were indistinguishable from nuclear histones by chromatographic analysis) occurred within minutes of exposure of $P388D_1$ cells to H_2O_2 (4). Release of nicotinamide occurred stoichiometrically with consumption of NAD.

The effect of inhibiting poly(ADP-ribose) polymerase by three agents, 3-aminobenzamide (3-ABA), nicotinamide, and theophylline, was then tested. Similar data were obtained with each inhibitor, but we have mostly reported results for the more specific 3-ABA. As shown in **Figure 4**, the 3-ABA prevented the fall in NAD levels, as expected, but also prevented in part the decrease in ATP concentration, the rise in intracellular Ca^{2+} levels, and cell death (5). The inactivation of GAPDH and mitochondria by H_2O_2 was insufficient to block ATP synthesis completely in these experiments. 3-ABA did not affect H_2O_2 levels.

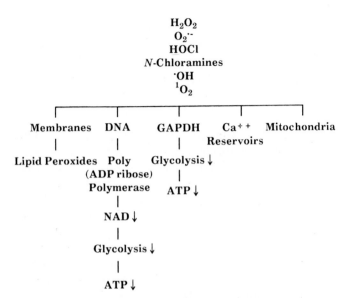

Figure 1. Functionally important primary targets of oxidants in target cells and biochemical consequences of the oxidant interaction with these targets. GAPDH = glyceraldehyde-3-phosphate dehydrogenase.

INHIBITION OF MITOCHONDRIAL OXIDATIVE PHOSPHORYLATION

Mitochondrial respiration (cyanide-sensitive oxygen consumption) in P388D$_1$ cells was inhibited in a dose-dependent manner by H$_2$O$_2$ exposure. The oligomycin-sensitive portion of the respiration demonstrated the greater sensitivity to oxidant injury, suggesting that the ATP–synthetase complex of the respiratory chain may be a target for injury by H$_2$O$_2$.

OXIDANT DAMAGE OF CELLULAR DNA

Since poly(ADP-ribose) polymerase is activated under conditions of DNA strand breakage, we reasoned that DNA damage might have occurred in

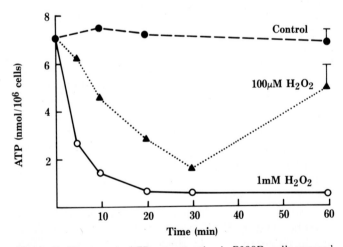

Figure 2. Decrease in ATP concentration in P388D$_1$ cells exposed to H$_2$O$_2$.

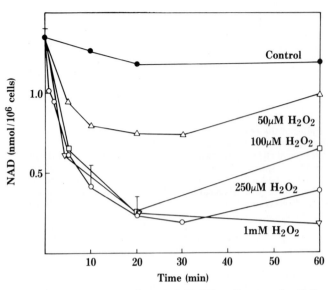

Figure 3. Decrease in NAD levels in P388D$_1$ cells exposed to H$_2$O$_2$.

cells exposed to oxidants. This has proved to be the case in all cell types assayed to date, and the DNA damage occurs within seconds of exposing the cells to oxidants (4).

A major unanswered question was that of the mechanisms by which oxidants damage DNA. Information available from the literature suggested that O$_2$$^{\cdot-}$ (6), as well as H$_2$O$_2$ and hydroxyl radical (·OH), could be responsible, although little information about HOCl, singlet O$_2$ (^{1}O$_2$), or N-chloramines was available. We first determined that reagent H$_2$O$_2$ could induce damage of cellular DNA, as measured by an alkaline unwinding assay. Human peripheral lymphocytes and P388D$_1$ cells were susceptible to micromolar concentrations of H$_2$O$_2$ (**Figure 5**) (4). Damage to cellular DNA developed within 20 seconds after exposure of the cells to H$_2$O$_2$ and reached a maximal effect in minutes. With catabolic removal of the H$_2$O$_2$ from the medium, repair of the DNA occurred over the succeeding hours in most, but not all, cell types. Exposure of several cell types (P388D$_1$ cells, human peripheral lymphocytes, GM1380 fibroblasts, and rabbit alveolar macrophages) to H$_2$O$_2$ revealed varied susceptibility of the DNA to damage by the H$_2$O$_2$. If H$_2$O$_2$ were the major oxidant species penetrating the cells to damage the DNA, then specific inhibition of catalase in the cytoplasm of the various cell types should produce cells of equal susceptibility. This proved to be the case. When these various cell types were first exposed to 3-amino-1,2,4-triazole to inhibit catalase (as well as myeloperoxidase in the neutrophils) and were then treated with various concentrations of H$_2$O$_2$, the cells showed greater susceptibility to DNA damage, and the degree of susceptibility was the same for all the cell types. In addition, in the absence of aminotriazole, the susceptibility of the cellular DNA

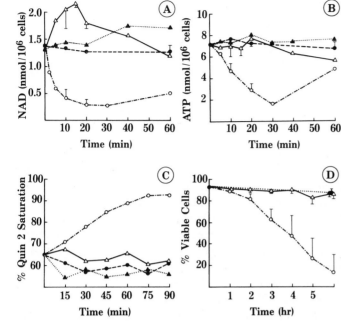

Figure 4. The capacity of 2.5 mM 3-aminobenzamide (3-ABA) to inhibit biochemical alterations induced by H_2O_2 in P388D$_1$ cells. Key: ●---● untreated; o--·o exposed to 250 μM H_2O_2; ▲····▲ treated with 2.5 mM 3-ABA; Δ——Δ treated with 2.5 mM 3-ABA followed by 250 μM H_2O_2. A) NAD levels. B) ATP levels. C) Intracellular Ca^{2+} levels as indicated by quin-2 fluorescence. D) Cell viability. (Data from reference 5.)

to various concentrations of H_2O_2 was inversely proportional to the activity of catalase in the cells.

Several oxidants generated by human monocytes were then assessed for their capacity to damage DNA in peripheral human lymphocytes. The ratio of monocytes to lymphocytes was 1:3. A strong correlation existed between the concentration of H_2O_2 in the extracellular medium and the degree of DNA strand breaks. Addition of catalase to the medium completely prevented the strand breaks in each system, but addition of superoxide dismutase (SOD) did not. These data suggest that H_2O_2 in the medium to which the target cells were exposed was responsible for initiating the DNA damage.

HOCl, *N*-chloramine, H_2O_2, and $^1O_2$ were then compared for their capacity to damage isolated PM2 DNA. (Isolated DNA was chosen to avoid intracellular variation in oxidant activity, such as from inactivation by cellular inhibitors and natural scavengers). While 100 μM H_2O_2 plus 30 μM iron ions induced an average of 55% strand breaks, 100 μM HOCl induced 5%, *N*-chloramine (100 μM HOCl plus 500 μM taurine) induced 6%, and a combination of 100 μM H_2O_2 and 100 μM HOCl (to generate $^1O_2$) induced 20%. Similarly, addition of 100 μM HOCl to P388D$_1$ cells failed to induce DNA damage, as measured by an alkaline unwinding assay.

These results support the conclusion that H_2O_2 is the dominant oxidant leading to DNA strand breaks. The data on cells in which intracellular catalase was

inhibited by aminotriazole suggest that H_2O_2 penetrates the cell, thereby gaining access to DNA. The H_2O_2 could conceivably induce damage directly or indirectly. Therefore, experiments were undertaken to examine this aspect.

PARTICIPATION OF HYDROXYL RADICAL IN DNA DAMAGE

Our attention turned to ·OH as the free radical most likely generated by the presence of H_2O_2 in the vicinity of nuclear DNA. H_2O_2 alone, at concentrations as high as 100 μM, failed to induce significant numbers of strand breaks in isolated PM2 DNA. However, abundant strand breaks were observed in the presence of Fe^{2+} (10 to 30 μM), especially when either ascorbate or $O_2^{·-}$ was added to reduce Fe^{3+} to Fe^{2+}. These results, in combination with other studies (e.g., references 7-9), strongly implicated the generation of ·OH from H_2O_2 as a mechanism. In whole P388D$_1$ cells, DNA damage, measured as strand breaks, was prevented by the chelation of iron using phenanthroline or desferrithiocin.

The apparent association of ·OH formation by the Fenton reaction and DNA damage was to this point based on indirect evidence. To determine more

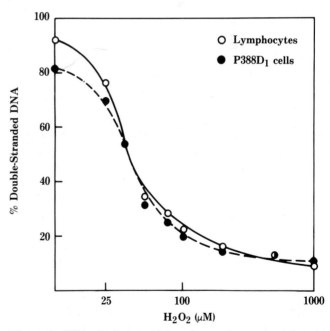

Figure 5. DNA single-strand breaks as determined by the alkaline unwinding technique. P388D$_1$ cells or human peripheral lymphocytes were incubated with different doses of H_2O_2 for 5 minutes at 37°C. H_2O_2 was removed by centrifugation; the cell pellet was resuspended in 450 μL ice-cold buffer; and 200 μL samples were lysed in alkaline medium. Ethidium bromide fluorescence was determined (excitation, 520 nm; emission, 590 nm) after a 45-minute incubation at 15°C. Results are the mean of three duplicate experiments. (Reproduced from reference 4, *The Journal of Clinical Investigation*, 1986:77:1312-1320, by copyright permission of the American Society for Clinical Investigation.)

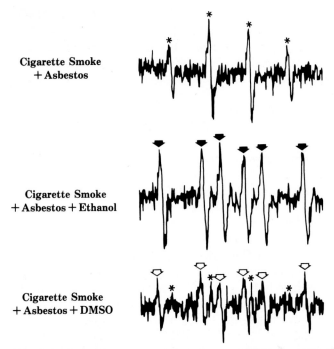

Figure 6. Electron paramagnetic resonance (EPR) spectra of DMPO adducts with ·OH (top), with α-hydroxyethyl radical from ethanol (middle), and with methyl radical from dimethylsulfoxide (bottom). The reaction mixture contained 0.8 μg PM2 DNA, 0.05 mg crocidolite asbestos, 10 μL cigarette smoke in phosphate-buffered saline. 100 mM DMPO was added. Asterisks in the upper and lower panels identify the DMPO-OH signal; the closed arrows in the middle panel identify the DMPO-α-hydroxyethyl signal; the open arrows in the bottom tracing identify the DMPO-methyl signal.

accurately if this association exists, we conducted experiments to measure ·OH levels at a time when DNA strand breaks occurred. We used electron paramagnetic resonance (EPR) spectroscopy with the spin trap dimethylpyrroline-*N*-oxide (DMPO). With H_2O_2, Fe^{2+}, and PM2 DNA, a 4-line spectrum appeared that was characteristic of the DMPO adduct with ·OH (7). A similar spectrum was observed utilizing cigarette smoke (a rich souce of H_2O_2) and asbestos (a rich source of iron) (**Figure 6**). A correlation was observed between the amount of DMPO–OH observed by EPR and the percentage of DNA with strand breaks (**Figure 7**). Since the DMPO–OH spectrum can be produced by mechanisms not involving ·OH, the secondary ·OH traps ethanol and dimethylsulphoxide (DMSO) were added to the mixtures described above. The resulting EPR spectra revealed the 6-line DMPO–α-hydroxyethyl signal and the 6-line DMPO–methyl signal, respectively (Figure 6). These patterns develop only when DMPO–OH is generated from ·OH, confirming that ·OH had been formed. Further confirmation was obtained by the observation that catalase (but not SOD), ·OH scavengers, and iron chelators inhibited both ·OH detection and DNA strand breaks. Complete inhibition of DNA strand breaks was observed with the addition of 3.5 μg catalase, 100 mM

DMSO, 100 mM mannitol, 100 mM sodium benzoate, 4 mM phenanthroline, and 4 mM desferrithiocin (10).

Because of the uncertainties in extrapolating the results in isolated DNA to whole cells, studies are now being devised to allow observation of ·OH generation in whole cells.

DNA DAMAGE BY PRODUCTS OF LIPID PEROXIDATION

Damage to DNA by the H_2O_2/·OH reaction may indeed play a major role in cellular injury and in altered function in the inflammatory response. In addition, products of lipid peroxidation induced by the interaction of ·OH with polyunsaturated fatty acids in the membranes of target cells may also contribute to the DNA damage. Ochi and Cerutti (11) emphasized the relationship of lipid hydroperoxides to the clastogenic agents released by stimulated monocytes. These collaborators have described the capacity of such factors, at concentrations of 10 to 20 μM, to induce DNA strand breaks in target cells. Our preliminary data support their conclusions. Unsaturated fatty acids (oleic, linoleic, linolenic, and arachidonic acids, 164 μM) induced DNA damage in GM1380 fibroblasts, and the amount of damage (leading to DNA strand breaks) corresponded to the degree of fatty acid unsaturation. The mechanism of DNA damage by this means remains uncertain, but the effect of the unsaturated fatty acids is clear. The importance of this mechanism in the inflammatory response remains to be determined.

CONCLUSIONS

The studies reviewed and the data described here support the hypothesis that, of various oxidants

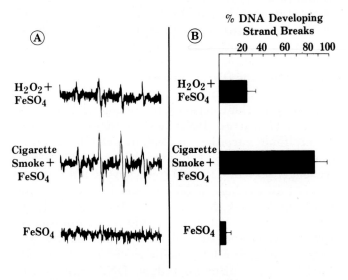

Figure 7. Correlation of the amount of DMPO-OH formed (A), as measured by electron paramagnetic resonance spectrometry, and the percentage of DNA strand breaks (B). The reaction mixture contained the following, in the combinations shown: 0.8 μg PM2 DNA, 10 μL cigarette smoke, 65 μM H_2O_2, and 30 μM $FeSO_4$.

generated by leukocytes during the inflammatory response, H_2O_2 is the most likely oxidant to penetrate target cells and reach the various cellular targets, including cell membranes, DNA, glyceraldehyde-3-phosphate dehydrogenase, Ca^{2+} reservoirs, and mitochondria. Considering oxidant damage to DNA, concentrations of H_2O_2 as low as 25 μM cause damage to DNA in target cells. Such concentrations are physiologically relevant since millimolar concentrations of H_2O_2 can be generated in the immediate vicinity of the target cells by stimulated neutrophils. Studies suggest that H_2O_2 acts indirectly through ·OH to damage DNA.

REFERENCES

1. Spragg RG, Hinshaw DB, Hyslop PA, Schraufstatter IU, Cochrane CG. Alterations in adenosine triphosphate and energy change in cultured endothelial and P388D$_1$ cells after oxidant injury. J Clin Invest 1985:76:1471-1476.

2. Hyslop PA, Hinshaw DB, Halsey WA Jr, et al. Mechanisms of oxidant mediated cell injury: the glycolytic and mitochondrial pathways of ADP phosphorylation are major intracellular targets inactivated by hydrogen peroxide. J Biol Chem 1988:263:1665-1675.

3. Hyslop PA, Hinshaw DB, Schraufstatter IU, Sklar LA, Spragg RG, Cochrane CG. Intracellular calcium homeostasis during hydrogen peroxide injury to cultured P388D$_1$ cells. J Cell Physiol 1986:129:356-366.

4. Schraufstatter IU, Hinshaw DB, Hyslop PA, Spragg RG, Cochrane CG. Oxidant injury of cells: DNA strand-breaks activate polyadenosine diphosphate-ribose polymerase and lead to depletion of nicotinamide adenine dinucleotide. J Clin Invest 1986:77:1312-1320.

5. Schraufstatter IU, Hyslop PA, Hinshaw DB, Spragg RG, Sklar LA, Cochrane CG. Hydrogen peroxide-induced injury of cells and its prevention by inhibitors of poly(ADP-ribose) polymerase. Proc Natl Acad Sci USA 1986:83:4908-4912.

6. Birnboim HC, Kanabus-Kaminska M. The production of DNA strand breaks in human leukocytes by superoxide anion may involve a metabolic process. Proc Natl Acad Sci 1985:82:6820-6824.

7. Floyd RA. DNA-ferrous iron catalyzed hydroxyl free radical formation from hydrogen peroxide. Biochem Biophys Res Comm 1981:99:1209-1215.

8. Frenkel K, Chrzan K, Troll W, Teebor GW, Steinberg JJ. Radiation-like modification of bases in DNA exposed to tumor promoter-activated polymorphonuclear leukocytes. Cancer Res 1986:46:5533-5540.

9. Mello Filho AC, Meneghini R. Protection of mammalian cells by o-phenanthroline from lethal and DNA-damaging effects produced by active oxygen species. Biochim Biophys Acta 1985:847:82-89.

10. Jackson J, Schraufstatter IU, Hyslop PA, et al. Role of oxidants in DNA damage: hydroxyl radical mediates the synergistic DNA damaging effects of asbestos and cigarette smoke. J Clin Invest 1987:80:1090-1095.

11. Ochi T, Cerutti PA. Clastogenic action of hydroperoxy-5, 8, 11,13-eicosatetraenoic acids on the mouse embryo fibroblasts C3H/10 T1/2. Proc Natl Acad Sci 1987:84:990-994.

QUESTIONS AND COMMENTS

Dr. Aron Fisher: The metabolic depression theory as the basis for O_2 toxicity has had a checkered history since it was first proposed 40 or so years ago. In some systems, there has been stimulation or no change in glycolysis and ATP generation until relatively late in toxicity. Is the altered metabolism cell- or stimulus-specific?

Dr. Charles Cochrane: We have no data on ATP levels in toxicity of cells caused by hyperoxia or on the metabolic events within cells during hypoxic injury, nor am I familiar with changes in DNA and related events.

Dr. Frank Bell: I have an interest in arterial smooth muscle cells. I'm wondering if you have had occasion to look at the susceptibility of arterial smooth muscle cells to hydrogen peroxide-induced DNA strand breakage and, if so, how you would rank the susceptibility of these cells relative to the susceptibility of other cell types you have examined.

Dr. Charles Cochrane: We have not looked at arterial smooth muscle cells, but from the studies on diverse cell types that are susceptible to DNA damage from low doses of external H_2O_2, I would guess that the DNA of those cells would be damaged.

Dr. Barry Halliwell: Your exciting results can be rationalized as a site-specific Fenton reaction using iron ions bound to the cellular DNA. This can be tested by soaking the cells in permeant chelating agents (e.g., phenanthroline) or by determining the products of ·OH attack on DNA using gas chromatography (GC)-mass spectrometry, as developed by Ames [Ann Int Med 1987:107:526-545] and by Dizdaroglu [Biochem J 1987:241:929-932]. Do you intend to carry out such studies?

Dr. Charles Cochrane: We are currently preparing to analyze DNA base changes by GC-mass spectroscopy. As to chelating agents, phenanthroline does inhibit cellular DNA damage caused by externally applied H_2O_2. The source of the iron, reacting in the presumed Fenton reaction at the surface of the DNA, remains unclear.

Dr. John Gutteridge: Fenton reactive iron can be released from heme proteins by organic peroxides and hydrogen peroxide.

Dr. Gerald Cohen: In the DNA strand-break experiments, to what extent does the added H_2O_2 alter the cellular steady-state level of reduced glutathione (GSH)? Does strand breakage require compromise of glutathione peroxidase activity?

Dr. Charles Cochrane: H_2O_2 in concentrations less than $100\,\mu$M can induce DNA damage (strand breaks) with little detectable loss of glutathione. There is rapid turnover of GSH to the oxidized form, but, in the presence of an intact pentose phosphate pathway, sufficient electron equivalents are forwarded in the glutathione pathway to maintain GSH in the reduced state. In our assays to date, the glutathione system does not greatly impede the action of H_2O_2 on DNA.

III. ISCHEMIC/TRAUMATIC INJURY AND OXYGEN RADICALS (Part 1)

Joseph C. Fantone, *Session Chairman*

GRANULOCYTE-MEDIATED ENDOTHELIAL INJURY:
Oxidant Damage Amplified by Lactoferrin and Platelet Activating Factor

Harry S. Jacob and Gregory M. Vercellotti

Studies investigating some mechanisms by which activated neutrophils can damage vascular endothelium are reviewed. Lactoferrin, a granule constituent, amplifies granulocyte-mediated endothelial damage by providing iron, by enhancing neutrophil adhesion to endothelium, and by generating hydroxyl radicals. Deferoxamine inhibits this effect, and apo-lactoferrin has no effect. The release of iron from lactoferrin upon exposure to superoxide is prevented by superoxide dismutase. Platelet activating factor (PAF), a granulocyte-stimulating product, can be produced by the endothelium in amounts that enhance the neutrophil-mediated damage to the endothelium itself. Minute amounts of PAF prime the polymorphonuclear neutrophil response to subsequently applied agonists, resulting in superoxide production, increased neutrophil adhesion, and elastase release. All of these actions are inhibited by PAF-receptor antagonists. These responses may be related to the three-fold increase in intracellular calcium concentrations in the PAF-primed neutrophils. Studies of the relation of granulocyte-mediated endothelial cytotoxicity to various clinical states may well lead to identification of inhibitors with therapeutic value.

OUR LABORATORY has maintained a consistent interest in the way that inflammatory cells, especially activated neutrophils, damage vascular endothelium. We believe granulocyte-mediated endothelial cytotoxicity is germane to a variety of clinical states, including immune complex vasculitis, some forms of the adult respiratory distress syndrome, the transient pulmonary dysfunction seen in hemodialyzed patients, and, perhaps most importantly, atherosclerosis (1-6). We and others have demonstrated that granulocytes can lyse cultured endothelial cells, both by releasing toxic oxygen species (7-10) and by the action of proteolytic enzymes (11,12). In the former case, which our group has tended to emphasize, oxygen species such as hydrogen peroxide (H_2O_2) (8), hydroxyl radical ($\cdot OH$) (13), and hypochlorous acid (HOCl) (11) have all been shown to mediate granulocyte-induced endothelial damage in vitro. In this paper, we review the roles of two factors in granulocyte-mediated vascular damage, lactoferrin and platelet activating factor.

LACTOFERRIN:
AN ENDOTHELIAL CYTOTOXIN

Recognizing that heavy metals enhance oxidation toxicity, we have investigated the role of iron in granulocyte-mediated vascular damage. Through the Haber-Weiss reaction, iron is known to catalyze the formation of $\cdot OH$ and ferryl radical (14,15); both are highly toxic and efficiently promote lipid peroxidation in cell membranes. That an iron moiety is involved in granulocyte-initiated oxidant damage to target cells is implied by our recently published findings (16) that "pure" (enzymatically generated) superoxide and peroxide are inefficient lysins of target red blood cells. In exploring this unexpected finding, we studied enucleated, agranular neutrophil cytoplasts (17), since they are excellent $O_2^{\cdot-}$ generators yet contain no lysosomal constituents (18). As with the "pure" oxidants, they also proved inefficient in lysing target cells. However, when we re-armed the cytoplasts with a single specific granule constituent, lactoferrin, marked hemolytic activity was reconstituted.

The obvious implications of these findings were that 1) the iron from lactoferrin somehow catalyzes production of extremely toxic oxygen species, such as $\cdot OH$, probably through the Haber-Weiss reaction and 2) lactoferrin iron may somehow be released as inorganic Fe^{2+}. In partial support, we found that deferoxamine (desferrioxamine B methanesulfonate) actually prevents granulocyte-mediated red cell hemolysis (16). We describe in this paper a mechanism by which free inorganic iron is released from neutrophil lactoferrin, and we demonstrate that this mechanism utilizes another neutrophil product, $O_2^{\cdot-}$, as a possible reducing agent for inorganic iron release. These results support data of others (19,20) that lactoferrin readily promotes $\cdot OH$ production--a conclusion that was previously controversial (21), since it was uncertain that lactoferrin could release free iron to act as a Fenton reagent. Our new results take on greater clinical relevance in view of the recent demonstrations of free lactoferrin in the sera of patients with diverse conditions involving endothelial damage, including hemodialysis (22), burns (23), and sepsis (24).

Lactoferrin Amplifies Endothelial Damage by Generating Hydroxyl Radicals

Granulocytes that are maximally stimulated to produce toxic oxidants (e.g., by exposure to phorbol esters) cause marked endothelial cytotoxicity, which is inhibited 80% by superoxide dismutase and catalase. That lactoferrin plays a critical role in this

From Division of Hematology, University of Minnesota Medical School, Minneapolis, Minnesota, USA.

Address correspondence to Dr. Harry S. Jacob, Division of Hematology, Department of Medicine, University of Minnesota, Box 480, Mayo Memorial Building, Minneapolis, Minnesota 55455, USA.

damage was documented by the addition of anti-lactoferrin antibody, which significantly depresses the injury. In further support, the addition of exogenous iron-saturated lactoferrin to stimulated granulocytes further enhances endothelial cell lysis, whereas addition of apo-lactoferrin is without effect. Moreover, deferoxamine significantly inhibits endothelial damage to an extent equal to that noted with anti-lactoferrin antibody.

In ancillary studies that exposed endothelial cells to lactoferrin-depleted neutrophil cytoplasts, we further showed a critical role for lactoferrin in granulocyte-mediated endothelial damage. Cytoplasts were used in numbers that produced amounts of $O_2^{\cdot-}$ virtually identical to those produced by stimulated parent neutrophils. These pseudocells caused minimal endothelial cell injury, but became highly cytotoxic when reconstituted with iron-saturated lactoferrin. Again, apo-lactoferrin showed no such enhancing effect.

In addition to acting as an iron donor, lactoferrin, a highly cationic protein, enhances effector/target cell apposition, resulting in a highly efficient exposure of target cells to granulocyte oxidants. Thus, lactoferrin-depleted neutrophil cytoplasts adhere poorly to endothelium, but increase their adhesion modestly when stimulated with phorbol esters; they become highly adherent after the addition of lactoferrin. Therefore, some of the enhanced endothelial damage caused by cytoplasts re-armed by lactoferrin is probably due to enhanced cytoplast adhesion to endothelium.

An equally important mechanism involves the ability of lactoferrin to enhance $\cdot$OH production by cytoplasts. Thus, neutrophil cytoplasts stimulated by phorbol esters produce virtually no $\cdot$OH, and this incapacity is not corrected by addition of apo-lactoferrin. In contrast, addition of iron-saturated lactoferrin stimulates $\cdot$OH production approximately 20-fold.

These data seem to contrast with those of others who showed that *soluble* iron-saturated lactoferrin does not catalyze $\cdot$OH production from its substrates, $O_2^{\cdot-}$ and H_2O_2, unless a chelator such as EDTA is present (21). That we found striking $\cdot$OH generation when lactoferrin was added to neutrophil cytoplasts suggested to us that simple binding of lactoferrin to membranes might alter the molecule in a manner that permits it to catalyze $\cdot$OH production. We tested this supposition by using red cell ghosts as extraneous model membranes. These membranes, as well as endothelial cells, were found to bind iron-saturated lactoferrin avidly, as detected by means of fluorescein-labeled, anti-lactoferrin antibody. The $\cdot$OH production by these lactoferrin-laden ghosts from enzymatically generated $O_2^{\cdot-}$ and H_2O_2 nearly doubled when compared to the production by lactoferrin-free ghosts ($P<.05$). We confirmed the observation of others (21) that uncomplexed, soluble lactoferrin is not able to catalyze $\cdot$OH production.

As might be predicted, significantly enhanced $\cdot$OH production that accompanies lactoferrin "chelation" to membranes, provokes marked lipid peroxidation in these same "innocent bystander" membranes. For instance, addition of iron-saturated lactoferrin to cultured endothelial cells significantly increases malondialdehyde formation when these cells are simultaneously incubated with $O_2^{\cdot-}$ plus H_2O_2. Furthermore, lactoferrin-depleted cytoplasts, which produce virtually no $\cdot$OH when stimulated with phorbol esters, do not provoke excessive lipid peroxidation; however, if re-armed with iron-saturated lactoferrin, these same cytoplasts foster marked lipid peroxidation.

Free Fe²⁺ is Released After Reduction by Superoxide

Since iron-saturated lactoferrin promotes lipid peroxidation in target membranes, which can be inhibited by deferoxamine, we felt it likely that the ferric form of iron in the protein might somehow be reduced to Fe^{2+} and then released from the protein. If so, $\cdot$OH and other toxic radicals might predictably be produced, which, in turn, should initiate lipid peroxidation. To document possible cleavage of free Fe^{2+} from the protein, we used a colorimetric assay that uses ferrozine, a specific ferrous-ion complexing agent. We found that spontaneous release of free ferrous iron from iron-saturated lactoferrin is negligible, but when lactoferrin is exposed to enzymatically generated $O_2^{\cdot-}$, free Fe^{2+} is released; this release is virtually completely inhibited by the simultaneous addition of superoxide dismutase. More relevantly, granulocytes stimulated to produce $O_2^{\cdot-}$ by phorbol esters also significantly amplify Fe^{2+} release from lactoferrin, whereas "resting" granulocytes release none. Release in the former case is also virtually completely prevented by superoxide dismutase.

Lactoferrin as an Endothelial Cytoxin: Conclusions

Our studies suggest the following sequence by which granulocyte-derived lactoferrin promotes endothelial damage: Lactoferrin, after its secretion from stimulated cells, binds to target endothelial cells probably because it is a strong cation; this binding is especially fostered by the close margination of stimulated granulocytes onto endothelium. Once bound, lactoferrin assumes a conformation that is not possible in the soluble form, which may permit it to release inorganic ferrous ion; this release, in turn, first requires reduction of the lactoferrin ferric iron by another product of stimulated neutrophils, $O_2^{.-}$. (Of note, this same reaction has also been shown recently (25) to free inorganic iron from ferritin.) We suggest that free ferrous iron then efficiently catalyzes production of $\cdot OH$ and perhaps other very toxic oxygen species, resulting in lipid peroxidation and lysis of the target endothelium.

PLATELET ACTIVATING FACTOR: AN ENHANCER OF ENDOTHELIAL DAMAGE

Until recently we have taken the rather chauvinistic view that endothelium acts as an inert substrate, awaiting assault by stimulated, marginated granulocytes. This chauvinism needs to be modified because of recent observations that endothelium, when perturbed by various agonists, produces the granulocyte-stimulating product, platelet activating factor (PAF). Of particular relevance to our interest in vascular injury syndromes are recent findings (26,27) that thrombin induces the synthesis and release of PAF from endothelium. Besides being produced by perturbed endothelial cells, this lipid mediator, 1-O-alkyl-2-acetyl-3-phosphocholine, is produced by other kinds of activated cells including basophils, monocytes, and neutrophils themselves. Originally named because of its capacity to aggregate and degranulate platelets in vivo, PAF is really far more potent as a neutrophil activator. This suggests that PAF, produced by mildly injured endothelium, might cause a positive feedback that would lead to even more neutrophil-mediated damage. In this regard, it is noteworthy that infusion of PAF into animals induces pulmonary sequestration of neutrophils, followed by increased vascular permeability (28).

Recent reports indicate that rather high concentrations of PAF directly promote the neutrophil production of toxic oxygen species, but the production of PAF by endothelium in vivo would presumably be in far lower amounts. Thus, we studied the effects of tiny concentrations of PAF on neutrophils. We found that miniscule amounts of PAF--five to six orders of magnitude lower than previously examined--*prime* neutrophils so that they then respond excessively to subsequent application of otherwise trivial concentrations of agonists. We demonstrated that this priming phenomenon aggravates neutrophil-mediated endothelial injury, and we emphasize the vicious scenario that may occur when vascular damage incites coagulation (thrombin generation), i.e., thrombin stimulates PAF synthesis, which, in turn, further stimulates marginated neutrophils to increase their attack on the vascular wall.

Since PAF may play an important amplifying role in granulocyte-mediated vascular injury, PAF antagonists might prove therapeutically important in the future. From the armamentarium of the barefoot doctors of China, several herbal remedies for ailments of the lung and heart have been pharmaceutically purified, and two botanicals have been found to contain potent PAF inhibitors. The seeds and leaves of the *Ginkgo biloba* tree, or "ya-chiao-pan," are the source of a powerful PAF receptor antagonist known by the pharmaceutical designation BN52021 (29). Another Chinese herb, "haifenteng," from a plant of the nightshade family has yielded two other PAF antagonists, kadsurenone and L-652 (30).

PAF Primes Granulocytes to Become Endothelial Cytotoxins

We pretreated granulocytes in priming experiments with various tiny concentrations of PAF for five minutes, followed by the addition of formyl-methionineleucinephenylalanine (FMLP), an oligopeptide chemotaxin that, by itself, is a very weak promoter of $O_2^{.-}$ production. Minute concentrations of PAF (10^{-10} to 10^{-11} M), when added alone, did not induce $O_2^{.-}$ production by neutrophils, but markedly provoked $O_2^{.-}$ production in these same cells when they were subsequently exposed to otherwise trivial levels of FMLP. In ancillary studies, PAF-primed, FMLP-stimulated neutrophils also released more elastase than cells exposed to FMLP alone. Finally, PAF-primed neutrophils became excessively adherent to monolayers of human endothelium. With a concentration of PAF that did not enhance polymorphonuclear neutrophil (PMN) adhesion more than that observed with buffer alone and a concentration of FMLP that increased adhesion by only 5%, neutrophil adhesion to endothelium was markedly increased.

The effects of PAF priming--increased neutrophil adhesion, $O_2^{.-}$ production, and elastase release--predict that primed neutrophils should be particularly efficient in causing endothelial lysis and detachment. Indeed, neither PAF nor FMLP, added alone at almost any concentration, cause any neutrophil-mediated lysis of cultured endothelial cells labeled with chromium 51. However, if neutrophils are first exposed to PAF and then to FMLP, they lyse endothelium significantly and, even more markedly, detach intact endothelial cells from their anchoring substratum. In ancillary studies, PAF was also found to prime neutrophil capacities for chemotaxis, aggregation, and surface expression of the adhesion-promoting receptor, CR3.

Mechanism of PAF Priming and Its Prevention

Priming by PAF is not stimulus-specific in that PAF equally primes neutrophil responses to FMLP, activated complement (C5a), phorbol esters, and opsonized zymosan particles. Priming is maximal within 5 minutes, and once the neutrophil is primed, PAF can be washed away prior to subsequent agonist stimulation without loss of effect. Neutrophil priming by PAF requires exposure of neutrophils to PAF before exposure to FMLP and involves a specific PAF receptor. That is, if the sequence of PMN exposure is reversed--FMLP first, followed by PAF--no enhancement of O_2^- production or elastase release can be demonstrated. Moreover, lyso-PAF, which lacks the acetate group at position 2 on the glycerol backbone, does not prime PMN functions. Finally, PAF must be taken up by specific neutrophil membrane receptors to exert its actions; for instance, if receptor function is blocked by incubation at 4°C, no priming occurs.

Since receptor-ligand signal transduction in various cells, including neutrophils, is usually mediated by changes in intracellular calcium and phosphatidyl-inositol turnover, we assayed Ca^{2+} fluxes in neutrophils and the changes induced by PAF priming. Using the calcium-sensitive probe Fura-2, we found that FMLP alone induced an approximate threefold increase in intracellular Ca^{2+} levels within 20 seconds, which returned to baseline in four minutes. However, if neutrophils were first primed with concentrations of PAF that have no effect on Ca^{2+} flux when used alone, they show markedly augmented increases in Ca^{2+} concentrations when subsequently stimulated with FMLP.

Because of the potential therapeutic relevance and to examine further the specificity of the PAF priming response, we investigated the recently described PAF receptor antagonists BN52021, kadsurenone, and L-652. These reagents were assayed for their capacity to inhibit PAF priming of neutrophils, particularly with regard to their enhanced mediation of endothelial injury. Micromolar concentrations of all three inhibitors were found to inhibit PAF-induced increments in neutrophil adhesion, O_2^- generation, and elastase release. Not surprisingly, the inhibitors all significantly protect endothelium labeled with chromium 51 from neutrophil damage, BN52021 being the most efficient.

PAF as an Endothelial Cytotoxin: Conclusions

The lipid mediator PAF not only directly activates neutrophils, but also, in much smaller quantities, primes PMN responses to stimuli such as FMLP and activated complement; this action results in excessive neutrophil adhesion to endothelial cells, O_2^- generation, and elastase release. Concomitantly, and of possible relevance to the pathogenesis of vascular damage, PAF-primed neutrophils cause excessive endothelial injury in vitro. PAF priming is receptor mediated, requires the intact PAF molecule, and is associated with enhanced intracellular Ca^{2+} flux. The PAF receptor antagonists BN52021, kadsurenone, and L-652 inhibit PAF-primed neutrophil adhesion, O_2^- generation, and elastase release, and, therefore, inhibit the resulting enhancement of neutrophil-mediated endothelial lysis and detachment. Since endothelium exposed to thrombin produces PAF, as do stimulated neutrophils themselves, powerful paracrine and autocrine amplifications of endothelial damage may occur during blood coagulation at sites of vascular injury. That is, we suggest that minute amounts of PAF, derived from endothelial cells perturbed by coagulation, can provoke otherwise trivially activated neutrophils to become lethal to endothelium, thereby aggravating vascular damage. We have supported this construct in a recent preliminary communication (31). These studies encourage us to suggest a possible therapeutic role for PAF inhibitors in vascular-damage syndromes, including atherosclerosis and some forms of the adult respiratory distress syndrome.

ADDENDUM

It has come to our attention that the manner by which lactoferrin is loaded with iron may affect its ability to accelerate ·OH generation (32). In the present studies, lactoferrin was slightly supersaturated (>100%) in a procedure that used ferric ammonium citrate to iron-load the protein.

REFERENCES

1. Hammerschmidt DE, Hudson LD, Weaver LJ, Craddock PR, Jacob HS. Association of complement activation and elevated plasma-C5a with adult respiratory distress syndrome: pathophysiological relevance and possible prognostic value. Lancet 1980:i:947-949.

2. Hammerschmidt DE, Harris PD, Wayland JH, Craddock PR, Jacob HS. Complement-induced granulocyte aggregation in vivo. Amer J Path 1981:102:146-150.

3. Craddock PR, Fehr J, Brigham KL, Kronenberg RS, Jacob HS. Complement and leukocyte mediated pulmonary dysfunction in hemodialysis. New Engl J Med 1977:296:769-774.

4. Jacob HS, Craddock PR, Hammerschmidt DE, Moldow CF. Complement-induced granulocyte aggregation: an unsuspected mechanism of disease. New Engl J Med 1980:302:789-794.

5. Craddock PR, Fehr J, Dalmasso AP, Brigham KL, Jacob HS. Hemodialysis leukopenia. Pulmonary vascular leukostasis resulting from complement activation by dialyzer cellophane membranes. J Clin Invest 1977:59:879-888.

6. Prentice RL, Szatrowski TP, Fujikura T, Kato H, Mason MW, Hamilton HH. Leukocyte counts and coronary heart disease in a Japanese cohort. Am J Epidemiol 1982:116:496-506.

7. Sacks T, Moldow CF, Craddock PR, Bowers TK, Jacob HS. Oxygen radicals mediate endothelial cell damage by complement-stimulated granulocytes. An in vitro model of immune vascular damage. J Clin Invest 1978:61:1161-1167.

8. Weiss SJ, Young J, LoBuglio AF, Slivka A, Nimeh NF. Role of hydrogen peroxide in neutrophil-mediated destruction of cultured endothelial cells. J Clin Invest 1981:68:714-721.

9. Martin WJ. Neutrophils kill pulmonary endothelial cells by a hydrogen peroxide-dependent pathway: an in vitro model of neutrophil-mediated lung injury. Am Rev Respir Dis 1984:130:209-213.

10. Harlan JM, Levine JD, Callahan KS, Schwartz BR, Harker LA. Glutathione redox cycle protects cultured endothelial cells against lysis by extracellularly generated hydrogen peroxide. J Clin Invest 1984:73:706-713.

11. Stroncek DF, Vercellotti GM, Huh PW, Jacob HS. Neutrophil oxidants inactivate alpha-1-protease inhibitor and promote PMN-mediated detachment of cultured endothelium: protection by free methionine. Arteriosclerosis 1986:6:332-340.

12. Harlan JM, Killen PD, Harker LA, Striker GE, Wright DC. Neutrophil-mediated endothelial injury in vitro: mechanisms of cell detachment. J Clin Invest 1981:68:1394-1403.

13. Varani J, Fligiel SEG, Till GO, Kunkel RG, Ryan US, Ward PA. Pulmonary endothelial cell killing by human neutrophils: possible involvement of hydroxyl radical. Lab Invest 1985:53:656-663.

14. Graf E, Mahoney JR, Bryant RG, Eaton JW. Iron catalyzed hydroxyl radical formation: stringent requirement for free iron coordination site. J Biol Chem 1984:259:3620-3624.

15. Halliwell B, Gutteridge JMC. Oxygen toxicity, oxygen radicals, transition metals and disease. Biochem J 1984:219:1-14.

16. Vercellotti GM, van Asbeck BS, Jacob HS. Oxygen radical-induced erythrocyte hemolysis by neutrophils: critical role of iron and lactoferrin. J Clin Invest 1985:76:956-962.

17. Roos D, Voetman AA, Meerhof LJ. Functional activity of enucleated human polymorphonuclear leukocytes. J Cell Biol 1983:97:368-377.

18. Korchak HM, Roos D, Giedd KN, et al. Granulocytes without degranulation: neutrophil function in granule-depleted cytoplasts. Proc Natl Acad Sci USA 1983:80:4968-4972.

19. Ambruso DR, Johnston RB. Lactoferrin enhances hydroxyl radical production by human neutrophils, neutrophil particulate fractions, and an enzymatic generating system. J Clin Invest 1981:67:352-360.

20. Bannister JV, Bannister WH, Hill HAO, Thornalley PJ. Enhanced production of hydroxyl radicals by the xanthine–xanthine oxidase reaction in the presence of lactoferrin. Biochim Biophys Acta 1982:715:116-120.

21. Winterbourn CC. Lactoferrin-catalysed hydroxyl radical production: additional requirement for a chelating agent. Biochem J 1983:210:15-19.

22. Hallgren R, Venge P, Wikstrom B. Hemodialysis-induced increase in serum lactoferrin and serum eosinophil cationic protein as signs of local neutrophil and eosinophil degranulation. Nephron 1981:29:233-238.

23. Wolach B, Coates TD, Hugli TE, Baehner RL, Boxer LA. Plasma lactoferrin reflects granulocyte activation via complement in burn patients. J Lab Clin Med 1984:103:284-293.

24. Gutteberg TJ, Haneberg B, Jorgensen T. The latency of serum acute phase proteins in meningococcal septicemia, with special emphasis on lactoferrin. Clin Chim Acta 1984:136:173-178.

25. Biemond P, van Eijk HG, Swaak AJG, Koster JF. Iron mobilization from ferritin by superoxide derived from stimulated polymorphonuclear leukocytes: possible mechanism in inflammation diseases. J Clin Invest 1984:73:1576-1579.

26. Prescott SM, Zimmerman GA, McIntyre TM. Human endothelial cells in culture produce platelet activating factor (1-alkyl-2-acetyl-sn-glycero-3-phosphocholine) when stimulated with thrombin. Proc Natl Acad Sci USA 1984:81:3534-3538.

27. Camussi G, Aglietta M, Malavasi F, et al. The release of platelet activating factor from human endothelial cells in culture. J Immunol 1983:131:2397-2403.

28. Handley DA, Arbeeny CM, Lee ML, VanValen RG, Saunders RN. Effect of platelet activating factor on endothelial permeability to plasma macromolecules. Immunopharmacology 1984:8:137-142.

29. Braquet P. Involvement of PAF-acether in various immune disorders using BN52021 (Ginkgolide B): a powerful PAF-acether antagonist isolated from Ginkgo biloba L. In: Braquet P, ed. Advances in prostaglandin, thromboxane and leukotriene research (vol 16). New York:Raven Press, 1986:179-198.

30. Shen TY, Hwang SB, Chang MN, et al. Characterization of a platelet-activating factor receptor antagonist isolated from haifenteng (Piper futokadsura): specific inhibition of in vitro and in vivo platelet-activating factor-induced effects. Proc Natl Acad Sci USA 1985:82:672-676.

31. Wickham NWR, Vercellotti GM, Yin HQ, Moldow CF, Jacob HS. Neutrophils are primed to release toxic oxidants by contact with thrombin-stimulated endothelium: role of endothelial cell-generated platelet activating factor. Clin Res 1987:35:603a.

32. Aruoma OI, Halliwell B. Superoxide-dependent and ascorbate-dependent formation of hydroxyl radicals from hydrogen peroxide in the presence of iron. Are lactoferrin and transferrin promoters of hydroxyl radical generation? Biochem J 1987:241:273-278.

QUESTIONS AND COMMENTS

Dr. John Gutteridge: Is there any evidence that lactoferrin is fully iron loaded in vivo?

Dr. Harry S. Jacob: Plasma levels of iron-containing lactoferrin have been shown to increase in patients during shock, after burns, or immediately after complement-activation with hemodialysis. The degree of lactoferrin iron saturation is unclear, however.

Dr. Irwin Fridovich: In the setting where you protected endothelial cells in culture, with superoxide dismutase (SOD) plus catalase, against attack by xanthine oxidase plus xanthine, did you test SOD or catalase separately?

Dr. Harry S. Jacob: The results when SOD or catalase were used alone were inconsistent; on some, but not all, occasions the single agent inhibited damage. Therefore, our published data has generally used the combination of the two enzymes.

Dr. Peter Ward: Do you know if $O_2^{\cdot-}$ can cause release of Fe^{3+} from lactoferrin, similar to the release of Fe^{2+} from lactoferrin that you have reported?

Dr. Harry S. Jacob: We have only monitored Fe^{2+} release by using the specific complexor, ferrozine. We have no data regarding Fe^{3+} release.

Dr. Peter Ward: In other experiments in which perfusion of lung with PAF predisposes the lung to accentuated damage by formyl peptide-activated PMN, is it known with what PAF is reacting in lung?

Dr. Harry S. Jacob: Inflammatory cells have specific membrane receptors for PAF. It is not known whether endothelium has similar receptors.

MYOCARDIAL ISCHEMIA AND REPERFUSION INJURY:
Oxygen Radicals and the Role of the Neutrophil

Paul J. Simpson, Joseph C. Fantone, and Benedict R. Lucchesi

There is a growing body of evidence that oxygen radicals can mediate myocardial tissue injury during ischemia and, in particular, during reperfusion. This paper reviews in vivo studies that have been instrumental in demonstrating this role of oxygen radicals and focuses on the role of the neutrophil as a mediator of myocardial damage. Upon reperfusion, neutrophils accumulate and produce an inflammatory response in the myocardium that is responsible, in part, for the extension of tissue injury associated with reperfusion. Studies associating the inhibition of neutrophil accumulation and adhesion with decreased infarct size support the hypothesis that a population of myocardial cells in the region at risk undergo irreversible changes upon reperfusion and the accumulation of neutrophils. This paper reviews studies of several pharmacological agents (ibuprofen, N-2-mercaptopropionyl glycine, allopurinol, prostacyclin, and prostanglandin analogues) that protect the myocardium from reperfusion injury. Possible mechanisms by which these agents act and directions of research that may lead to therapeutically useful approaches are also discussed.

OXYGEN-DERIVED FREE RADICALS and their metabolites are increasingly recognized for their contribution to tissue injury during myocardial ischemia and, in particular, during the phase of reperfusion in the presence of whole blood. The potential sources of toxic oxygen species during myocardial ischemia/reperfusion injury include mitochondrial electron transport systems (1,2), purine catabolism by xanthine oxidase (3), prostaglandin biosynthesis (4), and infiltration of phagocytes (neutrophils and monocytes).

Many components within the cell are susceptible to attack by free radicals. As suggested by Kako (5), the free radicals formed during ischemia or reperfusion may produce their deleterious effects by 1) peroxidizing cell membrane lipids and, thus, altering the structural integrity of the membrane, 2) peroxidizing the lipids involved in maintaining the microenvironment of membrane proteins, or 3) reacting both with proteins and with membrane lipids separately or concurrently.

The lipids that constitute the cell membrane, especially those lipids containing unsaturated double bonds, are susceptible to free radical attack, leading to the formation of lipid peroxides and aldehydes. A second important site of free radical attack is membrane protein involved in the transport of ions and the maintenance of the cellular ionic homeostasis, such as proteins with cysteinyl residues that have a critical role for enzymatic function. Wolff et al (6) have suggested that free radicals might alter proteins in several ways: 1) affecting specific amino acid residues in the protein, thereby leading to conformational changes and fragmentation or polymerization, 2) causing denaturation of the protein, or 3) rendering the protein more susceptible to hydrolysis. In addition, oxygen radicals and products of their reactions may alter the structure and function of RNA and DNA. It is apparent, therefore, that an excessive oxidant stress imposed upon the cell can lead to the chemical modification of essential components of the cell and potentially to altered function.

The role of oxygen radicals and their metabolites in neutrophil-dependent inflammatory reactions has been reviewed (7), and there is strong support for the concept that neutrophil-derived toxic oxygen species play a major role in myocardial injury associated with reperfusion of the ischemic heart (reviewed in reference 8). There is indirect and direct evidence indicating a significant role for free radicals in myocardial injury. The indirect evidence comes from studies using agents that interact with reactive metabolites of oxygen (e.g., superoxide dismutase (SOD), catalase, mercaptopropionyl glycine) or using agents that prevent the generation of free radical species (e.g., ibuprofen, BW 755C, nafazatrom, prostacyclin, iloprost, allopurinol), decreasing the amount of tissue destruction that occurs with myocardial ischemia and reperfusion. The direct evidence comes from more recent work using electron paramagnetic resonance (EPR) spectroscopy in samples from freeze-clamped hearts subjected to ischemia and reperfusion. Using isolated rabbit hearts subjected to global ischemia, Zweier and associates (9) demonstrated a sudden increase in free radical production upon reperfusion. In addition, in numerous studies, toxic oxygen species have been generated in vitro, and the functional responses of tissues (10-15) and enzymes (16-19) have been altered. The emphasis of this review will be on in vivo studies that have been instrumental in demonstrating the role of oxygen radicals as potential mediators of myocardial reperfusion injury.

From Departments of Pharmacology and Pathology, The University of Michigan Medical School, Ann Arbor, Michigan, USA.

Address correspondence to Dr. Benedict R. Lucchesi, Department of Pharmacology, M6322 Medical Sciences Building I, The University of Michigan Medical School, Ann Arbor, Michigan 48109, USA.

PHYSIOLOGICAL SIGNIFICANCE OF ULTIMATE MYOCARDIAL INFARCT SIZE

The stimulus for the development of therapeutic interventions directed towards the treatment of acute myocardial ischemia stems from the following observations: First, mortality among patients with acute myocardial infarction is influenced by the extent of left ventricular dysfunction, which is directly related to the amount of myocardium that becomes infarcted and thus nonfunctional (20,21). Second, reperfusion of the acutely ischemic myocardium decreases ultimate infarct size, as determined in experimental animals and presumably in patients. Patients who are treated and whose hearts are reperfused early (within 4 hours) after the onset of symptoms exhibit better functional recovery, as measured by a larger ejection fraction and smaller infarct size, assessed by the amount of intracellular enzymes released from the myocardium (22). It is now generally agreed that proper aggressive treatment of acute myocardial infarction should involve attempts to recanalize the obstructed coronaries, either by mechanical means such as percutaneous transluminal coronary angioplasty (PTCA) or by thrombolytic therapy with various agents (streptokinase, prourokinase, tissue-type plasminogen activator). If these two techniques are unsuccessful, surgical intervention (coronary artery bypass grafting) may be used (23).

DETERMINANTS OF ULTIMATE INFARCT SIZE

The size of the myocardial infarct that results after regional ischemia is directly related to the severity and duration of the ischemic insult (24-26). In the canine heart, coronary artery occlusion for more than 4 hours followed by reperfusion results in an infarct size that is essentially identical to the infarct that results after continued coronary artery occlusion for 24 hours. Coronary occlusion for less than 20 minutes is associated with prolonged ventricular dysfunction, a phenomenon referred to as *stunned myocardium* (27), in which the myocardium eventually recovers without evidence of myocardial cell injury. Since the degree of myocardial cellular necrosis increases with increasing duration of ischemia, it is apparent that early reperfusion of the ischemic myocardium will salvage potentially viable tissue (28).

When the ischemic interval is extended to 40 minutes, the extent of irreversibly injured tissue (infarct size) is directly related to the duration of the ischemia (24). Reimer and Jennings (25) described the *wavefront phenomenon* of advancing necrosis from the subendocardial to the subepicardial regions of the myocardium. The longer the deprivation of blood flow to the myocardium, the smaller the amount of tissue that can be recovered by reperfusion, with most of the remaining viable tissue being confined to the subepicardium. Thus, early reperfusion of the ischemic myocardium becomes essential if the goal of therapy is to prevent or decrease the extension of tissue damage associated with regional myocardial ischemia in the patient in whom a myocardial infarction is evolving.

CONCEPT OF MYOCARDIAL REPERFUSION INJURY

As a simple definition, myocardial reperfusion injury refers to irreversible cellular injury (necrosis) that results from the reintroduction of molecular oxygen at the time of organ reperfusion. In experimental studies, reperfusion of the ischemic myocardium results in an apparent acceleration of necrosis as manifested by cell swelling (29) and by the formation of contraction bands (30,31). However, additional studies suggest that, although essential for the ultimate survival of the myocardial cell, the sudden reintroduction of molecular oxygen may be detrimental to the once ischemic myocyte. This poses a paradox regarding the ideal approach to protecting the ischemic heart and gives rise to the concept of *myocardial reperfusion injury* (32,33). This injury is associated with a variety of events such as the calcium overload of cells that have pre-existing membrane defects, the influx of inflammatory cells (e.g., neutrophils), and the generation of oxygen radicals or other long-lived oxidants. Reperfusion injury in vivo probably results from the cumulative effects of these factors.

There is a complex interrelationship among the various factors that contribute to reperfusion injury. Oxygen radicals are produced by activated neutrophils that infiltrate ischemic and reperfused myocardium. Free radical scavengers, including SOD and catalase, decrease the contribution of superoxide ($O_2^{\cdot-}$) and hydroxyl radicals ($\cdot OH$) to myocardial cell injury (34,35). Another source of oxygen radicals and oxidants is the enzyme xanthine oxidase, which is localized within the vascular endothelium in many animal species (36). Xanthine dehydrogenase has been reported to undergo a conversion from its dehydrogenase to its oxidase form upon activation of a calcium-dependent protease (36-38). Upon reperfusion, xanthine oxidase is thought to utilize hypoxanthine as a substrate and molecular oxygen as an electron acceptor, thereby leading to the production of $O_2^{\cdot-}$ and H_2O_2 (**Figure 1**). Part of the support for this concept derives from the observation that allopurinol, an inhibitor of xanthine oxidase, has been reported to diminish tissue injury associated with reperfusion of the myocardium and other organs (see below and references 39 and 40).

In addition to the sources of free radicals listed above, cardiac myocytes have been proposed to be a production site of $O_2^{\cdot-}$ and H_2O_2 by mitochondrial metabolism or by the cyclooxygenase and lipoxygenase pathways during the cellular synthesis of arachidonic acid metabolites. Thus, the use of free radical scavengers could theoretically prevent cell injury caused by reactive oxygen species derived from one or more of these sources, and the efficacy of these scavengers in protecting the cell would depend upon their ability to gain access to the production site of the reactive oxygen species.

For the purpose of this discussion, we will use a strict definition of reperfusion injury, which considers the possibility that some or all of the ischemic myocytes that are not salvaged by reperfusion are viable at the time of reperfusion, but then are lethally altered by an imposed oxidative stress associated with the reintroduction of oxygenated blood and its cellular components. Thus, myocardial cells that were reversibly injured at the end of the ischemic interval, are subjected to unfavorable conditions during reperfusion, and the act of reperfusion itself leads to cell death. Myocardial cell death due to reperfusion injury may be different in mechanism from the type of cell death that results from prolonged myocardial ischemia.

THE CALCIUM AND OXYGEN PARADOXES

Two separate, but related, phenomena associated with reperfusion injury of the previously ischemic myocardium are the *calcium paradox* (41) and the *oxygen paradox* (30,42). When isolated hearts are perfused for brief periods with calcium-free buffer, and then reperfused with buffer containing physiological amounts of calcium ion, damage to the myocardial tissue occurs that is associated with calcium entry into the myocytes (41,43-46). The intracellular "calcium overload" of the heart has been postulated to be the cause of the calcium paradox. However, calcium entry may also occur secondary to ischemia/reperfusion-induced membrane disruption, such that calcium influx follows membrane damage and is not the proximate cause of the membrane injury. This suggests that alternative mechanisms may initiate the membrane damage associated with the calcium paradox, one possible mechanism being the production of oxygen intermediates, and suggests that the injury is not necessarily exclusively due to calcium overload (47).

In an analogous manner, the reintroduction of oxygen after a period of very low oxygen tension in the

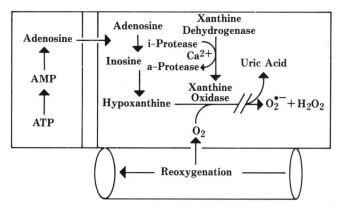

Figure 1. Scheme illustrating the role of xanthine oxidase in the production of $O_2^{\cdot-}$ and H_2O_2 after ischemia and reperfusion of the myocardium. (i-Protease = inactive; a-Protease = active)

isolated buffer-perfused heart is associated with the oxygen paradox (30,31,42). The oxygen paradox is characterized by the development of myocardial contracture upon reoxygenation of the ischemic myocardium and is accompanied by the release of intracellular enzymes (e.g., myocardial creatine kinase) in a pattern consistent with myocardial cell injury, which can be confirmed by light or electron microscopic examination of the tissue as well as by histochemical analysis. The same sequence of events does not occur if the ischemic heart is reperfused with a solution devoid of oxygen. Thus, the reintroduction of molecular oxygen is associated with an abrupt alteration in the integrity of the myocardial cell and an immediate decline or absolute loss of myocardial contractile function.

The two paradoxes are manifest by similar pathological changes that are energy dependent and result in contraction band necrosis secondary to intracellular accumulation of ionized calcium (48-50). The situation encountered clinically does not mimic the events seen with calcium-free perfusion, as occurs in the calcium paradox. The intact heart is not exposed to a calcium-free perfusate during myocardial ischemia and the evolution of an infarct or during reperfusion. The calcium paradox, therefore, may not be relevant. However, the oxygen paradox may be a relevant mechanism of myocardial damage.

With the intracellular accumulation of ionized calcium, several potentially deleterious processes are initiated. Calcium has been postulated to activate phospholipases, resulting in elevated concentrations of lysophospholipids, free fatty acids, and, potentially, arachidonic acid metabolites that may contribute to the myocardial cell damage. In addition, ATPases have been postulated to be activated by increased calcium entry into the cells, thus further jeopardizing myocyte viability by depleting energy stores. Calcium also activates many proteases, which can add to tissue destruction.

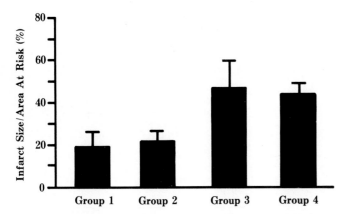

Figure 2. Effect of SOD plus catalase on the relative size of the myocardial infarct in the canine heart after ischemia and reperfusion. Open-chest anesthetized dogs were subjected to 90 minutes of regional myocardial ischemia followed by 24 hours of reperfusion. Groups 1-3 received SOD (5 mg/kg [2900 U/mg Sigma]) plus catalase (5 mg/kg [11,000 U/mg Sigma]) infused into the left atrial appendage. Group 4 received a saline infusion. Group 1 was administered the SOD plus catalase beginning 15 minutes before reperfusion and continuing 15 minutes after reperfusion. Group 2 was administered the SOD plus catalase for one hour beginning 15 minutes before reperfusion. Group 3 was administered the SOD plus catalase beginning 40 minutes after reperfusion. Infarct sizes in groups 1 and 2 were significantly smaller ($P < 0.05$) than those in groups 3 and 4. The bars indicate ± 1 SEM. (Plotted from data in reference 34.)

PROTECTION OF THE ISCHEMIC/REPERFUSED HEART BY SCAVENGERS OF OXYGEN RADICALS

The first suggestive evidence of the participation of oxygen radicals in myocardial reperfusion injury developed from the work of Shlafer et al (51) and Jolly et al (34). Shlafer and colleagues demonstrated that SOD plus catalase could reduce myocardial damage in the perfused isolated rabbit heart subjected to hypothermic global ischemia and reperfusion. Jolly et al (34) demonstrated that administration of SOD plus catalase to anesthetized dogs subjected to 90 minutes of coronary artery occlusion followed by 24 hours of reperfusion (**Figure 2**) reduced ultimate infarct size when the enzymes were administered before the induction of regional myocardial ischemia or when administered 15 minutes before myocardial reperfusion (Groups 1 and 2). In contrast, the enzymes were without benefit if they were infused 40 minutes after reperfusion had started (Group 3). These observations suggested that an extension of myocardial injury, in addition to that associated with the ischemia-induced myocardial cell death, was occurring very early during reperfusion and that the myocardial damage could be attenuated by pretreatment with free-radical metabolizing enzymes.

Werns et al (35) subsequently showed that the administration of SOD alone resulted in a 50% reduction of myocardial infarct size, whereas the administration of catalase alone did not result in a significant degree of myocardial salvage upon reperfusion. In a number of experimental studies (51,52) using isolated hearts, the ability of SOD to reduce ischemia/reperfusion damage (as measured by a variety of indices) has been confirmed. In a recent study, Werns et al (53) demonstrated that the administration of SOD in a dose regimen known to be effective in reducing ultimate infarct size in the canine heart did not affect wall thickening or scar formation when assessed six weeks after experimental myocardial infarction. Recently Ambrosio et al (54) showed that recombinant human SOD could reduce ultimate infarct size in the canine heart subjected to 90 minutes of regional ischemia followed by reperfusion, despite the fact that the enzyme was administered immediately upon reperfusion. The latter observation agrees with earlier observations (34) and strongly supports the view that an extension of myocardial injury occurs coincident with the onset of reperfusion.

Table 1 lists a number of additional studies of pharmacological interventions that support the concept that reactive products of oxygen are involved in the alteration of cardiac function or in the irreversible injury associated with myocardial ischemia and/or reperfusion.

In a recent study, Gallagher and associates (55), using the chronically instrumented dog subjected to three hours of regional myocardial ischemia, failed to show a protective effect of SOD on ultimate infarct size. This failure was most likely due to the degree of myocardial cell death associated with the three-hour ischemic interval, which may have left far too little myocardium that could be salvaged by the applied intervention (26,56). Hence, there must be a critical period of ischemia after which any intervention administered at the time of reperfusion is unlikely to reduce infarct size because the tissue has already undergone irreversible and cytotoxic effects from ischemia.

In support of this hypothesis, a recent study in our laboratory (26) demonstrated that four hours of regional ischemia in the canine heart followed by reperfusion results in a maximum extension of the ischemic injury which cannot be diminished by neutrophil depletion, an intervention that effectively decreases ultimate infarct size in the canine heart subjected to 90 minutes of ischemia followed by reperfusion (57,58). Therefore, it is important to evaluate the results of ischemia/reperfusion studies while recognizing that the ischemic interval is associated with an expanding wave front. The developing infarct can reach a maximum size, thereby circumventing reduction of the ultimate size by an intervention that prevents injury by a component associated with reperfusion.

It is apparent that there is growing support for the concept that myocardial ischemia, and in particular reperfusion injury, is accompanied by the formation of oxygen radicals, which overwhelm endogenous protective mechanisms and thereby exacerbate cell injury. An important issue that remains to be resolved is the source of these radicals. While it is known that activated neutrophils can generate toxic oxygen products, it is becoming clear that they are not the only potential source of the cytotoxic radicals, since free radical generation and protection by various scavengers are observed in studies using isolated hearts perfused with physiological salt solutions free of blood. More direct evidence for the generation of oxygen-derived free radicals by cardiac tissues comes from recent reports by Zweier et al (9,59), who used EPR spectroscopy to demonstrate the generation of oxygen-centered free radicals within seconds of restoring perfusion to the globally ischemic isolated heart which was perfused with a blood-free, buffered, physiologic salt solution. Of further interest, these authors were able to demonstrate that the EPR signal could be eliminated by the addition of SOD.

LOSS OF INTRACELLULAR ANTIOXIDANT DEFENSE MECHANISMS DURING MYOCARDIAL ISCHEMIA AND REPERFUSION

Cells and plasma contain a variety of antioxidant and free-radical scavenging molecules and enzymes which, under normal circumstances, help the cell to maintain an oxidizing environment while preventing the potentially deleterious effects of free radicals on cell membranes and organelles (60-70). Superoxide dismutase (60) enzymatically transforms $O_2^{\cdot-}$ to H_2O_2 and molecular oxygen. Under normal conditions, SOD is confined to the intracellular compartment.

Hydrogen peroxide is metabolized to water and oxygen by two important intracellular enzymes, catalase (61) and glutathione peroxidase (62). In addition, glutathione peroxidase metabolizes lipid hydroperoxides to alcohols. The enzymatic activity of the selenium-dependent glutathione peroxidase depends on the availability of reducing equivalents such as provided by glutathione. It is known that during myocardial ischemia, the concentrations of SOD, glutathione peroxidase, and glutathione decrease, thereby decreasing the ability of the cell to protect itself against the free radicals and H_2O_2 which are generated (17,18,63-65). Therefore, the ischemic myocardium is poorly prepared to cope with increased free radical and oxidant stress that occurs during reperfusion.

NEUTROPHILS AS MEDIATORS OF MYOCARDIAL CELL INJURY

Associated with reperfusion of the ischemic myocardium is a cellular reaction characterized by

Table 1. Some Pharmacological Interventions that Protect the Myocardium Against Neutrophil-Mediated Damage and/or Radical-Mediated Damage*

Agent	References
SOD (Superoxide dismutase)	14,35,120,141
SOD + Catalase	2,11,34,51,52
SOD + Mannitol	11,12,142
DMSO	14
Allopurinol	39,40
Coenzyme Q_{10}	143
Glucose-insulin-potassium	144
Lipoxygenase inhibitors	58,71,72,109,110
Neutrophil depletion	57,58,73,112
2-MPG	111,112
Dimethylthiourea	115
Prostacyclin	130-136
Iloprost	137,138
Anti-Mo1 monoclonal antibody	105

* Some interventions were shown to prevent cardiac enzyme release (14,51,141,144) or sarcolemmal damage (14), to restore depressed calcium uptake and ATPase activity in the sarcolemma (11,44), to maintain mitochondrial integrity and function (2,51,120), to prevent malondialdehyde formation (141), to improve cardiac function (15,51,52), or to decrease infarct size (34,35,39,40,58,71,72,105,109-112,115,131,135-138).

the accumulation of inflammatory cells and the production of inflammatory mediators in the reperfused myocardium. This inflammatory response is responsible, in part, for the extension of tissue injury associated with reperfusion of the previously ischemic myocardium (8,26,69-71).

A number of studies to date have documented the correlation between myocardial infarct size resulting from reperfusion and the extent of neutrophil infiltration (26,57,58,71-74). Neutrophils have been observed to infiltrate beginning with the onset of ischemic injury and to increase their numbers progressively throughout the evolution of a myocardial infarction for the first 24 hours (75,76). However, few investigators have attempted to confirm a causal relationship between neutrophil infiltration and infarct size. Mullane and coworkers (58) suggested that the infiltration of neutrophils precedes the development of myocardial cell necrosis. The formation of tissue edema, which accompanies the inflammatory response to ischemia, involves interactions that require the neutrophil for the full expression of the inflammatory response (77).

Chemotaxis and Activation of Neutrophils

In order for neutrophils to injure ischemic tissue, a chemical signal or chemoattractant must direct the neutrophil into the ischemic myocardial region. In 1971, Hill and Ward (78) established that, after ligation of a rat coronary artery, a tissue protease is released that can activate the third component of complement. Giclas and coworkers (79) confirmed that human heart subcellular membranes can activate complement. Since that time, there has been extensive confirmation that myocardial ischemia activates the complement system and that ischemia results in the migration of neutrophils into the myocardium (74,80,81).

Other chemotactic factors are generated during myocardial ischemia including the arachidonic acid-derived product, leukotriene B_4. Petrone and coworkers (82) determined that a potent chemotactic factor can be produced by $O_2^{\cdot-}$ acting upon a plasma protein. Additional studies indicate that an arachidonic acid derivative with chemotactic activity is produced upon exposure of arachidonic acid to $O_2^{\cdot-}$ (83). Hartmann et al (84) observed a 50% increase in chemotactic activity in the coronary sinus blood of dogs subjected to ligation of the left anterior descending coronary artery and correlated these changes with enzymatic and electrocardiographic indices of myocardial ischemia.

Further suggestion that the complement system is involved comes from the study of Maroko et al (85) in which complement was depleted by cobra venom factor after coronary ligation, resulting in a smaller amount of myocardium that eventually became infarcted. Pinckard and associates (80,81) confirmed these observations in a baboon model of myocardial infarction and documented with immunohistochemical methods the extensive localization of complement components (C3, C4, and C5) within the ischemic myocardium; this localization was not observed after decomplementation of the animal with cobra venom factor. Recent studies (86) have suggested that the membrane attack complex of complement is present within the ischemic myocardium of humans with acute myocardial infarctions as early as six hours after the onset of symptoms. The membrane attack complex consists of a stable macromolecular complex (C5b with C6, C7, and C8) that inserts into the membrane bilayer (with C9), forming a pore or channel through the membrane that permits bidirectional flow of ions and macromolecules, ultimately resulting in cell lysis. Thus, complement may have a direct as well as an indirect (neutrophil) effect on the sequential events associated with myocardial tissue injury and subsequent cell death.

A common pathophysiological finding in myocardial ischemic injury is endothelial damage to the coronary vascular bed, which leads to the extravasation of plasma and cellular components into the interstitial space. Polymorphonuclear leukocytes can adhere to and migrate through the endothelial cell layer and, thus, potentially have a role in mediating myocardial injury once they have gained access to the tissue space. The migration of these inflammatory cells is a time-dependent process in the presence of total occlusion; inflammatory cells enter the damaged myocardium slowly, becoming apparent at 24 hours after the onset of injury. On the other hand, reperfusion of the once ischemic tissue allows the inflammatory cells to have rapid access to the jeopardized myocardial region (58,71). The movement of neutrophils across the vascular wall may in itself be associated with permeability changes and injury to the vessel as a result of the injurious action of proteinases derived from the emigrating neutrophil. Evidence suggests that the migration of the neutrophil across the connective tissue barrier of the blood vessel depends on the action of proteolytic enzymes, which remain active even in the presence of plasma antiproteases (87-90).

Human neutrophils stimulated with phorbol myristate acetate and incubated with endothelial cells are known to be cytotoxic to the endothelial cells (91). Similar endothelial cytotoxic effects were elicited by the addition of postsecretory media from the activated neutrophils as well as the addition of a partially purified granule fraction from the inflammatory cells. The endothelial detachment was prevented by the addition of agents known to inhibit elastase and other serine proteinases. The inhibition of elastase by a_1-antiproteinase is markedly decreased by oxidants such as hypochlorous acid (HOCl) generated as a result of neutrophil H_2O_2 and myeloperoxidase activity, thus permitting elastase to promote extension of tissue injury. a_2-Macroglobulin is a second important plasma proteinase inhibitor, which, together with a_1-antiproteinase, accounts for over 90% of the proteinase-inhibiting capacity of serum. The a_2-macroglobulin accounts for over 50% of the inhibition of kallikrein. In addition, the neutrophil is capable of releasing the enzymes collagenase and gelatinase in latent forms, which become activated through both proteolytic and oxidative mechanisms. Thus, the activated neutrophil can use oxygen metabolites ($O_2^{\cdot-}$, H_2O_2, OCl$^-$) and proteinases in a cooperative manner to mediate tissue damage.

Adhesion-Promoting Cell Surface Glycoprotein Complexes

Pathophysiological conditions occur in which there is chemoattraction and enhanced binding of neutrophils to the surface of specific cells. Such conditions would be expected to enhance the opportunity for the inflammatory cells to induce tissue injury. It is becoming apparent that localization of complement components may enhance the attachment of neutrophils to the vascular endothelium after an ischemic insult to the tissue and that neutrophil attachment may be a prerequisite for neutrophil-mediated cellular injury (78-81). Leukocytes have cell surface glycoprotein molecules that are involved in cell-cell and cell-surface interactions. These include specific receptors for the Fc portion of immunoglobulin molecules, C3b (CR1 receptor), and a group of adhesion-promoting molecules collectively referred to as the CD11/CD18 complex, or LFA, antigens (92-94). Recent studies of the CD11/CD18 complex indicate that these molecules are heterodimers consisting of common beta subunits with distinct alpha subunits that confer molecular specificity. The Mo1 complex is present on human and animal phagocytic cells (neutrophils, monocytes, and macrophages) and is functionally similar to, or may be identical to, the receptor that recognizes C3bi (CR3 receptor) (**Figure 3**). Studies using monoclonal antibodies directed against Mo1 showed that it plays a functional role in promoting the attachment of neutrophils to a variety of substrates, including vascular endothelium and pulmonary alveolar epithelium (95), and in enhancing target cell injury (92-97). Moreover, activation of neutrophils by chemotactic factors increases the expression of these adhesion-promoting receptors (98,99), the net result of which is increased accumulation of neutrophils at the endothelial surface when tissue injury occurs. Recent studies by Gimbrone and colleagues (100-102) indicate that the expression of adherence-promoting molecules distinct from the CD11/CD18 complex on endothelial cell surfaces can be enhanced by inflammatory mediators (e.g., interleukin 1) and may also promote leukocyte sequestration at sites of tissue injury. In addition to resulting in destruction by neutrophil-derived products and proteolytic enzymes, activation of neutrophils within the vascular space has been suggested to result in the formation of cellular aggregates that can physically impair blood flow to the myocardial capillary bed and thereby further exacerbate the ischemic injury (73,103). Neutrophil accumulation in the vascular bed has been proposed to contribute to inadequate reflow or to the no-reflow phenomenon after brief periods of ischemia followed by reperfusion (104).

Neutrophils in Ischemia/Reperfusion Injury

Direct evidence for the role of neutrophils in myocardial infarction was initially provided by the study of Romson and associates (57). Dogs were depleted of circulating neutrophils before the

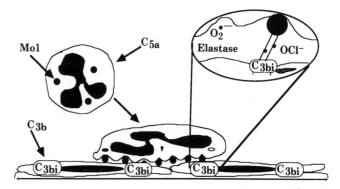

Figure 3. The theoretical role of Mo1 glycoprotein complex in neutrophil adherence to vascular endothelium. The C_{5a} activation of neutrophils increases the expression of these molecules (Mo1) as well as the activation of the neutrophils to produce $O_2^{\cdot-}$ and the degranulation that can damage the endothelial cells to which they are adhering.

induction of regional myocardial ischemia. Infarct size measured after 90 minutes of ischemia and six hours of reperfusion was 43% smaller in the neutrophil-depleted group compared to that in controls. Thus, a direct link was established between the ability of the host neutrophils to accumulate within the region of risk and the extent of tissue injury within the jeopardized myocardial zone. The importance of circulating polymorphonuclear leukocytes as mediators in ischemia/reperfusion myocardial injury has been documented in two other laboratories (58,73).

Based on these observations, we hypothesized that if neutrophil adherence could be inhibited, the recruitment and activation of neutrophils at sites of myocardial ischemia/reperfusion injury would be attenuated and the extent of the infarction would be decreased. Preliminary results from our study in canine hearts subjected to 90 minutes of ischemia followed by reperfusion show that the administration of an anti-Mo1 monoclonal antibody 45 minutes after the induction of regional myocardial ischemia significantly protects against reperfusion injury as measured by the size of myocardial infarct after six hours of reperfusion. Infarct size expressed as a percentage of the area of the myocardium at risk was reduced by 47% in the antibody-treated group compared to that in the control group, without significant differences in hemodynamic parameters (105). These data show that inhibition of neutrophil adhesion reduces the myocardial reperfusion injury and provide additional evidence for the important role of inflammatory cells in extending myocardial injury beyond that caused by the ischemia alone. These data also support the hypothesis that a significant number of myocardial cells in the region at risk are viable after a 90-minute ischemic period, but then progress to an irreversible state of injury upon reperfusion and the accumulation of polymorphonuclear leukocytes.

PHARMACOLOGICAL PROTECTION OF THE ISCHEMIC/REPERFUSED MYOCARDIUM

Ibuprofen

Studies by Romson et al (71) demonstrated the myocardial protective effect of the nonsteroidal anti-inflammatory agent ibuprofen. Ibuprofen decreased myocardial infarct size in the dog subjected to 60 minutes of coronary occlusion followed by 24 hours of reperfusion. The protective effect of ibuprofen was associated with decreased neutrophil accumulation in the myocardial region at risk.

That ibuprofen has a direct effect on neutrophils was indicated by more recent work in animals (106) in which activation of neutrophils by inflammatory mediators was inhibited by their previous exposure to ibuprofen. The protective effects of ibuprofen are unrelated to its ability to inhibit cyclooxygenase, as neither acetylsalicylic acid nor indomethacin could be demonstrated to decrease ultimate infarct size or to inhibit the release of $O_2^{\cdot-}$ by activated neutrophils (106). The same study demonstrated that the administration of a glucocorticoid did not reduce ultimate infarct size in this animal model of myocardial ischemia/reperfusion. Thus, it appears that ibuprofen, in contrast to indomethacin and acetylsalicylic acid, protects via a pharmacological mechanism that does not involve inhibition of prostanoid formation and that it may act directly upon the inflammatory cells by impairing their chemoattraction to the region and/or by impairing their ability to form and release inflammatory mediators. The clinical use of ibuprofen and related nonsteroidal anti-inflammatory agents to protect the ischemic heart must be evaluated in the context of potential deleterious effects on infarct healing and of the fibrotic response to these agents (107,108).

Subsequent studies have suggested that pharmacological interventions capable of inhibiting the lipoxygenase pathway of arachidonic acid metabolism also decrease myocardial infarct size, most probably through a mechanism related to the inhibition of neutrophil accumulation within the myocardium. Jolly and Lucchesi (109) showed that the dual cyclooxygenase-lipoxygenase inhibitor BW 755C (10 mg/kg) decreased myocardial infarct size by 50% as compared to the decrease in nontreated controls (in a canine model of 90 minutes of coronary occlusion followed by 24 hours of reperfusion). Mullane et al (58) demonstrated that decreased infarct size was associated with a BW 755C-induced decrease in leukocyte accumulation in the infarcted canine myocardium. Another agent that inhibits both the cyclooxygenase and lipoxygenase pathways, nafazatrom (BAY g6575), decreased infarct size in the dog after regional myocardial ischemia and reperfusion (72,110). The data indicate that the mechanism for decreasing infarct size is associated with decreased neutrophil accumulation in the myocardium.

N-2-Mercaptopropionyl Glycine

Mitsos and colleagues (111, 112) studied the independent effects of neutrophil depletion and of a sulfhydryl free-radical scavenger on the infarct size resulting from 90 minutes of regional myocardial ischemia and six hours of reperfusion. They observed that the sulfhydryl compound, N-2-mercaptopropionyl glycine (2-MPG), had neutrophil-independent protective effects in this animal model. Previous pharmacokinetic studies indicated that 2-MPG enters cells, where its effects may add to the cellular defense mechanisms directed against oxidative stress (113). Neutrophil depletion resulted in a 33% reduction in infarct size ($30.7 \pm 2.7\%$ SEM of the area at risk, $P < 0.01$) when compared to that in controls ($45.6 \pm 3.7\%$). Administration of 2-MPG to the neutropenic animal resulted in a further decrease in myocardial infarct size ($17 \pm 2.7\%$), a 63% decrease compared to the control value. This decrease was significant at $P < 0.01$ when compared either to control values or to values for neutrophil-depleted animals. Additional studies by Beyersdorf et al (114) showed that 2-MPG could prevent the hemodynamic, morphologic, and biochemical changes in the perfused isolated rat heart exposed to 90 minutes of hypoxia. These authors suggested that 2-MPG, by gaining access to the intracellular compartment, could protect the mitochondrial membrane from the toxic effects of oxygen radicals.

Other sulfhydryl-containing compounds can provide a similar protection, as illustrated by the recent report that dimethylthiourea decreases ultimate infarct size in a canine model of 90 minutes of regional ischemia followed by reperfusion (115). In the control group, the infarct size was $52.1 \pm 5.7\%$ of the area of risk; in the treated group, the infarct size was $28.8 \pm 5.7\%$. The size of the area at risk did not differ between the two groups. These data support the hypothesis that both intracellular and extracellular sources of reactive oxygen species may be important in mediating myocardial injury associated with ischemia and reperfusion and suggest that thiol compounds, because of their ability to gain access to the intracellular compartment as well as to the vascular and extracellular space, may provide an interesting approach to the development of cytoprotective agents.

Allopurinol, an Inhibitor of the Enzyme Xanthine Oxidase

Another potentially important source of oxygen radicals during myocardial ischemia and reperfusion is xanthine oxidase (38). Experiments demonstrating the protective effects of allopurinol in experimental models of myocardial ischemia have suggested that this enzyme is important in the generation of toxic oxygen species during myocardial reperfusion (39,116,117). Present within various tissues, the enzyme xanthine dehydrogenase is converted under conditions of ischemia, by a calcium-activated protease, to xanthine oxidase (the D-to-O conversion) (37,118). In addition, during ischemia, there is a buildup of purine metabolites from ATP and ADP. Thus, upon reperfusion, the required substrate, hypoxanthine, and the necessary electron acceptor, oxygen, are provided to the enzyme, leading to the formation of uric acid and, more importantly, to the generation of $O_2^{\cdot-}$ and H_2O_2. The localization of xanthine oxidase in the endothelial cell (119) provides it with an important locus for inducing tissue injury that could extend myocardial damage upon reperfusion beyond that already resulting from the ischemic insult.

Recently Werns et al (40) demonstrated an additive protective effect of allopurinol and SOD. Allopurinol (25 mg/kg, IV) was administered to one group of dogs that 18 hours later received a second dose (50 mg/kg) immediately before induction of regional myocardial ischemia for 90 minutes followed by six hours of reperfusion. A second group received vehicle. A third group received, in addition to allopurinol at the same dose and schedule as the first group, SOD (5 mg/kg), administered via the left atrium for one hour beginning 15 minutes before reperfusion. Allopurinol alone or allopurinol plus SOD reduced ultimate infarct size relative to that in control animals, with the greatest degree of myocardial salvage occurring in the group that received the combined treatment. These observations lend further support to the hypothesis that multiple sites of free radical production exist: an allopurinol-sensitive source (endothelial cell xanthine oxidase) and allopurinol-insensitive sources (e.g., polymorphonuclear leukocytes and mitochondria). Neutrophil-derived free radical attack may be controlled by providing an extracellular scavenger in the form of SOD, whereas the generation of $O_2^{\cdot-}$ derived from xanthine oxidase may be prevented by allopurinol. This concept is consistent with the earlier observations reported for 2-MPG administered to the neutropenic animal, in which the sulfhydryl compound provided an added degree of protection (111,112).

In vitro studies have shown that xanthine oxidase-derived free radicals can cause myocardial structural alteration and depress myocardial function (11,120). Myocardial xanthine oxidase activity has been suggested to be localized to the vascular endothelium (119). Controversial results have been reported (121) with respect to the efficacy of allopurinol in another experimental model of myocardial ischemia. Reimer and Jennings (121), with a 40-minute coronary occlusion model and administration of allopurinol beginning 30 minutes before occlusion and continuing until 40 minutes after reperfusion, failed to observe a protective effect with allopurinol. The efficacy of allopurinol perhaps can only be observed when one uses a pretreatment dosage regimen in which the drug is administered 12 to 18 hours before subjecting the heart to regional ischemia followed by reperfusion. This may be because time is required for accumulation of oxypurinol, the metabolite of allopurinol. Allopurinol is a competitive inhibitor of xanthine oxidase, and accumulation of large amounts of substrate (xanthine or hypoxanthine) within the ischemic myocardium may be sufficient to overcome the inhibitory action of the drug. In contrast, oxypurinol has a higher affinity for the enzyme and functions as a noncompetitive enzyme inhibitor. Thus, oxypurinol can more effectively inhibit xanthine oxidase regardless of the accumulated substrate concentration within the ischemic tissue.

Recent studies indicate that allopurinol (1 mM) protects against ischemia- and hypoxia-induced damage in the isolated rabbit heart subjected to hypothermic global ischemic arrest and subsequent reperfusion (122). Most interesting was the observation that the rabbit heart does not have detectable concentrations of either xanthine oxidase or xanthine dehydrogenase (123-125). In contrast, the rat heart has significant oxidase activity. Both rat and rabbit hearts derive significant protection from treatment with allopurinol (124-126). These data indicate that allopurinol may be protecting the ischemic rabbit myocardium from irreversible injury by mechanisms distinct from xanthine oxidase inhibition. One possibility is that allopurinol may act as a substrate for hypoxanthine-guanine phosphoribosyl transferase (HGPRT), which converts allopurinol to a ribonucleotide (126) that inhibits 5'-nucleotidase. This inhibition spares purine nucleotides by preventing the dephosphorylation of inosine and adenosine monophosphates, an action that would allow more efficient ATP resynthesis. In addition, it has been recently shown that oxypurinol may function as a scavenger of $\cdot$OH and of HOCl (127,128). Thus, allopurinol may possess multiple pharmacologic actions that protect the ischemic myocardium, and its salutary effects may not be related entirely or at all to inhibition of xanthine oxidase.

Prostacyclin, SC39902, Iloprost

PGI_2 and the E series prostaglandins have been reported to possess anti-inflammatory activity when examined in a variety of animal models (129). Both in vivo and in vitro, these prostaglandins alter the functional responses of a variety of inflammatory cells to inflammatory mediators (reviewed in reference 129). Recently, prostacyclin has been reported to be protective in a number of experimental models of myocardial ischemia (130-133). Lefer and coworkers (134) first suggested the usefulness of PGI_2 for the treatment of acute myocardial ischemia based on the ability of the prostanoid to inhibit platelet aggregation and to favorably alter myocardial oxygen supply and demand by increasing coronary artery blood flow and reducing systemic blood pressure, respectively. Melin and Becker (135) showed that PGI_2 protects the heart in the absence of an increase in collateral blood flow to the ischemic myocardium.

Since prostacyclin inhibits chemotaxis, the in vitro production of reactive oxygen species, and the release of degradative lysosomal enzymes from neutrophils (129), Simpson et al (136) hypothesized that the cytoprotective effect of PGI_2 in canine regional ischemia and reperfusion might be attributed to prostanoid alteration of the inflammatory reaction. In anesthetized dogs subjected to regional myocardial ischemia for 90 minutes and then reperfusion for six hours, prostacyclin (136) and a stable analogue, iloprost (137), diminished myocardial infarct size at the same doses that inhibited neutrophil function in vivo. Infarct size was, however, not decreased by the analogue SC 39902 despite the fact that it effectively inhibited ex vivo platelet aggregation and possessed the same hemodynamic properties as PGI_2. Furthermore, prostacyclin, in contrast to SC 39902, was shown to inhibit the activation of canine neutrophils in vitro, as determined by the production of $O_2^{\cdot-}$ (136). The ultimate size of the myocardial infarct was considered to be independent of the changes in collateral blood flow or myocardial oxygen demand, since neither prostacyclin nor SC 39902 increased collateral blood flow and both reduced blood pressure to the same extent. Iloprost was subsequently shown to have the same protective effect on infarct size as prostacyclin itself, in the same experimental model of myocardial infarction (137). In addition, the myocardial accumulation of neutrophils, as determined by myeloperoxidase activity in the region at risk, was suppressed by iloprost treatment. Furthermore, iloprost was shown to directly inhibit neutrophil production of $O_2^{\cdot-}$ in vitro.

A subsequent study was done to determine whether iloprost could produce sustained protection after 90 minutes of ischemia followed by 72 hours of reperfusion (138). Interestingly, a "time window" for neutrophil supressive therapy was found. Iloprost administered only during ischemia and for the first two hours of reperfusion resulted in no protection, but iloprost administered for the first 48 hours of perfusion was sufficient to reduce infarct size by 54%. In parallel studies, sustained neutrophil depletion for 48 hours with serial administration of anti-neutrophil antibody was required to reduce infarct size after 72 hours of reperfusion. Neutrophil depletion for only 24 hours did not inhibit the extent of the myocardial infarct at 72 hours.

The inhibition of neutrophil functional responses by prostacyclin and iloprost is thought to be secondary to the ability of these compounds to activate adenylate cyclase and increase cyclic AMP concentrations. Based upon our results with prostacyclin and iloprost, it may be important to explore other pharmacologic interventions known to elevate neutrophil concentrations of cyclic AMP (e.g., β-adrenergic agonists and/or phosphodiesterase inhibitors) for their ability to protect reperfused ischemic myocardium, and to determine whether the protective effect correlates with an inhibition of the associated inflammatory response and an inhibition of neutrophil function.

CONCLUSIONS

It is now accepted that early reperfusion of ischemic myocardium is an important consideration in an effort to reduce myocardial infarct size and decrease the associated morbidity and mortality. Experimental evidence suggests that within the myocardial region at risk, some myocardial cells are reversibly injured as a consequence of having been subjected to short periods (less than 3 hours) of ischemia. Within this population of cells, a fraction of the affected myocytes undergoes irreversible changes (cell death) upon reperfusion. Reperfusion injury, therefore, refers to cell death caused by reperfusion. The "lethal event" might be able to be attenuated or prevented by appropriate measures directed against the cytotoxic effects of reactive species of oxygen. The production sites of reactive oxygen species include phagocytic cells, myocardial tissue, especially the mitochondria of the reperfused myocyte (139), and vascular endothelium (the xanthine oxidase reaction). In addition, a therapeutic "time window" has been identified during which free radical scavengers or neutrophil suppressive therapy decreases the myocardial damage associated with reperfusion injury (138).

An alternative hypothesis has been put forth by Jennings et al (140), who propose that the development of contraction band necrosis during reperfusion occurs in irreversibly injured myocytes and that reperfusion injury does not involve cells that can be considered to be viable or reversibly injured. Jennings et al (140) are of the view that because of methodological limitations, it has not yet been demonstrated that reperfusion injury occurs in the sense that the final infarct size is due in part to myocytes that undergo a lethal event during the period of reperfusion. This view is at odds with the observations reported above, especially our studies involving supression of neutrophil function and adhesion (105,136-138), and suggests that more effort must be devoted to a better understanding of the role of the inflammatory mediators, phagocytic cells, and biochemical changes occuring in myocytes and endothelial cells at risk of injury during early periods of reperfusion.

Future investigations directed toward understanding the underlying mechanism(s) of cardioprotection afforded by many pharmacological interventions studied to date continues to be of interest. More intimate knowledge of the cardioprotective actions may aid in determining the cellular and subcellular sites of free radical production and may provide a better insight into developing an appropriate therapeutic approach to the patient in whom an acute myocardial infarction is evolving and who is being considered for thrombolytic therapy or myocardial revascularization.

ACKNOWLEDGMENT

These studies were supported by a grant (HL-19782) from the Heart, Lung, and Blood Institute of the National Institutes of Health.

REFERENCES

1. Boveris A, Chance B. The mitochondrial generation of hydrogen peroxide. Biochem J 1973:134:707-716.

2. Otani H, Tanaka H, Inoue T, et al. In vitro study on contribution of oxidative metabolism of isolated rabbit heart mitochondria to myocardial reperfusion injury. Circ Res 1984:55:168-175.

3. Bannister JV, Bannister WH, Hill HAO, Thornally PJ. Enhanced production of hydroxyl radicals by the xanthine-xanthine oxidase reaction in the presence of lactoferrin. Biochim Biophys Acta 1982:715:116-120.

4. Egan RW, Gale PH, Kuehl FA. Reduction of hydroperoxides in the prostaglandin biosynthetic pathway by a microsomal peroxidase. J Biol Chem 1979:254:3295-3302.

5. Kako KJ. Free radical effects on membrane protein in myocardial ischemia/reperfusion injury. J Mol Cell Cardiol 1987:19:209-212.

6. Wolff SP, Garner A, Dean RT. Free radicals, lipids and protein degradation. Trends Biochem Sci 1986:11:27-31.

7. Fantone JC, Ward PA. Role of oxygen-derived free radicals and metabolites in leukocyte-dependent inflammatory reactions. Am J Pathol 1982:107:397-418.

8. Lucchesi BR, Mullane KM. Leukocytes and ischemia-induced myocardial injury. Ann Rev Pharmacol Toxicol 1986:26:201-224.

9. Zweier JL, Rayburn BK, Flaherty JT, Weisfeldt ML. The effect of superoxide dismutase on free radical concentrations in post-ischemic myocardium. Circulation 1986:74(suppl II):371.

10. Hess ML, Okabe E, Kontos HA. Proton and free radical interaction with the calcium transport system of cardiac sarcoplasmic reticulum. J Mol Cell Cardiol 1981:13:767-772.

11. Hess ML, Okabe E, Ash P, Kontos HA. Free radical mediation of the effects of acidosis on calcium transport by sarcoplasmic reticulum in whole heart homogenates. Cardiovasc Res 1984:18:149-157.

12. Rowe GT, Manson NH, Caplan M, Hess ML. Hydrogen peroxide and hydroxyl radical mediation of activated leukocyte depression of cardiac sarcoplasmic reticulum: participation of the cyclooxygenase pathway. Circ Res 1983:53:584-591.

13. Sacks T, Moldow CF, Craddock PR, Bowers TK, Jacob HS. Oxygen radicals mediate endothelial cell damage by complement-stimulated granulocytes: in vitro model of immune vascular damage. J Clin Invest 1978:61:1161-1167.

14. Scott JA, Khaw BA, Locke E, Haber E, Homcy C. The role of free radical mediated processes in oxygen-related damage in cultured murine myocardial cells. Circ Res 1985:56:72-77.

15. Jackson CV, Mickelson JK, Pope TK, Rao PS, Lucchesi BR. O_2 free radical-mediated myocardial and vascular dysfunction. Am J Physiol 1986:251:H1225-H1231.

16. Guarnieri C, Flamigni F, Russonii-Calderara C. Glutathione peroxidase activity and release of glutathione from oxygen deficient perfused rat heart. Biochem Biophys Res Commun 1979:89:678-784.

17. Guarnieri C, Flamigni F, Calderera CM. Role of oxygen in the cellular damage induced by reoxygenation of hypoxic heart. J Mol Cell Cardiol 1980:12:797-808.

18. Rao PS, Mueller HS. Lipid peroxidation and acute myocardial ischemia. Adv Exp Med Biol 1983:161:347-363.

19. Julicher RHM, Tijburg LBM, Sterrenberg L, Bast A, Koomen JM, Noordhoek J. Decreased defence against free radicals in rat heart during normal reperfusion after hypoxic, ischemic and calcium free perfusion. Life Sci 1984:35:1281-1288.

20. Sobel BE, Bresnahan GF, Shell WE, Yoder RD. Estimation of infarct size in man and its relation to prognosis. Circulation 1972:46:640-648.

21. Rude RE, Muller JE, Braunwald E. Efforts to limit the size of myocardial infarcts. Ann Intern Med 1981:95:736-761.

22. Schwarz F, Schuler G, Katus H, et al. Intracoronary thrombolysis in acute myocardial infarction: duration of ischemia as a major determinant of late results after recanalization. Am J Cardiol 1982:50:933-937.

23. Braunwald E. The aggressive treatment of acute myocardial infarction. Circulation 1985:71:1087-1092.

24. Reimer KA, Lowe JE, Rasmussen MM, Jennings RB. The wavefront phenomenon of ischemic cell death. I. Myocardial infarct size vs duration of coronary occlusion in dogs. Circulation 1977:56:786-794.

25. Reimer KA, Jennings RB. The wave-front phenomenon of ischemic cell death. II. Transmural progression of necrosis within the framework of ischemic bed size (myocardium at risk) and collateral blood flow. Lab Invest 1979:40:663-644.

26. Jolly SR, Kane WJ, Hook BG, Abrams GD, Kunkel SL, Lucchesi BR. Reduction of myocardial infarct size by neutrophil depletion: effect of duration of occlusion. Am Heart J 1986:112:682-690.

27. Heyndrickx GR, Baig H, Nellens P, Leusen I, Fishbein MC, Vatner SF. Depression of regional blood flow and wall thickening after brief coronary occlusions. Am J Physiol 1978:234:H653-H659.

28. Koren G, Weiss AT, Hasin Y, et al. Prevention of myocardial damage in acute myocardial ischemia by early treatment with intravenous streptokinase. N Engl J Med 1985:313:1384-1389.

29. Jennings RB, Ganote CE, Kloner RA, Whalen DA Jr, Hamilton DG. Explosive swelling of myocardial cells irreversibly injured by transient ischemia. In: Fleckenstein A, Rona G, eds. Recent advances in studies on cardiac structure and metabolism. Baltimore: University Park Press, 1975:405-413. (Pathophysiology and morphology of myocardial cell alteration; vol 6).

30. Hearse DJ, Humphrey SM, Nayler WG, Slade A, Border D. Ultrastructural damage associated with reoxygenation of the anoxic myocardium. J Mol Cell Cardiol 1975:7:315-324.

31. Hearse DJ, Humphrey SM, Bullock GR. The oxygen paradox and the calcium paradox: two facets of the same problem? J Mol Cell Cardiol 1978:10:641-668.

32. Braunwald E, Kloner RA. Myocardial reperfusion: a double-edged sword? J Clin Invest 1985:76:1713-1719.

33. Nayler WG, Elz JS. Reperfusion injury: laboratory artifact or clinical dilemma? Circulation 1986:74:215-221.

34. Jolly SR, Kane WJ, Bailie MB, Abrams GD, Lucchesi BR. Canine myocardial reperfusion injury: its reduction by the combined administration of superoxide dismutase and catalase. Circ Res 1984:54:277-285.

35. Werns SW, Shea S, Driscoll EM, et al. The independent effects of oxygen radical scavengers on canine infarct size: reduction by superoxide dismutase but not catalase. Circ Res 1985:56:895-898.

36. Jarasch E-D, Bruder G, Heid HM. Significance of xanthine oxidase in capillary endothelial cells. Acta Physiol Scand 1986:Suppl 548:39-46.

37. Battelli MG, Della Corte E, Stirpe F. Xanthine oxidase type D (dehydrogenase) in the intestine and other organs of the rat. Biochem J 1972:126:747-749.

38. Parks DA, Granger DN. Xanthine oxidase:biochemistry, distribution and physiology. Acta Physiol Scand 1986:Suppl 548:87-99.

39. Chambers DE, Parks DA, Patterson G, et al. Xanthine oxidase as a source of free radical damage in myocardial ischemia. J Mol Cell Cardiol 1985:17:145-152.

40. Werns SW, Shea MJ, Mitsos SE, et al. Reduction of the size of infarction by allopurinol in the ischemic-reperfused canine heart. Circulation 1986:73:518-524.

41. Zimmerman AN, Hülsmann WC. Paradoxical influence of calcium ions on the permeability of the cell membranes in isolated rat heart. Nature 1966:211:646-647.

42. Hearse DJ, Humphrey SM, Chain EB. Abrupt reoxygenation of the anoxic potassium-arrested perfused rat heart: a study of myocardial enzyme release. J Mol Cell Cardiol 1973:5:395-407.

43. Alto E, Dhalla NS. Myocardial cation contents during induction of the calcium paradox. Am J Physiol 1979:237:H713-H719.

44. Nayler WG, Elz JS, Perry SE, Daly MJ. The biochemistry of uncontrolled calcium entry. Eur Heart J 1983:4(suppl H):29-41.

45. Nayler WG, Perry SE, Daly MJ. Cobalt, manganese and the calcium paradox. J Mol Cell Cardiol 1983:15:735-747.

46. Nayler WG, Perry SE, Elz JS, Daly MJ. Calcium, sodium and the calcium paradox. Circ Res 1984:55:227-237.

47. Ganote CE, Nayler WG. Editorial Review. Contracture and the calcium paradox. J Mol Cell Cardiol 1985:17:733-745.

48. Ganote CE, Grinwald PM, Nayler WG. 2,4-Dinitrophenol (DNP)-induced injury in calcium-free hearts. J Mol Cell Cardiol 1984:16:547-557.

49. VanderHeide RS, Angelo JP, Altschuld RA, Ganote CE. Energy dependence of contraction band formation in perfused hearts and isolated adult myocytes. Am J Pathol 1986:125:55-68.

50. Ganote CE, Sims MA. Parallel temperature dependence of contracture-associated enzyme release due to anoxia, 2,4-dinitrophenol (DNP), or caffeine and the calcium paradox. Am J Pathol 1984:116:94-106.

51. Shlafer M, Kane PF, Kirsh MM. Superoxide dismutase plus catalase enhances the efficacy of hypothermic cardioplegia to protect the globally ischemic, reperfused heart. J Thorac Cardiovasc Surg 1982:83:830-839.

52. Shlafer M, Kane PF, Wiggins VY, Kirsh MM. Possible role for cytotoxic oxygen metabolites in the pathogenesis of cardiac ischemic injury. Circulation 1982:66(suppl I):I85-I92.

53. Werns SW, Shea MJ, Vaporciyan A, et al. Superoxide dismutase does not cause scar thinning after myocardial infarction. J Am Coll Cardiol 1987:9:898-902.

54. Ambrosio G, Becker LC, Hutchins GM, Weisman HF, Weisfeldt ML. Reduction in experimental infarct size by recombinant human superoxide dismutase: insights into the pathophysiology of reperfusion injury. Circulation 1986:74:1424-1433.

55. Gallagher KP, Buda AJ, Pace D, Gerren RA, Shlafer M. Failure of superoxide dismutase and catalase to alter size of infarction in conscious dogs after 3 hours of occlusion followed by reperfusion. Circulation 1986:73:1065-1076.

56. Reimer KA, Jennings RB, Cobb FR, et al. Animal models for protecting the ischemic myocardium: results of the NHLBI cooperative study. Comparison of conscious and unconscious dog models. Circ Res 1985:56:561-665.

57. Romson JL, Hook BG, Kunkel SL, Abrams GD, Schork MA, Lucchesi BR. Reduction of the extent of ischemic myocardial injury by neutrophil depletion in the dog. Circulation 1983:67:1016-1023.

58. Mullane KM, Read N, Salmon JA, Moncada S. Role of leukocytes in acute myocardial infarction in anesthetized dogs: relationship to myocardial salvage by anti-inflammatory drugs. J Pharmacol Exp Ther 1984:228:510-522.

59. Zweier JL, Flaherty JT, Weisfeldt ML. Observation of free radical generation in the post-ischemic heart. Circulation 1985:72(suppl III):350.

60. McCord JM, Fridovich I. Superoxide dismutase: an enzymic function for erythrocuprein (hemocuprein). J Biol Chem 1969:244:6049-6055.

61. Roos D, Weening RS, Wyss SR, Aebi HE. Protection of human neutrophils by endogenous catalase: studies with cells from catalase deficient individuals. J Clin Invest 1980:65:1515-1522.

62. Chance B, Sies H, Boveris A. Hydroperoxide metabolism in mammaliam organs. Physiol Rev 1979:59:527-605.

63. Freeman B, Crapo J. Biology of disease: free radicals and tissue injury. Lab Invest 1982:47:412-426.

64. Meerson FZ, Kagan VE, Kozlow YP, Belkina LM, Arkhipenko YV. The role of lipid peroxidation in pathogenesis of ischemic damage and the antioxidant protection of the heart. Basic Res Cardiol 1982:77:465-485.

65. Tsan M, Danis EH, Del Vecchio PJ, Rosano CL. Enhancement of intracellular glutathione protects endothelial cells against oxidant damage. Biochem Biophys Res Commun 1985:127:270-276.

66. Barsacchi R, Pelosi G, Camici P, Bonaldo L, Maiorino M, Ursini F. Glutathione depletion increases chemiluminescence emission and lipid peroxidation in the heart. Biochim Biophys Acta 1984:804:356-360.

67. Al-Timimi DJ, Dormandy T. The inhibition of lipid autooxidation by human ceruloplasmin. Biochem J 1977:168:283-288.

68. Goldstein IM, Kaplan HB, Edelson HS, Weissmann G. Ceruloplasmin: a scavenger of superoxide anion radicals. J Biol Chem 1979:254:4040-4045.

69. Stocks J, Gutteridge JM, Sharp RJ, Dormandy TL. The inhibition of lipid autooxidation by human serum and its relation to serum proteins and alpha tocopherol. Clin Sci Mol Med 1974:47:223-233.

70. Dormandy TL. Free radical oxidation and antioxidants. Lancet 1978:1:647-650.

71. Romson JL, Hook BG, Rigot VH, Schork MA, Swanson DP, Lucchesi BR. The effect of ibuprofen on accumulation of indium-111-labeled platelets and leukocytes in experimental myocardial infarction. Circulation 1982:66:1002-1011.

72. Bednar M, Smith B, Pinto A, Mullane KM. Nafazatrom-induced salvage of ischemic myocardium in anesthetized dogs is mediated through inhibition of neutrophil function. Circ Res 1985:57:131-141.

73. Engler RL, Schmid-Schönbein GW, Pavelec RS. Leukocyte capillary plugging in myocardial ischemia and reperfusion in the dog. Am J Pathol 1983:111:98-111.

74. Rossen RD, Swain JL, Michael LH, Weakley S, Giannini E, Entman ML. Selective accumulation of the first component of complement and leukocytes in ischemic canine heart muscle: a possible initiator of an extra myocardial mechanism of ischemic injury. Circ Res 1988:57:119-130.

75. Mallory G, White P, Salcedo-Salgar J. The speed of healing myocardial infarction: a study of the pathologic anatomy in seventy-two cases. Am Heart J 1939:18:647-671.

76. Fishbein MC, Maclean D, Maroko PR. Histopathologic evolution of myocardial infarction. Chest 1978:73:843-849.

77. Wedmore CV, Williams TJ. Control of vascular permeability by polymorphonuclear leukocytes in inflammation. Nature 1981:289:646-650.

78. Hill JH, Ward PA. The phlogistic role of C3 leukotactic fragments in myocardial infarcts of rats. J Exp Med 1971:133:885-900.

79. Giclas PC, Pinckard RN, Olson MS. In vitro activation of complement by isolated heart subcellular membranes. J Immunol 1979:122:146-151.

80. Pinckard RN, O'Rourke RA, Crawford MH, et al. Complement localization and mediation of ischemic injury in baboon myocardium. J Clin Invest 1983:66:1050-1056.

81. McManus LM, Kolb WP, Crawford MH, O'Rourke RA, Grover FL, Pinckard RN. Complement localization in ischemic baboon myocardium. Lab Invest 1983:48:436-477.

82. Petrone WF, English DK, Wong K, McCord JM. Free radicals and inflammation: superoxide dependent activation of a neutrophil chemotactic factor in plasma. Proc Natl Acad Sci USA 1980:77:1159-1163.

83. Perez HD, Weksler BB, Goldstein IM. Generation of a chemotactic lipid from arachidonic acid by exposure to a superoxide-generating system. Inflammation 1980:4:313-328.

84. Hartmann JR, Robinson JA, Gunnar RM. Chemotactic activity in the coronary sinus after experimental myocardial infarction: effects of pharmacologic interventions on ischemic injury. Am J Cardiol 1977:40:550-555.

85. Maroko PR, Carpenter CB, Chiariello M, et al. Reduction by cobra venom factor of myocardial necrosis after coronary artery occlusion. J Clin Invest 1978:61:661-670.

86. Mathey DG, Schafer H, Schofer J, et al. Deposition of the terminal C5b-9 complement complex in infarcted areas of the human myocardium. Circulation 1986:74(suppl II):372 [Abstract].

87. Sugahara K, Cott GR, Parsons PE, Masons RJ, Sandhaus RA, Henson PM. Epithelial permeability produced by phagocytosing neutrophils in vitro. Am Rev Respir Dis 1986:133:875-881.

88. Russo RG, Liotta LA, Thorgeirsson U, Brundage R, Schiffmann F. Polymorphonuclear leukocyte migration through human amnion membrane. J Cell Biol 1981:91:459-467.

89. Weiss SJ, Regiani S. Neutrophils degrade subendothelial matrices in the presence of alpha-1-proteinase inhibitor: cooperative use of lysosomal proteinases and oxygen metabolites. J Clin Invest 1984:73:1297-1303.

90. Campbell E, Campbell M. Proteolysis by neutrophils while in contact with substrate. Chest 1986:89:S113.

91. Weiss SJ, Young J, LoBuglio AF, Slivka A, Nimeh NF. Role of hydrogen peroxide in neutrophil-mediated destruction of cultured endothelial cells. J Clin Invest 1981:68:714-721.

92. Arnaout MA, Dana N, Pitt J, Todd RF. Deficiency of two human leukocyte surface membrane glycoproteins (Mo1 and LFA-1). Fed Proc 1985:44:2664-2670.

93. Springer TA. The LFA-1, Mac-1 glycoprotein family and its deficiency in an inherited disease. Fed Proc 1985:44:2660-2663.

94. Anderson DC, Schamalstieg FC, Shearer W, et al. Leukocyte LFA-1, OKM1, p150,95 deficiency syndrome: functional and biosynthetic studies of three kindreds. Fed Proc 1985:44:2671-2677.

95. Simon RH, DeHart PD, Todd RF. Neutrophil-induced injury of rat pulmonary alveolar epithelial cell. J Clin Invest 1986:78:1375-1386.

96. Boogaerts MA, Yamada O, Jacob HS, Moldow CF. Enhancement of granulocyte-endothelial cell adherence and granulocyte-induced cytotoxicity by platelet release products. Proc Natl Acad Sci USA 1982:79:7019-7023.

97. Harlan JM. Leukocyte-endothelial interactions. Blood 1985:65:513-525.

98. Berger M, O'Shea J, Cross AS, et al. Human neutrophils increase expression of C3bi as well as C3b receptors upon activation. J Clin Invest 1984:74:1566-1571.

99. Tonnesen MG, Smedly LA, Henson PM. Neutrophil-endothelial cell interactions: modulation of neutrophil adhesiveness by complement fragments C5a and C5a des arg and formyl-methionyl-leucyl-phenylalanine in vitro. J Clin Invest 1984:74:1581-1592.

100. Bevilacqua MP, Pober JS, Majeau GR, Cotran RS, Gimbrone MA. Interleukin-1 (IL-1) induces biosynthesis and cell surface expression of procoagulant activity in human vascular endothelial cells. J Exp Med 1984:160:618-623.

101. Bevilacqua MP, Pober JS, Wheeler ME, Cotran RS, Gimbrone MA. Interleukin-1 activation of vascular endothelium: effects on procoagulant activity and leukocyte adhesion. Am J Pathol 1985:121:394-403.

102. Bevilacqua MP, Pober JS, Wheeler ME, Cotran RS, Gimbrone MA. Interleukin-1 acts on cultured human vascular endothelium to increase the adhesion of polymorphonuclear leukocytes, monocytes and related leukocyte cell lines. J Clin Invest 1985:76:2003-2011.

103. Jacob HS. The role of activated complement and granulocytes in shock states and myocardial infarction. J Lab Clin Med 1981:98:645-653.

104. Kloner RA, Ganote CE, Jennings RB, Reimer KA. The "no-reflow" phenomenon after temporary coronary occlusion in the dog. J Clin Invest 1974:54:1496-1508.

105. Simpson PJ, Todd RF III, Fantone JC, Mickelson JK, Griffin JD, Lucchesi BR. Reduction of experimental canine myocardial reperfusion injury by a monoclonal antibody (anti-Mo1, anti-CD11b) that inhibits leukocyte adhesion. J Clin Invest 1988:81:624-629.

106. Flynn J, Becker WK, Vercellotti GM, et al. Ibuprofen inhibits granulocyte responses to inflammatory mediators: a proposed mechanism for reduction of experimental myocardial infarct size. Inflammation 1984:8:33-44.

107. Brown EJ, Kloner RA, Shoen FJ, Hammerman H, Hale S, Braunwald E. Scar thinning due to ibuprofen administration after experimental myocardial infarct. Am J Cardiol 1983:51:877-883.

108. Jugdutt BI. Delayed effects of early infarct-limiting therapies on healing after myocardial infarction. Circulation 1985:72:907-914.

109. Jolly SR, Lucchesi BR. Effects of BW755C in an occlusion reperfusion model of ischemic myocardial injury. Am Heart J 1983:106:8:8-13.

110. Shea MJ, Murtagh JJ, Jolly SR, Abrams GD, Pitt B, Lucchesi BR. Beneficial effects of nafazatrom on ischemic reperfused myocardium. Eur J Pharmacol 1984:102:63-70.

111. Mitsos SE, Fantone JC, Gallagher KP, et al. Canine myocardial reperfusion injury: protection by a free radical scavenger, N-2-mercaptopropionyl glycine. J Cardiovasc Pharmacol 1986:8:978-988.

112. Mitsos SE, Askew TE, Fantone JC, et al. Protective effects of N-2-mercaptopropionyl glycine against myocardial reperfusion injury after neutrophil depletion in the dog: evidence for the role of intracellular-derived free radicals. Circulation 1986:73:1077-1086.

113. Chiba T, Kitoo H, Toshioka N. Studies on thiol and disulfide compounds I. Absorption, distribution, metabolism and excretion of 35-S-mercaptopropionylglycine. Yakugaku Zasshi [J Pharm Soc Jap] 1973:93:112-118.

114. Beyersdorf F, Zimmer G, Fuchs J, Kraft H, Veit P, Satter P. Improvement of myocardial function after global hypoxia by protection of the inner mitochondrial membrane. Arzneimittelforsch 1987:37:142-149.

115. Portz SJ, VanBenthuysen K, McMurtry I, Horwitz LD. Dimethylthiourea, a diffusable oxygen radical scavenger, reduces myocardial infarct size. Clin Res 1987:35:315A.

116. DeWall RA, Vasko KA, Stanley El, Kezdi P. Responses of the ischemic myocardium to allopurinol. Am Heart J 1971:82:362-370.

117. McCord JM, Roy RS. The pathophysiology of superoxide: roles in inflammation and ischemia. Can J Physiol Pharmacol 1982:60:1346-1352.

118. Battelli MG. Enzymic conversion of rat liver xanthine oxidase from dehydrogenase (D-form) to oxidase (O-form). FEBS Letters 1980:113:47-51.

119. Korthius RJ, Granger DN, Townsley MI, Taylor AE. The role of oxygen-derived free radicals in ischemia-induced increases in canine skeletal muscular vascular permeability. Circ Res 1985:57:599-609.

120. Burton KP, McCord JM, Ghai G. Myocardial alterations due to free radical generation. Am J Physiol 1984:246:H776-H783.

121. Reimer KA, Jennings RB. Failure of the xanthine oxidase inhibitor allopurinol to limit infarct size after ischemia and reperfusion in dogs. Circulation 1985:71:1069-1075.

122. Myers CL, Weiss SJ, Kirsh MM, Shlafer M. Involvement of hydrogen peroxide and hydroxyl radical in the "oxygen paradox": reduction of creatine kinase release by catalase, allopurinol or deferoxamine, but not by superoxide dismutase. J Mol Cell Cardiol 1985:17:675-684.

123. Grum CM, Ragsdale RA, Ketai LH, Shlafer M. Absence of xanthine oxidase or xanthine dehydrogenase in the rabbit myocardium. Biochem Biophys Res Commun 1986:141:1104-1108.

124. Grum CM, Ketai LH, Myers CL, Shlafer M. Purine efflux after cardiac ischemia: relevance to allopurinol cardioprotection. Am J Physiol 1987:252:H368-H373.

125. Yellon DM, Richard V, Hearse DJ, et al. The effect of allopurinol on myocardial infarct size in rat vs. rabbit: the contribution of xanthine oxidase. Fed Proc 1985:44:1480 [Abstract].

126. Nelson DJ, Bugge CJ, Krasny HC, Elion GB. Formation of nucleotides of (6-^{14}C)-allopurinol and (6-^{14}C)-oxypurinol in rat tissues and effects on uridine nucleotide pools. Biochem Pharmacol 1973:22:2003-2022.

127. Moorhouse CP, Grootveld M, Halliwell B, Quinlan JG, Gutteridge JMC. Allopurinol and oxypurinol are hydroxyl radical scavengers. FEBS Letters 1987:213:23-28.

128. Grootveld M, Halliwell B, Moorhouse CP. Action of uric acid, allopurinol and oxypurinol on the myeloperoxidase derived oxidant hypochlorous acid. Free Rad Res Commun 1988:4:69-76.

129. Fantone JC, Kunkel SL, Zurier RB. Effects of prostaglandins on in vivo immune and inflammatory reactions. In: Goodwin JS, ed. Prostaglandins and immunity. Boston: Martinez and Nijhoff, 1985:123-146.

130. Ogletree ML, Lefer AM, Smith JB, Nicolaou KC. Studies on the protective effect of prostacyclin in acute myocardial ischemia. Eur J Pharmacol 1979:56:95-103.

131. Jugdutt BI, Hutchins GM, Buckley BH, Becker LC. Dissimilar effects of prostacyclin, prostaglandin E$_1$, and prostaglandin E$_2$ on myocardial infarct size after coronary occlusion in conscious dogs. Circ Res 1981:49:685-700.

132. Ribeiro LGI, Brandon TA, Hopkins DG, Reduto LA, Taylor AA, Miller RR. Prostacyclin in experimental myocardial ischemia: effects on hemodynamics, regional myocardial blood flow, infarct size and mortality. Am J Cardiol 1981:47:835-840.

133. Araki H, Lefer AM. Role of prostacyclin in the preservation of ischemic myocardial tissue in the perfused cat heart. Circ Res 1980:47:757-763.

134. Lefer AM, Ogletree ML, Smith JB, Silver MJ, Nicolaou KC, Barnett WE, Gasic GP. Prostacyclin: a potentially valuable agent for preserving ischemic myocardial tissue in acute myocardial ischemia. Science 1978:200:52-54.

135. Melin JA, Becker LC. Salvage of ischemic myocardium by prostacyclin during experimental myocardial infarction. J Am Coll Cardiol 1983:2:279-286.

136. Simpson PJ, Mitsos SE, Ventura A, et al. Prostacyclin protects ischemic reperfused myocardium in the dog by inhibition of neutrophil activation. Am Heart J 1987:113:129-137.

137. Simpson PJ, Mickelson J, Fantone JC, Gallagher KP, Lucchesi BR. Iloprost inhibits neutrophil function in vitro and in vivo and limits experimental infarct size in the canine heart. Circ Res 1987:60:666-673.

138. Simpson PJ, Mickelson J, Fantone JC, Gallagher KP, Lucchesi BR. Sustained myocardial protection by iloprost with prolonged infusion in a canine model of temporary regional ischemia. Fed Proc 1987:46:1144.

139. Nishida T, Shibata H, Koseki M, et al. Peroxidative injury of the mitochondrial respiratory chain during reperfusion of hypothermic rat liver. Biochim Biophys Acta 1987:890:82-88.

140. Jennings RB, Reimer KA, Steenbergen C. Myocardial ischemia revisited: the osmolar load, membrane damage, and reperfusion. J Mol Cell Cardiol 1986:18:769-780.

141. Gaudel Y, Duvelleroy MA. Role of oxygen radicals in cardiac injury due to reoxygenation. J Mol Cell Cardiol 1984:16:459-470.

142. Stewart JR, Blackwell WH, Crute SL, Loughin V, Hess ML, Greenfield LJ. Prevention of myocardial ischemia/reperfusion injury with oxygen free-radical scavengers. Surg Forum 1982:33:317-320.

143. Nakamura Y, Takahashi M, Hayashi J, et al. Protection of ischemic myocardium with coenzyme Q_{10}. Cardiovasc Res 1982:16:132-137.

144. Hess ML, Okabe E, Poland J, Warner M, Stewart JR, Greenfield LJ. Glucose, insulin, potassium protection during the course of hypothermic global ischemia and reperfusion: a new proposed mechanism by the scavenging of free radicals. J Cardiovasc Pharm 1983:5:35-43.

QUESTION AND COMMENTS

Dr. Frank Bell: Other factors thought to affect infarct size relate to the accumulation of acyl Co A and fatty acids in the infarcted tissue. Have you ever attempted, in your models, to include such things as carnitine or carnitine analogues as possible modifiers of the lipid metabolism?

Dr. Paul Simpson: We have not attempted such treatment in our animal models. However, there is evidence that changing the myocardial lipid (fatty acid) metabolism can have beneficial effects during ischemia.

Dr. Peter A. Ward: With regard to the role of iron in ischemia reperfusion injury of dog myocardium, is there sufficient evidence to predict whether or not iron chelation will be protective?

Dr. Paul J. Simpson: There are studies showing that deferoxamine reduces injury in globally ischemic, reperfused, isolated hearts. To my knowledge, there is no evidence in vivo in the heart. That is, it hasn't been studied. But there is evidence that deferoxamine protects against neutrophil-dependent lung injury. Therefore, I would speculate that it would profit.

IV. ISCHEMIC/TRAUMATIC INJURY AND OXYGEN RADICALS (Part 2)

Harry S. Jacob, *Session Chairman*

MECHANISMS OF LIPID PEROXIDATION POTENTIATED BY ISCHEMIA IN BRAIN

Brant D. Watson and Myron D. Ginsberg

Identification of the primary mechanisms of tissue damage in ischemic cerebrovascular disease has proven to be elusive. This paper discusses the appropriateness of various methods commonly used to study free radicals in tissue and reviews various roles proposed for free radicals in ischemic damage of brain tissue. Current interest is focused on damage during reperfusion. Although reperfusion injury from free radical-induced peroxidation of lipids has been proposed as a fundamental mechanism of ischemic injury in several organ systems, it has not been definitively established for ischemic injury in the brain. Studies that have used indirect measures of free radical activity (decreased levels of ascorbate, increased levels of oxidized glutathione, and disappearance of unsaturated free fatty acids proportionate to their degree of unsaturation) have generated controversy; these methods either are not specific enough or are otherwise inappropriate for such studies. This paper summarizes the contributions from the authors' laboratory, emphasizing novel approaches and recent developments that address these issues.

DESPITE MUCH RESEARCH, the primary mechanisms leading to irreversible tissue damage in ischemic cerebrovascular disease remain to be identified. Certainly, deprivation of oxygen and nutrients will precipitate irreversible autolytic reactions leading to cell death in any tissue, provided that the degree and duration of ischemia are sufficient. Variations in the grade of ischemia and in the corresponding tissue response over time intimately influence the degree of metabolic recovery during and after attempts to resuscitate the tissue by reperfusion. These factors are particularly important in the brain, given its heterogeneity of structure and function.

FREE RADICALS AND LIPID PEROXIDATION

One plausible mechanism for inducing tissue damage is free radical-mediated lipid peroxidation (1-9). Free radicals are species containing one or more unpaired electrons. They often react avidly with susceptible molecules, such as unsaturated fatty acids, in order to regain the thermodynamically lowest energy state, defined by pairing of orbital electrons. The initiating radical usually achieves this by abstracting a hydrogen atom from a target molecule, giving rise to a new free radical. If the target molecule is an unsaturated fatty acid, available molecular oxygen can combine with the resultant

From Department of Neurology, University of Miami School of Medicine, Miami, Florida, USA.

Address correspondence to Dr. Brant D. Watson, Cerebral Vascular Disease Research Center, Department of Neurology (D4-5), University of Miami School of Medicine, PO Box 016960, Miami, Florida 33101, USA.

fatty acid radical to yield a peroxy radical. The peroxy radical is also reactive and can attain the paired-electron configuration by combining with a hydrogen atom from an adjacent molecule, forming a hydroperoxidized fatty acid molecule and, from its target molecule, another free radical. Continuation of this process, if it is not impeded by defense mechanisms, can lead to a chain of molecular alterations consisting, in the early stages, of peroxidized molecular products in unstable or inactivated configurations. These products include peroxidized lipids and proteins and numerous reactive degradation products (such as aldehydes) which facilitate intramolecular and intermolecular crosslinking among lipids and proteins. Consequent disorders in structure and function and loss of compartmentalization, most importantly in cell membranes (10-14), often presage cell death.

Despite the appeal of the lipid peroxidation process as a mechanism of tissue damage, obtaining evidence for its occurrence in vivo has proven very difficult. Most early research on lipid peroxidation was performed in vitro with peroxidation induced in tissue samples by adding ferrous ion and a reducing agent, usually ascorbic acid (15,16). Plausible mechanisms of radical chain initiation in vivo were unknown. In the 1960s the discovery that the enzymic functions of glutathione peroxidase (17) included the ability to detoxify lipid hydroperoxides (18,19) as well as hydrogen peroxide (H_2O_2) (20) strongly implied the existence of lipid peroxidation in vivo. Subsequently, the function of the copper-zinc protein erythrocuprein was discovered to be conversion of superoxide ($O_2^{\cdot-}$) into oxygen and H_2O_2 (21). This spurred a change in nomenclature-- erythrocuprein was renamed superoxide dismutase-- and reinforced the strong suspicion that free radical reactions are ubiquitous in vivo, despite the continued lack of direct evidence in terms of specific products known to be formed during lipid peroxidation in vitro. It is now known (22) that superoxide dismutase and glutathione peroxidase act synergistically to prevent or eliminate products arising from oxygen- or fatty acid-based radicals.

FREE RADICALS IN TISSUE INJURY: INFERENCE FROM PRODUCT MEASUREMENT

In view of the reactivity of free radicals, the steady-state concentrations of most free radicals are too low to measure directly; thus, their presence is usually inferred indirectly. A brief review of several such methods used for in vivo work in the brain is necessary in order to evaluate previous experiments. One indirect method is based on the disappearance of compounds known to react with free radicals. For example, antioxidant compounds such as a-tocopherol (vitamin E) (23,24), ubiquinones (25), and ascorbic acid are natural terminators of free radical-mediated chain processes; they serve as hydrogen atom donors to propagating radicals, but their resultant radicals do not appear to propagate reactive chains in vivo. The disappearance of antioxidants from metabolically compromised tissue has been used to implicate the participation of free radicals in tissue degradation. Similarly, the rate of disappearance of unsaturated free fatty acids after ischemia has been attributed to their peroxidation. The operative assumption is that the initial release of fatty acids from membrane phospholipids during ischemia (26-28), which occurs as a consequence both of phospholipase activation (29) and of inhibition of ATP-dependent fatty acid acylation (30-32), provides susceptible substrate during reoxygenation.

Another commonly used method is the thiobarbituric acid (TBA) test, in which aldehydes (e.g., malonaldehyde) arising from the decomposition of fatty acid hydroperoxides are reacted with TBA to form a colored product detectable by spectroscopy (33) or fluorimetry (34). Likewise, evidence that unsaturated fatty acids have been converted into radical intermediates can also be obtained by measuring the ultraviolet light absorption in the 235 nm region. Conversion of the fatty acids rearranges the fatty acid double bonds into a conjugated diene configuration, which absorbs at that wavelength (33-36). Finally, reciprocal changes in levels of reduced and oxidized glutathione have been interpreted to indicate lipid peroxidation (37). These changes are taken to reflect the reduction, at the expense of reduced glutathione, of lipid hydroperoxides to a-hydroxy fatty acids by glutathione peroxidase.

INITIAL SEARCHES FOR LIPID PEROXIDATION IN ISCHEMIC BRAIN IN VIVO

Originally, ischemic damage to central nervous system tissue was hypothesized to involve free radical-initiated chain processes originating from diffusible carriers of electrons in the mitochondrial respiratory chain (38,39). It was suggested that, during ischemia, these carriers become uncoupled from the electron transport chain and diffuse outward, where, in view of their radical-like character, they could initiate chain processes in the phospholipid matrix. However, the likely products of such a damage process, such as polymerized lipids or proteins, have not been detected during ischemia.

Decreases in ascorbyl radical levels were, however, found in a model of partial ischemia (38,39). Decreases in ascorbyl radical (measured in vitro as a dimethylsulfoxide adduct by electron spin resonance) between 1 and 24 hours after middle cerebral artery occlusion in cats were interpreted as evidence of ascorbic acid consumption during quenching of radical-mediated chain processes. However, subsequent measurements by others (40) of reduced and total ascorbic acid levels in a rat model of reversible global brain ischemia revealed no changes in either level during 30 minutes of ischemia or 24 hours of reperfusion. Although total glutathione concentrations steadily diminished throughout this time, oxidized glutathione (GSSG) levels were constant (40).

Measurement of TBA-reactive substances in a similar model of global ischemia in Wistar rats indicated no changes in amounts either during ischemia for up to 30 minutes or during recirculation for up to 72 hours (41). In contrast, the levels of TBA-reactive substances in hypertensive rats showing signs of stroke were double the levels in their healthy counterparts (42).

The potentially confounding influence of oxygen on ischemically induced biochemical alterations was suggested by the observation that the partially ischemic rat brain had a less satisfactory recovery of energy metabolites after blood recirculation than the totally ischemic brain (43). Subsequent work from our group (44), however, showed that when severe tissue lactic acidosis was prevented, complete ischemia proved to be more deleterious to postischemic recovery of tissue energy metabolism than did a comparable period of incomplete ischemia.

The apparently paradoxical deleterious effect of oxygen at low concentrations, as previously suggested by decreases in ascorbyl radical concentration (38,39), led to subsequent attempts to explain the apparently different effects of complete and incomplete ischemia in terms of lipid peroxidation, expressed as reciprocal changes in reduced glutathione (GSH) and GSSG levels (45). However, GSH levels decreased to the same extent during complete ischemia as during incomplete, whereas GSSG levels were unchanged in either case. Global forebrain ischemia of 30 minutes duration followed by recirculation for 30 or 90 minutes yielded similar results (45). A later attempt to distinguish the effects of complete ischemia from incomplete by measurement of fatty acid release during and after ischemia revealed no differences between these two types of cerebral insult (46).

At about the same time, Yoshida and coworkers in

our laboratory (47) observed increased levels of free fatty acids after 30 minutes of global forebrain ischemia in the rat. The most marked elevations were in the polyunsaturated species (arachidonic acid, 370-fold increase; docosahexaenoic acid, 44-fold), compared with 10- to 19-fold increases in saturated and monounsaturated fatty acid levels. Particularly rapid declines within 15 minutes of recirculation were observed for arachidonic and docosahexaenoic acids, reaching pre-ischemic levels at 30 minutes. These rapid decrements in polyunsaturated fatty acid levels at first suggested that these species were being subjected to lipid peroxidation in the early postischemic period.

This was further explored in a study of decapitation ischemia with aerobic or anaerobic incubation of tissue homogenates from rats maintained on diets containing various amounts of a-tocopherol (48). All deacylated fatty acid levels increased continuously throughout the ischemia and subsequent incubation periods; this change was not affected by the a-tocopherol status of the animal. The salient observation, however, was that *total* polyunsaturated fatty acid levels decreased during postischemic oxygen incubation of brain homogenates from a-tocopherol-deficient rats, indicating that esterified rather than free polyunsaturated fatty acids constituted the substrate pool for peroxidation (48). The previously observed preferential decline in free polyunsaturated fatty acids during recirculation was, therefore, reinterpreted as possibly due to other recirculatory events such as the differential rate of reacylation as the brain energy state recovers (49). This interpretation would, therefore, support the concept of two catabolic pathways for fatty acyl chains of phospholipids in the brain during ischemia and reoxygenation: the first, a hydrolysis of ester bonds yielding free fatty acids, which continues throughout ischemia and recirculation; the second, direct peroxidation of polyunsaturated acyl chains, which appears to be accentuated during postischemic reoxygenation and under conditions of a-tocopherol deficiency (48). However, the decrease of total unsaturated fatty acid levels in vivo after recirculation in rats initially subjected to reversible global brain ischemia could not be confirmed (unpublished data).

Recent studies in our laboratory have shown that, at the onset of ischemia, the preferential increases in the levels of arachidonic and stearic acids can be explained by phosphodiesteric cleavage of diphosphoinositide and monophosphoinositide and their subsequent deacylation by lipases, whereas in later ischemia, hydrolysis of other phospholipids plays a contributory role (50,51). The degradation and resynthesis of polyphosphoinositides and the formation of triacylglycerol arachidonate may be important in modulating free arachidonic acid levels in the brain during temporary ischemia (51).

LIPID PEROXIDATION DURING REPERFUSION OF ISCHEMIC BRAIN IN VIVO

In view of the generally equivocal or negative results accumulated up to 1982, the developing consensus was that little convincing evidence existed for free radical-based lipid peroxidation in ischemic brain injury in vivo. At this point our group reported the detection of conjugated dienes ipsilaterally in vivo 4 and 24 hours after embolic stroke in rats caused by intracarotid injection of microspheres (52). The advantages of the conjugated diene technique were that it reflected an early structural consequence of fatty acid peroxidation (33,35,36) and that lipid extraction from small amounts (less than 10 mg) of tissue sufficed for its spectroscopic detection. In addition, experiments with brain minces showed that conjugated dienes could be detected only upon incubation with oxygen, but that percentage losses in a-tocopherol and GSH concentrations were similar whether incubation was aerobic or anaerobic. Most importantly, no reciprocal increases in GSSG were observed (52).

This work was followed by the observation that a-tocopherol levels were decreased (by 20% at 15 minutes) during decapitation-induced ischemia in the rat (53). The levels of reduced ubiquinone-9 and -10 increased immediately after decapitation, but decreased at 15 minutes, whereas the levels of their oxidized forms increased continuously. Similar results were obtained when ischemia was produced in vivo by four-vessel occlusion for 30 minutes, followed by 15 or 30 minutes of recirculation (47). Brain a-tocopherol levels decreased to 93% of control with ischemia and to 87% of control during the early stages of recirculation. Reduced ubiquinone levels rapidly decreased by 20% to 23% upon recirculation. Although the altered levels of these antioxidant compounds were thought to indicate responsiveness to the initiation of free radical reactions, it would appear that oxygen was not likely involved in the maintenance of any radical chain processes.

From this initial evidence, the conjugated diene method appeared to be considerably more rigorous and a less equivocal indicator of lipid peroxidative processes and tissue oxygenation than the methods based on disappearance of antioxidant compounds. The conjugated diene values also suggested that the likeliest period of lipid peroxide formation was during recirculation of ischemic tissue (2). The operative rationale was that oxygen radicals would be produced by the interaction of oxygen with hyper-reduced respiratory chain components of ischemic mitochondria (54). This concept was supported by analyses in spontaneously hypertensive rats after three hours of cerebral ischemia induced by bilateral carotid artery ligation (55). The levels of TBA reactants were elevated at several times during the recirculation phase, and these increases could be mitigated by prior intravenous administration of a-tocopherol.

Subsequently, we refined the procedure for conjugated diene analysis (56,57) to permit quantitation in regional brain samples of 1 mg or less. Briefly, samples are punch-dissected with a hypodermic needle from the face of frozen coronal brain sections. After homogenization and total lipid extraction with a modified Bligh-Dyer procedure (52,58), the dried extracts are redissolved in heptane and their absorption spectra recorded between 190 nm and 330 nm with a computer-interfaced scanning spectrophotometer. Because of Rayleigh scattering by lipid aggregates (52,59), raw spectra display a background absorbance, which must be subtracted. For each brain region of interest, a library of composite, Rayleigh-corrected control spectra has been accumulated. These regional control spectra are normalized to, and then subtracted from, each corresponding Rayleigh-corrected ischemic sample spectrum. Difference spectra displaying a broad peak centered at 238 nm allow quantification of diene conjugation; spectral inflections in the 260 nm to 290 nm region, which represent higher-order conjugates, are also seen routinely (36).

Wistar rats were subjected to 30 minutes of high-grade reversible ischemia (2% to 3% of normal flow) by four-vessel occlusion (60) followed by recirculation for 0, 30, 60, or 240 minutes. Of a total of ten small samples obtained bilaterally from cortical and subcortical areas, only a small percentage (3%, 19%, 18%, and 10% of samples at the above times, respectively) exhibited conjugated diene spectra distinguishable from background; these conjugated diene concentrations were of the order of 1 μmol/g (57). No regions appeared to be preferentially vulnerable. The computer-averaged composite spectrum derived from all the samples from each animal was indistinguishable from the composite global control spectrum. This study indicated that lipid peroxidation occurred in a highly focal manner during the first hour of recirculation and that, had larger tissue samples been assayed (simulated by computer-averaging of regional spectra), no evidence for lipid peroxidation would have been detected owing to dilution of peroxide-containing foci.

In the same model, we demonstrated that regional Na^+, K^+-ATPase activity increased during high-grade forebrain ischemia and decreased with subsequent recirculation, but these responses were independent of the presence or absence of conjugated diene in the same small regional tissue samples (61).

Thus, lipid peroxidation did not appear to be the explanation for fluctuations in the activity of this enzyme with ischemia, possibly because the fraction of sampled tissue volume that contained conjugated dienes was small relative to the total volume sampled (61).

Given these results, some reasons can be proposed for the lack of evidence for lipid peroxidation in vivo when other methods were used. The tissue assays for TBA reactants (41) and for GSH and GSSG (40,45) required much greater amounts (at least 75 mg) of brain tissue than are required by the conjugated diene test. The negative results with the TBA and glutathione methods were duplicated by our simulation of large tissue volumes by the computer-averaging of discrete regional spectra. In hindsight, it appears appropriate to consider that such a heterogeneously structured organ as the brain might exhibit differential responses to a peroxidative insult, but our own inability to observe regional specificity suggests that the heterogeneity of response exists on a much smaller scale than we sampled. In addition, the lack of a reciprocal response by GSSG might be due to ischemia-induced inhibition of glutathione peroxidase, an enzyme dependent on glucose metabolism via the pentose phosphate pathway (17-20). The importance of sufficient levels of glucose and GSH to ensure hydroperoxide detoxification by the glutathione peroxidase system has been carefully delineated (62,63). Recirculation of ischemic tissue does not ensure normalization of glucose metabolism (64,65), and, during recirculation, the glutathione peroxidase pathway may operate suboptimally as well.

The influence of a-tocopherol on lipid peroxidation potentiated by brain ischemia was then examined more closely by means of dietary deficiency or supplementation of a-tocopherol (resulting in plasma a-tocopherol levels 4% of normal and 2.8 times normal, respectively). The a-tocopherol-deficient control group exhibited somewhat higher brain levels of TBA reactants than normal or supplemented groups, consistent with a slight increase in brain lipid peroxidation (66). Whereas decapitation ischemia or subsequent incubation of the brain in a nitrogen environment failed to produce major changes in TBA reactants, postdecapitation aerobic incubation produced increases in all groups. These increases were most pronounced in the a-tocopherol-deficient rats, intermediate in the normal group, and least in the supplemented animals. These data confirm that oxidative degradation of unsaturated lipids in brain membranes is dormant during ischemia itself and depends upon subsequent availability of oxygen. Furthermore, they confirm that endogenous a-tocopherol levels might be a means of modifying the burst of free radical generation occurring during oxygen reprovision. These data were confirmed in a subsequent in vitro study (48), in which postischemic aerobic incubation of brain tissue increased the levels of TBA reactants by sevenfold in the a-tocopherol-deficient group, by threefold in the normal group, and by twofold in the a-tocopherol-supplemented group. The increases in conjugated diene levels paralleled those of the TBA reactants. However, the suppressive effect of endogenous a-tocopherol on production of TBA reactants could not be confirmed in vivo (unpublished data).

SEARCH FOR LIPID PEROXIDATION IN EVOLVING BRAIN INFARCTION

Our original demonstration of postischemic lipid peroxidation in global brain ischemia prompted us to assess conjugated diene content in models more accurately representative of human thrombotic stroke. To this end, a reperfusible thrombotic stroke was induced in the territory of the middle cerebral artery (MCA) of the rat according to a modification of a previously published photochemical technique (67). In the modified method, singlet oxygen-mediated (Type II) photoperoxidation is initiated in the vascular endothelium; the resultant damage to the luminal membrane stimulates platelet adhesion and subsequent aggregation to the point of occlusion. The photothrombotic reaction is produced by focal irradiation of the MCA in conjunction with the intravenous administration of the photosensitizing dye rose bengal (68-70).

In MCA Occlusion Model 1 (69,70), a low power (0.9 mW) helium-neon laser (Particle Measurement Systems, Boulder, Colorado), operating at 543.5 nm, was used. In anesthetized male Sprague-Dawley rats, the MCA was exposed by subtemporal craniectomy, and the laser beam was focused through a pair of crossed cylindrical lenses transversely onto the MCA just distal to its rhinal branch, at an intensity of $10~W/cm^2$. Visual inspection showed that the thrombus formation was complete at 10 minutes of irradiation. In this model, we have found that reperfusion is possible by the topical application of 10^{-4} M nimodipine directly to the thrombosed segment.

In MCA Occlusion Model 2 (68,70), Wistar rats were irradiated with an argon ion laser (Lexel Model 95, Cooper LaserSonics, Palo Alto, California). The 514.5 nm argon beam was focused to yield a spot $350~\mu m$ long by $140~\mu m$ wide proximal to the rhinal branch of the MCA. A 5-minute irradiation at an incident intensity of $36~W/cm^2$ was used to induce complete occlusion by white thrombus. In this model, both common carotid arteries (CCA) were ligated, and partial reperfusion was instituted by removing the ligatures after one hour.

Table 1. Conjugated Diene in Two Models of Reperfusion After Middle Cerebral Artery (MCA) Occlusion*

	Recirculation Time (min)		
	0	5	15
MODEL 1: MCA photothrombotic occlusion for 1 hour in Sprague-Dawley rats			
No. of rats analyzed	3	--	5
No. positive for dienes	0	--	1
Diene incidence/total samples	0	--	1/60
Tissue diene concentration ($\mu mol/g$)	0	--	4.80
MODEL 2: MCA photothrombosis and 1 hour common carotid artery ligation in Wistar rats			
No. of rats analyzed	3	8	6
No. positive for dienes	0	2	3
Diene incidence/total samples	0	13/96	5/72
Tissue diene concentration ($\mu mol/g$; mean $\pm SD$)	0	4.28 ± 1.10	3.45 ± 1.60

* This table has been adapted from reference 70.

In each of these models, brains were assayed for conjugated diene after transcalvarial brain freezing in situ (71) and procurement of multiple, small, regional samples from ipsilateral and contralateral structures (61).

In Model 1, only one sample from eight brains (after one hour of MCA occlusion followed by 0, 5, or 15 minutes of recirculation) displayed the characteristic spectral peak of the conjugated diene structure (total incidence 1 in 60 samples) (Table 1). The most common finding in the analysis of the difference spectra was that the decrease in isolated double bonds (signified by a decrease in the differential absorbance in the 190 nm to 200 nm region) was correlated with a continuum of increased absorbance in the wavelength regions in which conjugated dienes and higher-order conjugates are normally observed.

In Model 2, positive spectral peaks corresponding to conjugated diene formation were observed, but only in 14% of samples taken at 5 minutes and in 7% of samples taken at 15 minutes of carotid recirculation after 1 hour of combined MCA and CCA occlusion. Oddly, most samples with detectable conjugated dienes were taken from areas contralateral to the photo-occluded MCA side (70). In a recent experiment in which rats were subjected to 25 minutes of four-vessel reversible forebrain occlusion and mild hypotension (known to produce consistent pathological changes in the ischemic striatum), no evidence for conjugated diene was found in any striatal sample (R. Busto, M.Y-T. Globus, B.D. Watson, and M.D. Ginsberg, unpublished data).

In other rats, torcular venous blood was sampled intermittently for conjugated diene, but in no case was it detected.

These studies suggest that lipid peroxidation, as assessed by conjugated diene formation, was not a major factor during the early stages of infarct formation. There are three possible explanations. One possibility is that the contribution of lipid peroxidation to postischemic neuronal injury may be expressed focally, perhaps only to the extent that free radical-mediated processes are not diluted or inhibited by the complex metabolic and hemodynamic factors operating during recirculation. A second possibility is that lipid peroxidation may occur globally, but that the chain process responsible for lipid peroxidation may be terminated after a small number of cycles, yielding conjugated dienes at levels below the spectroscopic detection threshold. A third possibility is that radical chain processes leading to peroxidation of acylated unsaturated fatty acids in cell membranes may be truly absent in the bulk of reperfused brain tissue and, therefore, may not induce tissue injury during the recovery phase.

FREE RADICALS AND LIPID PEROXIDATION IN BRAIN EDEMA IN VIVO

The role of free radicals and lipid peroxidation in brain edema has been investigated in an in vivo rat model of brain compression by transient application of an epidural Silastic mass (72,73). In this model, breakdown of the blood-brain barrier and increase in brain water content are observed during the first 24 hours after decompression. Brain swelling was shown to be greatest in animals deficient in α-tocopherol, and least in animals given α-tocopherol supplements. These results imply that edema can be modulated by the quenching of (unspecified) free radical processes. An alternative explanation is that α-tocopherol may act analogously to corticosteroids, by stabilizing cell membranes via physiochemical interactions between its phytyl side chain and the acyl chains of polyunsaturated phospholipids (23). The correlation of the magnitude of brain swelling with postdecompression decreases in brain total fatty acid levels (74) suggested a close relationship between disintegration of membrane phospholipids and edema formation. Conceivably, free radicals might initiate membrane lipid peroxidation and simultaneously activate deacylating enzymes, accounting for this generalized loss of fatty acid (74). In fact, an important function of phospholipase A_2 has been reported to be recognition and excision of peroxidized fatty acids from the membrane matrix, thus freeing them for reduction (and detoxification) by cytosolic glutathione peroxidase (3).

The concomitance of brain edema formation and fatty acid peroxidation mediated by the lipoxygenase pathway also has been investigated. Enhanced synthesis of the lipoxygenase metabolites leukotriene C_4 and D_4 in cerebral tissue was first reported to occur during postischemic reperfusion of gerbils (75). The recent correlation of increased amounts of several hydroxy-eicosatetraenoic fatty acids with maximal edema formation (at 72 hours after MCA occlusion in the rat) indicates that activation of the lipoxygenase pathway may be concomitant with edema formation (76). The development of brain edema in gerbils subjected to 20 minutes of bilateral carotid occlusion was accompanied by enhanced release of leukotriene B_4 during reperfusion; inhibition of the lipoxygenase pathway by nordihydroguaretic acid administered before induction of ischemia mitigated the degree of edema observed during reperfusion (77).

Despite the early finding that indomethacin, an inhibitor of the cyclooxygenase pathway, failed to affect edema produced by cortical freezing (78), subsequent work has generally suggested that activation of the cyclooxygenase pathway also contributes significantly to postischemic edema. The levels of several prostaglandins increased during recirculation in gerbils initially subjected to bilateral occlusion of the CCA; blockade of cyclooxygenase activity by indomethacin or aspirin inhibited the postischemic increases in prostaglandin synthesis (79). Further investigations with the gerbil model indicated that postischemic prostaglandin synthesis varied regionally and that the extent of edema formation also depended on the magnitude of reflow to ischemic zones (80).

THE OXYGEN RADICAL CASCADE DURING ISCHEMIA AND REPERFUSION

The evidence for free radical-mediated lipid peroxidation in ischemic brain injury has been discussed in terms of product analysis, and the difficulty of obtaining positive results in vivo with the TBA test, conjugated diene method, and levels of unsaturated fatty acids and antioxidant compounds has been described. In recent years, a different approach has emerged, based on the realization that oxygen participates in the *initiation* of free radical processes as well as their propagation (1,4-9,22,81-83). Radicals can be produced from molecular oxygen by stepwise addition of electrons, a process resulting in the oxygen radical cascade. The superoxide radical ($O_2^{\cdot-}$) is derived by single-electron reduction of oxygen; its dismutation product, H_2O_2, corresponds to doubly reduced oxygen. The next highest reduction state of oxygen is the hydroxyl radical ($\cdot OH$). Hydroxyl radical is extremely reactive; in particular, it reacts vigorously with unsaturated fatty acids by hydrogen atom abstraction

(84). For this reason, ·OH, or a species with similar reactivity, is thought to be the likely primary initiator of free fatty acid peroxidation. Perhydroxyl radical (HO_2·), which is the protonated form of O_2·⁻, may also be involved in chain initiation (84) under the acidic conditions known to occur in ischemia (85).

Several plausible mechanisms have been proposed for the generation of oxygen radicals during ischemia/reperfusion. In one mechanism, single electrons are shuttled in the mitochondrial respiratory chain by the mobile free radical ubisemiquinone (i.e., ubiquinone in its half-reduced form), which can be readily oxidized by molecular oxygen to yield O_2·⁻ (86). During ischemia, reducing equivalents accumulate in the mitochondrial respiratory chain (54). Upon reperfusion, a burst of O_2·⁻ may be released when incoming oxygen molecules react with the excess of ubisemiquinone radicals.

In another mechanism, prostaglandin synthetase performs two sequential reactions (87): peroxidation of arachidonic acid (cyclooxygenase activity) to form prostaglandin G_2, and subsequent reduction of its hydroperoxide group (hydroperoxidase activity) to yield prostaglandin H_2. During the latter reaction, enzyme-centered radical intermediates are formed which can be reduced by NADH or NADPH in a side reaction, oxidizing these nucleotides to their free radical counterparts. The interaction of molecular oxygen with nucleotide radicals forms O_2·⁻ in an interaction similar to that of oxygen with ubisemiquinone. In this mechanism, the ischemia-induced release of free fatty acids (46,47) provides an excessive amount of substrate for postischemic prostaglandin synthesis, which may now be accompanied by nucleotide radical-facilitated increases in O_2·⁻ formation.

The currently most discussed mechanism involves an irreversible transformation of xanthine dehydrogenase to xanthine oxidase during ischemia (81-83). Xanthine oxidase, catalyzing successive reactions of the ATP degradation products hypoxanthine and xanthine, produces O_2·⁻ in each step. Although this reaction sequence is often invoked to explain injury to tissue observed during reperfusion, the amount of reperfusion injury due to this mechanism must be assessed for each organ system, since the degradation of xanthine dehydrogenase to the oxidase is likely to occur at different, organ-specific rates.

Although the direct reactivity of O_2·⁻ itself is expressed mainly as its protonated form (HO_2·), its major contribution to cell toxicity is to generate H_2O_2. Hydrogen peroxide is susceptible to scission by ferrous ion (Fe^{2+}), yielding the extremely reactive ·OH according to the Fenton reaction (4-6,88). A similar reaction can occur with a fatty acid hydroperoxide in place of H_2O_2. This results in a fatty alkoxy radical, a species sufficiently reactive to sustain the chain reaction of lipid peroxidation (4-6,88).

Although iron is bound in the ferric (Fe^{3+}) form in vivo, it can be extracted in the ferrous form by reaction with O_2·⁻ (5). The peroxide/free radical reaction and the ferric/ferrous ion reaction, acting in concert, yield an overall reaction known either as the metal ion-catalyzed Haber-Weiss reaction or the superoxide-driven Fenton reaction (4-6). This reaction can be facilitated by iron ions released from proteins such as hemoglobin (89) and ferritin (25).

The "toxicities" of O_2·⁻ and H_2O_2 are, therefore, explained by their capacity to potentiate the production of species such as ·OH, which can initiate lipid peroxidation. With this mechanism, the alteration or destruction of many molecules can be effected by just one initiating radical. The danger represented by O_2·⁻ and H_2O_2 is augmented by the capacity of the latter to diffuse across cell membranes (8). Thus, a process leading to oxygen radical generation in one subcellular compartment may be transferred to other regions of the cell.

THE OXYGEN RADICAL CASCADE IN POSTISCHEMIC BRAIN INJURY

The hypothesis that tissue damage can be explained in terms of oxygen radical generation rapidly spawned a methodology complementary to the approach based on detection of products believed to result from lipid peroxidation. The hypothesis can be used in interpreting recent findings relevant to reperfusion injury in brain. Tissue edema and TBA reactants were produced in rat brain slices by adding polyunsaturated fatty acids, and these effects were accompanied by O_2·⁻ production and eliminated by the addition of superoxide dismutase (90). Subsequent application of a hydroxyl radical-generating system (xanthine or hypoxanthine reacting with xanthine oxidase and chelated ferric ion) to rat brain preparations in vitro facilitated release of free fatty acids, tissue swelling, degradation of membrane phospholipids, and production of TBA reactants (91). Finally, infusion of the mixture of radical-generating components into rat brain in vivo induced breakdown of the blood-brain barrier, leading to edema and neuronal death (92). These results, and the findings described above (74,76,77) regarding the role of cyclooxygenase or lipoxygenase metabolism in producing brain edema in vivo, can be reinterpreted as due to an accelerated activity (resulting from an excess of substrate fatty acid) either of the hydroperoxidase component of the cyclooxygenase pathway or of the lipoxygenase pathway. The peripheral generation of O_2·⁻ and initiation of the oxygen radical cascade leading to lipid peroxidation would be concomitantly stimulated (87).

Ischemia is also characterized by an acidotic state induced by the conversion of glucose to lactate (2). To explore a possible connection between ischemia-induced lactic acidosis and free radical formation, brain homogenates were incubated at lowered pH in the presence of ferrous ion (85). Between pH 6.0 and 6.5, TBA reactant levels were greatly increased, while tissue a-tocopherol levels and polyunsaturated fatty acid (both free and bound) levels decreased. In interpreting these results, HO_2· was suggested to be an initiator of the lipid peroxidation. Alternatively, the release of protein-bound iron at lowered pH was proposed to contribute to the stimulation of lipid peroxidation. The latter possibility was invoked (93) to explain the development of infarction in a rat model of reversible global forebrain ischemia in which cerebral lactic acidosis was exacerbated by hyperglycemia (94). In contrast, in the context of resuscitation following ischemia induced by cardiac arrest, it was found that the release of iron from cerebral stores and the formation of TBA reactants occurred concomitantly during reperfusion (95). Inasmuch as iron-catalyzed lipid peroxidation can be suppressed during reperfusion by administration of the iron chelator deferoxamine (desferrioxamine B methanesulfonate) (88), it has been conjectured that resuscitation strategies based on knowledge of postischemic reactions injurious to tissue may mitigate the high incidence of central nervous system injury following resuscitation (96).

TOPICS FOR FURTHER RESEARCH

Ascertaining the response of brain tissue to pre-ischemic or postischemic manipulation of the oxygen radical pathway is attracting increasing interest. Of parallel interest are studies of brain trauma induced by percussion (97) or hypertension (98). It has been shown, by administration of specific inhibitors, that the cyclooxygenase pathway participates in the development of morphologically observed injury to vascular endothelium. Similar vascular abnormalities, as well as the consequent loss of blood-brain barrier integrity and the extravasation of plasma proteins, could be induced by topical administration of arachidonate (98-100) and quenched by scavengers of O_2·⁻ (97,99) or by suppression of O_2·⁻ transport via the anion channel (99). These results eventually led to the proposal (cited above) that stimulation of the oxygen radical cascade occurs when an excess of cyclooxygenase substrates amplifies prostaglandin synthesis, generating O_2·⁻ by nucleotide radical reduction of oxygen in a side reaction during prostaglandin hydroperoxidase activity (87). From these observations, the main radical-related contribution to cerebral injury is postulated to occur in the vascular space, with the parenchyma being injured secondarily by transport of superoxide-induced reactions into the intracellular space.

Since organic antioxidants or enzymes included in the reperfusate are not likely to gain uniform access to all ischemic zones, an unresolved question remains: Is any significant parenchymal contribution to reperfusion-induced brain injury due either to oxygen radicals themselves or to reactions initiated by them leading to lipid peroxidation? Determination of the relative contributions of these scenarios requires a technique which can detect the earliest appearance of oxygen radicals and their reaction products in reperfused tissue. An example of this approach in vitro is the detection of oxygen radicals by a fluorescence technique. Radicals released during the respiratory burst (101) of neutrophils stimulated with phorbol myristate ester can be detected by the oxidation of nonfluorescent 2',7'-dichlorofluorescin to fluorescent 2',7'-dichlorofluorescein (102). This test (103), and another more sensitive version (104), has been shown in vitro to be specific for the hydroperoxide moiety and to be considerably more sensitive than the spectrophotometric conjugated diene assay. With such a test, the association of morphologic signs of pre-ischemic and postischemic brain damage might be correlated with oxygen radical-induced lipid peroxidation. Finally, the question of the development of lipid peroxidation in time, its microscopic heterogeneity or homogeneity, and its location vis-a-vis the vascular or parenchymal space may finally be addressed and perhaps resolved.

ACKNOWLEDGMENT

These studies were supported by USPHS Grants NS05820, NS23244, NS22603, and by American Heart Association Grant-in-Aid 85-1258. Dr. Ginsberg is the recipient of a Jacob Javits Neuroscience Investigator Award.

REFERENCES

1. Tappel AL. Lipid peroxidation damage to cell components. Fed Proc 1973:32:1870-1874.

2. Siesjö BK. Cell damage in the brain: a speculative synthesis. J Cereb Blood Flow Metab 1981:1:155-185.

3. Sevanian A, Hochstein P. Mechanism and consequences of lipid peroxidation in biological systems. Ann Rev Nutr 1985:5:365-390.

4. Slater TF. Free-radical mechanisms in tissue injury. Biochem J 1984:222:1-15.

5. Halliwell B, Gutteridge JMC. Oxygen toxicity, oxygen radicals, transition metals and disease. Biochem J 1984:219:1-14.

6. Halliwell B, Gutteridge JMC. Oxygen free radicals and iron

in relation to biology and medicine: some problems and concepts. Arch Biochem Biophys 1986:246:501-514.

7. Fridovich I. The biology of oxygen radicals. Science 1978:201:875-880.

8. Freeman BA, Crapo JD. Biology of disease: free radicals and tissue injury. Lab Invest 1982:47:412-426.

9. Proctor PH, Reynolds ES. A review: free radicals and disease in man. Physiol Chem Phys Med NMR 1984:16:175-195.

10. Thaw HH, Hamberg H, Brunk UT. Acute and irreversible injury following exposure of cultured cells to reactive oxygen metabolites. Eur J Cell Biol 1983:31:46-54.

11. Noronha-Dutra AA, Steen EM. Lipid peroxidation as a mechanism of injury in cardiac myocytes. Lab Invest 1982:47:346-353.

12. Yagi K, Ohkawa H, Ohishi N, Yamashita M, Nakashima T. Lesion of aortic intima caused by intravenous administration of linoleic acid hydroperoxide. J Appl Biochem 1981:3:58-65.

13. Anderson WR, Tan WC, Takatori T, Privett OS. Toxic effects of hydroperoxide injections on rat lung: a light microscopical and ultrastructural study. Arch Pathol Lab Med 1976:100:154-162.

14. Pasquali-Ronchetti I, Bini A, Botti B, De Alojsio G, Fornieri C, Vannini V. Ultrastructural and biochemical changes induced by progressive lipid peroxidation on isolated microsomes and rat liver endoplasmic reticulum. Lab Invest 1980:42:457-468.

15. Barber AA, Bernheim F. Lipid peroxidation: its measurement, occurrence, and significance in animal tissues. Adv Gerontol Res 1967:2:355-403.

16. Plaa GL, Witschi H. Chemicals, drugs, and lipid peroxidation. Ann Rev Pharmacol 1976:16:125-141.

17. Mills GC. Glutathione peroxidase and the destruction of hydrogen peroxide in animal tissues. Arch Biochem Biophys 1960:86:1-5.

18. Little C, O'Brien PJ. An intracellular GSH-peroxidase with a lipid peroxide substrate. Biochem Biophys Res Comm 1968:31:145-150.

19. Christophersen BO. Formation of monohydroxy-polyenic fatty acids from lipid peroxides by a glutathione peroxidase. Biochim Biophys Acta 1968:164:35-46.

20. Cohen G, Hochstein P. Glutathione peroxidase: the primary agent for the elimination of hydrogen peroxide in erythrocytes. Biochemistry 1963:2:1420-1428.

21. McCord JM, Fridovich I. Superoxide dismutase: an enzymatic function for erythrocuprein (hemocuprein). J Biol Chem 1969:244:6049-6055.

22. Chance B, Sies H, Boveris A. Hydroperoxide metabolism in mammalian organs. Physiol Rev 1979:59:527-605.

23. Lucy JA. Functional and structural aspects of biological membranes: a suggested structural role for vitamin E in the control of membrane permeability and stability. Ann NY Acad Sci 1972:203:4-11.

24. Mead JF. Free radical mechanisms of lipid damage and consequences for cellular membranes. In: Pryor WA, ed. Free radicals in biology: vol 1. New York: Academic Press, 1976:51-68.

25. Mellors A, Tappel AL. The inhibition of mitochondrial peroxidation by ubiquinone and ubiquinol. J Biol Chem 1966:241:4353-4356.

26. Bazán NG. Effects of ischemia and electroconvulsive shock on free fatty acid pool in the brain. Biochim Biophys Acta 1970:218:1-10.

27. Marion J, Wolfe LS. Origin of the arachidonic acid released post-mortem in rat forebrain. Biochim Biophys Acta 1979:574:25-32.

28. Porcellati G, De Medio GE, Fini C, et al. Phospholipid and its metabolism in ischemia. In: Neuhoff V, ed. Proceedings of the European society for neurochemistry. Weinheim: Verlag Chemie, 1978:285-303.

29. Edgar AD, Strosznajder J, Horrocks LA. Activation of ethanolamine phospholipase A_2 in brain during ischemia. J Neurochem 1982:39:1111-1116.

30. Bazán NG. Free arachidonic acid and other lipids in the nervous system during early ischemia and after electroshock. Adv Exp Med Biol 1976:72:317-335.

31. Sun GY, Su KL, Der OM, Tang W. Enzymic regulation of arachidonate metabolism in brain membrane phosphoglycerides. Lipids 1979:14:229-235.

32. Yoshida S, Harik SI, Busto R, Santiso M, Martinez E, Ginsberg MD. Free fatty acids and energy metabolites in ischemic cerebral cortex with noradrenaline depletion. J Neurochem 1984:42:711-717.

33. Dahle LK, Hill EG, Holman RT. The thiobarbituric acid reaction and the autoxidations of polyunsaturated fatty acid methyl esters. Arch Biochem Biophys 1962:98:253-261.

34. Yagi K. A simple fluorometric assay for lipoperoxide in blood plasma. Biochem Med 1976:15:212-216.

35. Holman RT, Burr GO. Spectrophotometric studies of the oxidation of fats. VI. Oxygen absorption and chromophore production in fatty esters. J Am Chem Soc 1946:68:562-566.

36. Klein RA. The detection of oxidation in liposome preparations. Biochim Biophys Acta 1970:210:486-489.

37. Chance B, Nishiki K, Oshino N. Glutathione release, an indicator of hyperoxic stress. In: Jobsis FF, ed. Oxygen and physiological function. Dallas: Professional Information Library, 1977:388-402.

38. Demopoulos H, Flamm E, Seligman M, Power R, Pietronigro D, Ransohoff J. Molecular pathology of lipids in CNS membranes. In: Jobsis FF, ed. Oxygen and physiological function. Dallas: Professional Information Library, 1977:491-508.

39. Demopoulos HB, Flamm ES, Pietronigro DD, Seligman ML. The free radical pathology and the microcirculation in the major central nervous system disorders. Acta Physiol Scand 1980:Suppl 492:91-119.

40. Cooper AJL, Pulsinelli WA, Duffy TE. Glutathione and ascorbate during ischemia and post-ischemic reperfusion in rat brain. J Neurochem 1980:35:1242-1245.

41. MacMillan V. Cerebral Na^+, K^+-ATPase activity during exposure to and recovery from acute ischemia. J Cereb Blood Flow Metab 1982:2:457-465.

42. Tomita I, Sano M, Serizawa S, Ohta K, Katou M. Fluctuation of lipid peroxides and related enzyme activities at time of stroke in stroke-prone spontaneously hypertensive rats. Stroke 1979:10:323-326.

43. Nordström CH, Rehncrona S, Siesjö BK. Effects of phenobarbital in cerebral ischemia. II. Restitution of cerebral energy state, as well as of glycolytic metabolites, citric acid cycle intermediates and associated amino acids after pronounced incomplete ischemia. Stroke 1978:9:335-343.

44. Yoshida S, Busto R, Martinez E, Scheinberg P, Ginsberg MD. Regional brain energy metabolism after complete versus incomplete ischemia in the rat in the absence of severe lactic acidosis. J Cereb Blood Flow Metab 1985:5:490-501.

45. Rehncrona S, Folbergrová J, Smith DS, Siesjö BK. Influence of complete and pronounced incomplete cerebral ischemia and subsequent recirculation on cortical concentrations of oxidized and reduced glutathione in the rat. J Neurochem 1980:34:477-486.

46. Rehncrona S, Westerberg E, Åkesson B, Siesjö BK. Brain cortical fatty acids and phospholipids during and following complete and severe incomplete ischemia. J Neurochem 1982:38:84-93.

47. Yoshida S, Abe K, Busto R, Watson BD, Kogure K, Ginsberg MD. Influence of transient ischemia on lipid-soluble antioxidants, free fatty acids and energy metabolites in rat brain. Brain Res 1982:245:307-316.

48. Yoshida S, Busto R, Watson BD, Santiso M, Ginsberg MD. Post-ischemic cerebral lipid peroxidation in vitro: modification by dietary vitamin E. J Neurochem 1985:44:1593-1601.

49. Sun GY. Metabolism of arachidonate and stearate injected simultaneously into the mouse brain. Lipids 1977:12:661-665.

50. Ikeda M, Yoshida S, Busto R, Santiso M, Ginsberg MD. Polyphosphoinositides as a probable source of brain free fatty acids accumulated at the onset of ischemia. J Neurochem 1986:47:123-132.

51. Yoshida S, Ikeda M, Busto R, Santiso M, Martinez E, Ginsberg MD. Cerebral phosphoinositide, triacylglycerol, and energy metabolism in reversible ischemia: origin and fate of free fatty acids. J Neurochem 1986:47:744-757.

52. Kogure K, Watson BD, Busto R, Abe K. Potentiation of lipid peroxides by ischemia in rat brain. Neurochem Res 1982:7:437-454.

53. Abe K, Yoshida S, Watson BD, Busto R, Kogure K, Ginsberg MD. α-Tocopherol and ubiquinones in rat brain subjected to decapitation ischemia. Brain Res 1983:273:166-169.

54. Kogure K, Busto E, Schwartzman RJ, Scheinberg P. The dissociation of cerebral blood flow, metabolism, and function in the early stages of developing cerebral infarction. Ann Neurol 1980:8:278-290.

55. Yamamoto M, Shima T, Uozumi T, Sogabe T, Yamada K, Kawasaki T. A possible role of lipid peroxidation in cellular damages caused by cerebral ischemia and the protective effect of alpha-tocopherol administration. Stroke 1983:14:977-982.

56. Ginsberg MD, Watson BD, Yoshida S, et al. Aspects of tissue injury in cerebral ischemia. In: Reivich M, Hurtig HI, eds. Cerebrovascular diseases. New York: Raven Press, 1983:237-247.

57. Watson BD, Busto R, Goldberg WJ, Santiso M, Yoshida S, Ginsberg MD. Lipid peroxidation in vivo induced by reversible global ischemia in rat brain. J Neurochem 1984:42:268-274.

58. Bligh EG, Dyer WJ. A rapid method of lipid extraction and purification. Can J Biochem Physiol 1959:37:911-917.

59. Jenkins FA, White HE. Fundamentals of optics. New York: McGraw-Hill, 1957:457.

60. Pulsinelli WA, Brierley JB. A new model of bilateral hemispheric ischemia in the unanesthetized rat. Stroke 1979:10:267-272.

61. Goldberg WJ, Watson BD, Busto R, Kurchner H, Santiso M, Ginsberg MD. Concurrent measurement of (Na^+, K^+)-ATPase activity and lipid peroxides in rat brain following reversible global ischemia. Neurochem Res 1984:9:1737-1747.

62. Schraufstatter IU, Hinshaw DB, Hyslop PA, Spragg RG, Cochrane CG. Glutathione cycle activity and pyridine nucleotide levels in oxidant-induced injury of cells. J Clin Invest 1985:76:1131-1139.

63. Harlan JM, Levine JD, Callahan KS, Schwartz BR, Harker LA. Glutathione redox cycle protects cultured endothelial cells against lysis by extracellularly generated hydrogen peroxide. J Clin Invest 1984:73:706-713.

64. Globus MY-T, Ginsberg MD, Harik SI, Busto R, Dietrich WD. Role of dopamine in ischemic striatal injury: metabolic evidence. Neurology 1987:37:1712-1719.

65. Pulsinelli WA, Levy DE, Duffy TE. Regional cerebral blood flow and glucose metabolism following transient forebrain ischemia. Ann Neurol 1982; 11:499-502.

66. Yoshida S, Busto R, Santiso M, Ginsberg MD. Brain lipid peroxidation induced by postischemic reoxygenation in vitro: effect of vitamin E. J Cereb Blood Flow Metab 1984:4:466-469.

67. Watson BD, Dietrich WD, Busto R, Wachtel MS, Ginsberg MD. Induction of reproducible brain infarction by photochemically initiated thrombosis. Ann Neurol 1985:17:497-504.

68. Watson BD, Prado R, Dietrich WD, Busto R, Scheinberg P, Ginsberg MD. Mitigation of evolving cortical infarction in rats by recombinant tissue plasminogen activator following photochemically induced thrombosis. In: Powers WJ, Raichle ME, eds. Cerebrovascular diseases. New York: Raven Press, 1987:317-330.

69. Nakayama H, Dietrich WD, Watson BD, Prado R, Busto R, Ginsberg MD. Pharmacologically induced recirculation following experimental middle cerebral artery thrombosis: histopathological consequences. J Cereb Blood Flow Metab 1987:7 (Suppl 1):S23.

70. Watson BD, Prado R, Nakayama H, Busto R, Santiso M, Ginsberg MD. Does early reperfusion of MCA territory destined for infarction following thrombotic stroke in rats induce global lipid peroxidation? J Cereb Blood Flow Metab 1987:7(Suppl 1):S11.

71. Pontén U, Ratcheson RA, Salford LG. Optimal freezing conditions for cerebral metabolites in rats. J Neurochem 1973:21:1127-1138.

72. Yoshida S, Busto R, Ginsberg MD, et al. Compression-induced brain edema: modification by prior depletion and supplementation of vitamin E. Neurology (NY) 1983:33:166-172.

73. Ishii S, Hayner R, Kelly WA, Evans JP. Studies of cerebral swelling. II. Experimental cerebral swelling produced by supratentorial extradural compression. J Neurosurg 1959:16:152-166.

74. Yoshida S, Busto R, Abe K, Santiso M, Ginsberg MD. Compression-induced brain edema in rats: effect of dietary vitamin E on membrane damage in the brain. Neurology 1985:35:126-130.

75. Moskowitz MA, Kiwak KJ, Hekimian K, Levine L. Synthesis of compounds with properties of leukotrienes C_4 and D_4 in gerbil brains after ischemia and reperfusion. Science 1984:224:886-889.

76. Usui M, Asano T, Takakura K. Identification and quantitative analysis of hydroxy-eicosatetraenoic acids in rat brains exposed to regional ischemia. Stroke 1987:18:490-494.

77. Dempsey RJ, Roy MW, Cowen DE, Maley ME. Lipoxygenase metabolites of arachidonic acid and the development of ischaemic cerebral oedema. Neurol Res 1986:8:53-56.

78. Pappius BM, Wolfe LS. Some further studies on vasogenic edema. In: Pappius HM, Feindel W, eds. Dynamics of brain edema. New York: Springer-Verlag, 1976:138-143.

79. Gaudet RJ, Levine L. Transient cerebral ischemia and brain prostaglandins. Biochem Biophys Res Commun 1979:86:893-901.

80. Iannotti F, Crockard A, Ladds G, Symon L. Are prostaglandins involved in experimental ischemic edema in gerbils? Stroke 1981:12:301-306.

81. Bulkley GB. The role of oxygen free radicals in human disease processes. Surgery 1983:94:407-411.

82. McCord JM, Roy RS. The pathophysiology of superoxide: roles in inflammation and ischemia. Can J Physiol Pharmacol 1982:60:1346-1352.

83. McCord JM. Oxygen-derived free radicals in post-ischemic tissue injury. New Eng J Med 1985:312:159-163.

84. Bielski BHJ, Arudi RL, Sutherland MW. A study of the reactivity of HO_2/O_2^- with unsaturated fatty acids. J Biol Chem 1983:258:4759-4761.

85. Siesjö BK, Bendek G, Koide T, Westerberg E, Wieloch T. Influence of acidosis on lipid peroxidation in brain tissues in vitro. J Cereb Blood Flow Metab 1985:5:253-258.

86. Turrens JF, Alexandre A, Lehninger AL. Ubisemiquinone is the electron donor for superoxide formation by complex III of heart mitochondria. Arch Biochem Biophys 1985:237:408-414.

87. Kukreja RC, Kontos HA, Hess ML, Ellis EF. PGH synthase and lipoxygenase generate superoxide in the presence of NADH or NADPH. Circ Res 1986:59:612-619.

88. White BC, Krause GS, Aust SD, Eyster GE. Post-ischemic tissue injury by iron-mediated free radical lipid peroxidation. Ann Emerg Med 1985:14:804-809.

89. Gutteridge JMC. Iron promoters of the Fenton reaction and lipid peroxidation can be released from haemoglobin by peroxides. FEBS Lett 1986:201:291-295.

90. Chan PH, Fishman RA. Transient formation of superoxide radicals in polyunsaturated fatty acid-induced brain swelling. J Neurochem 1980:35:1004-1007.

91. Chan PH, Yurko M, Fishman RA. Phospholipid degradation and cellular edema induced by free radicals in brain cortical slices. J Neurochem 1982:38:525-531.

92. Chan PH, Schmidley JW, Fishman RA, Longar SM. Brain injury, edema, and vascular permeability changes induced by oxygen-derived free radicals. Neurology 1984:34:315-320.

93. Pulsinelli WA, Kraig RP, Plum F. Hyperglycemia, cerebral acidosis, and ischemic brain damage. In: Plum F, Pulsinelli W, eds. Cerebrovascular diseases. New York: Raven Press, 1985:201-210.

94. Pulsinelli WA, Waldman S, Rawlinson D, Plum F. Moderate hyperglycemia augments ischemic brain damage: a neuropathologic study in the rat. Neurology 1982:32:1239-1246.

95. Krause GS, Joyce KM, Nayini NR, et al. Cardiac arrest and resuscitation: brain iron delocalization during reperfusion. Ann Emerg Med 1985:14:1037-1043.

96. Babbs CF. Role of iron ions in the genesis of reperfusion injury following successful cardiopulmonary rescuscitation: preliminary data and a biochemical hypothesis. Ann Emerg Med 1985:14:777-783.

97. Kontos HA, Wei EP. Superoxide production in experimental brain injury. J Neurosurg 1986:64:803-807.

98. Kontos HA. Oxygen radicals in cerebral vascular injury. Circ Res 1985:57:508-516.

99. Kontos HA, Wei EP, Ellis EF, et al. Appearance of superoxide anion radical in cerebral extracellular space during increased prostaglandin synthesis in cats. Circ Res 1985:57:142-151.

100. Wei EP, Ellison MD, Kontos HA, Povlishock JT. O_2 radicals in arachidonate-induced increased blood-brain barrier permeability to proteins. Am J Physiol 1986:251:H693-H699.

101. Fantone JC, Ward PA. Polymorphonuclear leukocyte-mediated cell and tissue injury. Hum Pathol 1985:16:973-978.

102. Bass DA, Parce JW, Dechatelet LR, Szejda P, Seeds MC, Thomas M. Flow cytometric studies of oxidative product formation by neutrophils: a graded response to membrane stimulation. J Immunol 1983:130:1910-1917.

103. Cathcart R, Schwiers E, Ames BN. Detection of picomole levels of hydroperoxides using a fluorescent dichlorofluorescein assay. Anal Biochem 1983:134:111-116.

104. Yamamoto Y, Brodsky MH, Baker JC, Ames BN. Detection and characterization of lipid hydroperoxides at picomole levels by high-performance liquid chromatography. Anal Biochem 1987:160:7-13.

THE ROLE OF OXYGEN RADICAL-INDUCED LIPID PEROXIDATION IN ACUTE CENTRAL NERVOUS SYSTEM TRAUMA

Edward D. Hall and J. Mark Braughler

Most neuronal degeneration subsequent to central nervous system (CNS) trauma apparently results not from the primary injury but from secondary processes. This paper reviews biochemical, physiological, and pharmacological evidence supporting the concept that oxygen radical-induced lipid peroxidation plays a key role in this degeneration. Studies of oxygen radical formation and of lipid peroxidation have shown that these are early post-traumatic events. Inhibition of post-traumatic lipid peroxidation by administration of glucocorticoids or antioxidants was associated with inhibition of post-traumatic cerebral ischemia or decreased blood flow and with preservation of nerve function in various models of CNS trauma. These studies suggest that lipid peroxidation is a key factor and not an epiphenomenon. Further studies evaluating the effects of various steroids on injured brain or spinal cord have shown that the beneficial effects of these compounds are correlated not with glucocorticoid activity but with an ability to inhibit lipid peroxidation.

IT IS GENERALLY BELIEVED that a major portion of post-traumatic neuronal necrosis after brain or spinal cord injury does not result from diffuse primary injury, but rather from a secondary process. The vast majority of human spinal cord injuries do not involve actual physical transection of the spinal cord, but are contusive or compressive injuries (1). Many experimental studies of blunt spinal injury have shown that while a certain degree of direct mechanical damage to blood vessels and nerve cells occurs, a large amount of the post-traumatic destruction is due to a progressive secondary pathophysiological process. The injury appears to set in motion a series of molecular events that lead to gradual tissue (e.g., vascular and neuronal) degeneration, thus destroying the anatomical substrate necessary for neurological recovery. The initial structural integrity of the spinal cord at the injury site, however, suggests that functional recovery could be facilitated by a therapy that interrupted the molecular processes involved in the secondary degeneration. For those of us interested in identifying more effective agents for early treatment of acute central nervous system (CNS) trauma, both cerebral and spinal, at least a partial understanding of the mechanism or mechanisms of secondary post-traumatic neuronal destruction is a necessary prerequisite.

Over the past ten years, a large body of evidence

From Central Nervous System Diseases Research Unit, The Upjohn Company, Kalamazoo, Michigan, USA.

Address correspondence to Dr. Edward D. Hall, CNS Diseases Research Unit, 7251-209-4, The Upjohn Company, Kalamazoo, Michigan 49001, USA.

obtained from a wide variety of experimental studies of acute CNS trauma strongly suggests that oxygen radical-induced lipid peroxidation plays a key role in the progressive secondary neuronal degeneration that follows blunt injury. This view was originally put forth by Demopoulos and colleagues (2). The discussion which follows is a review of old and new evidence derived from biochemical, physiological, and pharmacological experiments.

BIOCHEMICAL EVIDENCE OF EARLY LIPID PEROXIDATION IN THE ACUTELY INJURED SPINAL CORD

Extensive biochemical data document the occurrence of oxygen radical formation and lipid peroxidation as early post-traumatic events in the experimentally injured spinal cord. Perhaps the most straightforward experimental approach has been to demonstrate, using the thiobarbituric acid test, increased concentrations of the breakdown products of peroxidized polyunsaturated fatty acids after blunt spinal injury. Demopoulos and colleagues (3) first reported a fivefold to tenfold increase in the content of thiobarbituric acid reaction (TBAR) products in cat spinal cord homogenates at 18 hours after a severe contusion injury. More recently, a 70% increase in spinal TBAR products was observed as early as 30 minutes after compressive injury in rats (4). Similar studies in our laboratories showed that incubation of homogenates of cat spinal cord tissue removed as early as five minutes after contusion injury produced significantly more TBAR products than did homogenates from uninjured controls (**Figure 1**). This shows that a spinal cord milieu conducive to tissue damaging lipid peroxidation exists very early after cord injury.

Tissue cholesterol is also susceptible to post-traumatic oxygen free-radical attack. Demopoulos et al (5) reported a 25% decrease in cat spinal cord cholesterol content at one hour after contusion injury together with the appearance of 2,4,6-cholestatriene, a cholesterol oxidation product, which was not detectable in uninjured cord samples. Anderson et al (6) observed a similar decline (15%) in cat spinal cord cholesterol content as early as five minutes after a compressive injury, suggesting that cholesterol oxidation occurs rapidly after blunt spinal trauma.

An additional approach to the measurement of

lipid peroxidation in the injured cord has been to utilize as a biochemical marker for oxidative events the exquisite sensitivity of guanylate cyclase to activation by oxygen radicals and lipid peroxides (7,8). With this technique we observed a doubling of cyclic guanosine monophosphate (cGMP) content in cat spinal cords at 30 minutes after contusion injury (9). This result has been confirmed by Kurihara (4), who found a 50% increase in cGMP content of the compressed spinal cord of the rat as early as 30 minutes after injury.

Another indicator of post-traumatic lipid peroxidation is a decrease in tissue antioxidant levels (e.g., ascorbate, a-tocopherol). Indeed, results of this approach support the hypothesis that intense lipid peroxidation of spinal tissue occurs within the first minutes to hours after cord injury. For example, a gradual decline in tissue levels of reduced ascorbate coincided with an increase in levels of oxidized ascorbate in the contused spinal cord of the cat (10). At one hour after injury, levels of reduced ascorbate had fallen by 37%, whereas levels of oxidized ascorbate more than doubled. Similarly, the a-tocopherol content of injured spinal cord was shown to decrease significantly within five minutes after compressive cord trauma in cats (11). A reasonable hypothesis explaining this decline in spinal antioxidant levels is that the antioxidants are consumed as the result of a sharp increase in oxygen radical levels and lipid peroxidation within the injured tissue.

One of the earliest functional consequences of tissue lipid peroxidation is inhibition of the activities of various phospholipid-dependent membrane enzymes such as $Na^+ + K^+$-ATPase (12,13). Considering this, the most impressive indicator of the very early occurrence of post-traumatic spinal lipid peroxidation may be the finding of a significant loss of $Na^+ + K^+$-ATPase activity in gray matter as early as five minutes after spinal cord contusion in dogs (14). A similar decrease in $Na^+ + K^+$-ATPase activity was observed in synaptosomes prepared from contused spinal cords from cats (15,16) and compressed spinal cords from rats (4). The probability that this acute loss of "sodium pump" activity is due to post-traumatic lipid peroxidation is supported by the work of Anderson and Means (17) in which an inhibition of $Na^+ + K^+$-ATPase activity induced by intraspinal microinjection of ferrous chloride was closely correlated (r = 0.97) with tissue TBAR product formation.

ROLE OF MICROVASCULAR LIPID PEROXIDATION IN POST-TRAUMATIC CNS ISCHEMIA

The identification of lipid peroxidation as an important factor in the acute phase of CNS injury,

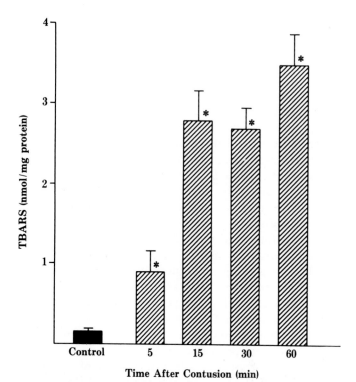

Figure 1. In vitro lipid peroxidation (measured by TBAR product formation) in homogenates of contused spinal cords removed from cats at different times after injury. Injured segments (L-3) of spinal cord were rapidly removed and frozen in liquid N_2 at the indicated times after contusion. Control tissue was from uninjured animals. The frozen segments were thawed and homogenized in 10 volumes of 100 mM potassium phosphate buffer pH 7.0. TBAR product formation in homogenates was determined after a 60-minute incubation of homogenates at 37°C as described in reference 33. Each point represents the mean ± SE for 5 animals. The asterisks indicate significant differences (P<0.05) between the injured and uninjured tissue, as calculated by one-way analysis of variance (ANOVA).

rather than simply an epiphenomenon, depends upon the successful demonstration of its association with post-traumatic pathophysiological events. Recent pharmacological investigations have, in fact, provided strong support for a role of progressive microvascular lipid peroxidation in the development of post-traumatic CNS ischemia, which is generally believed to contribute to secondary tissue degeneration, e.g., in injured spinal cord.

The first of these investigations found a close correlation between the ability of a single large intravenous (IV) dose of the glucocorticoid methylprednisolone to inhibit spinal cord lipid peroxidation (5,9,11,18) and to retard the gradual decline in white matter blood flow that follows severe blunt trauma (19,20). For both effects, the optimal dose was 30 mg/kg indicating that the dose which significantly diminishes lipid peroxidation is also associated with a decrease in post-traumatic ischemia. Moreover, the methylprednisolone dose-response for inhibition of post-traumatic spinal lipid peroxidation and ischemia was essentially identical to that for the concomitant prevention of early (one hour) postinjury lactic acid accumulation (21).

Even more to the point of trying to establish a role for lipid peroxidation in the development of post-traumatic spinal cord ischemia are studies that examined the effect of intensive antioxidant dosing on the progressive decline in white matter blood flow after contusion injury in cats (22). Cats were pretreated with daily, high, oral doses of a-tocopherol (vitamin E, 1000 IU) and selenium (50 µg) for five days prior to spinal contusion injury, an antioxidant regimen earlier demonstrated to protect the cat spinal cord from peroxidative damage by microinjection of ferrous chloride (17). In untreated cats, moderately severe spinal contusion injury resulted in a progressive decrease in white matter blood flow from near normal levels immediately after injury to 53.5% below the pre-injury level four hours later. In contrast, a-tocopherol and selenium pretreatment prevented any post-traumatic decrease in white matter perfusion (22). Further experiments have shown that the administration of a single 25 mg/kg IV dose of ascorbic acid, while not as effective as the more intensive a-tocopherol and selenium pretreatment, also significantly retarded development of post-traumatic spinal cord ischemia (23).

As noted earlier, the post-traumatic loss of endogenous spinal cord ascorbate (10) and a-tocopherol (11) may represent increased utilization of these antioxidants in response to injury-triggered lipid peroxidation. The ability of exogenous high doses of these same antioxidants to retard post-traumatic spinal cord ischemia strongly supports a causal role for lipid peroxidation in its development.

A similar role for oxygen radicals has been observed for post-traumatic cerebral microvascular damage. Kontos and coworkers (24) showed that fluid percussion head injury in cats produced early (one hour) endothelial lesions in cerebral cortical arterioles whose formation was correlated with pathological vasodilation and a reduced vasoconstrictor responsiveness to hypercapnia. Formation of the endothelial lesions, with the associated physiological abnormalities, was inhibited by topical application of the free radical scavengers superoxide dismutase, nitroblue tetrazolium, or mannitol, suggesting that oxygen radicals are the pathophysiological mediators. The radicals may be generated in response to an injury-induced increase in brain cyclooxygenase activity, an increase known to occur because the cortical levels of various prostaglandins are also increased after injury (25). Consistent with this interpretation is the fact that pretreatment with cyclooxygenase inhibitors such as indomethacin also prevents the secondary post-traumatic cortical microvascular damage (24).

ROLE OF MICROVASCULAR LIPID PEROXIDATION IN POSTHEMORRHAGIC BRAIN ISCHEMIA

Subarachnoid hemorrhage, a common sequela of severe cerebral (or spinal) injury, is associated with a progressive secondary decrease in CNS blood flow, which, if severe enough, becomes ischemia. This phenomenon is referred to clinically as vasospasm, based upon angiographic demonstration of decreased diameters of the major cerebral arteries. However, numerous experimental studies have also documented a defect in microvascular perfusion, which is probably due to a direct influence of blood-derived mediators on brain arterioles in addition to the major vessels. Although a number of factors may be mechanistically involved in ischemia development after subarachnoid hemorrhage (26), considerable evidence supports vascular lipid peroxidation as a causal factor. For example, a close correlation between the lipid hydroperoxide content of cerebrospinal fluid (CSF) and the onset of post-subarachnoid hemorrhage vasospasm has been found in both animals and man (27).

Thus, in a fashion similar to the studies discussed earlier concerning post-traumatic spinal cord ischemia (22,23), we have also investigated in cats the ability of intensive antioxidant pretreatment to prevent the progressive decrease in cerebral blood flow after experimental subarachnoid hemorrhage. Cats were pretreated with a-tocopherol (1000 IU) for five days followed by intracisternal injection of 0.5 mL/kg of fresh unheparinized autologous arterial blood. In untreated animals, this resulted in a progressive decrease in cerebral blood flow (caudate nucleus), which reached a level of approximately 50% below normal at three hours after subarachnoid hemorrhage. In a-tocopherol-treated cats, this decrease in blood flow was almost completely prevented (**Figure 2**). No significant differences in cardiovascular function or blood gas levels were observed between the two groups, suggesting that the protective effect of a-tocopherol was directly on the cerebral vasculature and not secondary to other physiological alterations. This pharmacological result supports a role for an oxygen radical-lipid peroxidation process in the development of posthemorrhagic ischemia. In further support of this view, Asano et al (28) have shown that acute administration of the antioxidant 1,2-bis(nicotinamide)-propane can promptly reverse acute or chronic vasospasm in dogs after subarachnoid hemorrhage.

ROLE OF LIPID PEROXIDATION IN POST-TRAUMATIC AXONAL DEGENERATION

In addition to involvement in microvascular damage and consequent development of ischemia in

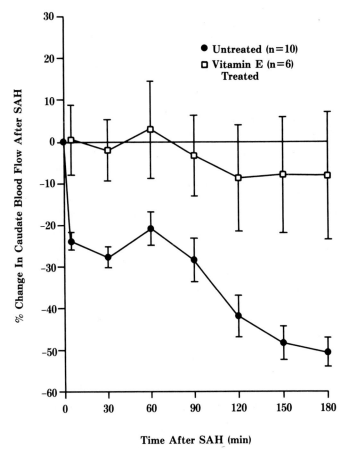

Time After SAH (min)

Figure 2. Time course of changes in caudate nuclear blood flow (measured by hydrogen clearance) after experimental subarachnoid hemorrhage (SAH) in untreated versus a-tocopherol (vitamin E)-treated cats. Values indicate mean ± SE. The absolute caudate blood flow was 50.3 ± 3.2 mL/100 g per minute in the untreated cats compared to 55.8 ± 8.4 in the a-tocopherol-treated cats. A repeated-measure ANOVA comparing the overall time courses showed a highly significant treatment effect (P < 0.0005, F ratio = 16.59, degrees of freedom = 1, 14).

the injured spinal cord and brain, lipid peroxidation may also be directly involved in the degeneration of spinal axons after injury. Recent studies in one of our laboratories have examined this possibility in the anterograde (Wallerian) degeneration of surgically sectioned motor nerve fibers in the cat. Specifically, the surgical transection of soleus motor axons at the greater sciatic foramen, followed 48 hours later by an assessment of neuromuscular function in the in vivo soleus nerve-muscle preparation, provides a reproducible model for studying the early consequences of neuronal degeneration (29-32). In this model, the degenerating motor axons and nerve terminals display subtle, but important, defects in neuromuscular transmission and excitability that can be quantified by a number of functional tests. Previous studies with this model have shown that intensive pretreatment with glucocorticoids such as triamcinolone (30) or methylprednisolone (31) can retard the degenerative process as evidenced by a significant preservation of neuromuscular function at 48 hours after sectioning of the axon.

In more recent experiments, an attempt has been made to investigate pharmacologically the possible role of lipid peroxidation in the anterograde degeneration process (29). Prior to nerve section, cats were intensively pretreated with daily oral doses of a-tocopherol (200 IU) and selenium (50 μg); this selenium dose was the same as that in the studies of post-traumatic spinal cord ischemia (22), whereas the a-tocopherol dose was lower. This treatment retarded the anterograde degeneration process significantly. A preservation of neuromuscular function was observed, as measured by the greater soleus muscle contractile response to low-frequency nerve stimulation and by a better maintenance of tetanic contractile tension during high-frequency nerve stimulation (**Figure 3**). Although biochemical correlates are needed to support these functional results, the ability of antioxidant dosing to slow the anterograde degenerative process suggests that lipid peroxidation may be a fundamental mechanism of neuronal degeneration after injury.

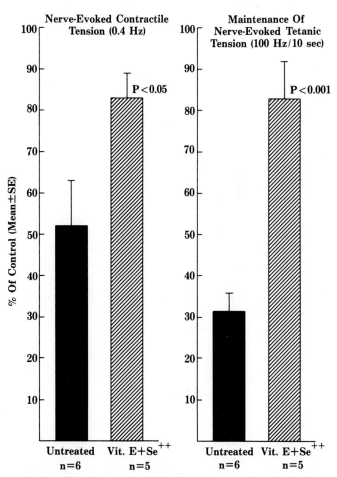

Figure 3. Effects of intensive pretreatment with a-tocopherol (vit E) and selenium (Se[+]) on nerve-evoked isometric contractile tension and maintenance of maximal tetanic (100 Hz/10 sec) tension in nerve-sectioned soleus nerve-muscle preparations in vivo, measured 48 hours after sectioning. The values are the percent (mean ± SE) of control values (measured in normal preparations with intact nerves). The P values were derived by one-way ANOVA.

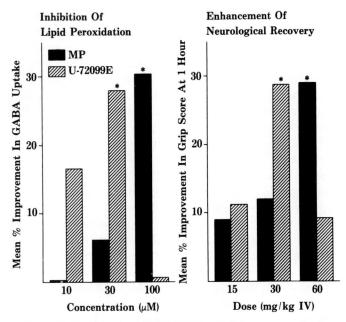

Inhibition Of
Lipid Peroxidation

Enhancement Of
Neurological Recovery

Figure 4. Enhancement of ^{14}C-GABA uptake by rat synaptosomes (by inhibition of the xanthine/xanthine oxidase-induced peroxidative impairment of GABA uptake) and enhancement of early neurological recovery in severely head-injured mice by the glucocorticoid methylprednisolone (MP) or the nonglucocorticoid U-72099E. The asterisks indicate significant differences compared with no treatment, as calculated by Duncan's multiple range test. The correlation coefficient between the percent improvement in GABA uptake and the percent improvement in grip score was 0.93 ($P<0.008$) when the values for percent improvement in GABA uptake for the two steroids were combined for each concentration and when the values for percent improvement in grip score for the two steroids were combined for each dose.

The demonstrated ability of some glucocorticoids to inhibit neuronal lipid peroxidation directly (33) also supports an antioxidant mechanism for the slowing of motor nerve degeneration by intensive glucocorticoid dosing (30,31). Likewise, for the injured spinal cord, the early and repeated administration of methylprednisolone in doses sufficient to decrease lipid peroxidation has recently been shown in both rats (34) and cats (6) to result in significantly greater long-term structural preservation after blunt cord injury.

CORRELATION OF STEROID EFFECTS IN CNS TRAUMA WITH INHIBITION OF LIPID PEROXIDATION

As discussed earlier, a clear dose-response correlation has been demonstrated between the ability of the glucocorticoid methylprednisolone to inhibit spinal cord lipid peroxidation (9,18) and to retard the development of post-traumatic spinal cord ischemia (19-21). Moreover, methylprednisolone doses that successfully inhibit spinal cord lipid peroxidation have also been reported to enhance recovery of spinal extracellular calcium concentrations (20); to attenuate neurofilament

degradation (15); to decrease injury-induced arachidonate release, prostanoid formation, and cholesterol loss (6); and to facilitate short- (20) and long-term (6) neurophysiological recovery after spinal cord injury.

In vitro studies have shown that not all glucocorticoids inhibit lipid peroxidation in CNS tissue, nor are those that inhibit this process equipotent as membrane antioxidants (33). For example, methylprednisolone optimally inhibits lipid peroxidation in isolated rat brain synaptosomes at a concentration of $100\,\mu$M. Prednisolone is a less powerful lipid peroxidation inhibitor, with an optimal concentration of $300\,\mu$M. However, the prototype glucocorticoid hydrocortisone is an ineffective inhibitor of lipid peroxidation in vitro over a broad range of concentrations (10-3000 μM). It is interesting to note that the effectiveness of these three glucocorticoids as inhibitors of lipid peroxidation in CNS tissue is highly predictive of their ability to enhance early neurological recovery of mice after a moderately severe concussive head injury (35). Methylprednisolone worked best in this model at a dose of 30 mg/kg IV; prednisolone produced a significant improvement in recovery at 60 mg/kg IV; and hydrocortisone had no effect even at a dose of 120 mg/kg IV.

Recent work has focused on the possibility that a nonglucocorticoid steroid might duplicate the efficacy of methylprednisolone in models of CNS trauma and neuronal membrane damage from lipid peroxidation. Several steroids have been shown to be devoid of glucocorticoid-related activities (as measured by ACTH suppression in cultured pituitary cells, suppression of body weight gain in mice, and thymic involution) related to their lack of a β-hydroxyl group in position 11 of the steroid nucleus. One of these, U-72099E (17,21-dihydroxy-11a-*tert*-butyl-acetoxy-1,4-pregnadiene-3,20-dione-21-hemisuccinate, sodium salt) has been studied in detail and compared with methylprednisolone in the protection of CNS neuronal membranes from lipid peroxidation in vitro and the promotion of early neurological recovery in severely head-injured mice (36). In studies in which xanthine and xanthine oxidase were used to peroxidatively impair rat brain synaptosomal uptake of γ-aminobutyric acid (GABA), methylprednisolone and U-72099E caused a concentration-dependent preservation of GABA uptake by inhibiting lipid peroxidation. U-72099E is three times more potent than methylprednisolone, with an optimum concentration of $30\,\mu$M compared with $100\,\mu$M for methylprednisolone.

Consistent with its greater potency as an inhibitor of neuronal membrane lipid peroxidation, U-72099E significantly improved early neurological recovery in severely head-injured mice at an optimal IV dose of

30 mg/kg; methylprednisolone improved recovery at a dose of 60 mg/kg IV (**Figure 4**). Although not definitive, these results support the hypothesis that the action of certain steroids in protecting the injured nervous system is independent of glucocorticoid activity, but is closely correlated with an ability to inhibit post-traumatic lipid peroxidation. Furthermore, these results support the view that lipid peroxidation is a critical acute pathophysiological phenomenon in the injured nervous system.

REFERENCES

1. Windle WF. Concussion, contusion and severance of the spinal cord. In: Windle WF, ed. The spinal cord and its reaction to traumatic injury. New York: Dekker, 1980:205-218.

2. Demopoulos HB, Milvy P, Kakari S, Ransohoff J. Molecular aspects of membrane structure in cerebral edema. In: Reulen JH, Schuermann K, eds. Steroids and brain edema. Vienna: Springer-Verlag, 1972:29-39.

3. Milvy P, Kakari S, Campbell JB, Demopoulos HB. Paramagnetic species and radical products in cat spinal cord. Ann NY Acad Sci 1973:222:1102-1111.

4. Kurihara M. Role of monoamines in experimental spinal cord injury in rats: relationship between Na^+-K^+-ATPase and lipid peroxidation. J Neurosurg 1985:62:743-749.

5. Demopoulos HB, Flamm ES, Seligman ML, Pietronigro DD, Tomasula J, De Crescito V. Further studies on free-radical pathology in the major central nervous system disorders: effect of very high doses of methylprednisolone on the functional outcome, morphology and chemistry of experimental spinal cord impact injury. Can J Physiol Pharmacol 1982:60:1415-1424.

6. Anderson DK, Saunders RD, Demediuk P, Dugan LL, Braughler JM, Hall ED, et al. Lipid hydrolysis and peroxidation in injured spinal cord: partial protection with methylprednisolone or vitamin E and selenium. CNS Trauma 1985:2:257-267.

7. Braughler JM, Mittal CK, Murad F. Effects of thiols, sugars and proteins on nitric oxide activation of guanylate cyclase. J Biol Chem 1979:254:12450-12454.

8. Murad F, Arnold WP, Mittal CK, Braughler JM. Properties and regulation of guanylate cyclase and some proposed functions for cyclic GMP. In: Greengard P, Robison GA, eds. Advances in cyclic nucleotide research, vol 11. New York: Raven Press, 1979:175-204.

9. Hall ED, Braughler JM. Effects of intravenous methylprednisolone on spinal cord lipid peroxidation and $Na^+ + K^+$-ATPase activity: dose-response analysis during 1st hour after contusion injury in the cat. J Neurosurg 1982:57:247-253.

10. Pietronigro DD, Hovsepian M, Demopoulos HB, Flamm ES. Loss of ascorbic acid from injured feline spinal cord. J Neurochem 1983:41:1072-1076.

11. Saunders RD, Dugan LL, Demediuk P, Means ED, Horrocks LA, Anderson DK. Effects of methylprednisolone and the combination of alpha tocopherol and selenium on arachidonic acid metabolism and lipid peroxidation in traumatized spinal cord tissue. J Neurochem 1987:49:24-31.

12. Kovachich GB, Mishra OP. Partial inactivation of Na, K, -ATPase in cortical brain slices incubated in normal Krebs-Ringer phosphate medium at 1 and 10 atm oxygen pressure. J Neurochem 1981:36:333-335.

13. Sun AY. The effect of lipoxidation on synaptosomal $(Na^+ + K^+)$-ATPase isolated from the cerebral cortex of squirrel monkey. Biochem Biophys Acta 1972:266:350-360.

14. Clendenon NR, Allen H, Gordon WA, Bingham WG Jr. Inhibition of $Na^+ + K^+$-activated ATPase activity following experimental spinal cord trauma. J Neurosurg 1978:49:563-568.

15. Braughler JM, Hall ED. Effects of multi-dose methylprednisolone sodium succinate administration on injured cat spinal cord neurofilament degradation and energy metabolism. J Neurosurg 1984:61:290-295.

16. Goldman SS, Elowitz E, Flamm ES. Effect of traumatic injury on membrane phosphatase activity in cat spinal cord. Exp Neurol 1983:82:650-662.

17. Anderson DK, Means ED. Iron-induced lipid peroxidation in spinal cord: protection with mannitol and methylprednisolone. J Free Rad Biol Med 1985:1:59-64

18. Hall ED, Braughler JM. Acute effects of intravenous glucocorticoid pretreatment on the in vitro peroxidation of cat spinal cord tissue. Exp Neurol 1981:73:321-324.

19. Hall ED, Wolf DL, Braughler JM. Effects of a single large dose of methylprednisolone sodium succinate on experimental post-traumatic spinal cord ischemia: dose-response and time-action analysis. J Neurosurg 1984:61:124-130.

20. Young W, Flamm ES. Effect of high-dose corticosteroid therapy on blood flow, evoked potentials, and extracellular calcium in experimental spinal injury. J Neurosurg 1982:57:667-673.

21. Braughler JM, Hall ED. Lactate and pyruvate metabolism in injured cat spinal cord before and after a single large intravenous dose of methylprednisolone. J Neurosurg 1983:59:256-261.

22. Hall ED, Wolf DL. A pharmacological analysis of the pathophysiological mechanisms of post-traumatic spinal cord ischemia. J Neurosurg 1986:64:951-961.

23. Hall ED, Braughler JM. Role of lipid peroxidation in post-traumatic spinal cord degeneration: a review. CNS Trauma 1987:3:281-294.

24. Kontos HA, Wei EP, Ellis EF, Povlishock JT, Dietrich WD. Prostaglandins in physiological and in certain pathological responses of the cerebral circulation. Fed Proc 1981:40:2326-2330.

25. Ellis EF, Wright KF, Wei EP, Kontos HA. Cyclooxygenase products of arachidonic acid metabolism in cat cerebral cortex after experimental concussive brain injury. J Neurochem 1981:37:892-896.

26. Cook DA. The pharmacology of cerebral vasospasm. Pharmacology 1984:29:1-16.

27. Sano K, Asano T, Tanishima T, Sasaki T. Lipid peroxidation as a cause of cerebral vasospasm. Neurol Res 1980:2:253-272.

28. Asano T, Sasaki T, Koide T, Takakura K, Sano K. Experimental evaluation of the beneficial effect of an antioxidant on cerebral vasospasm. Neurol Res 1984:6:49-53.

29. Hall ED. Intensive anti-oxidant pretreatment retards motor nerve degeneration. Brain Res 1987:413:175-179.

30. Hall ED, Riker WF, Baker T. Beneficial action of glucocorticoid treatment on neuromuscular transmission

during early motor nerve degeneration. Exp Neurol 1983:79:488-496.

31. Hall ED, Wolf DL. Methylprednisolone preservation of motor nerve function during early degeneration. Exp Neurol 1984:84:715-720.

32. Okamoto M, Riker WF Jr. Motor nerve terminals as the site of initial function changes after denervation. J Gen Physiol 1969:53:70-80.

33. Braughler JM. Lipid peroxidation-induced inhibition of γ-aminobutyric acid uptake in rat synaptosomes: protection by glucocorticoids. J Neurochem 1985:44:1282-1288.

34. Iizuka H, Iwasaki Y, Yamamoto T, Kadoya S. Morphometric assessment of drug effects in experimental spinal cord injury. J Neurosurg 1986:65:92-98.

35. Hall ED. High-dose glucocorticoid treatment improves neurological recovery in head-injured mice. J Neurosurg 1985:62:882-887.

36. Hall ED, McCall JM, Chase RL, Yonkers PA, Braughler JM. A non-glucocorticoid steroid analog of methylprednisolone duplicates its high dose pharmacology in models of central nervous system trauma and neuronal membrane damage. J Pharmacol Exp Ther 1987:242:137-142.

QUESTIONS AND COMMENTS

Dr. Richard Johnston, Jr.: What do you know about the mechanism of the protective effect of methylprednisolone sodium succinate or the corticosteroid analog?

Dr. Edward Hall: We believe that both methylprednisolone and the nonglucocorticoid analog U-72099E inhibit membrane lipid peroxidation by inserting into the membranes and protecting susceptible lipids from oxygen radical insult. This view of steroid membrane insertion was originally put forth by Demopoulos in relation to antioxidant effects of steroids and still seems tenable. Interestingly, the twofold greater potency of U-72099E compared to methyprednisolone as an inhibitor of CNS tissue lipid peroxidation correlates with its greater lipid solubility, which is consistent with a membrane insertion mechanism. However, not all lipid-soluble steroids are effective inhibitors of lipid peroxidation in vitro or protective in CNS trauma models. Prednisolone is effective, but hydrocortisone, which in contrast to prednisolone and methylprednisolone lacks the 1,2 double bond in the steroid A ring, is ineffective. However, the role of the delta 1,4 A ring in the activity is unknown.

CALCIUM AND LIPID PEROXIDATION

J. Mark Braughler

Although both lipid peroxidation and Ca^{2+} have been implicated as important contributors to the cell damage caused by physical trauma or ischemia, their possible interaction has not, until recently, been addressed. Studies reported here have shown in cell and cell-free systems that lipid peroxidation and Ca^{2+} may synergistically damage biological membranes. In purified rat brain synaptosomes, iron-dependent lipid peroxidation was associated with an accumulation of Ca^{2+} by the synaptosome that depended on the dose of Fe^{2+}. In the absence of detectable membrane lipid peroxidation, the Ca^{2+} uptake could also be stimulated in synaptosomes by the addition of oxidized arachadonic acid. Deferoxamine inhibited the iron-dependent uptake of Ca^{2+}, but various Ca^{2+} channel blocking agents did not. In cultured spinal cord neurons, iron-dependent lipid peroxidation was accompanied by an accumulation of Ca^{2+} and a parallel release of arachadonic acid into the culture medium. In purified brain synaptosomes, Ca^{2+} enhanced the rate of lipid peroxidation under conditions where the rate is usually slow. These data, as well as data from other studies reviewed in this paper, support the hypothesis that lipid peroxidation and Ca^{2+} are intimately and inseparably involved in the pathogenesis of cell injury by oxygen radicals.

BOTH LIPID PEROXIDATION and Ca^{2+} have been implicated as important contributory factors to cell damage resulting from either physical trauma or ischemia. Until recently, however, their possible interaction in the pathophysiology of cell death has not been directly addressed. Although hypotheses concerning the involvement of either lipid peroxidation or Ca^{2+} abound, each has classically been considered separately.

In the case of lipid peroxidation, there is almost universal agreement that peroxidation of unsaturated fatty acids within membranes will disrupt membrane function and destroy cells. The involvement of lipid peroxidation in traumatic or ischemic cell damage has, on the other hand, been a subject of considerable debate. While the formation of oxygen radicals and the peroxidation of lipids during complete ischemia is considered impossible (1-4), complete ischemia rarely occurs. Furthermore, even during the development of total ischemia, oxygen gradients within tissues would exist as available oxygen is utilized. In addition, the phenomenon of reperfusion injury is becoming increasingly recognized as primarily an oxygen radical injury (5-7). Investigators from many laboratories continue to provide a growing body of evidence, based upon a variety of experimental approaches, for the involvement of lipid peroxidation in ischemic and traumatic cell injury (5-11).

From Central Nervous System Diseases Research Unit, The Upjohn Company, Kalamazoo, Michigan, USA.

Address correspondence to Dr. J. Mark Braughler, CNS Diseases Research Unit, 7251-209-5, The Upjohn Company, Kalamazoo, Michigan 49001, USA.

As for Ca^{2+}, shortly after the onset of ischemia or trauma, extracellular Ca^{2+} concentrations fall dramatically, resulting in intracellular Ca^{2+} accumulation (1,3,12-14). The calcium-dependent activation of phospholipases with subsequent release of free fatty acids from membranes and activation of the arachidonic acid cascade represents an early and readily quantifiable event in ischemic tissue (1,2,4,14,15). Other Ca^{2+} effects leading to the demise of the cell include inhibition of mitochondrial respiratory activity, activation of calcium-dependent proteases, which may catalyze conversion of xanthine dehydrogenase to xanthine oxidase (16), and the degradation of neurofilament and myelin proteins in neuronal tissue (17,18).

In a few laboratories, some studies of the role of lipid peroxidation in cell death have implicated a concurrent involvement of Ca^{2+}. For example, Casini et al (19,20) have shown that the cytotoxic effects of carbon tetrachloride or bromobenzene are linked to lipid peroxidation and depend upon the concentration of extracellular Ca^{2+}. In other studies, Barsacchi et al (21) have reported that exposure of isolated perfused rat hearts to organic hydroperoxides results in cellular damage morphologically identical to that associated with a pathological increase in intracellular Ca^{2+} levels. Such studies suggest that lipid peroxidation and Ca^{2+} are intimately linked as mediators of cell death.

CALCIUM ENHANCEMENT OF MEMBRANE DAMAGE BY LIPID PEROXIDATION

Perturbations in neurotransmitter uptake, mitochondrial function, and enzyme activity have been reported to occur during either primary ischemia or ischemia secondary to traumatic injury (2,10,22,23). Each of these ischemic effects can be duplicated in vitro by lipid peroxidation. For example, initiation of lipid peroxidation has been shown to decrease neurotransmitter uptake by brain synaptosomes or brain slices (24,25), inhibit respiration of isolated brain mitochondria (26), and inhibit $Na^+ + K^+$-ATPase activity in cultured spinal cord neurons and brain slices (25,27). We in our laboratory (28) have used a number of experimental systems to examine the interaction between lipid peroxidation and Ca^{2+} as mediators of functional membrane damage. In purified rat brain synaptosomes and mitochondria and in cultured fetal mouse spinal cord neurons, Ca^{2+} was found to

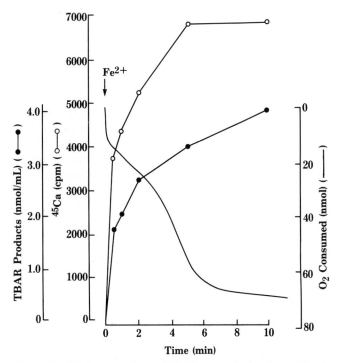

Figure 1. Calcium uptake and lipid peroxidation in rat brain synaptosomes with addition of Fe^{2+}. Synaptosomes prepared in Krebs buffer as described (9) were incubated in Krebs buffer at 37°C (0.1 mg synaptosomal protein/mL). Reactions also contained 1.5 mM $CaCl_2$ and were initiated by the addition of 200 μM Fe^{2+} (38). Ca^{2+} uptake was assayed by the addition of 1.4 μM $^{45}Ca^{2+}$ (800 mCi/mmol). Reactions were stopped by the addition of 2 mL ice cold Ca^{2+}-free Krebs buffer containing 1 mM $LaCl_3$. Samples were filtered and washed, and $^{45}Ca^{2+}$ content was determined by scintillation counting. TBAR product formation (●-●) and O_2 uptake (——) were determined as described elsewhere (38). The earliest time point for Ca^{2+} uptake (o-o) and TBAR product formation was 5 seconds after the addition of Fe^{2+}. Data are means of triplicate determinations from a representative experiment.

enhance markedly the lipid peroxidation-mediated damage to specific indices of membrane function. Subsequent studies by Malis and Bonventre (29) supported these observations by demonstrating that Ca^{2+} could potentiate oxygen radical injury to renal mitochondria. These results prompted more detailed studies of the interaction of lipid peroxidation and Ca^{2+}.

LIPID PEROXIDATION ENHANCEMENT OF MEMBRANE CALCIUM PERMEABILITY

The effects of lipid peroxidation on the permeability of cell membranes to Ca^{2+} were examined in purified rat brain synaptosomes. Addition of 200 μM Fe^{2+} to synaptosomes in Krebs buffer resulted in a rapid stimulation of lipid peroxidation as demonstrated by the consumption of oxygen from the medium and by the formation of thiobarbituric acid reactive (TBAR) products (**Figure 1**). Coupled with this acceleration of lipid peroxidation by Fe^{2+} was a rapid accumulation of Ca^{2+} by the synaptosomes. The explosive nature of

the change in Ca^{2+} permeability of the membrane was indicated by the fact that within 5 seconds after the addition of Fe^{2+}, the Ca^{2+} content of the synaptosomes was increased nearly fourfold compared with the content in synaptosomes not exposed to Fe^{2+}. The increased Ca^{2+} uptake was coincident with a burst in oxygen consumption and TBAR product formation.

The enhanced permeability of synaptosomal membranes to Ca^{2+} that was induced by the addition of Fe^{2+} was directly related to lipid peroxidation. Both lipid peroxidation and Ca^{2+} uptake were stimulated by Fe^{2+} in a dose-dependent manner (**Figure 2**). A comparison of the Fe^{2+}-dependent increase in TBAR product formation and the Ca^{2+} uptake revealed a correlation coefficient of 0.986 ($P < 0.002$) indicating that the Ca^{2+} influx was tightly associated with the formation of lipid peroxidation products.

Philipson and Ward (30) have reported that the permeability of sarcolemmal vesicles to Ca^{2+} is increased by fatty acids. In those studies, unsaturated fatty acids were more potent stimulators of passive Ca^{2+} permeability than saturated fatty acids. Furthermore, the degree of fatty acid unsaturation was positively correlated with the increase in Ca^{2+} permeability, and arachidonic acid was significantly more potent than linolenic acid. In theory, fatty acids or their oxidation products may act as ionophores by altering the phospholipid environment of the membrane (31) either through detergent-like

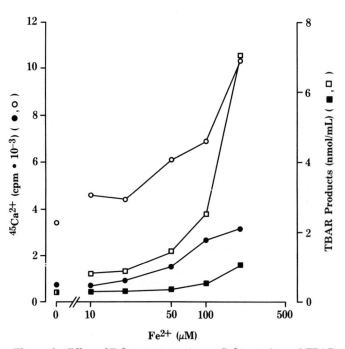

Figure 2. Effect of Fe^{2+} concentration on Ca^{2+} uptake and TBAR product formation. Assays were conducted as in Figure 1 except that reactions were initiated by the addition of the concentration of Fe^{2+} indicated. Ca^{2+} uptake by synaptosomes (●, o) and TBAR product formation (■, □) were determined at either 5 seconds (●, ■) or 2 minutes (o, □) after the addition of Fe^{2+}.

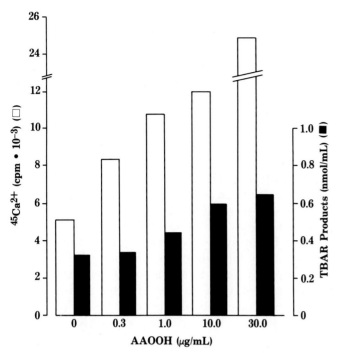

Figure 3. Effect of oxidized arachidonic acid (AAOOH) on Ca^{2+} uptake and TBAR product formation. Assays were conducted as in Figure 1. AAOOH was prepared by incubation of arachidonic acid (Nu Chek Prep, Elysian, Minnesota) for 72 hours at 45°C under a stream of air. Reactions were initiated by the addition of AAOOH in ethanol. Ca^{2+} uptake and TBAR product formation were determined at 1 minute.

Table 1. Effects of Various Agents on Lipid Peroxidation-Induced Ca^{2+} Uptake by Brain Synaptosomes*

Addition (μM)	$^{45}Ca^{2+}$ Uptake (cpm)		
	Control (no Fe^{2+})	Fe^{2+} (200 μM)	Net Increase with Fe^{2+}
None	2821 ± 173	5250 ± 129	2429 ± 44
Deferoxamine (500)	3366 ± 315	3275 ± 263***	ND[†, ††]
Verapamil (30)	2203 ± 426	4615 ± 44	2412 ± 382
Nifedipine (30)	1745 ± 195[†]	4877 ± 270	3132 ± 75
Cinnarizine (30)	1127 ± 296[†]	3049 ± 286**	1922 ± 10

* $^{45}Ca^{2+}$ uptake was determined as described for Figure 1 in the presence of the addition indicated. Reactions were terminated at 2 minutes after the addition of 200 μM Fe^{2+}. Values are means ±SD of three experiments. Statistical evaluation by ANOVA.
[†] $P<0.05$ compared with no addition.
** $P<0.05$ compared with Fe^{2+} alone.
[††] ND = no difference detected between control and Fe^{2+} values.

actions or by directly binding Ca^{2+} (32). In this regard, oxidized arachidonic acid at concentrations as low as 0.3 μg/mL (approximately 1 μM) stimulated Ca^{2+} uptake by brain synaptosomes without causing a substantial increase in the formation of TBAR products (**Figure 3**). The results from these and other studies suggest that lipid peroxidation may increase the permeability of membranes to Ca^{2+} through the formation and release of fatty acids and their oxidation products.

DEFEROXAMINE INHIBITION OF Fe^{2+}-DEPENDENT CALCIUM UPTAKE

Deferoxamine (desferrioxamine B methanesulfonate) inhibits lipid peroxidation and prevents the formation of lipid peroxidation reaction products under a variety of experimental conditions involving iron (33). Addition of 500 μM deferoxamine to incubations containing synaptosomes and 200 μM Fe^{2+} in Krebs buffer completely blocked TBAR product formation. Deferoxamine also blocked Fe^{2+}-dependent uptake of Ca^{2+} (**Table 1**). In contrast, various Ca^{2+} channel blocking agents, while in some instances significantly decreasing Ca^{2+} uptake in the absence of Fe^{2+}, did not affect the Ca^{2+} uptake attributable to lipid peroxidation (Table 1).

The failure of Ca^{2+} channel blockers to inhibit the iron-dependent accumulation of Ca^{2+} suggested that changes in membrane permeability to Ca^{2+} resulted from lipid peroxidation-induced damage which opened nonspecific channels or holes within the membrane. Chien et al (34) have presented evidence that sarcolemmal vesicles isolated from ischemic myocardium have an increased permeability to Ca^{2+} that was associated with depletion of phosphatidylcholine. It is possible that degradation of membrane phospholipids leads to changes in the structural integrity of membranes sufficient to alter their permeability characteristics. Certainly, the nonspecificity of the Ca^{2+} influx resulting from lipid peroxidation may be related to generalized deterioration of membrane structure and the membrane lipid components.

LIPID PEROXIDATION AND INCREASED ARACHIDONIC ACID RELEASE FROM CELLS

Au et al (35) have examined the stimulation of membrane phospholipase A_2 activity in isolated brain capillaries by oxygen radicals. In their studies, an exogenous oxygen radical-generating system (xanthine oxidase/hypoxanthine/ADP-Fe^{3+}) induced a significant degradation of membrane phospholipids that was mediated by an activation of phospholipase A_2. The degradation of phospholipid was coincident with an increase in free fatty acid concentrations, particularly of the 20:4 and 22:6 acids, with substantial increases also seen in 18:1 and 18:2 acids. Interestingly, EGTA (ethylene glycol bis(β-aminoethyl ether)-N,N,N',N'-tetraacetic acid) abolished the action of oxygen radicals on phospholipid breakdown and fatty acid release, suggesting a role for extracellular Ca^{2+} in the activation of phospholipase A_2 by oxygen radicals.

The effects of lipid peroxidation on Ca^{2+} uptake

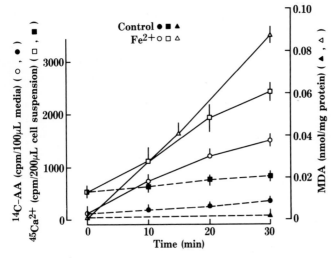

Figure 4. Ca^{2+} uptake, arachidonic acid (AA) release, and TBAR product formation in cultured spinal cord neurons. Fetal mouse spinal cord neurons (28) were preincubated for 4 hours with 160 μCi [^{14}C]-AA (60 mCi/mmol) to label membrane phospholipids. After preincubation, cultures were rinsed with Krebs buffer and incubated in fresh Krebs buffer for another 30 minutes at 35°C. After this incubation, 10 μM $^{45}Ca^{2+}$ (800 mCi/mmol) was added. Ca^{2+} uptake ($\square$, $\blacksquare$) was determined at the times indicated by washing cells twice in Ca^{2+}-free Krebs containing 1 mM LaCl$_3$ and dissolving cells in 1 N NaOH for counting. Protein was determined as described elsewhere (28). Arachidonic acid release into the incubation medium (o, $\bullet$) was assessed by scintillation counting of 100 μL aliquots of the medium. TBAR product (MDA) formation in cells ($\triangle$, $\blacktriangle$) was determined by washing cells in fresh Krebs buffer and then adding 500 μL of 0.8 N HCl containing 12.5% trichloroacetic acid and 0.05% butylated hydroxytoluene. Cells were removed by scraping, and TBAR product concentration was determined as described elsewhere (38). Data are mean ± SE of duplicate assays from four cultures.

and arachidonic acid release from intact cells have been examined in cultured spinal cord neurons. Addition of Fe^{2+} to cultured cells resulted in lipid peroxidation as evidenced by the formation of TBAR products (**Figure 4**). The increased formation of lipid peroxidation products was accompanied by an accumulation of intracellular Ca^{2+} and a parallel release of arachidonic acid into the culture medium. These studies agree with those of Au et al (35) and argue for the participation of Ca^{2+} in the release of fatty acid in response to a peroxidative insult.

While it is generally believed that Ca^{2+} mobilization is crucial for the activation of phospholipases, studies by Sevanian and coworkers have argued differently (36,37). In a recent report, Sevanian and Kim (36) demonstrated that phospholipase A$_2$ can be activated in the absence of Ca^{2+} by the presence of peroxidized fatty acids in the phospholipids. The degree of phospholipase activation was correlated with the extent of lipid peroxidation as measured by the formation of TBAR products. Interestingly, although phospholipase A$_2$ has been shown to have a preference for removing oxidized fatty acids from phospholipids (37), once activated by the presence of oxidized lipid, phospholipase activity

is relatively indiscriminate and will catalyze the release of intact fatty acids as well. These results indicate that lipid peroxidation may induce the degradation of phospholipids by at least two mechanisms, one involving Ca^{2+} and one requiring the presence of oxidized lipid.

CALCIUM ENHANCEMENT OF LIPID PEROXIDATION RATES

In addition to enhancing the damage to membrane function resulting from lipid peroxidation, Ca^{2+} may also enhance lipid peroxidation rates. **Figure 5** shows the rate of lipid peroxidation in purified brain synaptosomes as measured by the uptake of O_2 following the addition of Fe^{2+}. In previous studies, Braughler et al (38) have demonstrated that in unbuffered saline lipid peroxidation proceeds slowly after the addition of 200 μM Fe^{2+}. Under such conditions, lipid

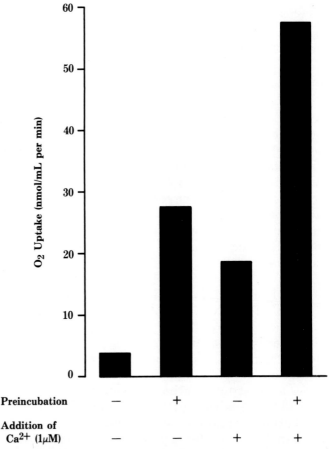

Figure 5. Enhancement of Fe^{2+}-dependent lipid peroxidation by Ca^{2+}. Brain synaptosomes were prepared in unbuffered 0.9% NaCl (pH adjusted to 7.0) and incubated at 37°C in 0.9% NaCl (synaptosomal protein 0.1 mg/mL). Lipid peroxidation during the first 10 minutes after the addition of 200 μM Fe^{2+} was measured by the consumption of O_2 as described elsewhere (38). In some cases, synaptosomes were preincubated for 5 minutes in the presence or absence of 1 μM Ca^{2+}, as indicated, prior to addition of Fe^{2+}. Data are expressed as the mean linear rate of O_2 consumption during the 10 minutes after addition of Fe^{2+}.

UPJOHN SYMPOSIUM / OXYGEN RADICALS April 1987

peroxidation depends upon formation of a suitable Fe^{2+}/Fe^{3+} ratio. The importance of the iron ratio in the initiation of lipid peroxidation has subsequently been supported by similar studies by Minotti and Aust (39). Under the conditions described for Figure 5, little peroxidation occurred during a 20-minute incubation in the presence of Fe^{2+} as evidenced by the slow rate of O_2 consumption and TBAR product formation (see also reference 38). The rate of lipid peroxidation was markedly increased, however, by the addition of $1\,\mu M$ Ca^{2+}. Similar results were obtained with Ca^{2+} concentrations as low as $0.1\,\mu M$; concentrations of $10\,\mu M$ and higher maximally stimulated lipid peroxidation (not shown). Preincubation of the synaptosomes for five minutes either in the absence or presence of Ca^{2+} further enhanced the rate of lipid peroxidation in comparison to that observed with nonpreincubated synaptosomes. The effects of Ca^{2+} on the rate of lipid peroxidation were not apparent when optimal iron conditions (such as an optimal Fe^{2+}/Fe^{3+} ratio) were used to stimulate lipid peroxidation (not shown). Clearly, however, under certain in vitro conditions where lipid peroxidation rates are slow, stimulation or acceleration of lipid peroxidation by Ca^{2+} can be observed.

CONCLUSIONS

The pathophysiology of traumatic and ischemic cell injury is, at our current level of understanding, a complex chain of cellular events which synergistically and relentlessly leads to the demise of affected cells. Based upon the results reported here, the concept of an intimate interaction between lipid peroxidation and Ca^{2+} in the pathophysiology of ischemic cell death fits well into such a scheme. Lipid peroxidation, either under less than optimal conditions or perhaps occurring quite explosively and intensely in discrete cellular domains, may be expected to alter membrane permeability to Ca^{2+} by several mechanisms. An increased concentration of Ca^{2+} intracellularly could theoretically act either to enhance lipid peroxidation reactions further or to stimulate the degradation of phospholipids. In addition, a Ca^{2+}-independent activation of phospholipid breakdown may exist. Once fatty acids begin to be released from membranes, they may bring more Ca^{2+} into the cells by acting as ionophores. Further enhancement of membrane Ca^{2+} permeability would be expected to result directly from the disruption of membrane phospholipids. The metabolism of released fatty acids to prostaglandins and other eicosanoids is known to result in the generation of oxygen radicals and lipid hydroperoxides, which may themselves further aggravate the spread of ischemic injury (3,4,31,40-42). It is clear that a complex relationship between Ca^{2+}

and lipid peroxidation may exist, which fits well within the scheme of pathological events associated with ischemic cell injury. The data presented in this report, as well as numerous studies by others, support the hypothesis that Ca^{2+} and lipid peroxidation are intimately involved in certain types of cellular injury. Certainly, whenever oxygen radicals are involved in membrane damage, Ca^{2+} must be suspected as a participant.

REFERENCES

1. Bhakoo KK, Crockard HA, Lascelles PT. Regional studies of changes in brain fatty acids following experimental ischaemia and reperfusion in the gerbil. J Neurochem 1984:43:1025-1031.

2. Hillered L, Siesjo BK, Arfors KE. Mitochondrial response to transient forebrain ischemia and recirculation in the rat. J Cereb Blood Flow Metab 1984:4:438-446.

3. Siesjo BK. Cell damage in the brain: a speculative synthesis. J Cereb Blood Flow Metab 1981:1:155-185.

4. Siesjo BK. Cerebral circulation and metabolism. J Neurosurg 1984:60:883-908.

5. Chan PH, Schmidley JW, Fishman RA, Longar SM. Brain injury, edema, and vascular permeability changes induced by oxygen-derived free radicals. Neurology 1984:34:315-320.

6. Goldberg WJ, Watson BD, Busto R, Kurchner H, Santiso M, Ginsberg MD. Concurrent measurement of (Na^+, K^+)-ATPase activity and lipid peroxides in rat brain following reversible global ischemia. Neurochem Res 1984:9:1737-1747.

7. Watson BD, Busto R, Goldberg WJ, Santiso M, Yoshida S, Ginsberg MD. Lipid peroxidation in vivo induced by reversible global ischemia in rat brain. J Neurochem 1984:42:268-274.

8. Hall ED, Braughler JM. Effects of intravenous methylprednisolone on spinal cord lipid peroxidation and Na^+, K^+-ATPase activity: dose-response analysis during the first hour after contusion injury in the cat. J Neurosurg 1982:57:247-253.

9. Imaizumi S, Kayama T, Suzuki J. Chemiluminescence in hypoxic brain. The first report: correlation between energy metabolism and free radical reactions. Stroke 1984:15:1061-1065.

10. Kurihara M. Role of monoamines in experimental spinal cord injury in rats: relationship between Na^+, K^+-ATPase and lipid peroxidation. J Neurosurg 1985:62:743-749.

11. Seligman ML, Flamm ES, Goldstein BD, Poser RG, Demopoulos HB, Ransohoff J. Spectrofluorescent detection of malonaldehyde as a measure of lipid free radical damage in response to ethanol potentiation of spinal cord trauma. Lipids 1977:12:945-950.

12. Farber JL. Biology of disease: membrane injury and calcium homeostasis in the pathogenesis of coagulative necrosis. Lab Invest 1982:47:114-123.

13. Stokes BT, Fox P, Hallinden G. Extracellular calcium activity in the injured spinal cord. Exp Neurol 1983:80:561-572.

14. Young W, Yen V, Blight A. Extracellular calcium ionic

activity in experimental spinal cord contusion. Brain Res 1982:253:105-113.

15. Crockard HA, Bhakoo KK, Lascelles PT. Regional prostaglandin levels in cerebral ischaemia. J Neurochem 1982:38:1311-1314.

16. Roy RS, McCord JM. Superoxide and ischemia: conversion of xanthine dehydrogenase to xanthine oxidase. In: Greenwald R, Cohen G, eds. Proceedings of the third international conference on superoxide and superoxide dismutase. New York: Elsevier, 1983:145-153.

17. Banik NL, Hogan EL, Whetstine LJ, Balentine JD. Changes in myelin and axonal proteins in $CaCl_2$-induced myelopathy in rat spinal cord. CNS Trauma 1984:1:131-137.

18. Braughler JM, Hall ED. Effects of multidose methylprednisolone sodium succinate administration on injured cat spinal cord neurofilament degradation and energy metabolism. J Neurosurg 1984:61:290-295.

19. Casini AF, Farber JL. Dependence of the carbon tetrachloride-induced death of cultured hepatocytes on the extracellular calcium concentration. Am J Pathol 1981:105:138-148.

20. Casini AF, Giorli M, Hyland RJ, Serroni A, Gilfor D, Farber JL. Mechanisms of cell injury in the killing of cultured hepatocytes by bromobenzene. J Biol Chem 1982:257:6721-6728.

21. Barsacchi R, Camici P, Bottigli U, et al. Correlation between hydroperoxide-induced chemiluminescence of the heart and its function. Biochim Biophys Acta 1983:762:241-247.

22. Enseleit WH, Domer FR, Jarrott DM, Baricos WH. Cerebral phospholipid content and Na^+,K^+-ATPase activity during ischemia and postischemic reperfusion in the Mongolian gerbil. J Neurochem 1984:43:320-327.

23. Strong AJ, Tomlinson BE, Venables GS, Gibson G, Hardy JA. The cortical ischaemic penumbra associated with occlusion of the middle cerebral artery in the cat. II. Studies of histopathology, water content and in vitro neurotransmitter uptake. J Cereb Blood Flow Metab 1983:3:97-108.

24. Braughler JM. Lipid peroxidation-induced inhibition of γ-aminobutyric acid uptake in rat brain synaptosomes: protection by glucocorticoids. J Neurochem 1985:44:1282-1288.

25. Chan PH, Kerlan R, Fishman RA. Reductions of γ-aminobutyric acid and glutamate uptake and Na^+, K^+-ATPase activity in brain slices and synaptosomes by arachidonic acid. J Neurochem 1983:40:309-316.

26. Hillered L, Ernster L. Respiratory activity of isolated rat brain mitochondria following in vitro exposure to oxygen radicals. J Cereb Blood Flow Metab 1983:3:207-214.

27. Anderson DK, Means ED. Iron-initiated lipid peroxidation in murine spinal cord cultures. Soc Neurosci Abstr 1985:11:523.

28. Braughler JM, Duncan LA, Goodman T. Calcium enhances in vitro free radical-induced damage to brain synaptosomes, mitochondria, and cultured spinal cord neurons. J Neurochem 1985:45:1288-1293.

29. Malis CD, Bonventre JV. Mechanism of calcium potentiation of oxygen free radical injury to renal mitochondria: a model for post-ischemic and toxic mitochondrial damage. J Biol Chem 1986:261:14201-14208.

30. Philipson KD, Ward R. Effects of fatty acids on Na^+-Ca^{2+} exchange and Ca^{2+} permeability of cardiac sarcolemmal vesicles. J Biol Chem 1985:260:9666-9671.

31. Siesjo BK, Wieloch T. Molecular mechanisms of ischemic brain damage: Ca^{2+}-related events. In: Plum F, Pulsinelli W, eds. Cerebrovascular diseases. New York: Raven Press, 1985:187-198.

32. Watras J, Messineo FC, Herbette LG. Mechanisms of fatty acid effects on sarcoplasmic reticulum. I. Calcium-fatty acid interaction. J Biol Chem 1984:259:1319-1324.

33. Aust SD, Morehouse LA, Thomas CE. Role of metals in oxygen radical reactions. J Free Rad Biol Med 1985:1:3-25.

34. Chien KR, Reeves JP, Buja LM, Bonte F, Parkey RW, Willerson JT. Phospholipid alterations in canine ischemic myocardium: temporal and topographical correlations with Tc-99m-PPi accumulation and an in vitro sarcolemmal Ca^{2+} permeability defect. Circ Res 1981:48:711-719.

35. Au AM, Chan PH, Fishman RA. Stimulation of phospholipase A_2 activity by oxygen-derived free radicals in isolated brain capillaries. J Cell Biochem 1985:27:449-453.

36. Sevanian A, Kim E. Phospholipase A_2 dependent release of fatty acids from peroxidized membranes. J Free Rad Biol Med 1985:1:263-271.

37. Sevanian A, Stein RA, Mead JF. Metabolism of epoxidized phosphatidylcholine by phospholipase A_2 and epoxide hydrolase. Lipids 1981:16:781-789.

38. Braughler JM, Duncan LA, Chase RL. The involvement of iron in lipid peroxidation: importance of ferric to ferrous ratios in initiation. J Biol Chem 1986:261:10282-10289.

39. Minotti G, Aust SD. The requirement for iron (III) in the initiation of lipid peroxidation by iron (II) and hydrogen peroxide. J Biol Chem 1987:262:1098-1104.

40. Demopoulos HB, Flamm ES, Petronigro DD, Seligman ML. The free radical pathology and the microcirculation in the major central nervous system disorders. Acta Physiol Scand 1980:Suppl 492:91-119.

41. Sano K, Asano T, Tanishima T, Sasaki T. Lipid peroxidation as a cause of cerebral vasospasm. Neurol Res 1980:2:253-272.

42. Lands WE. Interactions of lipid hydroperoxides with eicosanoid biosynthesis. J Free Rad Biol Med 1985:1:97-101.

V. PHAGOCYTIC CELLS, OXYGEN RADICALS, AND ORGAN INJURY

Richard B. Johnston, Jr., *Session Chairman*

IMMUNE COMPLEXES, OXYGEN RADICALS, AND LUNG INJURY

Peter A. Ward, Kent J. Johnson, Jeffrey S. Warren, and Robin G. Kunkel

The pathogenesis of the acute lung injury resulting from the deposition of immune complexes differs depending on whether the immune complex contains IgG or IgA antibodies. This paper describes the differences and proposes some mechanisms explaining these differences. For example, the IgG immune complex-induced injury depends on the presence of neutrophils, whereas the IgA-related injury does not. This difference may play a role in the different sensitivities of each system to superoxide dismutase (SOD); the insensitivity of the IgG-related injury to SOD may reflect the greater amount of superoxide generated in this system (by the large number of recruited neutrophils), overwhelming the ability of SOD to dispose of superoxide. Further studies of the IgA-related injury show that toxic oxygen products are generated by alveolar but not interstitial macrophages. For both IgG- and IgA-related injuries, macrophages appear to be primed by soluble products (released by activated macrophages), so that the production of toxic oxygen products is enhanced when the macrophages are subsequently stimulated by immune complexes. These studies are beginning to identify and untangle the complicated and interlinked pathways by which immune complexes induce lung damage.

THE TRIGGERING of an acute inflammatory response in the lungs of rats, by deposits of immune complexes containing IgG antibody, results in a complicated series of humoral and cellular reactions culminating in acute lung injury. It has been known for some time that immune complex deposition in dermal vessel walls generates products of complement activation that increase vascular permeability and bring about recruitment of neutrophils from the blood. Indeed, depletion of complement or of neutrophils abrogates immune complex-induced tissue injury (1-3). Because superoxide dismutase (SOD) protects against immune complex-induced vascular injury (4,5), one suggestion is that superoxide ($O_2^{\cdot-}$) and perhaps other oxygen products directly participate in producing the injury. Another suggestion is that $O_2^{\cdot-}$ may act indirectly, by generating a chemotactic lipid that amplifies the recruitment of neutrophils and thereby intensifies the inflammatory response (4,6). SOD has transient protective effects against lung injury induced by the deposition of IgG-containing immune complexes (7). Catalase, however, has sustained protective effects, suggesting that H_2O_2 or its derivatives are important in the events leading to injury. Recently, we have demonstrated that immune complexes containing IgA also produce oxygen radical-mediated acute lung

From Department of Pathology, The University of Michigan Medical School, Ann Arbor, Michigan, USA.

Address correspondence to Dr. Peter A. Ward, Department of Pathology, The University of Michigan Medical School, M5240 Medical Science I, Box 0602, Ann Arbor, Michigan 48109-0602, USA.

injury (8), but the effector cells in this reaction appear to be tissue macrophages rather than neutrophils (9). In this paper, we compare and contrast the pathogenic events involved in acute lung injury mediated by IgG- and IgA-containing immune complexes.

MEDIATORS REQUIRED FOR IMMUNE COMPLEX-INDUCED LUNG INJURY

Murine IgG and IgA monoclonal antibodies, each of which is reactive with the same hapten (dinitrophenol coupled to an albumin carrier), as well as polyclonal IgG rabbit antibody to bovine serum albumin, all induce acute lung injury in rats when the antibody is delivered into the airways, followed by intravenous injection of antigen. Our recent studies have defined the mediators required for this damage (**Table 1**). To deplete the complement levels, we used cobra venom factor, and to deplete the number of blood neutrophils, we used antibody specifically reactive with the rat neutrophil. The acute lung injury (defined by an increased vascular permeability and by morphometric analysis) produced by monoclonal IgG antibody depends on the availability of both neutrophils and complement. A similar pattern of mediator requirements is found in lung injury induced with rabbit polyclonal IgG antibody to bovine serum albumin. However, acute lung injury produced by IgA-immune complexes requires complement but not neutrophils: neutrophil depletion did not diminish the intensity of lung injury, whereas complement depletion had protective effects similar to those found when IgG-immune complexes are used.

The morphological features of lungs injured by immune complexes were determined by transmission electron microscopy (**Figure 1**). IgG-Immune complexes have caused considerable alveolar and vascular injury as shown by the presence of proteinaceous material and red cells within the alveolar compartment (Figure 1A). Neutrophils are prominent within the microvascular and interstitial compartments (solid arrowheads). In contrast, lungs damaged by IgA-immune complexes (Figure 1B) show few if any neutrophils within the tissue. Evidence of injury is found in the presence of red cells and fibrin (solid arrows) within the alveolar compartment. The extensive damage to, or destruction of, alveolar epithelial cells seen at higher magnifications (data not shown) exposes the alveolar wall basement membrane to the alveolar compartment. In IgA-immune complex-induced reactions, alveolar

Table 1. Mediators Required for IgG- and IgA-Immune Complex-Induced Lung Injury In the Rat*

Immune Complex	Source	Reduction (%) in Injury[†]	
		With Neutrophil Depletion	With Complement Depletion
Monoclonal IgG	Mouse	76.9	61.5
Polyclonal IgG	Rabbit	86.3	66.3
Monoclonal IgA	Mouse	7.6	64.1

* Based on data in references 7 and 8.
† As measured by changes in vascular permeability.

macrophages are prominent and found within alveolar spaces (Figure 1B, open arrows). Thus, there are distinctive morphological differences between the acute lung injury produced by IgG- or by IgA-immune complexes. These are entirely compatible with the data for mediator requirements (Table 1).

EVIDENCE FOR THE ROLE OF OXYGEN-DERIVED PRODUCTS IN IMMUNE COMPLEX-INDUCED LUNG INJURY

Previous studies have provided clear evidence that the lung injury produced in rats by polyclonal

IgG-immune complexes involves oxygen-derived species (5,7). The data (**Table 2**) show that catalase has strong protective effects against lung injury caused by the deposition of IgG-immune complexes. Although SOD demonstrated protective effects at one and two hours, these effects had disappeared by three hours after deposition of the IgG-immune complex (5). Recent evidence suggests that IgG-immune complex-induced injury in rat lung is iron-dependent, as demonstrated by the ability of deferoxamine (desferrioxamine B methanesulfonate) to protect against injury (Table 2). Further details of the steps involved in the pathogenesis of IgG-immune complex-mediated lung injury are not known at present.

For lung injury induced by IgA-immune complex, both catalase and SOD had pronounced protective effects, as did the hydroxyl radical (·OH) scavenger dimethysulfoxide (Table 2). Animals pretreated with deferoxamine were also highly protected against the injury, whereas those treated with iron-saturated deferoxamine had no protection. These data suggest that mediator requirements for IgA-immune complex-induced lung injury include the generation of $O_2^{·-}$ and H_2O_2 and the availability of iron. It is possible that oxygen-containing iron radicals (ferryl and perferryl ions) or ·OH may be the key products

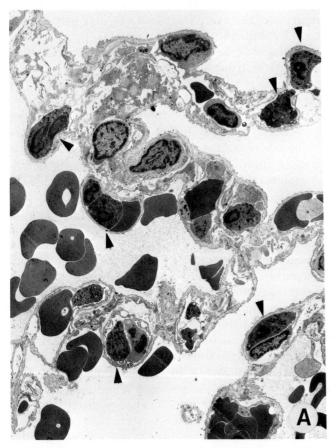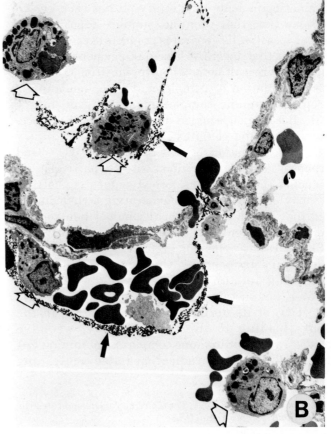

Figure 1. Transmission electron microscopy of rat lungs 2 hours after deposition of immune complexes containing IgG (frame A) or IgA (frame B). Neutrophils (solid arrowheads) are common in the IgG immune complex-induced reaction, whereas alveolar macrophages (open arrows) and fibrin (solid arrows) are prominent in the IgA-immune complex-induced reaction. (Uranyl acetate, lead citrate, X2100)

Table 2. Patterns of Oxygen Metabolite Involvement in Immune Complex-Induced Lung Injury*

Immune Complex Model	Addition†	Reduction (%) in Lung Injury at 3 hr**
IgG	Catalase	78
	Superoxide dismutase	0
	Deferoxamine	53
IgA	Catalase	95.5
	Superoxide dismutase	87.8
	Dimethyl sulfoxide	100
	Deferoxamine	77.3
	Iron-saturated deferoxamine	0

* Data from references 5, 7, 8, and 9 and, for the IgG-immune complex–deferoxamine experiment, from unpublished data (J.S. Warren, K.J. Johnson, and P.A. Ward).

† Amount of reagents used: catalase 44 000 U, superoxide dismutase 46 000 U, dimethyl sulfoxide 2 mL, deferoxamine 10 mg.

** As measured by changes in vascular permeability.

involved in tissue damage in the lung. The strong protective effects of dimethylsulfoxide would be consistent with a role for ·OH. The possibility that myeloperoxidase-derived products such as hypochlorous acid (HOCl), chloramines, or dichloramines are related to the injury does not explain the requirement for iron. In addition, the very low content of myeloperoxidase in alveolar macrophages suggests that halide-dependent products of H_2O_2 may not be a major contributor to the lung injury, although some role for halide derivatives cannot be ruled out.

In an attempt to define more clearly the sources of oxygen products involved in the model of IgA-immune complex-induced injury, we have used a histochemical technique in which cerium chloride forms an electron-dense product (cerium perhydroxide) in the presence of H_2O_2 (10). In brief, cerium chloride is instilled into rat lungs at the time of sacrifice (two hours after airway instillation of IgA antibody, which was followed immediately by intravenous injection of antigen). The lungs are inflated with glutaraldehyde and then processed for transmission electron microscopy. Characteristic results of these studies are shown in **Figures 2** and **3**. The electron-dense (black) particles (Figure 2A, open and solid arrows) represent cerium perhydroxide which, in turn, reflects the presence of H_2O_2. These particles are distributed along the surface of the alveolar wall that is covered

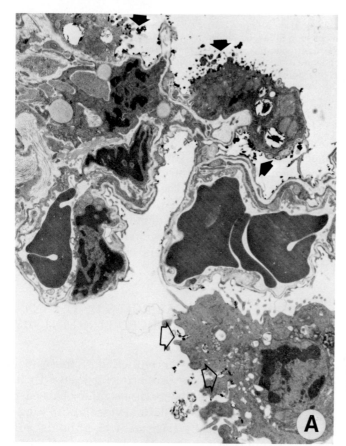 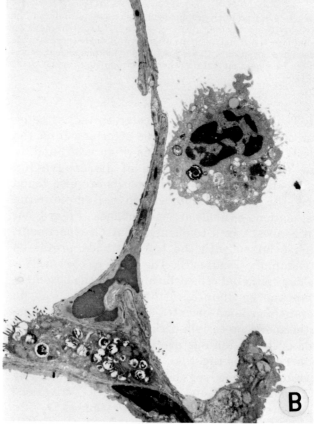

Figure 2. Transmission electron microscopy of IgA-immune complex-induced injured rat lung at 2 hours. In frame A, electron-dense particles of cerium perhydroxide are present along alveolar macrophages (open arrows) and alveolar epithelial cells (solid arrows). These particles indicate the presence of H_2O_2. In frame B, catalase was co-instilled with the IgA antibody. No morphological evidence of injury is found; there are no deposits of cerium perhydroxide. (Uranyl acetate, lead citrate; A, X6000; B, X4300)

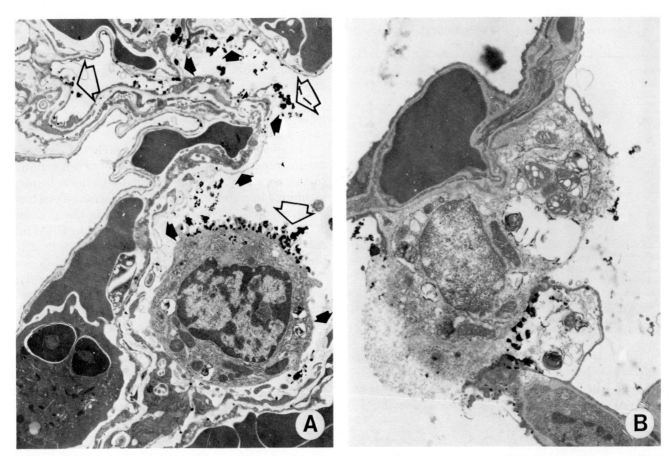

Figure 3. Electron micrographic evidence of oxidant-induced injury in rat lung following deposition of IgA-immune complexes. Cerium perhydroxide deposits indicate the presence of H_2O_2. In frame A, cerium perhydroxide deposits (open arrows) are found along the surface of an alveolar type II cell and along the alveolar wall where there is evidence of denudation of the basement membrane (solid arrows). No deposits are seen in association with the vascular polymorphonuclear neutrophils. In frame B, a disintegrating alveolar epithelial cell has separated from the basement membrane where electron-dense cerium perhydroxide deposits are present. (Uranyl acetate, lead citrate; A, X7250; B, X9150)

with Type I and Type II alveolar epithelial cells. Some of the latter appear to be detaching from the underlying basement membrane (Figure 3A) and, in some areas, show evidence of disintegration (Figure 3B). Electron-dense deposits are also found along the surface and within cell membrane invaginations of alveolar macrophages (Figure 2A, open arrows). In a companion control experiment, catalase mixed with the IgA antibody protected against injury (Figure 2B). There was no evidence for alveolar epithelial cells detaching from the basement membrane or disintegrating, and there was no interstitial edema or intra-alveolar hemorrhage. Furthermore, no cerium perhydroxide deposits were found. These findings are consistent with recent studies (9) showing that alveolar macrophages, harvested from the lungs of rats undergoing injury by IgA-immune complexes, are in a state of "activation" as revealed by spontaneous generation of $O_2^{\cdot-}$ in vitro and supernormal production of $O_2^{\cdot-}$ after addition of phorbol ester in vitro.

The absence of electron dense deposits within the interstitial (Figure 2A) and vascular (Figure 3A)

compartments suggests that the alveolar macrophages, but not interstitial macrophages or blood neutrophils, are the source of the toxic oxygen products responsible for the lung injury. Companion control studies in which the rats did not receive antigen injections have demonstrated that the electron-dense products shown in Figure 2 require the presence of both antigen and antibody (data not shown).

POSSIBLE BIOLOGICAL ROLES OF $O_2^{\cdot-}$ IN IMMUNE COMPLEX-INDUCED LUNG INJURY

There is a large body of conflicting evidence about the role of $O_2^{\cdot-}$ in the induction of acute tissue injury. As described above, tissue injury caused by IgG-immune complexes in dermal vessels or in lung is greatly diminished by treatment of animals with SOD, although in the lung the protective effects of SOD are transient. The protective effects of SOD appear to be related to a diminished influx of neutrophils into tissues (4,5); this is consistent with the concept that $O_2^{\cdot-}$ is somehow involved in the recruitment of neutrophils, perhaps through generation of a chemotactic lipid (4,6). On this basis, $O_2^{\cdot-}$ would only be functioning indirectly to produce tissue injury by amplifying the recruitment of neutrophils. The transient nature of the protective effects of SOD could be explained by the overriding action of C5a, which would be generated in progressively increasing amounts as more immune complexes became deposited in the lung tissue and more complement activation occurred. In time, C5a would replace the functional role of a superoxide-generated chemotactic lipid.

In contrast, in acute lung injury induced by IgA-immune complexes, SOD has sustained protective effects (Table 2). This paradox might be explained by the data in **Figure 4**, where the amounts of $O_2^{\cdot-}$ generated in lung have been calculated from the numbers of inflammatory cells involved in the IgG- and IgA-induced lung damage. The numbers are based on actual measurements of the numbers of inflammatory cells retrieved from bronchoalveolar lavage and from direct in vitro measurements of the superoxide-generating capacities of neutrophils and lung macrophages (8,11). Because of the lack of measurable recruitment of neutrophils into IgA-immune complex-induced reactions, the $O_2^{\cdot-}$ would be generated by the alveolar macrophages in an amount we estimated to be approximately 100 nmol in a two-hour period. In contrast, because of the large number of neutrophils recruited into the alveolar compartment of lungs injured by deposition of IgG-immune complexes, the amounts of $O_2^{\cdot-}$ generated were calculated to be considerably higher (at least threefold higher) than that produced by alveolar macrophages. Accordingly, in the IgA-immune complex-induced reaction, virtually all $O_2^{\cdot-}$ generated could be intercepted by externally administered SOD, causing immediate dismutation to H_2O_2, whereas in the IgG-immune complex-induced reaction, the dismutation of the larger quantities of $O_2^{\cdot-}$ by SOD would be less efficient. Assuming that $O_2^{\cdot-}$ plays a key role in promoting the reduction (and thus the availability) of ferritin-associated iron from Fe^{3+} to Fe^{2+}, the differences in total amounts of $O_2^{\cdot-}$ generated in the two models of immune complex-induced lung injury may explain why SOD is so much more effective in protecting against IgA-immune complex-induced lung injury.

These speculations assume that iron, as Fe^{2+}, must become available in order to facilitate formation of $\cdot OH$ (9). It is possible that $O_2^{\cdot-}$ could play different roles in the pathogenesis of acute tissue injury triggered by immune complexes, one role involving formation of a chemotactic lipid and the other related to making iron available for the reduction of H_2O_2 to $\cdot OH$.

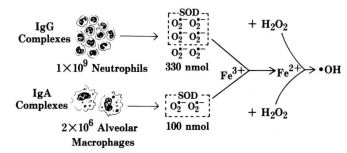

Figure 4. Postulated explanation for the sustained protective effects of superoxide dismutase (SOD) against lung injury induced by IgA-immune complexes but not by IgG-immune complexes. Externally administered SOD may be unable to dispose of the greater amounts of $O_2^{\cdot-}$ generated by the neutrophils in the IgG-related injury.

POSSIBLE ROLE OF MACROPHAGE PRODUCTS IN OXYGEN RADICAL-MEDIATED INJURY

There is abundant evidence that products of activated macrophages play a key role in tissue injury. As indicated above, oxygen products from tissue macrophages and rat neutrophils seem to be important in the development of acute lung injury after deposition of IgA- or IgG-immune complexes. Evidence is accumulating that products of stimulated macrophages, including interleukin-1 (IL-1) and tumor necrosis factor (TNF), may directly stimulate neutrophils and monocytes to generate oxygen radicals (12,13). Experiments to investigate the role of macrophage products in immune complex-induced lung injury have been carried out. Rat alveolar macrophages (5×10^5 cells) were exposed to IgG-immune complexes in the presence or absence of supernatant fluids from alveolar macrophages that had been permitted to phagocytose opsonized zymosan particles. In the presence of these supernatant fluids, the amount of $O_2^{\cdot-}$ generated over a 30-minute period was approximately 44% more than that generated in the absence of the fluids (**Figure 5**). Supernatant fluids from zymosan-stimulated macrophages did not themselves induce $O_2^{\cdot-}$ generation in macrophages (Figure 5), and supernatant fluids from nonstimulated macrophages did not enhance $O_2^{\cdot-}$ production by immune complex-activated alveolar macrophages (data not shown). Thus, supernatant fluids from zymosan-stimulated macrophages can enhance $O_2^{\cdot-}$ production by alveolar macrophages activated with immune complexes.

The possibility was pursued that the effects described in Figure 5 might be related to macrophage products such as IL-1 or TNF. Experiments were carried out using recombinant human TNF or purified human IL-1. The results are shown in **Figure 6**. Human IL-1 enhanced $O_2^{\cdot-}$ responses in rat alveolar macrophages incubated with immune complexes, whereas IL-1 in the absence of the immune complexes

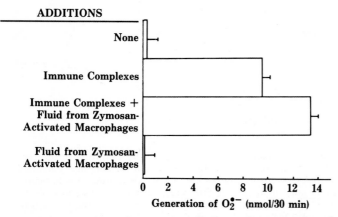

ADDITIONS

Figure 5. The effect of supernatant fluids on the generation of $O_2^{\cdot-}$ (mean $\pm$SE) by rat alveolar macrophages. The addition of supernatant fluids from stimulated rat alveolar macrophages enhanced $O_2^{\cdot-}$ generation by other alveolar macrophages incubated with IgG-immune complexes.

did not cause $O_2^{\cdot-}$ responses exceeding the control values. Human TNF was less effective, but enhanced $O_2^{\cdot-}$ responses somewhat in rat alveolar macrophages incubated in the presence, but not in the absence, of immune complexes.

As illustrated in **Figure 7**, these data suggest that products of stimulated alveolar macrophages may exert positive feedback effects on $O_2^{\cdot-}$ responses of macrophages undergoing activation by immune complexes or other agonists. In other words, contact of rat alveolar macrophages with supernatant fluids from stimulated macrophages, with TNF or with IL-1, "primes" the macrophages for a supernormal $O_2^{\cdot-}$ response initiated by subsequent contact with immune complexes. The combined effects of this positive feedback (Figure 7) and the direct stimulatory effects of immune complexes on macrophages could amplify the generation of toxic oxygen products. C5a has also been found to prime

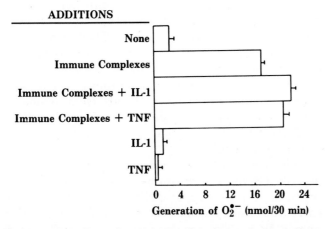

ADDITIONS

Figure 6. The effects of recombinant human interleukin-1 (IL-1) and recombinant human tumor necrosis factor (TNF) on the generation of $O_2^{\cdot-}$ (mean $\pm$SE) by rat alveolar macrophages. The addition of IL-1 and TNF enhanced $O_2^{\cdot-}$ generation by alveolar macrophages incubated with IgG-immune complexes.

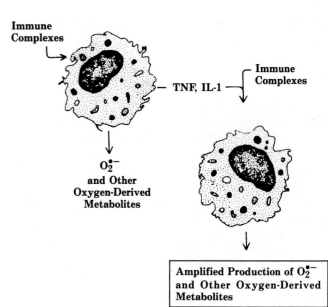

Figure 7. Proposed steps by which the $O_2^{\cdot-}$ production of lung macrophages stimulated by immune complexes is amplified by a positive feedback mechanism. Immune complexes stimulate macrophages to generate $O_2^{\cdot-}$ and also to release tumor necrosis factor (TNF) and interleukin-1 (IL-1). The TNF and IL-1 prime other macrophages so that when those macrophages are, in turn, stimulated by immune complexes, $O_2^{\cdot-}$ production is amplified.

macrophages for enhanced $O_2^{\cdot-}$ production in the presence of immune complexes (data not shown).

Although direct proof of the mechanism for IgA-immune complex-induced acute lung injury is not yet available, we propose the following sequence of pathogenic events:

1. Deposition of IgA-immune complexes, resulting in limited complement activation and C5a generation and the activation of alveolar macrophages by immune complexes;
2. Release of IL-1 or TNF or both from macrophages;
3. Priming of other alveolar macrophages by C5a, IL-1, and TNF;
4. Contact of these primed alveolar macrophages with IgA-immune complexes, resulting in enhanced oxygen radical generation; and, finally,
5. Tissue injury.

SUMMARY

Our studies have identified differences in the pathogenesis of the lung damage induced by IgG-immune complexes and by IgA-immune complexes: the two types of damage have different mediator requirements and have somewhat different sensitivities to compounds that alter oxygen radical metabolism. Although these studies have begun to answer some of the questions about the mechanisms by which immune complex-induced lung damage occurs, they also reveal that this damage is mediated by remarkably complicated and interlinked pathways.

REFERENCES

1. Cochrane CG, Weigle WO, Dixon FJ. The role of polymorphonuclear leukocytes in the initiation and cessation of the Arthus vasculitis. J Exp Med 1959:110:481-494.

2. Ward PA, Cochrane CG. Bound complement and immunologic injury of blood vessels. J Exp Med 1965:121:215-234.

3. Ward PA, Hill JH. Biologic role of complement products: complement-derived leukotactic activity extractable from lesions of immunologic vasculitis. J Immunol 1972:108:1137-1145.

4. Petrone WF, English DK, Wong K, McCord JM. Free radicals and inflammation: superoxide dependent activation of a neutrophil chemotactic factor in plasma. Proc Natl Acad Sci USA 1980:77:1159-1163.

5. McCormick JR, Harkin MM, Johnson KJ, Ward PA. Suppression by superoxide dismutase of immune complex-induced pulmonary alveolitis and dermal inflammation. Am J Pathol 1981:102:55-61.

6. Perez HD, Weksler BB, Goldstein IM. Generation of a chemotactic lipid from arachidonic acid by exposure to a superoxide-generating system. Inflammation 1980:4:313-328.

7. Johnson KJ, Ward PA. Role of oxygen metabolites in immune complex injury of lung. J Immunol 1981:126:2365-2369.

8. Johnson KJ, Wilson BS, Till GO, Ward PA. Acute lung injury in rat caused by immunoglobulin A immune complexes. J Clin Invest 1984:74:358-369.

9. Johnson KJ, Ward PA, Kunkel RG, Wilson BS. Mediation of IgA-induced lung injury in the rat: role of macrophages and reactive oxygen products. Lab Invest 1986:54:499-506.

10. Briggs RT, Drath DB, Karnovsky ML, Karnovsky MJ. Localization of NADH oxidase on the surface of human polymorphonuclear leukocytes by a new cytochemical method. J Cell Biol 1975:67:566-586.

11. Ward PA, Duque RE, Sulavik MC, Johnson KJ. In vitro and in vivo stimulation of rat neutrophils and alveolar macrophages by immune complexes. Am J Pathol 1983:110:297-309.

12. Maly FE, Kapp A, Walker C, DeWeck AL. Induction of granulocyte chemiluminescence by a mediator derived from human monocytes. Lymphokine Res 1986:5:21-33.

13. Tsujimato M, Yokota S, Vilcek J, Weissmann G. Tumor necrosis factor provokes superoxide anion generation from neutrophils. Biochem Biophys Res Commun 1986:137:1094-1100.

QUESTIONS AND COMMENTS

Dr. Charles Cochrane: Earlier electron microscopic studies revealed damage to endothelial cells in dermal Arthus reactions (blebbed retractions) along with lysis of the underlying basement membrane. Does this support the possibility that different mechanisms of injury of endothelial cells exist in immune complex damage in the dermis?

Dr. Peter Ward: There unquestionably is evidence of damage of endothelial cells and vascular basement membrane in dermal Arthus reactions. Our data suggest this may occur by oxygen radical-independent reactions, perhaps in part similar to the observations of Henson and coworkers in 1986 [Smedly LA, Tonnesen MG, Sandhaus RA, et al. Neutrophil-mediated injury to endothelial cells: enhancement by endotoxin and essential role of neutrophil elastase. J Clin Invest 1986:77:1233-1239], who found that human polymorphonuclear neutrophils can kill microvascular endothelial cells from human foreskin in a manner independent of oxygen radicals. If this were relevant in our model in rat skin, then the vascular basement membrane could be readily degraded by proteolysis secondary to secreted lysosomal proteases from polymorphonuclear neutrophils.

Dr. Charles Cochrane: With the activation of complement in the IgA-dependent injury and with the protection worked by complement depletion, it is of interest that neutrophils were not attracted to the lesion and activated by C5a.

Dr. Peter Ward: We believe that IgA complexes activate the alternative complement pathway in an inefficient manner, generating enough C5a to prime the resident alveolar macrophages for enhanced $O_2^{\cdot-}$ response after contact with IgA immune complexes. However, we speculate that there is not sufficient C5a generated to recruit neutrophils.

Dr. Herbert Johnson: Can you use the cerium chloride staining procedures to stain oxygen reactive products in lavaged lung cells to show activation as you showed in tissue with endothelial cells and polymorphonuclear neutrophils?

Dr. Peter Ward: This technique should be applicable, but we have not used it for this purpose. However, lavaged alveolar macrophages do show evidence in vitro of both enhanced basal and enhanced stimulated production of $O_2^{\cdot-}$ in animals undergoing IgA-immune complex-induced lung injury.

Dr. Richard Johnston: In the IgA-complex model, what is the ligand for macrophage release of $O_2^{\cdot-}$? As far as I know, Fc receptors for IgA have not been identified yet on macrophages, and binding through CR1 or CR3 should not induce the respiratory burst. At least it does not in peritoneal macrophages or cultured human monocytes.

Dr. Peter Ward: There are suggestions in the literature that macrophages may have Fc receptors for IgA. We have not examined alveolar macrophages for either Fc-*a* receptors or CR1/CR3 receptors. C5a and IgA-immune complexes cause enhanced $O_2^{\cdot-}$ responses. Whether these are receptor mediated, we cannot say.

THE ROLE OF OXYGEN RADICALS IN KIDNEY DISEASE

Kent J. Johnson, Ahmed Rehan, and Peter A. Ward

Relatively little is known about the role of free radicals in renal disease. Because glomerulonephritis is apparently triggered by an immune complex and mediated by leukocytes, leukocyte-generated oxygen radicals may be responsible for much of the tissue injury. In neutrophil-dependent models of glomerulonephritis, hydrogen peroxide appears to be responsible for much of the glomerular injury. However, further studies have not provided evidence for the superoxide or hydroxyl radical involvement found in other organ systems, but have suggested that myeloperoxidase-generated compounds such as hypochlorous acid may be important. The role of oxygen radicals in macrophage-dependent models remains unclear; in initial studies, catalase had no protective effect even though there was evidence of lipid peroxidation. In renal tubular cell injury induced by ischemia, oxygen radicals are apparently involved. The findings in these renal studies do not necessarily follow the patterns found in other tissues. It is becoming increasingly clear that oxygen radical species implicated as being primarily responsible for injury in one system may not be the responsible species in another. Care must be taken in extrapolating information from one system to another.

IT HAS LONG BEEN APPRECIATED that certain types of human renal diseases, in particular those affecting the glomerulus, appear to be mediated by immunologic mechanisms. As early as 1907, an immune basis was suspected for the glomerulo-nephritis occurring as a result of bacterial infections such as scarlet fever (1). This hypothesis was verified in the 1950s when the development of techniques such as immunofluorescence and electron microscopy revealed immune complex deposition in the glomeruli of many patients with various types of glomerulonephritis (2). Also, at about this time classic experimental models such as serum sickness were developed that clearly showed initiation of the glomerular injury secondary to the formation or deposition of immune complexes in the glomeruli (3,4). Today we appreciate that most types of human glomerulonephritis are immunologically mediated, with evidence of immune complex deposition in the glomeruli (5). Indeed, human and experimental glomerulonephritis, in particular lupus nephritis, represent perhaps the best examples of immune complex diseases.

In light of these findings, it is surprising how little is known about the mediation of these diseases. Complement appears to be involved in some types of human as well as experimental glomeronephritis

From Department of Pathology, The University of Michigan Medical School, Ann Arbor, Michigan, USA.

Address correspondence to Dr. Kent J. Johnson, Department of Pathology, The University of Michigan Medical School, M7520D Box 0602, Ann Arbor, Michigan 48109-0602, USA.

(6,7). There is also evidence that phagocytes (neutrophils, macrophages) accumulate in the glomeruli and are the source of mediators responsible for much of the glomerular injury. What these mediators are is unclear. With this in mind, the following discussion presents preliminary data about the role of oxygen radicals in the pathogenesis of glomerulonephritis. Some attention will also be given to the evidence for oxygen radical involvement in other types of renal disease, in particular, in acute renal failure where evidence is emerging that oxygen radicals are involved in the tubular cell injury.

THE ROLE OF OXYGEN RADICALS IN GLOMERULONEPHRITIS

We first review studies of oxygen radical production by cells normally present in the renal glomerulus and then look at the evidence implicating oxygen radicals as an important mediator of the tissue injury seen in glomerulonephritis.

Oxygen Radical Production by the Normal Renal Glomerulus

Recent studies have shown that isolated normal glomeruli produce oxygen radicals when appropriately stimulated in vitro. In studies by Shah (8), isolated rat glomeruli stimulated with phorbol myristate acetate (PMA) showed evidence of oxygen radical generation as assessed by chemiluminescence. When inhibitors or scavengers of oxygen radicals were used, the pattern of inhibition of the chemiluminescence suggested that superoxide ($O_2^{\cdot-}$), hydrogen peroxide (H_2O_2), and the hydroxyl radical ($\cdot OH$) were all produced. Thus, this study was the first to show that the normal glomerulus has the capacity to produce free radicals.

The relevance of this observation is unclear, but it has long been known that some mesangial cells are phagocytic, and a primary function of these cells may be the uptake and clearance of particulate materials, including immune complexes, from the circulation (9). One would expect that these phagocytic cells, like other phagocytic cells, would have a membrane-associated NADPH oxidase system and, therefore, could release oxygen radicals during phagocytosis. In fact, recent studies of isolated mesangial cells demonstrated that they produce oxygen radicals during phagocytosis (10). Thus, the production of oxygen radicals by the cells could be responsible for the initial glomerular injury after the deposition of immune complexes. This generation of free radicals might also be involved in the subsequent production of other inflammatory mediators such as prostaglandins and complement, which may in turn lead to recruitment of leukocytes from the blood into the glomeruli. In support of this hypothesis, initial studies have found that oxygen radicals stimulate prostaglandin production by the glomerulus (10,11). Thus, the ability of the normal glomerulus to produce oxygen radicals may be an important first step in the sequence of events in glomerulonephritis.

Oxygen Radicals in Neutrophil-Dependent Models of Glomerulonephritis

Most types of glomerulonephritis appear "proliferative," with increased numbers of cells present mostly within mesengial regions. A variable percentage of these cells are neutrophils, which is not surprising since an acute inflammatory response is involved. Large numbers of neutrophils are characteristically seen in acute poststreptococcal nephritis, as well as in certain types of lupus nephritis.

Some animal models of glomerulonephritis have clearly illustrated the ability of neutrophils to induce glomerular injury and proteinuria. Perhaps the best examples are the classic studies by Cochrane, Dixon, and colleagues (see, for example, reference 12) in the early 1960s. They demonstrated that the early or heterologous phase of anti-glomerular basement membrane (anti-GBM) nephritis or nephrotoxic nephritis was neutrophil-dependent, since prior depletion of neutrophils largely prevented development of the glomerular injury and proteinuria. Other experimental models of neutrophil-dependent glomerulonephritis have since been developed (13-15).

After these initial observations, surprisingly little work has been done to define further the nature of this neutrophil-dependent glomerular injury. It was generally assumed that neutrophil proteases were responsible for the glomerular injury, since Cochrane (16) showed that rabbits with nephritis had evidence of protease activity in their urine and that isolated glomerular basement membranes in vitro could be degraded by neutrophil proteases. However, direct evidence of protease involvement was not obtained. There are no convincing in vivo studies showing suppression of glomerular injury by antiproteases.

Not until the late 1970s did investigators begin to look at the role of oxygen radicals in glomerulonephritis. In a preliminary study, Stokes and McCord (17) induced glomerulonephritis in mice by a single injection of preformed immune complexes. Administration of superoxide dismutase (SOD)

decreased the degree of cellular proliferation in the glomeruli, suggesting that $O_2^{\cdot-}$ was somehow involved in the recruitment of blood neutrophils and macrophages into the glomeruli. SOD was also tested in another murine model of immune complex glomerulonephritis (18) and again was found to lessen the severity of glomerular injury. These studies were the first to suggest a role for oxygen radicals, specifically $O_2^{\cdot-}$, in the mediation of glomerular injury. The reason for the decreased glomerular cellularity with SOD is suggested by subsequent studies in vitro, where $O_2^{\cdot-}$ appears to induce the formation of chemotactic factors from lipids, including arachidonic acid (19,20).

With this background in mind, we in our laboratory decided to explore in greater detail the role of oxygen radicals in neutrophil-dependent glomerulonephritis. In our initial study, we used the classic anti-GBM nephritis model with its clear-cut neutrophil dependence in the early or heterologous phase. We were able to show (**Figure 1**) that addition of catalase prior to the development of the glomerulonephritis markedly diminished the degree of proteinuria. This protective effect was dose dependent, and the maximal reduction in proteinuria was 75%. Morphologically the glomeruli of the catalase-treated animals showed large numbers of neutrophils, as expected, but little glomerular injury (**Figure 2**). These studies were the first to show that H_2O_2 and/or its metabolic products are capable of inducing glomerular injury and proteinuria (21).

Studies were also done to assess the protective effects of SOD, $\cdot$OH scavengers, and iron chelators. Neither SOD nor dimethylsulphoxide (DMSO) (Figure 1) nor the iron chelator deferoxamine (desferrioxamine B methanesulfonate) showed any protective effect. Thus, although H_2O_2 is implicated in this model of glomerulonephritis, we were unable to implicate either $O_2^{\cdot-}$ or $\cdot$OH.

Other experimental models of neutrophil-dependent glomerular injury developed in our laboratory and elsewhere have also implicated H_2O_2 as a critical mediator of glomerular injury. We developed a model of neutrophil-dependent glomerular injury in rats by infusing PMA into the renal artery. The resulting glomerulonephritis and proteinuria were neutrophil dependent and could be suppressed by the addition of catalase but not of SOD (14). In a third model of neutrophil-dependent glomerular injury, one secondary to systemic complement activation, we were again able to protect with catalase but not with SOD, DMSO, or deferoxamine, again suggesting that the generation of H_2O_2 is central to the development of the glomerular injury and proteinuria (15).

Even though our studies were not able to show any evidence for $\cdot$OH involvement in glomerular

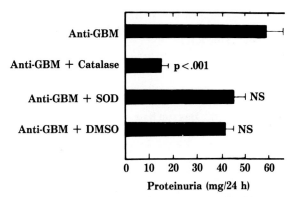

Figure 1. Protective effects of oxygen radical inhibitors for suppressing proteinuria in neutrophil-dependent glomerular injury in the rat. The following amounts of inhibitors were given: catalase 40 mg, SOD 40 mg, DMSO 2 mL. Only catalase significantly inhibited proteinuria, compared to the proteinuria with anti-GBM treatment alone.

injury, another laboratory has provided preliminary evidence that $\cdot$OH might be involved in the spontaneous glomerular injury seen in NZB lupus mice; DMSO protected against the progression of the glomerular injury in these animals (22). There is also some evidence that other metabolic products of H_2O_2, namely, the myeloperoxidase-generated products such as hypochlorous acid (HOCl) may be involved in the development of glomerular injury. Couser and colleagues (23) found that infused myeloperoxidase, which is cationic, would bind to glomeruli, which normally have a high net negative charge due to their negatively charged glycoproteins. The subsequent infusion of H_2O_2 in low doses, which by itself induced little or no glomerular injury, would induce proteinuria in the presence of myeloperoxidase. In another study (24), these investigators also found evidence of halogenation products in the glomeruli of animals with a neutrophil-dependent, immune complex-induced glomerulonephritis. These studies have extended our concept of the role of oxygen-derived products in neutrophil-dependent glomerular injury and suggest that HOCl is also important. Except for the one preliminary observation cited earlier (22), the inability of our laboratory and others to incriminate the $\cdot$OH radical in renal injury is very different from oxygen radical-dependent injury in other organ systems such as the lung, where $\cdot$OH is clearly implicated (25-26). The reasons for this discrepancy are not clear, but the oxygen radical species implicated in tissue injury appear to differ

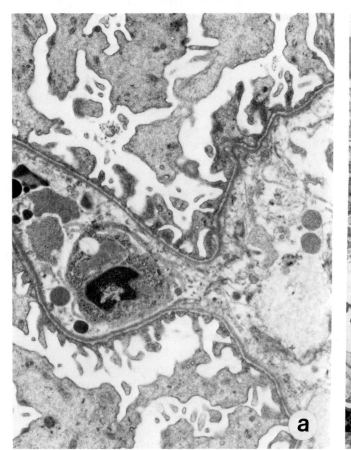

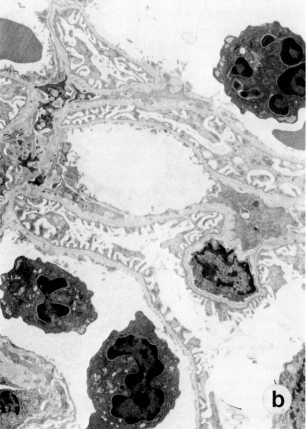

Figure 2. Morphological studies of catalase suppression of glomerular injury in the rat. a) A high-power view of a glomerular capillary loop in a rat with anti-GBM nephritis. A neutrophil is present in the capillary loop along with evidence of endothelial cell injury and partial effacement of the epithelial cell foot processes (transmission electron microscopy, X11,500). b) A typical glomerulus from an animal with anti-GBM nephritis treated with catalase. Numerous neutrophils are present in the glomerular capillary loops, but there is little endothelial or epithelial cell alteration (transmission electron microscopy, X5000).

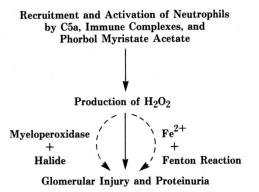

Recruitment and Activation of Neutrophils
by C5a, Immune Complexes, and
Phorbol Myristate Acetate

Production of H_2O_2

Myeloperoxidase Fe^{2+}
    +   +
Halide   Fenton Reaction

Glomerular Injury and Proteinuria

Figure 3. Postulated pathophysiology of neutrophil-dependent, oxygen radical-mediated glomerular injury.

somewhat, depending on the organ system involved. **Figure 3** is a flow diagram of our current knowledge about the role of oxygen-derived species in neutrophil-dependent glomerular injury.

Oxygen Radicals in Macrophage-Dependent Models of Glomerulonephritis

It now seems well established that the monocyte/macrophage cell is the most important effector cell in proliferative glomerulonephritis. Macrophages are normally present in the renal mesangium, depending on the species examined, and are thought to be responsible for the phagocytic and macromolecular clearing ability of the mesangium (9-10). In glomerulonephritis, both in humans and in experimental animals, monocytes/macrophages from the circulation accumulate in the glomeruli and are the main cells responsible for the increased cellularity seen in acute glomerulonephritis (27-29).

There is good experimental evidence that macrophages are largely responsible for much of the glomerular injury and proteinuria. Macrophage depletion studies have shown a protective effect in many of the classic models of glomerulonephritis, including the delayed or autologous phase of anti-GBM nephritis as well as serum sickness (30-32). Thus, macrophages clearly are critical effector cells in most types of glomerulonephritis. What is presently not known is which of the many inflammatory mediators produced by these cells are responsible for the glomerular injury.

Since oxygen radicals are implicated in macrophage-dependent lung injury (26,33), we decided to look at their role in a macrophage-dependent model of glomerulonephritis: the IgG-induced autologous anti-GBM nephritis model. A single injection into rats of sheep IgG antibody made against rat GBM caused massive proteinuria, with an initial peak of proteinuria in the first 24 hours corresponding to the neutrophil-dependent heterologous phase, followed by a second peak of proteinuria 5 to 7 days after injection corresponding to

Table 1. Catalase Suppression of Heterologous but not Autologous Proteinuria in the Anti-GBM Nephritis Model in the Rat

Treatment	Day	No. of Rats	Total Protein Excretion in Urine* (mg/24 h)	Inhibition (%)
Anti-GBM antibody	1	4	373.30 ± 22.90	--
Anti-GBM antibody plus PEG:catalase†	1	4	33.67 ± 12.63	99
Anti-GBM antibody	5	4	194.99 ± 68.35	--
Anti-GBM antibody plus PEG:catalase	5	4	159.00 ± 53.59	NS**
Anti-GBM antibody	7	7	170.52 ± 57.26	--
Anti-GBM antibody plus PEG:catalase	7	7	153.44 ± 31.78	NS

* Mean ± SD
† The amount of PEG:catalase given was 10 000 units every 48 hours.
** NS = no significant difference.

the macrophage-dependent autologous phase (**Table 1**). The administration of polyethyleneglycol (PEG)-catalase daily to these animals almost completely eliminated the early proteinuria, confirming our previous observations (21). However, catalase had no clear effect on the autologous phase proteinuria. These initial studies do not confirm a role for oxygen-derived species in this model of macrophage-dependent glomerular injury.

Possible complicating factors include the fact that this model of tissue injury occurs over days instead of hours, raising the possibility that effective therapeutic levels of catalase were not present. Also the large size of the PEG-catalase (M_r greater than 10^6) may impede its ability to get into the mesangium where the macrophages are located. In fact, size restriction may be a critical factor; we have found that PEG-catalase does not effectively inhibit the inflammation in a model of pancreatitis, whereas unconjugated catalase does, suggesting that PEG-catalase may not infuse as readily into the sites of inflammation. Further studies must be done to determine definitively whether oxygen radicals play a role in macrophage-dependent glomerular injury.

Even though we are presently unable to show a direct inhibition by oxygen radical scavengers, there is evidence of oxygen radical generation in the kidneys of these animals. The urine of rabbits with anti-GBM nephritis contained lipid peroxidation products (as fluorochrome fluorescent products), whose peak concentration corresponded to the peak concentration of protein in the urine (**Figure 4**). Normal rabbit urine or baseline urine from rabbits given the anti-GBM antibody to induce nephritis do not contain these fluorescent products. Thus, the development of anti-GBM nephritis in these animals is associated with evidence of lipid peroxidation, suggesting that oxygen radicals are being generated in the glomeruli. Further studies need to be done with oxygen radical scavengers and iron chelators.

OXYGEN RADICALS IN TUBULOINTERSTITIAL DISEASE AND ACUTE RENAL FAILURE

Renal tubulointerstitial inflammation is a significant component of many types of renal lesions including bacterial pyelonephritis as well as such presumably immunologically mediated processes as drug-induced interstitial nephritis, transplant rejection, and processes associated with various types of glomerulonephritis (34). No matter what causes the tubulointerstitial diseases, they are all characterized by damage to the renal tubular epithelial cells, which is the primary cause of the clinical syndrome of acute renal failure (35-36). The injury is presumably caused by inflammatory mediators, but there are few definitive studies identifying the mediators involved.

One study by Paller et al (37) has looked at the role of oxygen radicals in renal tubular cell injury and acute renal failure induced by ischemia. Acute renal failure with tubular cell injury was induced in rats by occlusion of the renal artery and subsequent reperfusion. Animals receiving SOD, dimethyl-thiourea (DMTU), or allopurinol just prior to the ischemic event had significantly better renal function than untreated controls, as manifested by lower plasma creatinine concentrations and higher renal blood flow. However, catalase had no protective effect. Morphologically the animals that received SOD, DMTU, or allopurinol showed less severe tubular epithelial cell injury, and fewer of those rats died. These studies were the first to show that oxygen radicals are involved in one type of renal tubular cell injury, that induced by ischemia. This finding is not surprising, since good evidence exists that ischemic/reperfusion injury in other organs such as the heart is due to the generation of oxygen radicals (38-42). For other causes of tubular cell injury, particularly those involving immunologic reactions, no definitive data exist, although studies are presently underway in many laboratories to assess the role of oxygen radicals in these types of injury.

CONCLUSIONS

Compared with what is known for other organ systems such as the lung, there is little information about the role of oxygen radicals in the pathogenesis of kidney injury. Most of the available information comes from studies of the various experimental

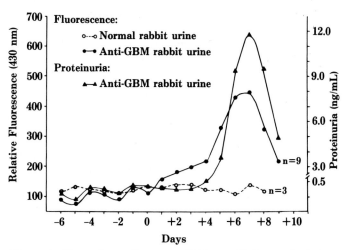

Figure 4. Fluorochrome fluorescent lipid peroxidation products in the urine of rabbits with anti-GBM nephritis.

models of glomerulonephritis, where H_2O_2 and perhaps myeloperoxidase products such as HOCl have been implicated in the pathogenesis of neutrophil-dependent models of glomerulonephritis. Regarding macrophage-dependent models of glomerulonephritis, not enough studies have been done to determine the role of oxygen radicals, even though initial studies have been negative. Finally, in the study of injury to other parts of the kidney, namely, the tubulointerstitial region, there is preliminary evidence of oxygen radical involvement in the acute tubular cell injury induced by ischemia.

One of the interesting observations made in our studies is that mediation of oxygen radical-dependent tissue injury and, in particular, the oxygen-derived species implicated as being primarily responsible for the injury appear to differ in various regions of the body. This is best illustrated by comparing oxygen radical-dependent, immune-complex tissue injury in various tissues. As shown in **Table 2**, the effector cell and the oxygen radical species implicated as being responsible for the injury differ somewhat with body system. For example, acute lung injury induced by IgG-immune complexes depends both on complement and on neutrophils, with catalase or iron chelators providing the greatest degree of protection, but SOD not providing protection (43). Conversely, although IgA-induced lung injury also appears to be complement dependent and mediated by oxygen radicals, macrophages rather than neutrophils appear to be the critical effector cell, and the pattern of inhibition suggests that O_2^{-}, H_2O_2, and ·OH are all involved (26). In the dermal Arthus reaction induced by IgG immune complexes, neutrophils are the critical effector cells, but catalase has no inhibitory effect and only SOD shows consistent early inhibition (44). Finally, in the kidney, the acute IgG-induced heterologous anti-GBM nephritis model is neutrophil dependent, with H_2O_2 implicated most

Table 2. Mediation of Experimental Immune Complex-Induced Tissue Injury in Various Organ Systems

Organ System	Mediator Characteristics					
	Complement Dependent	Neutrophil Dependent	Macrophage Dependent	Inhibited by SOD	Inhibited by Catalase	Iron Dependent
Lung						
IgG-immune complex injury	yes	yes	no	no	yes	yes
IgA-immune complex injury	yes	no	yes	yes	yes	yes
Skin						
IgG-immune complex injury (Arthus reaction)	yes	yes	no	yes	no	unknown
Kidney						
IgG-immune complex glomerulonephritis						
Anti-GBM nephritis heterologous phase	yes	yes	no	no	yes	no
Anti-GBM nephritis autologous phase	no	no	yes	unknown	no	unknown

strongly as the primary oxidant and little evidence for $O_2^{\cdot-}$ or $\cdot OH$ involvement (21). Caution should, therefore, be exercised when extrapolating data from one organ system to another.

REFERENCES

1. Schick B. Die Nachkrankheiten des scharlachs. Jahrb Kinderheil 1907;65:132-73.

2. Mellors RC, Ortega LG. Analytical pathology. III. New observations on the pathogensis of glomerulonephritis, lipid nephrosis, periarteritis nodosa and secondary amyloidasis in man. Am J Pathol 1956;32:455-499.

3. Cochrane CG. Immune complex mediated tissue injury. In: Cohen S, Ward PA, McCluskey RT, eds. Mechanisms of immunopathology. New York: John Wiley, 1979;29-48.

4. Dixon FJ, Feldman JD, Vasquez JJ. Experimental glomerulonephritis: the pathogenesis of a laboratory model resembling the spectrum of human glomerulonephritis. J Exp Med 1961:113:899-920.

5. Wilson CB. Recent advances in the immunological aspects of renal disease. Fed Proc 1977;36:2171-2175.

6. Arroyave CM. The complement system in pediatric renal disease. Paediatrician 1979:8:349-363.

7. Johnson KJ, Striker G, Killen P. Immunopathology of glomerular disease. In: Ward PA, ed. Handbook of inflammation: vol 4. North Holland: Elsevier, 1983;1-36.

8. Shah SV. Light emission by isolated rat glomeruli in response to phorbol myristate acetate. J Lab Clin Med 1981:98:46-57.

9. Schreiner GF, Kiely JM, Cotran RS, Unanue ER. Characterization of resident glomerular cells in the rat expressing Ia determinants and manifesting genetically restricted interactions with lymphocytes. J Clin Invest 1981:68:920-931.

10. Baud L, Hagege J, Sraer J, Rondeau E, Perez J, Ardaillou R. Reactive oxygen production by cultured rat glomerular mesangial cells during phagocytosis is associated with stimulation of lipoxygenase activity. J Exp Med 1983:158:1836-1852.

11. Dunn MJ. The role of arachidonic acid metabolites in glomerulonephritis. In: Bertani T, Remuzzi G, eds. Glomerular injury 300 years after Morgagni. Milan:Wichtig Editore, 1983;77.

12. Cochrane CG, Unanue ER, Dixon FJ. A role of polymorphonuclear leukocytes and complement in nephrotoxic nephritis. J Exp Med 1965;122:99-116.

13. Couser WG. Mechanisms of glomerular injury in immune-complex disease. Kidney Int 1985;28:569-583.

14. Rehan A, Johnson KJ, Kunkel RG, Wiggens RC. Role of oxygen radicals in phorbol myristate acetate-induced glomerular injury. Kidney Int 1985;27:503-511.

15. Rehan A, Wiggins RC, Kunkel RG, Till GO, Johnson KJ. Glomerular injury and proteinuria in rats after intrarenal injection of cobra venom factor: evidence for the role of neutrophil-derived oxygen free radicals. Amer J Pathol 1986:123:57-66.

16. Cochrane CG. Immunologic tissue injury mediated by neutrophilic leukocytes. Adv Immunol 1968:9:97-162.

17. Stokes SH, McCord JM. Prevention of immune complex induced glomerulonephritis by superoxide dismutase. Alabama J Med Sci 1979:16:33.

18. Jennette JC, Hyson CP, Iskander SS. Palliative effect of superoxide dismutase in heterologous protein induced glomerulonephritis [Abstract]. Fed Proc 1982;41:335.

19. Petrone WF, English DK, Wong K, McCord JM. Free radicals and inflammation: the superoxide-dependent activation of a neutrophil chemotactic factor in plasma. Proc Natl Acad Sci USA 1980:77:1159-1163.

20. Perez HD, Goldstein JM. Generation of a chemotactic lipid from arachidonic acid by exposure to a superoxide generating system [Abstract]. Fed Proc 1980;34:1170.

21. Rehan A, Johnson KJ, Wiggins RC, Kunkel RG, Ward PA. Evidence for the role of oxygen radicals in acute nephrotoxic nephritis. Lab Invest 1984:51:396-403.

22. Kaplan BS, Milner LS, de Chardarevian JP, Goodyear PR, Fong JSC. Early dimethylsulfoxide administration

ameliorates glomerular disease in NZB WF 1, Lupus mice [Abstract]. Kidney Int 1985:27:214.

23. Johnson RJ, Klebanoff SJ, Couser WG. The myeloperoxidase-hydrogen peroxide-halide system: a new mediator of glomerulonephritis (GN) [Abstract]. Kidney Int 1986:29:278.

24. Couser WG, Johnson RJ, Adler S, Ochi RF, Kelbanoff SJ. The myeloperoxidase-hydrogen peroxide-halide system: evidence for participation in neutrophil-mediated glomerulonephritis [Abstract]. Kidney Int 1986:29:271.

25. Ward PA, Till GO, Kunkel R, Beauchamp C. Evidence for the role of hydroxyl radical in complement and neutrophil dependent tissue injury. J Clin Invest 1983:72:789-801.

26. Johnson KJ, Ward PA, Kunkel RG, Wilson BS. Mediation of IgA induced lung injury in the rat: role of macrophages and reactive oxygen products. Lab Invest 1986:54:499-506.

27. Morita T, Kihara I, Oite T, Yamamoto T. Participation of blood borne cells in rat Masugi nephritis. Acta Pathol JPN 1976:26:409-422.

28. Sano M. Participation of monocytes in glomerulonephritis in acute serum sickness of rabbit. Acta Pathol JPN 1976:26:423-433.

29. Atkins RC, Holdsworth SR, Glasgow EF, Matthews FE. The macrophage in human rapidly progressive glomerulonephritis. Lancet 1976:i:830-832.

30. Holdsworth SR, Neale TJ, Wilson CB. Abrogation of macrophage dependent injury in experimental glomerulonephritis in the rabbit: use of antimacrophage serum. J Clin Invest 1981:68:686-698.

31. Hunsicker LG, Shearer TP, Plattner SB, Weisenburger D. The role of monocytes in serum sickness nephritis. J Exp Med 1979:150:413-425.

32. Holdsworth SR, Neale TJ, Wilson CB. The participation of macrophages and monocytes in experimental immune complex glomerulonephritis. Clin Immunol Immunopathol 1980:15:510-524.

33. Johnson KJ, Ward PA. Acute and progressive lung injury after contact with phorbol myristate acetate. Amer J Pathol 1982:107:29-35.

34. Cotran RS, Rubin RH, Tolkoff-Rubin NE. Tubulointerstitial diseases. In: Brenner BM, Rector FC, eds. The kidney. 3rd ed. Philadelphia: WB Saunders, 1985:1143.

35. Weinburg JM, Humes HD. Acute renal failure. In: Salez K, Whelton A, eds. Acute renal failure: correlation between morphology and function. New York: Marcel Decker, 1983:179-194.

36. Venkatachalam MA. Pathology of acute renal failure. In: Brenner BM, Stein JH, eds. Acute renal failure. New York: Churchill Livingston, 1980:79-107.

37. Paller MS, Hoidal JR, Ferris TF. Oxygen free radicals in ischemic acute renal failure in the rat. J Clin Invest 1984:74:1156-1164.

38. Flamm ES, Demopoulos HB, Seligman ML, Poser RG, Ransohoff J. Free radicals in cerebral ischemia. Stroke 1978:9:445-447.

39. Kogure K, Watson BD, Busto R, Abe K. Potentiation of lipid peroxides by ischemia in rat brain. Neurochem Res 1982:7:437-454.

40. Guarnieri C, Flamigni F, Caldarera CM. Role of oxygen in the cellular damage induced by re-oxygenation of hypoxic heart. J Mol Cell Cardiol 1980:12:797-808.

41. Granger DN, Rutili G, McCord JM. Superoxide radicals in feline intestinal ischemia. Gastroenterology 1981:81:22-29.

42. Demopoulos HB, Flamm ES, Pietronigro DD, Seligman ML. The free radical pathology and the microcirculation in the major central nervous system disorders. Acta Physiol Scand 1980:Suppl 492:91-119.

43. Johnson KJ, Ward PA. Role of oxygen metabolites in immune complex injury of lung. J Immunol 1981:126:2365-2369.

44. Fligiel SEG, Ward PA, Johnson KJ, Till GO. Evidence for a role of hydroxyl radical on immune-complex-induced vasculitis. Amer J Pathol 1984:115:375-382.

QUESTIONS AND COMMENTS

Dr. Charles Cochrane: Despite your data on lack of protection by radical scavengers and deferoxamine in the autologous nephritis, you have wisely listed the role of free radicals and iron-catalyzed reactions as unknown. I would suggest determining if primary targets of oxidants such as glyceraldehyde-3-phosphate dehydrogenase or DNA bases are affected in glomerular cells with and without treatment by inhibitors.

Dr. Kent Johnson: I certainly do not mean to imply that reactive oxygen products are not increased in the pathogenesis of macrophage-dependent glomerular injury. Our results are tentative, and it certainly would be of interest to look for intracellular oxidant-induced changes in these glomeruli.

Dr. Richard Johnston: Can you direct antiproteinases to sites of damage in your model for macrophage-induced damage?

Dr. Kent Johnson: No studies have been done in this regard. Antiproteases conceivably would preferentially localize in the glomeruli if they were made cationic, and this might be a way of specifically directing antiprotease into the glomeruli.

Dr. Richard Johnston: Do patients with a_1-antiproteinase deficiency have a different pattern of damage if they get glomerulonephritis (compared to that in otherwise normal patients who get glomerulonephritis), or is there any hint of increased frequency of renal disease in these people?

Dr. Kent Johnson: There is no evidence that I am aware of that patients with a_1-antiproteinase deficiency have any increased incidence of renal disease, specifically of glomerulonephritis. Furthermore, no data are available that these patients have more severe glomerulonephritis than individuals with normal levels of protease inhibitors.

TUMOR NECROSIS FACTOR AND REACTIVE OXYGEN SPECIES:
Implications for Free Radical-Induced Tissue Injury

Ian A. Clark, Cassandra M. Thumwood, Geeta Chaudhri, William B. Cowden, and Nicholas H. Hunt

In addition to causing direct tissue damage, free radicals may also act indirectly through cytokines such as tumor necrosis factor (TNF). This paper reviews the evidence for several of the possible functional points of contact between oxygen radicals and TNF. For example, the expression of interleukin-2 receptors on T lymphocytes, necessary for T cell proliferation, may depend on free radicals and on TNF. Likewise, evidence suggests that free radicals might provide a positive signal for the release of TNF. Examples of types of tissue injury that probably involve the interplay of free radicals and TNF (such as the adherence of neutrophils to vascular endothelium, dyserythropoiesis, cerebral malaria in mice, and various models of autoimmune disease) are also reviewed. Clearly, studies to define the exact mechanisms of free radical generation and action in biological systems must now also consider the interrelationships between the free radicals and cytokines like TNF.

MUCH EFFORT HAS BEEN DIRECTED towards defining the exact mechanisms of free radical generation in biological systems and how these radicals can cause tissue damage. Nevertheless, to understand what happens in vivo we must also explore the interactions between free radicals and the array of lymphokines and monokines secreted by stimulated leukocytes. A clear grasp of the in vivo activities of any of these agents, radical or cytokine, will not, in our view, be attained without first appreciating their interrelated influences on various biological processes, including tissue damage. This contribution attempts to bridge the gap, giving special attention to the various roles of tumor necrosis factor (TNF).

TUMOR NECROSIS FACTOR

TNF is a polypeptide hormone (M_r 17 000) released from monocytes and macrophages. This form is sometimes termed TNFa, to distinguish it from a similar molecule produced by activated lymphocytes, previously referred to as lymphotoxin, now often termed TNFβ. TNFa (henceforth referred to as TNF) was first described as an undefined functional entity with antitumor activity (1) and has been proposed by us (2,3) and others (4) to be involved in the host response to malaria, promoting both parasite death and host immunopathologic changes. TNF was later shown to be identical to cachectin (5), a monokine that causes hypertriglyceridemia and cachexia (6) by suppressing the activity of lipoprotein lipase (7).

TNF influences many biological functions and, at low concentrations, performs such useful tasks as helping to increase the expression of histocompatibility antigens (8,9) (necessary to initiate many immune responses) and of receptors for epidermal growth factor on fibroblasts (10). The expression of class II histocompatibility antigens is not always beneficial: in the presence of interferon-γ (IFN-γ), TNF has recently been reported to induce expression of these antigens on pancreatic islet β-cells where they normally are not found (11). These cells might then present their own surface autoantigens to helper T cells, initiating their autoimmune destruction, leading to diabetes. When injected, TNF can mimic many of the pathological effects of sepsis, causing both tissue damage and severe functional alterations (12,13). TNF is also regarded as a mediator of inflammation (14). The ability of antibody specific for TNF to inhibit most of the dramatic changes associated with experimental endotoxicity (15) is consistent with these arguments. The apparent activities of TNF in endotoxicity are reminiscent of those proposed for platelet-activating factor (PAF). Both, for example, cause thrombocytopenia, neutrophil aggregation, and superoxide secretion by neutrophils, so it is not surprising that TNF has been suggested to induce release of PAF (12,14). Excellent reviews on TNF are readily available (14,16).

As we might suspect, TNF acts collaboratively with other cytokines. For example, its functions are closely interwoven with those of IFN-γ, a product of activated T lymphocytes. IFN-γ can increase the release of TNF from macrophages (17,18), enhance the expression of the receptors necessary for cells to recognize TNF (19,20), and act synergistically at the effector level (10,21). Interleukin-2 (IL-2), another product of activated T lymphocytes, also enhances release of TNF (17).

Among the many recently uncovered properties of TNF is its ability to sensitize neutrophils (22) and monocytes (M. Parant and C. Jupin, Centre National de la Récherche Scientifique, Paris, personal communication) to agents that induce these cells to release reactive forms of oxygen. It now seems, as discussed later, that this will prove to be only one of

From Department of Zoology and John Curtin School of Medical Research, The Australian National University, Canberra, ACT 2601, Australia.

Address correspondence to Dr. Ian A. Clark, Department of Zoology, The Australian National University, Canberra, ACT 2601, Australia.

several functional points of contact between oxygen radicals and TNF.

FREE RADICAL AND TNF ACTIVATION OF T LYMPHOCYTES

In view of the wealth of in vitro supportive evidence, it seems logical to use iron chelators and radical scavengers in vivo to help establish whether free radical-mediated processes are contributing to tissue damage in disease states. It is now evident that interpretation can be difficult because radical involvement can occur at several levels. One level that has previously been unsuspected, but for which we now have substantial in vitro evidence, is in the activation of T lymphocytes before they proliferate. As discussed later, this could have relevance in autoimmune or infectious conditions.

There is ample evidence that the proliferation of T lymphocytes requires iron, but its function has been unclear. Deferoxamine (desferrioxamine B methylsulfonate) inhibition of T lymphocyte proliferation has been explained (23) by the removal of the iron required as a cofactor by ribonucleotide reductase, an enzyme essential for DNA synthesis. The association of chemiluminescence with thymocyte activation by concanavalin A (24) prompted us to examine whether the capacity of iron to catalyze reduction of hydrogen peroxide to more reactive radical species could be involved. Our test system was a one-way mixed lymphocyte reaction, in which lymphocytes from two histologically incompatible strains of mice are cultured after one batch of cells has been irradiated to prevent their subsequent proliferation (25). These irradiated cells provide the allogeneic tissue antigens, or alloantigens, to which the other lymphocytes respond by activation and proliferation, two discrete processes.

We found that, as well as being inhibited in a dose-dependent manner by four structurally unrelated iron chelators (one of which was deferoxamine), these cultures were also inhibited by butylated hydroxyanisole (BHA) in micromolar amounts (25) (**Figure 1**). Further investigation showed that none of these agents inhibited production of interleukin-1 (IL-1) or IL-2, but that all profoundly decreased the expression of receptors for IL-2 on T lymphocytes (**Figure 2**). The expression of these receptors must be induced on the surface of T lymphocytes and be occupied by IL-2 molecules before the series of events that induce T lymphocytes to proliferate can continue. As evidence against ribonucleotide reductase being the site of iron removal or of BHA action, we found that once IL-2 receptors were present and IL-2 was available, none of these agents, in the concentrations that profoundly

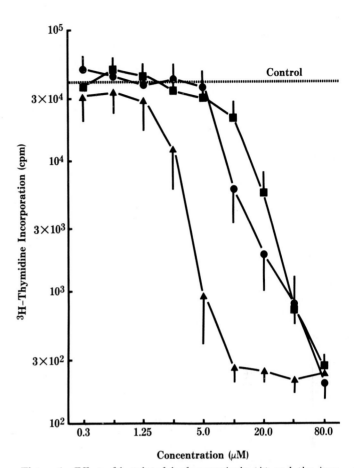

Figure 1. Effect of butylated hydroxyanisole (▲) and the iron chelators pyridoxal isonicotinyl hydrazine (●) and octanohydroxamic acid (■) on the incorporation of ³H-thymidine in mixed lymphocyte reaction cultures. Reprinted with permission of *The Journal of Immunology* from reference 25.

inhibited activation of T lymphocytes, could inhibit proliferation (25). These results argue (indirectly) for free radicals being essential, at some early stage before IL-2 receptors are expressed, to act as positive mediators in the activation of T lymphocytes exposed to alloantigens. These principles also hold true when T lymphocytes are stimulated by mitogens (G. Chaudhri, unpublished data) and therefore may require consideration in any attempt to modify an autoimmune or infectious disease by administering iron chelators or free radical scavengers.

A recent report (26) indicates that one of the immunoregulatory functions of TNF is to increase the expression of high-affinity receptors for IL-2 on T lymphocytes. One as yet unexplored, but (in view of the evidence in the next section) distinct, possibility is that the antioxidants we added to our mixed lymphocyte cultures could have been inhibiting production of TNF by accessory cells, and that this could have contributed to our observations. Furthermore, the capacity of small amounts of endotoxin to enhance the mixed lymphocyte reaction (27) could reflect its TNF-inducing properties (1).

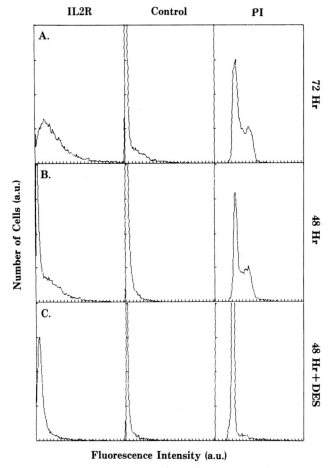

IL2R   **Control**   **PI**

A.   72 Hr

B.   48 Hr

C.   48 Hr + DES

Number of Cells (a.u.)

Fluorescence Intensity (a.u.)

Figure 2. Flow microfluorometric analysis of concanavalin A-stimulated lymph node cells. Fluorescence profiles show IL-2 receptor (IL2R) expression (first panel) and control profiles (second panel) at 72 hr (A), 48 hr (B), and 48 hr in the presence of 20 μM deferoxamine (DES) (C). Three other iron chelators and butylated hydroxanisole produced the same outcome. The DNA content of the three cell populations is shown by the propidium iodide (PI) profiles in the third panel. Reprinted with permission of *The Journal of Immunology* from reference 25.

FREE RADICALS MAY HELP RELEASE TNF

There is ample circumstantial evidence on which to base a prediction that the generation of free radicals is closely connected with the generation of TNF: for example, many agents that induce cells to emit chemiluminescence also cause TNF release. Sendai virus (28,29), concanavalin A (24,17), and phorbol myristate acetate (30,31) are good examples. The antitumor drug bleomycin provides another line of evidence. This agent generates oxygen radicals (32) and sensitizes animals to the harmful effects of endotoxin (33), which are mostly mediated by TNF (15). Without endotoxin present, however, bleomycin induces side effects (33) very similar to those induced in phase I human trials with parenteral TNF (34). This is consistent with the observation (33) that leukocytes incubated with bleomycin release an endogenous pyrogen. Like IL-1, TNF possesses this activity, and indeed induces IL-1 release (35).

Table 1. Effect of hydroxyl radical scavengers on TNFβ (lymphotoxin) production induced by phorbol myristate acetate (PMA)*

Scavenger	Concentration	% Inhibition[†]
Dimethylsulfoxide	2%	47 ±13 (4)
Thiourea	5 mM	61 ± 5 (3)
Mannitol**	50 mM	59 ± 7 (3)
Tetramethylurea	5 mM	77 ± 6 (2)
Urea	5 mM	9 ±16 (2)

* Reprinted with permission of the authors from reference 41.
† Percent inhibition ± S.E. The numbers of experiments are shown in parenthesis. The PMA concentration was 20 μg/mL.
** Mannitol was added 60 minutes before PMA induction.

Another unexplained finding that fits this concept is the ability of vitamin E supplements to increase the diminished lipoprotein lipase activity seen in experimental diabetes (36). Since vitamin E scavenges radicals, and the synthesis of lipoprotein lipase is inhibited by TNF (as cachectin), this model could be further studied. The insulin resistance of diabetes is also consistent with the presence of cachectin (37). Finally, the ability of endotoxin to increase production of superoxide (38) and to induce TNF (1) could, by these concepts, be seen as links in the same chain of events. It is notable that *Corynebacterium parvum* primes for both of these products in vivo (39,40).

The most direct published evidence that free radicals might be providing a positive signal for the release of TNF comes from work on the mechanism of TNFβ (lymphotoxin) release (41). This mediator, which has about 30% homology in its amino acid sequence with TNF (42), occupies the same cellular receptors (43) and hence shares many of the functions of TNF (e.g., reference 44).

Various hydroxyl radical scavengers inhibit generation of TNFβ by cells (**Table 1**). Table 1 also shows that urea, an agent structurally related to thiourea and tetramethylurea, but a poor radical scavenger, was inactive. The NADPH oxidase system was activated during release of TNFβ. Another group has shown that oxidation of terminal galactose residues on the surface of human monocytes (using galactose oxidase or sodium periodate) induces release of a monokine that can signal T lymphocytes to release IFN-γ (45). TNF is the only monokine known at present to possess this property (46,26). Like TNF (and unusual among cytokines), their monokine was not species specific. New data from our laboratory consistent with a radical-mediated step in TNF release include its enhancement by hydrogen peroxide and inhibition by deferoxamine and BHA (G. Chaudhri and I.A. Clark, unpublished data).

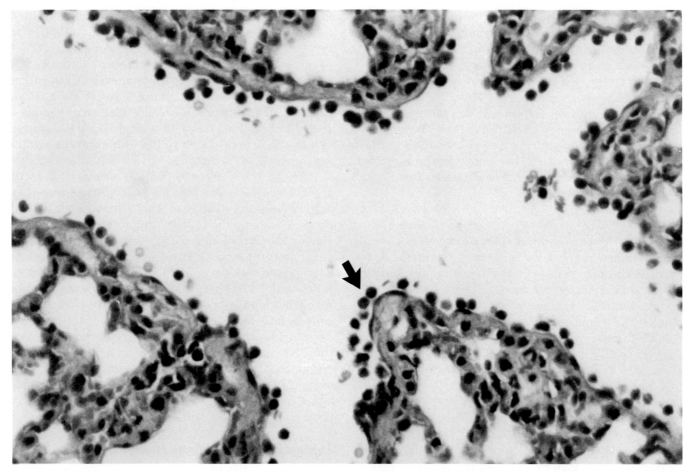

Figure 3. Neutrophils adhering to the endothelium of a mouse infected with *Plasmodium vinckei* with a low parasitemia 5 hours after intravenous injection of 10 μg of recombinant human TNF. Uninjected mice do not show this change until the parasite load is 7 to 8 times higher.

TISSUE INJURY AND THE INTERPLAY OF FREE RADICALS AND TNF

Certain histological changes common to various diseases can be reproduced in vivo by either free radical generators or TNF.

Endothelial Cell Damage From Neutrophils

Neutrophils adhere to vascular endothelium, which may be injured by reactive oxygen species released from the neutrophils (47,48). This phenomenon, seen in pulmonary vessels in burns, sepsis, and trauma, as well as in falciparum malaria (49), has been studied closely from a free radical viewpoint. The direct observation of neutrophils adhering to vessel walls in the hamster cheek pouch after perfusion with radical generators (50) provides a model that seems sufficient to explain adherent neutrophils in oxygen toxicity (51) and paraquat poisoning (52).

If, however, radicals promote generation of TNF, as suggested in the preceding section, this monokine could be involved in even the simplest in vivo model of neutrophil-mediated endothelial damage. Recent experiments in a well-defined in vitro system have shown that recombinant TNF will cause neutrophils to aggregate (53) and to adhere to vascular endothelium (53,54). Treatment of either the neutrophils or the endothelium is sufficient to cause aggregation and adherence, and exposure to as little as 2 ng/mL of TNF initiates changes that require no protein or RNA synthesis, yet lead to maximal adherence four hours later (54). This adherence works well in vivo (**Figure 3**) (12). Subsequent studies (55) have implicated the CDw18 membrane antigen complex on the neutrophil surface as the site of this adherence. It will be instructive to see if the neutrophil adherence seen in oxygen toxicity (51) and ischemia/reperfusion injury (56) also involves the CDw18 antigen.

Clearly, repeating the earlier experiments involving neutrophils and endothelial damage (48,50), using recombinant TNF and antibody that neutralizes TNF as additional variables, will be informative. It seems reasonable to predict that reactive oxygen species and TNF will prove to have interdependent roles in these in vivo events, the initial radical production helping to induce the TNF that then causes neutrophils to adhere (54) and also sensitizes them to agents that provoke them to release further reactive oxygen (22). Indeed, there is evidence that TNF can directly provoke generation of superoxide by neutrophils (57). Thus TNF could act as an amplifying loop for reactive oxygen species in this system, which may also involve PAF. We should note that TNF can injure endothelial cells directly (58,59) and that, at very low concentrations, it is chemotactic for monocytes and neutrophils (60).

Dyserythropoiesis

Dyserythropoiesis contributes to the anemia seen in patients with chronic infections, malaria, and certain tumors, with distinctive changes being observed in erythroid precursors. These changes also occur in the bone marrow of vitamin E-deficient monkeys (61) and pigs (62). Inhibition of erythroid colony formation can be duplicated in vitro by enzymatically produced reactive oxygen or by stimulated neutrophils (63). On the other hand, there is ample evidence that both crude (64,65) and recombinant TNF (66) can suppress development of erythroid colonies in vitro, and we have recently found (I.A. Clark, unpublished data) that the malformed erythroid precursors seen in malaria can be reproduced in vivo by injecting recombinant TNF. Thus the interactions discussed earlier, with radicals both generating TNF (41,45) and being generated by TNF (22,57), may each need to be considered in an attempt to understand acquired dyserythropoiesis.

Cerebral Malaria In Mice Infected With
Plasmodium berghei (ANKA Strain)

Mice infected with non-ANKA strains of *P. berghei* withstand high (70%) parasitemias before they become ill, and then exhibit no cerebral symptoms or histological changes. For unknown reasons *P. berghei* ANKA causes, in most strains of mice, a distinct syndrome in which severe cerebral signs and pathological changes develop at much lower (7% to 15%) parasitemias. Monocytes adhere to the endothelial cells of cerebral vessels, and scattered foci of hemorrhage follow endothelial injury (67). Although not providing a close parallel to the early events in human cerebral malaria, this model continues to be studied because no other nonhuman model is available.

To investigate the possibility that reactive oxygen species might be contributing to the vascular damage, we fed to mice, from 7 days before infection until the end of the experiment, a diet containing either 0.75% BHA or 0.5% ethoxyquin. Instead of dying with cerebral symptoms 7 to 10 days after infection, as did

mice fed the control diet, those fed the supplemented diets lived for 20 to 30 days after infection (68). The increased longevity was not a consequence of suppressed parasitemia, and cerebral pathological changes were absent. Others have recently reported this same outcome after giving a single injection of rabbit antibody specific for mouse TNF on either day 4 or day 7 of the infection (69). These authors also used serum TNF levels to predict which mice would develop cerebral symptoms.

Where these agents (68,69) are acting is at present unclear. One obvious possibility is that they are influencing events at the site of endothelial injury, but in the light of the information in the earlier sections of this paper, this clearly is not the only interpretation. Since the cerebral pathological changes do not develop in mice that do not have functional T lymphocytes (70,71), the antioxidants may (additionally or solely) inhibit activation of these cells in vivo, as we have found in vitro (25). As noted earlier, this could operate by blocking production of the TNF that enhances expression of IL-2 receptors (26) or that stimulates leukocytes to release reactive oxygen (22,57). Likewise, antibody to TNF could operate at each of these levels, as well as by preventing direct damage to endothelium (58, 59).

Models For Autoimmune Diseases

There now seems little doubt that suppressing free radical fluxes will inhibit the development of experimental neurological pathological changes, since in addition to our original experiments with deferoxamine in experimental allergic encephalitis (72), others have used superoxide dismutase, catalase, and the organoselenium compound ebselen to inhibit experimental allergic neuritis also in the rat (73). In addition, current work in our laboratory indicates prolonged survival in a hyperacute model of experimental allergic encephalitis (in which pertussis is used instead of complete Freund's adjuvant) in rats given BHA in ALZET osmotic pumps (L. Hansen, N.H. Hunt, and W.B. Cowden, unpublished data). This same diet significantly increased the longevity of MRL/lpr mice (**Figure 4**), a strain that innately develops an autoimmune state similar to systemic lupus erythematosus. An obvious interpretation of all these experiments in vivo is that free radical-induced tissue damage mediated by leukocytes is being directly inhibited. But since T lymphocyte activation is probably necessary in all of these models (as it is in cerebral malaria caused by *P. berghei*), the apparent role of free radicals in this activation must also be taken into account. Furthermore, it is yet to be established whether neutralizing antibody against TNF has the same influence on these disease models as has been reported for murine cerebral malaria (69).

UPJOHN SYMPOSIUM/OXYGEN RADICALS April 1987

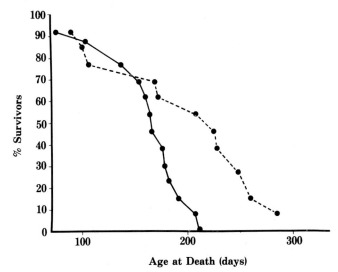

Figure 4. Longevity of MRL/lpr strain mice fed a diet containing 0.75% butylated hydroxyanisole (BHA) (---) or a control diet (—). The diets were fed to breeding pairs before and during gestation and suckling and to the offspring throughout life. Each point represents the time of death of one mouse.

If so, it uncovers another possible role for modulators of radical fluxes in these systems, and, in antibody to TNF, reveals a tool with wide application.

A further level of complexity is placed on the relationship between free radicals and TNF by the possibility, raised recently (74), that when TNF causes cellular injury it does so by generating radicals intracellularly. Attenuation of TNF toxicity by the metal chelator *o*-phenanthroline (75) and by azide and dinitrophenol (76) supports this possibility.

CONCLUSIONS

The interrelationships between radical species and cytokines, particularly TNF, must be more completely understood if the outcome of in vivo experiments using iron chelators and radical scavengers is to be interpreted correctly. Their roles in T cell activation need particular attention in infectious and autoimmune diseases.

ACKNOWLEDGMENT

This study received support from the malaria component of the UNDP/World Bank/WHO Special Programme for Research and Training in Tropical Diseases and from the National Health and Medical Research Council of Australia. We also thank Elizabeth Jackson, who kindly typed this manuscript.

REFERENCES

1. Carswell EA, Old LJ, Kassel RL, Green S, Fiore N, Williamson B. An endotoxin-induced serum factor that causes necrosis of tumors. Proc Natl Acad Sci USA 1975:72:3666-3670.

2. Clark IA. Does endotoxin cause both disease and parasite death in acute malaria and babesiosis? Lancet 1978:i:75-77.

3. Clark IA, Virelizier J-L, Carswell EA, Wood PR. Possible importance of macrophage-derived mediators in acute malaria. Infect Immun 1981:32:1058-1066.

4. Taverne J, Dockrell HM, Playfair JHL. Endotoxin-induced serum factor kills malaria parasites in vitro. Infect Immun 1981:33:83-89.

5. Beutler B, Greenwald D, Hulmes JD, et al. Identity of tumor necrosis factor and the macrophage-secreted factor cachectin. Nature 1985:316:552-554.

6. Hotez PJ, Le Trang N, Fairlamb AH, Cerami A. Lipoprotein lipase suppression in 3T3-LI cells by a hemoprotozoan-induced mediator from peritoneal exudate cells. Para Immunol 1984:6:203-209.

7. Beutler B, Mahoney J, Le Trang N, Pekala P, Cerami A. Purification of cachectin, a lipoprotein lipase-suppressing hormone secreted by endotoxin-induced RAW 264.7 cells. J Exp Med 1985:161:984-995.

8. Collins T, Lapierre LA, Fiers W, Strominger JL, Pober JS. Recombinant human tumor necrosis factor increases mRNA levels and surface expression of HLA-A, B antigens in vascular endothelial cells and dermal fibroblasts in vitro. Proc Natl Acad Sci USA 1986:83:446-450.

9. Pfizenmaier K, Scheurich P, Schluter C, Kronke M. Tumor necrosis factor enhances HLA-A, B, C and HLA-DR gene expression in human tumor cells. J Immunol 1987:138:975-980.

10. Palombella VJ, Yamashiro DJ, Maxfield FR, Decker SJ, Vilcek J. Tumor necrosis factor increases the number of epidermal growth factor receptors on human fibroblasts. J Biol Chem 1987:262:1950-1954.

11. Pujol-Borrel R, Todd I, Doshi M, et al. HLA Class II induction in human islet cells by interferon-γ plus tumour necrosis factor or lymphotoxin. Nature 1987:326:304-306.

12. Tracey KJ, Beutler B, Lowry SF, et al. Shock and tissue injury induced by recombinant human cachectin. Science 1986:234:470-474.

13. Tracey KJ, Lowry SF, Fahey TJ. Cachectin/tumor necrosis factor induces lethal shock and stress hormone responses in the dog. Surg Gynecol Obstet 1986:164:415-422.

14. Beutler B, Cerami A. Cachectin: more than a tumor necrosis factor. N Engl J Med 1987:316:379-385.

15. Beutler B, Milsark IW, Cerami A. Passive immunization against cachectin/tumor necrosis factor protects mice from lethal effects of endotoxin. Science 1985:229:869-871.

16. Beutler B, Cerami A. Cachectin and tumour necrosis factor as two sides of the same biological coin. Nature 1986:320:584-588.

17. Nedwin GE, Svedersky LP, Bringman TS, Palladino MA, Goeddel DV. Effect of interleukin-2, interferon-γ, and mitogens on the production of tumor necrosis factors α and β. J Immunol 1985:135:2492-2497.

18. Collart MA, Belin D, Vassalli J-D, De Kossodo S, Varsalli P. γ-Interferon enhances macrophage transcription of the tumor necrosis factor/cachectin, interleukin 1, and urokinase genes, which are controlled by short-lived repressors. J Exp Med 1986:164:2113-2118.

19. Aggarwal BB, Eessalu TE, Hass PE. Characterization of receptors for human tumour necrosis factor and their regulation by interferon. Nature 1985:318:665-667.

20. Ruggiero V, Tavernier J, Fiers W, Baglioni C. Induction of

the synthesis of tumor necrosis factor receptors by interferon-γ. J Immunol 1986:136:2445-2450.

21. Chang RJ, Lee SH. Effects of interferon-γ and tumor necrosis factor-α on the expression of an Ia antigen on a murine macrophage cell line. J Immunol 1986:137:2853-2856.

22. Klebanoff SJ, Vadas MA, Harlan JM et al. Stimulation of neutrophils by tumor necrosis factor. J Immunol 1986:136:4220-4225.

23. Hoffbrand AV, Ganeshaguru K, Hooton JWL, Tattersall MHN. Effect of iron deficiency and desferrioxamine on DNA synthesis in human cells. Br J Haematol 1976:33:515-526.

24. Wrogemann K, Weidemann MJ, Peskar BA, Staudinger H, Rietschel ET, Fischer H. Chemiluminescence and immune activation. 1. Early activation of rat thymocytes can be monitored by chemiluminescence measurements. Eur J Immunol 1978:8:749-752.

25. Chaudhri G, Clark IA, Hunt NH, Cowden WB, Ceredig R. Effects of antioxidants on primary alloantigen-induced T cell activation and proliferation. J Immunol 1986:137:2646-2652.

26. Scheurich P, Thoma B, Ucer U, Pfizenmaier K. Immunoregulatory activity of recombinant human tumor necrosis factor (TNF)-α: induction of TNF receptors on human T cells and TNF-α-mediated enhancement of T cell responses. J Immunol 1987:138:1786-1790.

27. Spear GT, Teodorescu M. Enhancement of human MLR by very low concentrations of lipopolysaccharide and blocking of this enhancement by polymyxin B. J Immunol Methods 1984:73:321-327.

28. Peterhans E. Sendai virus stimulates chemiluminescence in mouse spleen cells. Biochem Biophys Res Comm 1979:91:383-392.

29. Aderka D, Holtmann H, Toker L, Hahn T, Wallach D. Tumor necrosis factor induction by Sendai virus. J Immunol 1986:136:2938-2942.

30. Janco RL, English D. Regulation of monocyte oxidative metabolism: chemotactic factor enhancement of superoxide release, hydroxyl radical generation, and chemiluminescence. J Lab Clin Med 1983:102:890-898.

31. Kobayashi Y, Asada M, Osawa T. Production of lymphotoxin and tumour necrosis factor by a T-cell hybridoma. Immunology 1987:60:213-217.

32. Tom WM, Montgomery MR. Biochemical and morphological assessments of bleomycin pulmonary toxicity in rats. Toxicol Appl Pharmacol 1980:53:64-74.

33. Dinarello CA, Ward SB, Wolff SM. Pyrogenic properties of bleomycin (NSC-125066). Cancer Chemother Rep 1973:57:393-398.

34. Spriggs DR, Sherman ML, Kufe DW, Frei E. Tumour necrosis factor: clinical trials and future directions. In: Bock G, Whelan J, Marsh J, eds. Tumour necrosis factor and related cytotoxins. Ciba Foundation Symposium No. 131. Philadelphia: John Wiley, 1987:206-207.

35. Dinarello CA, Cannon JG, Wolff SM, et al. Tumor necrosis factor (cachectin) is an endogenous pyrogen and induces production of interleukin 1. J Exp Med 1986:163:1433-1450.

36. Pritchard KA, Patel ST, Karpen CW, Newman HAI, Panganamala RV. Triglyceride-lowering effect of dietary vitamin E in streptozocin-induced diabetic rats: increased lipoprotein lipase activity in livers of diabetic rats fed high dietary vitamin E. Diabetes 1986:35:278-281.

37. Pekala P, Kawakami M, Vine W, Lane MD, Cerami A. Studies of insulin resistance in adipocytes induced by macrophage mediator. J Exp Med 1983:157:1360-1365.

38. Pabst MJ, Johnston RB. Increased production of superoxide anion by macrophages exposed in vitro to muramyl dipeptide or lipopolysaccharide. J Exp Med 1980:151:101-114.

39. Johnston RB, Godzik CA, Cohn ZA. Increased superoxide anion production by immunologically activated and chemically elicited macrophages. J Exp Med 1978:148:115-127.

40. Green S, Dobrjansky A, Carswell EA, et al. Partial purification of a serum factor that causes necrosis of tumors. Proc Natl Acad Sci USA 1976:73:381-385.

41. Kobayashi Y, Asada M, Osawa T. Mechanism of phorbol myristate acetate-induced lymphotoxin production by a human T cell hybridoma. J Biochem 1984:95:1775-1782.

42. Pennica D, Nedwin GE, Hayflick JS, et al. Human tumour necrosis factor: precursor structure, expression and homology to lymphotoxin. Nature 1984:312:724-729.

43. Kull FC, Jacobs S, Cuatrecasas P. Cellular receptor for ^{125}I-labeled tumor necrosis factor: specific binding, affinity labeling, and relationship to sensitivity. Proc Natl Acad Sci USA 1985:82:5756-5760.

44. Wong GH, Goeddel DV. Tumour necrosis factors α and β inhibit virus replication and synergize with interferons. Nature 1986:323:819-822.

45. Antonelli G, Blalock JE, Dianzani F. Generation of a soluble IFN-γ inducer by oxidation of galactose residues on macrophages. Cell Immunol 1985:94:440-446.

46. Wong HW, Goeddel DV. Interferon-γ induces the expression of tumor necrosis factor/lymphotoxin and vice versa. 6th Internat Cong Immunol, Toronto [Abstracts] 1986:365.

47. Till GO, Johnson KJ, Kunkel R, Ward PA. Intravascular activation of complement and acute lung injury: dependence on neutrophils and toxic oxygen metabolites. J Clin Invest 1982:69:1126-1135.

48. Ward PA, Till GO, Kunkel R, Beauchamp C. Evidence for role of hydroxyl radical in complement and neutrophil-dependent tissue injury. J Clin Invest 1983:72:789-801.

49. Macpherson GG, Warrell MJ, White NJ, Looareesuwan S, Warrell DA. Human cerebral malaria: a quantitative ultrastructural analysis of parasitized erythrocyte sequestration. Am J Path 1985:119:385-401.

50. Del Maestro RF, Thaw HH, Bjork J, Planker M, Arfors K-E. Free radicals as mediators of tissue injury. Acta Physiol Scand 1980:Suppl 492:43-57.

51. Fox RB, Hoidal JR, Brown DM, Repine JE. Pulmonary inflammation due to oxygen toxicity: involvement of chemotactic factors and polymorphonuclear leukocytes. Am Rev Resp Dis 1981:123:521-523.

52. Schoenberger CI, Rennard SI, Bitterman PB, Fukuda Y, Ferrans VJ, Crystal RG. Paraquat-induced pulmonary fibrosis: role of the alveolitis in modulating the development of fibrosis. Am Rev Resp Dis 1984:129:168-173.

53. Larrick JW, Fendly BM, Gray O, Toy K, Senyk G. Tumor necrosis factor (TNF) activates and aggregates human granulocytes. Blood 1985:66(suppl 1):89a.

54. Gamble JR, Harlan JM, Klebanoff SJ, Vadas MA. Stimulation of the adherence of neutrophils to umbilical vein endothelium by human recombinant tumor necrosis factor. Proc Natl Acad Sci USA 1985:82:8867-8871.

55. Pohlman TH, Stanness KA, Beatty PG, Ochs HD, Harlan JM. An endothelial cell surface factor induced in vitro by lipopolysaccharide, interleukin 1, and tumor necrosis factor-α increases neutrophil adherence by a CDw18-dependent mechanism. J Immunol 1986:136:4548-4553.

56. Romson JL, Hook BG, Kunkel SL, et al. Reduction of the extent of ischemic myocardial injury by neutrophil depletion in the dog. Circulation 1983:67:1016-1023.

57. Tsujimoto M, Yokota S, Vilcek J, Weissmann G. Tumor necrosis factor provokes superoxide anion generation from neutrophils. Biochem Biophys Res Comm 1986:137:1094-1100.

58. Stolpen AH, Guinan EC, Fiers W, Pober JS. Recombinant tumor necrosis factor and immune interferon act singly and in combination to reorganize human vascular endothelial cell monolayers. Am J Path 1986:123:16-24.

59. Sato N, Goto T, Haranaka K, et al. Actions of tumor necrosis factor on cultured vascular endothelial cells: morphological modulation, growth inhibition and cytotoxicity. J Natl Cancer Inst 1986:75:1113-1121.

60. Ming WJ, Bersani L, Mantovani A. Tumor necrosis factor is chemotactic for monocytes and polymorphonuclear leukocytes. J Immunol 1987:138:1469-1474.

61. Porter FS, Fitch CD, Dinning JS. Vitamin E deficiency in the monkey. IV. Further studies of the anemia with emphasis on bone marrow morphology. Blood 1962:20:471-477.

62. Lynch RE, Hammar SP, Lee GR, Cartwright GE. The anemia of vitamin E deficiency in swine: an experimental model of the congenital dyserythropoietic anemias. Am J Hematol 1977:2:145-148.

63. Schulman JC, Vercellotti G, Jacob HS, Zanjani ED. Anemia of chronic inflammation: role of inflammatory cell oxidants in erythropoietic depression and its reversal by intact red blood cells. Blood 1985:66(suppl 1):55a.

64. Shah RG, Green S, Moore MAS. Colony stimulating and inhibiting activities in mouse serum after Corynebacterium parvum-endotoxin treatment. J Reticuloendothel Soc 1978:23:29-41.

65. Sassa S, Kawakami M, Cerami A. Inhibition of the growth and differentiation of erythroid precursor cells by an endotoxin-induced mediator from peritoneal macrophages. Proc Natl Acad Sci USA 1983:80:1717-1720.

66. Abboud S, Gerson SL, Berger NA. The effect of recombinant human tumor necrosis factor on normal human progenitor cells. Blood 1985:66(suppl 5):124a.

67. Rest JR. Cerebral malaria in inbred mice: a new model and its pathology. Trans Roy Soc Trop Med Hyg 1982:76:410-415.

68. Clark IA, Chaudhri G, Thumwood CM, Hunt NH, Cowden WB. Free radicals in malarial immunopathology. In: Rice-Evans C, ed. Free radicals, oxidant stress and drug action. London: Richelieu Press, 1987:237-255.

69. Grau GE, Fajardo LF, Piguet P-F, Allet B, Lambert P-H, Vassalli P. Tumor necrosis factor (cachetin) as an essential mediator in murine cerebral malaria. Science 1987:237:1210-1212.

70. Finley RW, Mackey LJ, Lambert P-H. Virulent P. berghei malaria: prolonged survival and decreased cerebral pathology in cell-deficient nude mice. J Immunol 1982:129:2213-2218.

71. Grau GE, Piguet P-F, Engers HD, Louis JA, Vassalli P, Lambert P-H. L3T4$^+$ T lymphocytes play a major role in the pathogenesis of murine cerebral malaria. J Immunol 1986:137:2348-2354.

72. Bowern N, Ramshaw IA, Clark IA, Doherty PC. Inhibition of autoimmune neuropathological process by treatment with an iron-chelating agent. J Exp Med 1984:160:1532-1543.

73. Hartung HP, Schafer B, Heininger K, Toyka KV. Reduced oxygen species induce functional deficits and tissue damage in experimental allergic neuritis. Abstracts of Biennial SFRR Meeting, Dusseldorf, July 1986:66.

74. Jones GRN. Free radicals in immunological killing: the case of tumor necrotizing factor (TNF). Med Hypoth 1986:21:267-271.

75. Ruff MR, Gifford GE. Tumour necrosis factor. In: Pick E, ed. Lymphokines, vol 2. New York: Academic Press, 1981:235-272.

76. Matthews N, Watkins JF. Tumour necrosis factor from the rabbit. 1. Mode of action, specificity and physicochemical properties. Br J Cancer 1978:3:302-309.

QUESTIONS AND COMMENTS

Dr. Richard Johnston, Jr.: Could you speculate on the possible involvement of oxidants in mediating the cachexia that is associated with TNF? Perhaps the oxidant-induced metabolic damage described by Cochrane and colleagues is the final result of TNF (cachectin) activity.

Dr. Ian Clark: The cachexia and the oxidant-induced metabolic damage are conceivably linked by oxidants inducing TNF secretion, but the cachexia is thought to be related to inhibition of lipoprotein lipase and related enzymes, and I have seen no evidence that these are selectively blocked in oxidant stress.

OXYGEN RADICALS AND PARKINSON'S DISEASE

Gerald Cohen

The accelerated loss of pigmented neurons seen in Parkinson's disease may result, in part, from an increased catabolism of the catecholamine dopamine within the remaining neurons. Catabolism of dopamine by monoamine oxidase within nerve terminals produces hydrogen peroxide; increased catabolism could produce amounts of hydrogen peroxide that damage the neuron directly or indirectly through the formation of hydroxyl radicals. This paper describes experiments that led to and have tested this working hypothesis. Studies in vitro and in vivo that either increase dopamine concentrations in nerve terminals or that inhibit dopamine metabolism support this hypothesis. The dopamine catabolism hypothesis of neuronal damage provides a valuable guide for the design of experiments to investigate mechanisms of altered neuronal function in central nervous system disorders that affect catecholamine neurons.

PARKINSON'S DISEASE is characterized by an accelerated senescence of pigmented neurons in the pars compacta of the substantia nigra. These neurons synthesize and secrete dopamine (3,4-dihydroxyphenylethylamine, a catecholamine) as their neurotransmitter. The neurons project to the striatum, where they regulate motor activity. Pigmentation within the cell bodies is due to the presence of neuromelanin, which is believed to be formed by the polymerization of dopamine.

We all lose melanized nigrostriatal neurons through an apparently natural process as we age. When about 80% of the neurons are lost, tremor and rigidity appear, symptoms that are the hallmarks of Parkinson's disease. For reasons that have not yet been clarified, the loss of melanized dopamine neurons appears to be accelerated in Parkinson's disease. Studies of twins have tended to rule out genetic factors. Some investigators are considering the possible action of environmental toxins in accelerating the demise of dopamine neurons.

A working hypothesis has been developed, based on studies of catecholamine neurons in laboratory experiments, that the natural metabolism of dopamine within nerve terminals can produce an oxidative stress that promotes neuronal senescence. Emphasis is placed upon the turnover of dopamine by monoamine oxidase, an enzyme that generates hydrogen peroxide (H_2O_2) as a metabolic end-product. The H_2O_2 can act directly as a cellular oxidant and can also serve as a precursor of the reactive hydroxyl

From Department of Neurology, Mount Sinai School of Medicine, City University of New York, New York, USA.

Address correspondence to Dr. Gerald Cohen, Department of Neurology and Graduate School in Biomedical Sciences, Mount Sinai School of Medicine, City University of New York, Fifth Avenue and 100th Street, New York, New York 10029, USA.

radical ($\cdot$OH). Experimental evidence supports the view that dopamine turnover is amplified as dopamine neurons are lost.

THE WORKING HYPOTHESIS

Oxidative deamination of dopamine by monoamine oxidase, present in the outer membrane of mitochondria, is the main catabolic pathway for dopamine within dopamine nerve terminals. The reaction leads to formation of H_2O_2:

$$\text{Dopamine} + O_2 + H_2O \rightarrow$$
$$\text{3,4-dihydroxyphenylacetaldehyde} + NH_3 + H_2O_2 \quad [1]$$

The average concentration of dopamine in a dopamine nerve terminal is estimated to be 50 mM (1). A major portion is stored in vesicles, where the dopamine is protected from catabolism. The cytoplasmic pool of dopamine is, however, subject to oxidation by monoamine oxidase. This cytoplasmic pool is transiently elevated by the reuptake of released neurotransmitter, which is the immediate fate of a major fraction of the released dopamine. Thus, natural physiologic processes associated with neurotransmitter release can lead to an oxidative stress mediated by monoamine oxidase and H_2O_2 (2). This H_2O_2 can induce damage directly, e.g., by oxidizing sulfhydryl groups of proteins, and can act indirectly by forming oxy-radicals, namely, superoxide ($O_2^{\cdot-}$) and $\cdot$OH.

Hefti et al (3) provided experimental evidence that dopamine turnover is increased in rats with partial lesions of the substantia nigra. In their experiments, nigral dopamine neurons were destroyed in a dose-dependent manner by intranigral injection of 6-hydroxydopamine, a nerve toxin. The formation of acidic metabolites of dopamine (used as an index of monoamine oxidase activity) was measured and related to the number of surviving nerve terminals in the striatum. A marked increase was observed as the loss of neurons approached 80%. This observation reflects known feedback regulatory phenomena, such as increased neuronal firing rates (after partial denervation) and increased biosynthetic activity (allosteric change in tyrosine hydroxylase), which together increase the amount of dopamine released per unit of time from the surviving dopamine neurons. Since a portion of the released dopamine is recaptured and metabolized within the dopamine nerve terminals, the steady-state levels of H_2O_2 in

Table 1. Detection of Hydroxyl Radicals with Methional During the Autoxidation of Dialurate or 6-Hydroxydopamine (6-OH-DA)*

Cell Toxin	Ethylene (nmol)[†]
Dialurate (0.1 mM)	1.53
6-OH-DA (0.1 mM)	2.79

* The methional concentration was 1 mM. The experiments were run in an acetate buffer, pH 6.4. Data from reference 6.
[†] Ethylene gas production was measured by head-space gas chromatography.

Table 2. Prevention of Alloxan-Induced Diabetes in Mice by Hydroxyl Radical Scavengers*

Treatment[†]	Blood Glucose[**] (mg/100 mL)
Untreated control	120
Alloxan (50 mg/kg, IV)	445
Ethanol (4 g/kg, IP) + Alloxan	107
Thiourea (3 g/kg, IP) + Alloxan	147

* Data from reference 7.
[†] Ethanol was given 30 minutes before and thiourea 2 hours before alloxan.
[**] Blood glucose concentrations were measured 72 hours after alloxan was given.

surviving dopamine terminals may increase fivefold after destruction of 80% of the neuronal population.

Hence, we are led to consider the possibility that loss of nigrostriatal neurons in human subjects, either as a result of the natural aging process or due to some unspecified intracellular or environmental stress, sets the stage for a self-generated oxidative stress. The net result could be an accelerated rate of senescence of the surviving nigrostriatal neurons. In this model, the natural physiological activity of dopamine neurons (release, reuptake, and catabolism of the neurotransmitter) adds to and accelerates neuronal senescence.

EXPERIMENTS LEADING TO THE WORKING HYPOTHESIS

Alloxan and 6-hydroxydopamine are two well-known cellular toxins. Alloxan (a quinoidal compound) and its reduced form, dialuric acid (a polyhydroxylated compound), induce a diabetic state in experimental animals by destroying the insulin-producing β-cells of the pancreas. 6-Hydroxydopamine (a polyhydroxylated compound) and its oxidized forms (o- and p-quinones) destroy catecholamine neurons.

Dialuric acid and 6-hydroxydopamine are unstable in the presence of oxygen and undergo rapid spontaneous reactions (autoxidation) at or near neutral pH to form quinodal compounds. Ascorbate recycles the quinoidal products by reducing them to the hydroxylated compounds and thus augments both oxygen consumption and the production of reactive oxygen species (4). The production of $O_2^{-\cdot}$ in this in vitro system was documented by experiments with superoxide dismutase (5). The generation of highly reactive $\cdot OH$ was detected in experiments in vitro (**Table 1**) (6) with what has become a standard method, ethylene gas production from methional or from 2-keto-4-methylthiobutyrate. In other experiments not shown in Table 1, ethylene production was suppressed by catalase, superoxide dismutase, and competitive scavengers of $\cdot OH$.

Do alloxan and 6-hydroxydopamine induce cell damage by generating $\cdot OH$? To test this possibility, experimental animals were pretreated with $\cdot OH$ scavengers (7,8). Protection by the scavengers against diabetes caused by alloxan or against peripheral sympathectomy caused by 6-hydroxydopamine would be prima facie evidence for the involvement of $\cdot OH$. In the experiments with alloxan (**Table 2**), the scavengers protected mice against the elevation in blood glucose that reflects the loss of insulin-producing cells. In addition, protection against degranulation of the pancreatic β-cells was observed histologically. In the experiments with 6-hydroxydopamine (**Table 3**), the scavengers diminished the loss of catecholamine uptake that reflects the loss of sympathetic (noradrenergic) nerve terminals in the left atrium. Protection of the nerve plexus in the iris was also observed by fluorescence histochemistry. These, and additional experiments by other investigators (e.g., 9,10), provide strong evidence for $\cdot OH$-mediated cellular damage by alloxan and 6-hydroxydopamine.

Although 5,7-dihydroxytryptamine was originally developed as a toxin for serotonin neurons, experimental studies showed that it also destroys

Table 3. Protection Against Peripheral Sympathectomy from 6-Hydroxydopamine (6-OH-DA) in Mice by Hydroxyl Radical Scavengers*

Treatment[†]	% of Nerve Plexus Remaining
Untreated control	100
6-OH-DA (4 mg/kg, IV)	41
Ethanol (4 g/kg, IP) + 6-OH-DA	59[**]
6-OH-DA (10 mg/kg, IV)	17
PTTU (200 mg/kg, IP) + 6-OH-DA	68[**]

* Data from reference 8.
[†] The scavengers were injected 1 hour before 6-OH-DA was given. The sympathetic innervation of the left atrium was measured quantitatively by the uptake of tritium-labeled norepinephrine. PTTU is phenylthiazolylthiourea, a $\cdot OH$ scavenger that can penetrate into sympathetic neurons.
[**] The scavenger provided significant protection (P<0.01).

Table 4. Protection Against Peripheral Sympathectomy from 5,7-Dihydroxytryptamine (5,7-DHT) in Mice by Hydroxyl Radical Scavengers or Monoamine Oxidase Inhibitor*

Treatment[†]	% of Nerve Plexus Remaining
Untreated control	100
5,7-DHT (40 mg/kg, IV)	35
Ethanol (4 g/kg, IP)+5,7-DHT	73**
PTTU (200 mg/kg, IP)+5,7-DHT	60**
Nialamide (50 mg/kg, IP)+5,7-DHT	80**

* Data from reference 11.
† Protective agents were injected 1 hour before 5,7-DHT was given. The sympathetic innervation of the left atrium was measured quantitatively by the uptake of tritium-labeled norepinephrine. PTTU is phenylthiazolylthiourea, a ·OH scavenger. Nialamide is a monoamine oxidase inhibitor.
** The protective agents provided significant protection (P<0.01).

Table 5. Protection of Dopamine (DA) Nerve Terminals by α-Methyl-p-Tyrosine Methyl Ester (AMPT) in Experimental Stroke in Gerbils*

Treatment[†]	Viable DA Nerve Terminals (% of Control)
Untreated control	100
Stroke	27
AMPT (250 mg/kg, IP)+Stroke	54**
AMPT (400 mg/kg, IP)+Stroke	82**

* Data from reference 14.
† The AMPT was injected 6 hours before left carotid artery ligation. Nerve terminal viability at 16 hours after carotid ligation was assessed by synaptosomal uptake of tritium-labeled dopamine.
** The AMPT provided significant protection (P<0.01).

catecholamine neurons. To test the possibility that 5,7-dihydroxytryptamine mediates neuronal damage by generating ·OH, experimental animals were pretreated with ·OH scavengers before 5,7-dihydroxytryptamine was injected (11). The ·OH scavengers ethanol and phenylthiazolylthiourea prevented the loss of the catecholamine uptake by sympathetic nerve terminals that innervate the left atrium (**Table 4**). Nialamide, an inhibitor of monoamine oxidase, was also protective; other investigators (12) have observed protection by pargyline, another monoamine oxidase inhibitor. These results imply formation of neurodestructive amounts of ·OH from the H_2O_2 that is generated by monoamine oxidase in the presence of 5,7-dihydroxytryptamine.

EXPERIMENTS EMANATING FROM THE WORKING HYPOTHESIS

If the degradation of endogenous catecholamines by monoamine oxidase produces an oxidant stress (via H_2O_2 production), then limiting catabolism by monoamine oxidase could be protective. Therefore, attempts to limit catecholamine levels or metabolism by monoamine oxidase were undertaken in several forms of experimental neurotoxicity.

Cerebral ischemia in the Mongolian gerbil provides a valuable experimental model for unilateral ischemic stroke. In gerbils lacking an intact circle of Willis (about 40% of the population), occlusion of one common carotid artery results in ischemic stroke in that hemisphere, while the contralateral hemisphere is essentially (but not entirely) unaffected. Thus, damage to neurons in the ischemic hemisphere can be assessed by comparison to control neurons in the contralateral hemisphere, within a single animal. In an initial study with this model, the damage to

dopamine nerve terminals was compared with that to terminals that secrete glutamate or γ-aminobutyrate (GABA) as neurotransmitters. Damage to dopamine terminals was more pronounced than damage to glutamate or GABA terminals (13), even when these terminals exist side by side in the same brain region (the striatum).

These and other observations led to evaluation of α-methyl-p-tyrosine methyl ester (AMPT, an inhibitor of tyrosine hydroxylase) as an agent that might protect dopamine nerve terminals (14). By inhibiting tyrosine hydroxylase, dopamine levels are depleted and dopamine catabolism by monoamine oxidase is minimized. AMPT provided significant protection against ischemic neuronal damage in the Mongolian gerbil model (**Table 5**). These results imply that endogenous dopamine mediates damage to cerebral terminals in experimental ischemia. It is important to note that, although ischemic tissue is hypoxic, it is not anoxic. Hence, oxidative phenomena, such as monoamine oxidase activity, can continue. A variety of factors emanating from the hypoxic state could predispose neurons to increased damage from generated H_2O_2.

Although these experimental results are provocative, they do not establish monoamine oxidase activity as a factor in the neurotoxic mechanism. Protection of both glutamate and serotonin neurons was also observed (not shown in Table 5). This unexpected protection of non-catecholamine nerve terminals is not easily explained by diminished catabolism of dopamine. Further studies are required to distinguish between a direct protective action of AMPT in brain and a protection mediated by elimination of endogenous catecholamines (i.e., elimination of catabolic pathways or elimination of neurotransmitter actions). It is of great interest that AMPT also blocks the neurodegenerative actions of methamphetamine on dopamine neurons in rodents (15). It seems likely that similar neurochemical mechanisms are involved in damage induced by brain ischemia and by methamphetamine.

Another model derives from the parkinsonism reported (16,17) in young adults who deliberately ingested illicit meperidine analogs contaminated with a synthetic byproduct, 1-methyl-4-phenyl-1,2,3,6-tetrahydropyridine (MPTP). The parkinsonian symptoms have been attributed to the destruction of dopamine neurons in the pars compacta of the substantia nigra.

The monkey is the one animal species that exhibits a sensitivity to low doses of administered MPTP. However, organotypic cultures of embryonic rat mesencephalon, which contain the equivalent of the pars compacta dopamine cell bodies, are also sensitive to MPTP. Studies (18) with organotypic cultures showed that monoamine oxidase inhibitors protect dopamine neurons against the neurodegenerative actions of MPTP as measured by dopamine uptake (**Table 6**) and confirmed by fluorescence microscopy. These observations led to studies in monkeys (19), which showed that the monoamine oxidase inhibitors pargyline and deprenyl protected against the action of MPTP in vivo (Table 6). This protection in monkeys was confirmed by measurements of the levels of dopamine and its metabolites in the striatum. Moreover, the protected monkeys appeared behaviorally normal; they did not develop akinesia and could not be distinguished from control animals that had not received MPTP.

These results show that monoamine oxidase activity is intimately involved in the appearance of neurodegenerative changes. However, work by others along two lines indicates that dopamine catabolism by monoamine oxidase is not involved. First, diminution of dopamine levels by treatment with the tyrosine hydroxylase inhibitor AMPT is not protective in rodents (20). Second, monoamine oxidase (specifically, monoamine oxidase B) converts MPTP to 1-methyl-4-phenylpyridine (MPP^+) (21). Considerable evidence has linked MPP^+ to the neurodegenerative process. Thus, catabolism of dopamine by monoamine oxidase as a major component in the neurotoxic mechanism in MPTP toxicity is not strongly supported.

Nevertheless, the working hypothesis concerning dopamine turnover and peroxidative stress has proven to be a valuable guide for the design of experiments to intervene in neurodegenerative changes. In both models studied, either depleting brain dopamine levels (in cerebral ischemia) or inhibiting monoamine oxidase (in MPTP toxicity) was associated with protection of dopamine neurons in vivo. Even though, in both instances, alternative explanations for the mechanisms of protection appear probable, the turnover of dopamine by monoamine oxidase activity and the potential toxicity associated

Table 6. Protection by Monoamine Oxidase Inhibitors Against Destruction of Dopamine (DA) Neurons by 1-Methyl-4-Phenyl-1,2,3,6-tetrahydropyridine (MPTP)*

Treatment[†]	Viable DA Nerve Terminals (% of Control)
Embryonic Rat Mesencephalon in Vitro	
Untreated control	100
MPTP (10 μM for 7 days)	15
Pargyline (10 μM) + MPTP	58**
Monkeys in Vivo	
Untreated control	100
MPTP (350 μg/kg, IV, for 3 days)	6
Deprenyl + MPTP	100**
Pargyline + MPTP	148**

* Data from references 18 and 19.
† Nerve terminal viability was assessed by uptake of tritium-labeled dopamine by intact rat mesencephalic cultures or by synaptosomes prepared from monkey caudate.
** The MAO inhibitors (pargyline, deprenyl) provided significant protection ($P < 0.025$ for rat mesencephalon; $P < 0.01$ for monkey caudate).

with H_2O_2 production in the nervous system warrant further detailed study.

RECENT EXPERIMENTS CONCERNING THE WORKING HYPOTHESIS

The need for a direct assessment of H_2O_2 production during the catabolism of dopamine by monoamine oxidase in nerve terminals led to further experiments (22). A major cellular mechanism for the detoxification of H_2O_2 is the glutathione peroxidase/glutathione reductase pathway. In reducing H_2O_2 to H_2O, glutathione peroxidase converts reduced glutathione (GSH) to oxidized glutathione (GSSG). Increased steady-state levels of GSSG can provide an index of oxidative stress.

The level of GSSG in rodent brain is quite low, constituting less than 1% of the total glutathione (23). An attempt was made to detect conversion of GSH to GSSG during catabolism of dopamine by nerve terminals in the striatum. Reserpine was used to block the storage of dopamine in synaptic vesicles. In this way, the degradation of dopamine was selectively activated, so that experimental changes would reflect monoamine oxidase activity and H_2O_2 production within dopamine nerve terminals.

The experiments were designed to evaluate the formation of GSSG when exogenous dopamine is taken up into the nerve terminals by the axonal membrane transport system or when dopamine is synthesized within the nerve terminal from added L-dopa (3,4-dihydroxyphenylalanine), which penetrates into nerve terminals where it is

Table 7. Oxidized Glutathione (GSSG) Levels in Rat Striatal Synaptosomes After Treatment with Reserpine and Dopamine (DA) or Reserpine and L-Dopa*

	Increase in GSSG over Control Levels[†]	
Treatment	pmol/mg of Original Tissue	% Increase
Reserpine+DA (n=11)	4.07±0.46	22.9±2.6
Reserpine+L-Dopa (n=7)	5.89±0.56	30.0±2.5

* Data from reference 22.
[†] The values are the mean ±SEM. The GSSG levels in control samples were 18.77±1.79 pmol/mg original tissue in experiments with DA and 21.54±1.65 pmol/mg in experiments with L-dopa. The differences compared to control values in each set of experiments were significant (P<0.05; paired t-test).

decarboxylated to form dopamine. Because reserpine prevents storage, the dopamine is catabolized by intraneuronal monamine oxidase.

To study the processes in nerve terminals, experiments were carried out with a synaptosomal preparation from the striatum of rats (22). Aliquots of the preparation were incubated with glucose and reserpine phosphate in the presence of either dopamine or L-dopa. At the end of the incubation period, the synaptosomal pellet was isolated and homogenized in 0.4 M perchloric acid. The supernatant was analyzed for GSSG concentration by a modification of the method of Tietze (24).

The steady-state level of GSSG increased significantly during incubation with either reserpine plus dopamine or reserpine plus L-dopa (**Table 7**). The rise in GSSG was detected despite the presence of glucose, which supports the reduction of GSSG by glutathione reductase. These results signify an intracellular flux of H_2O_2 when exogenous dopamine is taken up into reserpinized nerve terminals or when dopamine is synthesized in situ from added L-dopa.

In additional experiments, synaptosomes were incubated with clorgyline, an inhibitor of monoamine oxidase. Clorgyline prevented the increase in GSSG levels, which means that the H_2O_2 was generated by monoamine oxidase. In other experiments with L-dopa, synaptosomes were incubated with carbidopa, an inhibitor of dopa decarboxylase. Carbidopa significantly suppressed the rise in GSSG, indicating that H_2O_2 formation depends on the decarboxylation of L-dopa to dopamine within the nerve terminals.

The observed increase in steady-state levels of GSSG during oxidative deamination of dopamine by monoamine oxidase supports the working hypothesis about dopamine catabolism and oxidative stress.

CONCLUSIONS

Peroxides and oxy-radicals are toxic in the nervous system, and they could play a prominent role in a variety of nervous system disorders. The H_2O_2 generated by autoxidation or by the action of monoamine oxidase has been implicated as a causative or ancillary factor in the degeneration of catecholamine neurons by neurotoxins. In Parkinson's disease, an accelerated turnover of dopamine may provoke an oxidative stress within surviving dopamine terminals.

Measurable increases in GSSG concentrations have been observed in organs such as liver exposed to peroxides (25). These observations are taken to indicate the presence of an oxidative stress. We have observed an increase in GSSG concentrations during the catabolism of dopamine by monoamine oxidase in dopamine nerve terminals. These observations support the working hypothesis about the role of monoamine oxidase during dopamine turnover in Parkinson's disease. These experiments provide insights into mechanisms that may be responsible for neuronal senescence or other alterations in neuronal function in central nervous system disorders that affect catecholamine neurons.

REFERENCES

1. Anden N-E, Fuxe K, Hamberger B, Hokfelt T. A quantitative study of the nigro-neostriatal dopamine neuron system in the rat. Acta Physiol Scand 1966:67:306-312.

2. Cohen G. The pathobiology of Parkinson's disease: biochemical aspects of dopamine neuron senescence. J Neural Transm 1983:19(suppl):89-103.

3. Hefti F, Melamed E, Wurtman RJ. Partial lesions of the dopaminergic nigrostriatal system in rat brain: biochemical characterization. Brain Res 1980:195:123-137.

4. Heikkila RE, Cohen G. Cytotoxic aspects of the interaction of ascorbic acid with alloxan and 6-hydroxydopamine. Ann NY Acad Sci 1975:258:221-230.

5. Heikkila RE, Cohen G. 6-Hydroxydopamine: evidence for superoxide radical as an oxidative intermediate. Science 1973:181:456-457.

6. Cohen G, Heikkila RE, MacNamee D. The generation of hydrogen peroxide, superoxide radical and hydroxyl radical by 6-hydroxydopamine, dialuric acid, and related cytotoxic agents. J Biol Chem 1974:249:2447-2452.

7. Heikkila RE, Winston B, Cohen G, Barden H. Alloxan-induced diabetes: evidence for the hydroxyl radical as a cytotoxic intermediate. Biochem Pharmacol 1976:25:1085-1092.

8. Cohen G, Heikkila RE, Allis B, et al. Destruction of sympathetic nerve terminals by 6-hydroxydopamine: protection by 1-phenyl-3-(2-thiazolyl)-2-thiourea, diethyldithiocarbamate, methimazole, cysteamine, ethanol and n-butanol. J Pharmacol Exp Ther 1976:199:336-352.

9. Grankvist K, Marklund S, Taljedal I-B. Superoxide dismutase is prophylactic against alloxan diabetes. Nature 1981:294:158-160.

10. Graham DG, Tiffany SM, Bell WR Jr, Gutknecht WF. Autoxidation versus covalent binding of quinones as the mechanism of toxicity of dopamine, 6-hydroxydopamine and related compounds towards C1300 neuroblastoma cells in vitro. Mol Pharmacol 1978:14:644-653.

11. Allis B, Cohen G. The neurotoxicity of 5,7-dihydroxytryptamine in the mouse atrium: protection by 1-phenyl-3-(2-thiazolyl)-2-thiourea and by ethanol. Eur J Pharmacol 1977:43:269-272.

12. Creveling CR, Lundstrom J, McNeal ET, Tice L, Daly JW. Dihydroxytryptamines: effects on noradrenergic function in mouse heart in vivo. Mol Pharmacol 1975:11:211-222.

13. Weinberger J, Cohen G. The differential effects of ischemia on the active uptake of dopamine, gamma-aminobutyric acid and glutamate by brain synaptosomes. J Neurochem 1982:38:963-968.

14. Weinberger J, Nieves-Rosa J, Cohen G. Nerve terminal damage in cerebral ischemia: protective effect of alpha-methyl-para-tyrosine. Stroke 1985:16:864-870.

15. Schmidt CJ, Ritter JK, Sonsalla PK, Hanson GR, Gibb JW. Role of dopamine in the neurotoxic effects of methamphetamine. J Pharmacol Exp Ther 1985:233:539-544.

16. Davis GC, Williams AC, Markey SP, et al. Chronic parkinsonism secondary to intravenous injection of meperidine analogues. Psychiatry Res 1979:1:249-254.

17. Langston JW, Ballard P, Tetrud JW, Irwin I. Chronic parkinsonism in humans due to a product of meperidine-analog synthesis. Science 1983:219:979-980.

18. Mytilineou C, Cohen G. 1-Methyl-4-phenyl-1,2,3,6-tetrahydropyridine destroys dopamine neurons in explants of rat embryo mesencephalon. Science 1984:225:529-531.

19. Cohen G, Pasik P, Cohen B, Leist A, Mytilineou C, Yahr MD. Pargyline and deprenyl prevent the neurotoxicity of 1-methyl-4-phenyl-1,2,3,6-tetrahydropyridine (MPTP) in monkeys. Eur J Pharmacol 1984:106:209-210.

20. Fuller RW, Hemrick-Luecke SK. Effects of amfonelic acid, alpha-methyltyrosine, Ro 4-1284 and haloperidol pretreatment on the depletion of striatal dopamine by 1-methyl-4-phenyl-1,2,3,6-tetrahydropyridine in mice. Res Commun Chem Pathol Pharmacol 1985:48:17-25.

21. Chiba K, Trevor AL, Castagnoli N Jr. Metabolism of the neurotoxic tertiary amine, MPTP, by brain monoamine oxidase. Biochem Biophys Res Commun 1984:120:574-578.

22. Spina MB, Cohen G. Oxidative stress during dopamine catabolism by monoamine oxidase (MAO): increased levels of oxidized glutathione (GSSG) [Abstract 2296]. Fed Proc 1987:46:709.

23. Slivka A, Spina MB, Cohen G. Reduced and oxidized glutathione in human and monkey brain. Neurosci Lett 1987:74:112-118.

24. Tietze F. Enzymic method for the quantitative determination of nanogram amounts of total and oxidized glutathione: applications to mammalian blood and other tissues. Anal Biochem (US) 1969:27:502-522.

25. Sies H. Hydroperoxides and thiol oxidants in the study of oxidative stress in intact cells and organs. In: Sies H, Ed. Oxidative stress. London: Academic Press, 1985:73-90.

CHAIRMAN'S CONCLUDING REMARKS

A RADICAL APPROACH TO HUMAN DISEASE

Barry Halliwell

THIS HAS BEEN an enormously valuable and stimulating conference, reporting new developments both in basic science and in its clinical applications. The free radical field illustrates well the value of supporting basic scientific research; it has been a highly productive research area, in part because of its multidisciplinary nature. The basic chemistry of superoxide ($O_2^{\cdot-}$) and hydroxyl ($\cdot OH$) radicals was laid down many years ago by radiation chemists (reviewed in reference 1); the basic features of the mechanism of lipid peroxidation were elucidated by scientists at the British Rubber Producers Association (reviewed in reference 2); combustion chemists use free radical scavengers to diminish "knock" in petrol-driven engines; and some of the most detailed chemical work on lipid peroxides and food antioxidants has been carried out by food scientists (3). We are surrounded by plastics, often the products of free-radical chain polymerizations, and paint our houses with paints that harden by a free radical mechanism. Indeed, all human life depends on an atmospheric free radical, the dioxygen molecule (O_2).

In 1954 Gerschman and Gilbert (reviewed in reference 4) proposed that most of the damaging effects of elevated oxygen concentrations in living organisms could be attributed to the formation of free radicals. However, this idea did not capture the interest of many biologists and clinicians until the discovery in 1969 of an enzyme specific for the catalytic removal of a free radical (5 and reviewed in reference 6). That enzyme is, of course, superoxide dismutase. The pioneering work of McCord and Fridovich (5) has led to the present conference and to many fundamental scientific discoveries. These include greater understanding of how phagocytes kill intruders (7), of how bacteria adapt during the transition from anaerobic to aerobic life, of why some lactobacilli accumulate manganese ions, of how toxins such as paraquat, alloxan, and 6-hydroxydopamine damage cells (8,9), and of how human tissues may be injured by chronic inflammation (9,10).

The free radical field is often "sold" nowadays by its medical implications, which are, indeed, very important, but I also make a plea for it as a major

coherent field of basic science that welds together chemistry, biology, and medicine. Many scientists unfamiliar with free radicals regard the field as highly specialized, esoteric, or irrelevant to mainstream biology, biochemistry, and medicine. In fact, it is just the opposite! One cannot approach an understanding of toxicology without considering drug-derived radicals, nor can one gain a complete understanding of inflammation by disregarding phagocyte-derived oxidants (7-9). The damage to proteins during x-ray crystallography or lyophilization, the "going off" of adrenalin on the bench or cysteine in cell culture media, the tainting of milk exposed to copper ions, and the persistent background cellular damage (to such molecules as DNA) produced by ionizing radiation are *all* processes involving radicals (9).

I am particularly pleased to see, therefore, that the newer developments in collaborative research are linking what have previously been treated as completely different research areas. Some scientists working on prostaglandins and leukotrienes now consider the interaction between such molecules and $O_2^{\cdot-}$ or lipid peroxides (11). The ability of platelet activating factor (12) and tumor necrosis factors (13) to modify oxidant production by phagocytes has been discussed in detail at this meeting, as has the role of oxidants in T-lymphocyte activation (13). The precise role played by radicals in such disorders as rheumatoid arthritis (10) or in immune injury to the kidney (14) and lung (15) is not yet clear, but they *are* involved and they interact with prostaglandins, leukotrienes, interleukins, and other modulators of immune function (10-15). Only further *multidisciplinary* research will clarify what is going on and the relevance to human disease of the animal models that are being used. Radiation chemists are beginning to work with biochemists and immunologists to clarify, at the molecular level, the precise damage that is done to molecules such as DNA (16) and proteins (17) by radicals such as $\cdot OH$. Identification of "fingerprints" of radical attack, diagnostic of the damaging species, may result from this work.

After the discovery of superoxide dismutase, much research concentrated on the pathways for the generation of $O_2^{\cdot-}$ within cells, on the nature of the damage that can be done by this radical (6,18), and on the mechanism of oxygen radical production by phagocytes (7). Superoxide is known to accelerate the

From Department of Biochemistry, University of London King's College, London, United Kingdom.

Address correspondence to Dr. Barry Halliwell, Department of Biochemistry, University of London King's College, Strand Campus, London WC2R 2LS, United Kingdom.

metal ion-dependent formation of highly reactive ·OH from H_2O_2 according to the metal-catalyzed Haber-Weiss reaction, (sometimes called superoxide-driven Fenton chemistry, if the metal is iron), which may be written in a grossly simplified form as follows:

$$O_2^{\cdot-} + Fe^{3+} \text{ (or } Cu^{2+}) \text{ chelate} \rightarrow$$
$$O_2 + Fe^{2+} (Cu^+) \text{ chelate} \quad [1]$$

$$Fe^{2+}(Cu^+) \text{ chelate} + H_2O_2 \rightarrow$$
$$Fe^{3+}(Cu^{2+}) \text{ chelate} + \cdot OH + OH^- \quad [2]$$

Net reaction:

$$O_2^{\cdot-} + H_2O_2 \xrightarrow[\text{catalyst}]{Fe/Cu} \cdot OH + OH^- + O_2 \quad [3]$$

The role of ·OH in mediating the toxicity of $O_2^{\cdot-}$ and H_2O_2 has often been discussed at this meeting, but some of the basic chemistry involved is not yet clear. It can only be clarified by chemists and biochemists working in collaboration. For example, alternatives to ·OH, such as ferryl species, are still being proposed as the reactive radical formed in the Fenton reactions. I say only that any such alternative species must react efficiently with all the ·OH scavengers shown to be effective in biochemical systems, must combine with spin traps to give the "·OH" spin adduct, must abstract hydrogen atoms to initiate lipid peroxidation, and must be able to react with aromatic compounds to give the same product profile that is produced by ·OH (19). Ferryl, perferryl, or $Fe^{2+}/Fe^{3+}/O_2$ species have yet to be demonstrated to do any of these things. Borg (20) pointed out at the conference that mechanisms such as that written in equations 1-3 ignore competing reactions that become very significant when high concentrations of such metals as iron are present. For example, a large excess of Fe^{2+} (100 μM or more) can *depress* ·OH formation in Fenton systems because of the fast reaction shown below.

$$Fe^{2+} + \cdot OH \rightarrow Fe^{3+} + OH^- \quad [4]$$

How much catalytic (equation 3) metal ion is available in vivo? Preliminary attempts to answer this question for iron have used the bleomycin method (reviewed in reference 2), and the answers are in the low micromolar range (5 μM or less except in iron-overload disease). Hence, in vitro experiments on lipid peroxidation and ·OH formation that use 50 μM to 200 μM concentrations of iron complexes give results whose biological relevance is questionable (20). It has been argued (2,21) that the rate of radical reactions in vivo may be limited by the supply of redox-active metal ions, so that increased liberation of such metal ions from storage pools

during cellular damage could accelerate reactions such as lipid peroxidation.

Papers presented at the conference (22-24) discussed the importance of free radical reactions in cerebral injury due to trauma or to ischemia/reperfusion. Some areas of the brain are rich in iron, and cerebrospinal fluid has no iron-binding capacity (2,21), so increased free radical reactions related to iron release upon injury to the nervous system may play an important role in postinjury tissue deterioration (21). This role might be amenable to therapeutic intervention using antioxidants, metal-chelating agents, or molecules combining the properties of both (24). Deferoxamine (desferrioxamine B methanesulfonate), the first chelator to be suggested for use in this way (25), is now known to be unsuitable (21) for human treatment (except for iron overload), and I was fascinated to hear at the conference of some of the newer compounds that are undergoing development and testing.

Biochemists spent considerable time in the 1970s and early 1980s debating the chemical nature of the transition metal ions that could accelerate radical reactions, such as ·OH formation, in vivo (reviewed in reference 10). It is now clear that organisms try to keep such metal ions safely sequestered, since they can convert several poorly reactive species into highly reactive ones (**Table 1**). Thus iron within ferritin, transferrin, or lactoferrin does not easily participate in radical reactions (2,21). However, $O_2^{\cdot-}$ can mobilize some iron from ferritin (2,27); H_2O_2 easily degrades hemoglobin to release iron (2); and cellular injury liberates the intracellular mobile iron pools. Thus oxidant stress (from excess $O_2^{\cdot-}$ and H_2O_2 formation) can *create* its own catalytic metal ions, as seems to occur in the inflamed rheumatoid joint (28). Even transferrin can be persuaded to give up its iron in a catalytic form, at low pH values (29). Iron bound to lactoferrin does not seem to be available to stimulate ·OH formation and lipid peroxidation in free solution at physiological pH (2,29). However, work presented by Jacob and Vercellotti (12) suggests that binding of lactoferrin to the membranes of certain target cells can labilize iron from the protein, making the cells very susceptible to being killed by $O_2^{\cdot-}$ and H_2O_2. This would be a clear example of a site-specific reaction: ·OH is formed at a point where the metal catalyst is located and then attacks molecules at or very close to that point (2,20,21). Another example is provided by the work of Cochrane et al (30), who reported that treatment of human cells with H_2O_2 causes rapid DNA damage that seems to be mediated by ·OH (19,30). If that is the case (and comparable results have also been obtained by another group (31)), it means either that the DNA within the nucleus already has bound to it metal ions that can generate ·OH from any H_2O_2

that survives to enter the nucleus, or that the H_2O_2 treatment liberates metal ions within the cell that quickly attach to the DNA. Modern techniques (e.g., reference 16) can be used to investigate the products of DNA damage produced within cells by H_2O_2 to see if the products are diagnostic for attack by ·OH.

There was considerable debate at the conference (2,20,27) concerning the mechanism of iron-stimulated lipid peroxidation in biological membranes and in liposomes. There was no disagreement about the results, but about their interpretation. Thus ·OH *can* initiate lipid peroxidation by hydrogen atom abstraction. However, lipid peroxidation in liposomes or microsomes, stimulated by adding Fe^{2+}, Fe^{3+}-ADP, Fe^{2+}/Fe^{3+} mixtures, or Fe^{3+} and ascorbic acid, is not usually inhibited by adding catalase or scavengers of ·OH (2,24,27). It thus seems that under the usual conditions in which peroxidation is studied in vitro (that is, ambient O_2 and high concentrations of added iron complexes (20)), ·OH does not play a role in what is observed. Aust (27) made the interesting proposal that an $Fe^{2+}/Fe^{3+}/O_2$ complex is the initiator of peroxidation in these systems. This explains many experimental results (24,27), although such a complex has yet to be isolated and characterized. Gutteridge (2) argued that the liposomes and microsomes studied always contain some preformed lipid peroxide, so that first-chain initiation by ·OH is no longer required and that added metal complexes (including the proposed $Fe^{2+}/Fe^{3+}/O_2$ complex) are acting largely by decomposing lipid peroxides into chain-propagating peroxy and alkoxy radicals (Table 1). Careful experiments with EDTA, which appears to inhibit this lipid peroxide decomposition but stimulates ·OH formation, were consistent with this proposal (2). Borg (20) pointed out that Fe^{2+}, Fe^{3+}, and their various chelates have different lipophilicities and thus different tendencies to enter membranes and generate reactive species inside them. As explained previously, he also criticized the high iron concentrations being used. I believe that this problem will only be resolved by expert chemists studying the interaction of defined radical species and metal complexes with highly purified, peroxide-free lipids, along the lines of experiments recently performed with $HO_2·$, the protonated form of $O_2^{·-}$ (32). Obtaining peroxide-free lipids, however, is a very difficult process.

Increases in the amounts of various "markers" of lipid peroxidation is the evidence most frequently quoted for a role played by free radicals in human disease, perhaps because methods exist for measuring these markers. Gutteridge (2) critically reviewed the diene conjugation and thiobarbituric acid (TBA) methods, pointing out their many pitfalls. Fortunately, more specific methods are on the horizon

Table 1. Role of Metal Ions in Converting Less Reactive Species to More Reactive Species

Superoxide ($O_2^{·-}$) Hydrogen peroxide (H_2O_2)	$\xrightarrow{Fe/Cu^*}$	Hydroxyl radical (·OH)
Lipid peroxides (ROOH)	$\xrightarrow{Fe/Cu^\dagger}$	Alkoxy (RO·), peroxy ($RO_2·$) radicals Cytotoxic aldehydes
Thiols (RSH)	$\xrightarrow{Fe/Cu\ plus\ O_2^{**}}$	Thiyl radical (RS·) $O_2^{·-}$, H_2O_2, ·OH
NAD(P)H	$\xrightarrow{Fe/Cu\ plus\ O_2^{**}}$	NAD(P)·, $O_2^{·-}$, H_2O_2, ·OH
Catecholamines Some other "autoxidizable" molecules	$\xrightarrow{Fe/Cu/Mn\ plus\ O_2^{**}}$	$O_2^{·-}$, H_2O_2, ·OH, semiquinones (or equivalent radicals derived from the oxidizing compounds)

* The iron- or copper-catalysed Haber-Weiss reaction
† Lipid peroxide decomposition is metal-ion dependent and eventually produces highly cytotoxic products such as 4-hydroxy-2,3-*trans*-nonenal and less toxic ones such as malondialdehyde (26).
** Most so-called autoxidations are stimulated by traces of transition metal ions and proceed by free radical mechanisms.

(4,19,26). However, cellular oxidant injury can frequently occur without detectable lipid peroxidation (2,10). For example, paraquat injures lung by increased intracellular formation of $O_2^{·-}$ and H_2O_2 (6,18), yet lipid peroxidation appears to be a late stage in this tissue injury rather than a primary cause of it (19,33). A similar comment applies to several other toxins (10,19,21,33). The presentation of Cochrane et al (30) illustrated this point; cellular injury by H_2O_2 in their system was due to DNA damage and its metabolic consequences, not to lipid peroxidation. **Figure 1** illustrates how Ca^{2+} decompartmentalization and lipid peroxidation can be secondary consequences of oxidant attack on molecules such as DNA. Again, we should speak no longer in general terms of oxidants "damaging cells and tissues," but ask what targets are being attacked and why they are so sensitive (19).

I have spent a long time considering ·OH and metal ions, so I must return to $O_2^{·-}$ for a moment and address the question, "Is all the toxicity of $O_2^{·-}$ mediated by its facilitation of ·OH formation?" I think not. Fridovich (6,34) reminded us of some cellular targets that are directly attacked by $O_2^{·-}$, including dihydroxyacid dehydratase. The protonated form of $O_2^{·-}$, $HO_2·$, is reactive enough to initiate peroxidation of fatty acids (35), although whether this occurs in *biological* membranes remains to be established. What convinces me that there is more to $O_2^{·-}$ than just ·OH formation is the massive

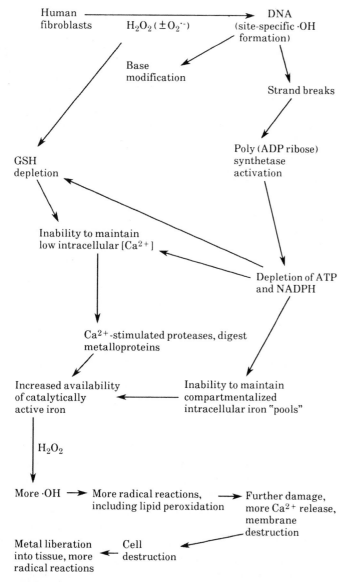

Figure 1. Interrelationship of oxidant damaging mechanisms.

evidence, from adaptation, mutation, genetic engineering, and comparative biochemistry studies (6,34,36,37), that superoxide dismutase is a major cellular antioxidant. Since this enzyme acts catalytically only on $O_2^{\cdot-}$, it follows that $O_2^{\cdot-}$ is well worth removing even at the expense of forming H_2O_2. Thus, although metal ion-dependent formation of $\cdot OH$ is, I believe, an important mechanism of $O_2^{\cdot-}$ toxicity, it does not explain everything.

I have already discussed the exciting results presented at the conference describing the role of oxidants in immune injury and in damage to the central nervous system by trauma or by ischemia/reperfusion. This new information may lead to therapeutic advances. Equally exciting is the work presented on the role of oxidants in ischemia/reperfusion in heart (38). Ischemia itself injures cells and, if continued for a sufficiently long period, will kill them. However, reperfusion after a

brief period of ischemia, although beneficial in the long term, gives an initial insult to the tissues upon reoxygenation that involves $O_2^{\cdot-}$, H_2O_2, and $\cdot OH$ (35,38). This phenomenon has been demonstrated not only in heart (35,38) and brain (23), but also in skin, intestine, and pancreas (33). Simpson et al (38) emphasized the importance of protecting against reoxygenation injury during streptokinase infusion, or other thrombolytic therapies, and in the preservation of organs for transplantation. Their review (38) of potential protective mechanisms emphasized the interaction of oxidants, Ca^{2+} ions, and arachidonic acid-derived products from phagocytes in producing reperfusion damage in vivo.

In conclusion, I wish to thank The Upjohn Company for its generous support of both the Conference and the publication of the proceedings. I am sure we have all found it to be a worthwhile exercise.

REFERENCES

1. Butler J, Land EJ, Swallow AJ. Chemical mechanisms of the effects of high energy radiation on biological systems. Radiat Phys Chem 1984:24:273-282.

2. Gutteridge JMC. Lipid peroxidation: some problems and concepts. In: Halliwell B, ed. Oxygen radicals and tissue injury symposium [Proceedings]. Bethesda: Federation of American Societies for Experimental Biology, 1988.

3. Daniel JW. Metabolic aspects of antioxidants and preservatives. Xenobiotica 1986:16:1073-1078.

4. Gerschman R. Historical introduction to the "free radical theory" of oxygen toxicity. In: Gilbert DL, ed. Oxygen and living processes, an interdisciplinary approach. New York: Springer Verlag, 1981:44-46.

5. McCord JM, Fridovich I. Superoxide dismutase. An enzymic function for erythrocuprein (hemocuprein). J Biol Chem 1969:224:6049-6055.

6. Fridovich I. The biology of oxygen radicals: general concepts. In: Halliwell B, ed. Oxygen radicals and tissue injury symposium [Proceedings]. Bethesda: Federation of American Societies for Experimental Biology, 1988.

7. Babior BM, Curnutte JT, Okamura N. The respiratory burst oxidase of the human neutrophil. In: Halliwell B, ed. Oxygen radicals and tissue injury symposium [Proceedings]. Bethesda: Federation of American Societies for Experimental Biology, 1988.

8. Cohen G. Oxygen radicals and Parkinson's disease. In: Halliwell B, ed. Oxygen radicals and tissue injury symposium [Proceedings]. Bethesda: Federation of American Societies for Experimental Biology, 1988.

9. Halliwell B, Gutteridge JMC. Free radicals in biology and medicine. Oxford: Clarendon Press, 1985.

10. Halliwell B, Gutteridge JMC. The importance of free radicals and catalytic metal ions in human diseases. Mol Aspects Med 1985:8:89-193.

11. Sedor JR. Free radicals and prostanoid synthesis. J Lab Clin Med 1986:108:521-522

12. Jacob HS, Vercellotti GM. Granulocyte-mediated endothelial injury: oxidant damage amplified by lactoferrin

and platelet activating factor. In: Halliwell B, ed. Oxygen radicals and tissue injury symposium [Proceedings]. Bethesda: Federation of American Societies for Experimental Biology, 1988.

13. Clark IA, Thumwood CM, Chaudhri G, Cowden WB, Hunt NH. Tumor necrosis factor and reactive oxygen species: implications for free radical-induced tissue injury. In: Halliwell B, ed. Oxygen radicals and tissue injury symposium [Proceedings]. Bethesda: Federation of American Societies for Experimental Biology, 1988.

14. Johnson KJ, Rehan A, Ward PA. The role of oxygen radicals in kidney disease. In: Halliwell B, ed. Oxygen radicals and tissue injury symposium [Proceedings]. Bethesda: Federation of American Societies for Experimental Biology, 1988.

15. Ward PA, Johnson KJ, Warren JS, Kunkel RG. Immune complexes, oxygen radicals, and lung injury. In: Halliwell B, ed. Oxygen radicals and tissue injury symposium [Proceedings]. Bethesda: Federation of American Societies for Experimental Biology, 1988.

16. Dizdaroglu M, Dirksen ML, Jiang H, Robbins JH. Ionizing-radiation-induced damage in the DNA of cultured human cells: identification of 8,5-cyclo-2-deoxyguanosine. Biochem J 1987:241:929-932.

17. Wolff SP, Dean RT. Fragmentation of proteins by free radicals and its effect on their susceptibility to enzymic hydrolysis. Biochem J 1986:234:399-403.

18. Fisher AB. Intracellular production of oxygen-derived free radicals. In: Halliwell B, ed. Oxygen radicals and tissue injury symposium [Proceedings]. Bethesda: Federation of American Societies for Experimental Biology, 1988.

19. Halliwell B, Grootveld M. The measurement of free radical reactions in humans. Some thoughts for future experimentation. FEBS Lett 1987:213:9-14.

20. Borg DC, Schaich KM. Iron and iron-derived radicals. In: Halliwell B, ed. Oxygen radicals and tissue injury symposium [Proceedings]. Bethesda: Federation of American Societies for Experimental Biology, 1988.

21. Halliwell B, Gutteridge JMC. Oxygen free radicals and iron in relation to biology and medicine: some problems and concepts. Arch Biochem Biophys 1986:246:501-514.

22. Hall ED, Braughler JM. The role of oxygen radical-induced lipid peroxidation in acute central nervous system trauma. In: Halliwell B, ed. Oxygen radicals and tissue injury symposium [Proceedings]. Bethesda: Federation of American Societies for Experimental Biology, 1988.

23. Watson BD, Ginsberg MD. Mechanisms of lipid peroxidation potentiated by ischemia in brain. In: Halliwell B, ed. Oxygen radicals and tissue injury symposium [Proceedings]. Bethesda: Federation of American Societies for Experimental Biology, 1988.

24. Braughler JM. Calcium and lipid peroxidation. In: Halliwell B, ed. Oxygen radicals and tissue injury symposium [Proceedings]. Bethesda: Federation of American Societies for Experimental Biology, 1988.

25. Gutteridge JMC, Richmond R, Halliwell B. Inhibition of the iron-catalysed formation of hydroxyl radicals from superoxide and of lipid peroxidation by desferrioxamine. Biochem J 1979:184:469-472.

26. Esterbauer H, Koller E, Slee RG, Koster JF. Possible involvement of the lipid-peroxidation product 4-hydroxynonenal in the formation of fluorescent chromolipids. Biochem J 1986:239:405-409.

27. Aust SD. Sources of iron for lipid peroxidation in biological systems. In: Halliwell B, ed. Oxygen radicals and tissue injury symposium [Proceedings]. Bethesda: Federation of American Societies for Experimental Biology, 1988.

28. Halliwell B, Gutteridge JMC, Blake D. Metal ions and oxygen radical reactions in human inflammatory joint disease. Phil Trans Roy Soc Lond Series B 1985:311:659-671.

29. Aruoma OI, Halliwell B. Superoxide-dependent and ascorbate-dependent formation of hydroxyl radicals from hydrogen peroxide in the presence of iron. Are lactoferrin and transferrin promoters of hydroxyl radical generation? Biochem J 1987:241:273-278.

30. Cochrane CG, Schraufstatter IU, Hyslop P, Jackson J. Cellular and biochemical events in oxidant injury. In: Halliwell B, ed. Oxygen radicals and tissue injury symposium [Proceedings]. Bethesda: Federation of American Societies for Experimental Biology, 1988.

31. Mello Filho AC, Meneghini R. In vivo formation of single-strand breaks in DNA by hydrogen peroxide is mediated by the Haber-Weiss reaction. Biochim Biophys Acta 1984:781:56-63.

32. Bielski BHJ, Arudi RL, Sutherland MW. A study of the reactivity of HO_2/O_2^- with unsaturated fatty acids. J Biol Chem 1983:258:4759-4761.

33. Eklow-Lastbom L, Rossi L, Thor H, Orrenius S. Effects of oxidative stress caused by hyperoxia and diquat: a study in isolated hepatocytes. Free Rad Res Commun 1986:2:57-68.

34. Fridovich I. Biological effects of the superoxide radical. Arch Biochem Biophys 1986:247:1-11.

35. McCord JM. Oxygen-derived free radicals in post-ischemic tissue injury. New Engl J Med 1985:312:159-163.

36. Farr SB, D'Ari R, Touati D. Oxygen-dependent mutagenesis in E coli lacking superoxide dismutase. Proc Natl Acad Sci US 1986:83:8268-8272.

37. Cutler RG. Antioxidants, aging and longevity. In: Pryor WA, ed. Free radicals in biology. London: Academic Press, 1984:6:371-428.

38. Simpson PJ, Fantone JC, Lucchesi BR. Myocardial ischemia and reperfusion injury: oxygen radicals and the role of the neutrophil. In: Halliwell B, ed. Oxygen radicals and tissue injury symposium [Proceedings]. Bethesda: Federation of American Societies for Experimental Biology, 1988.

PARTICIPANTS AND CONTRIBUTORS

PARTICIPANTS AND CONTRIBUTORS

Steven D. Aust, Ph.D.
Director
Biotechnology Center
Utah State University
Logan, Utah 84322-4430
United States

Bernard M. Babior, M.D., Ph.D.
Head, Division of Biochemistry
Department of Basic and Clinical Research
Research Institute of Scripps Clinic
10666 North Torrey Pines Road
La Jolla, California 92037
United States

Frank P. Bell, Ph.D.
Metabolic Diseases Research
7250-209-3
The Upjohn Company
Kalamazoo, Michigan 49001
United States

Donald C. Borg, M.D.
Senior Scientist
Medical Research Center
Brookhaven National Laboratory
Upton, Long Island, New York 11973
United States

J. Mark Braughler, Ph.D.
Senior Research Scientist
CNS Diseases Research
7251-209-5
The Upjohn Company
Kalamazoo, Michigan 49001
United States

Peter Chelune, B.S.
Medical Sciences Liaison
9278 VanRick
The Upjohn Company
Kalamazoo, Michigan 49001
United States

Ian A. Clark, B.V.Sc., Ph.D.
Department of Zoology
The Australian National University
Canberra, ACT 2601
Australia

Charles G. Cochrane, M.D.
Department of Immunology
Research Institute of Scripps Clinic
10666 North Torrey Pines Road
La Jolla, California 92037
United States

Gerald Cohen, Ph.D.
Department of Neurology
Mount Sinai School of Medicine
Fifth Avenue and 100th Street
New York, New York 10029
United States

Joseph C. Fantone, M.D.
Department of Pathology
M4227 Medical Science Building I
The University of Michigan Medical School
Ann Arbor, Michigan 48109-0602
United States

Aron B. Fisher, M.D.
Professor of Physiology and Medicine
Institute for Environmental Medicine
University of Pennsylvania School of Medicine
14 John Morgan Building
36th and Hamilton Walk
Philadelphia, Pennsylvania 19104-6068
United States

Irwin Fridovich, Ph.D.
James B. Duke Professor
Department of Biochemistry
Duke University Medical Center
Durham, North Carolina 27710
United States

J. Kenneth Gibson, Ph.D.
Cardiovascular Diseases Research
7243-209-3
The Upjohn Company
Kalamazoo, Michigan 49001
United States

Myron D. Ginsberg, M.D.
Professor of Neurology
Director, Cerebral Vascular Disease Research Center
Department of Neurology (D4-5)
University of Miami School of Medicine
P.O. Box 016960
Miami, Florida 33101
United States

John M. C. Gutteridge, Ph.D., D.Sc.
Division of Chemistry
National Institute for Biological Standards and Control
Blanche Lane, South Mimms, Potters Bar
Hertfordshire, EN6 3QG
United Kingdom

Edward D. Hall, Ph.D.
Senior Research Scientist
CNS Diseases Research
7251-209-4
The Upjohn Company
Kalamazoo, Michigan 49001
United States

Barry Halliwell, D.Phil., D.Sc.
Department of Biochemistry
University of London King's College
Strand Campus
London, WC2R 2LS
United Kingdom

Harry S. Jacob, M.D.
Division of Hematology
Department of Medicine
University of Minnesota
Box 480, Mayo Memorial Building
Minneapolis, Minnesota 55455
United States

Herbert G. Johnson, Ph.D.
Hypersensitivity Diseases Research
7244-25-3
The Upjohn Company
Kalamazoo, Michigan 49001
United States

Kent J. Johnson, M.D.
Department of Pathology
M7520D Box 0602
The University of Michigan Medical School
Ann Arbor, Michigan 48109
United States

Richard B. Johnston, Jr., M.D.
Professor and Chairman
Department of Pediatrics
University of Pennsylvania
Children's Hospital of Philadelphia
34th and Civic Center Boulevard
Philadelphia, Pennsylvania 19104
United States

Gary Mahnke, B.S.
Drug Study Manager
Medical Sciences Liaison
9273 VanRick
The Upjohn Company
Kalamazoo Michigan 49001
United States

Joe M. McCord, Ph.D.
Department of Biochemistry
College of Medicine
University of South Alabama
Mobile, Alabama 36688
United States

Robert G. Schaub, Ph.D.
Senior Scientist
Cardiovascular Diseases Research
7243-209-4
The Upjohn Company
Kalamazoo, Michigan 49001
United States

Paul J. Simpson, Ph.D.
Department of Pathology
M4227 Medical Science Building I
The University of Michigan Medical School
Ann Arbor, Michigan 48109
United States

Peter A. Ward, M.D.
Godfrey D. Stobbe Professor of Pathology
Professor and Chairman, Department of Pathology
The University of Michigan Medical School
M5240 Medical Science Building I, Box 0602
Ann Arbor, Michigan 48109-0602
United States

Brant D. Watson, Ph.D.
Cerebral Vascular Disease Research Center
Department of Neurology (D4-5)
University of Miami School of Medicine
P.O. Box 016960
Miami, Florida 33101
United States

Gerald R. Zins, Ph.D.
Director, Hairgrowth Research
7235-209-3
The Upjohn Company
Kalamazoo, Michigan 49001
United States